Alfred Webb.

REBEL

BETWEEN

SPIRIT AND LAW

REBEL BETWEEN SPIRIT AND LAW

Ahmad Zarruq, Sainthood, and Authority in Islam

Scott Kugle

Indiana University Press

Bloomington and Indianapolis

This book is a publication of

Indiana University Press
601 North Morton Street
Bloomington, IN 47404-3797 USA

http://iupress.indiana.edu

Telephone orders 800-842-6796
Fax orders 812-855-7931
Orders by e-mail iuporder@indiana.edu

The paper used in this publication meets the minimum requirements of American National Standard for Information Sciences—Permanence of Paper for Printed Library Materials, ANSI Z39.48-1984.

Manufactured in the United States of America

Library of Congress Cataloging-in-Publication Data

Kugle, Scott Alan, date
Rebel between spirit and law : Ahmad Zarruq, sainthood, and authority in Islam / Scott Kugle.
p. cm.
Includes bibliographical references and index.
ISBN 0-253-34711-4 (cloth : alk. paper) 1. Zarruq, Ahmad ibn Ahmad, d. 1493. 2. Sufis—Morocco—Biography. 3. Sufism—Africa, North—History. 4. Islam and politics—Africa, North—History. I. Title.
BP80.Z25K84 2006
297.4092—dc22

2005032223

1 2 3 4 5 11 10 09 08 07 06

This study is dedicated to my father, J. Alan Kugle,
who lives by the law,
and to Shaykh Rasheed al-Hasan Kaleemi Jeeli,
who keeps alive the spirit.

Contents

Maps

Preface

Across the Islamic world, saints and the institutions of their Sufi followers excite emotional reactions. The oscillation between the heaping of accolades upon saints and the condemnation of them left me amazed and confused. During my residence among Muslims in Morocco, Egypt, Pakistan, and India, I encountered societies still punctuated by the personalities of saints. Their tombs were landmarks and sanctuaries of quiet in the desperate rush of urban life, whether they were domed architectural masterpieces or shanties of folksy kitsch. Their poetry filled the literary canons and saturated the lyrics of popular music. They even lived as current moral exemplars with communities of devoted followers (though saints have become increasingly hidden and marginalized in modernizing Muslim societies).

While I was struggling up the hill to one of India's largest pilgrimage destinations, an old man engaged me in conversation. Our goal was the once-lonely tomb of a Muslim saint, Muᶜīn al-Dīn Chishtī, whose death anniversary draws hundreds of thousands of pilgrims. Some of these pilgrims come with the expectation of spiritual experiences, some with simple devotion, and some with an eye only for festivities. As we neared the tomb enclosure, the old man looked around at the surging crowds and said, "Muᶜīn al-Dīn was a real saint, not like this rag-tag crowd of pretenders who weep and slobber—look at what a state Sufis have come to!" Just one year earlier, in May 1997, on the other side of the Islamic world, I attended a conference in Casablanca entitled *The Heart-Pulling Power of Sufism in the Modern World* (Quwwat Jadhb al-Taṣawwuf fīʾl-ᶜĀlam), organized by the Butshīshī Sufi community (a branch of the Qādirī lineage that is very active at present in Morocco). There, a college teacher in philosophy stood at the podium to deliver his talk, but was continually overpowered by his own words and broke down in waves of ecstatic weeping. The audience, young and old, students and professionals, stood in applause and confirmation.

These extreme reactions point out the ambivalence of saints within Islamic societies. There are many Muslims who, overwhelmed by the changes brought by modern life, are convinced that saints no longer exist. Others claim the banner of reform and assert that saints and Sufis have wrecked Islam by rotting its core. Reformers who engage modernity depict saints as cult figures of "popular piety" that is misguided at best, possibly heretical, or at worst is ruining Islam from within. They focus their anger against forces of oppression from outside their religious community on scapegoats within the community; within modern reformist discourse, the figure of the saint bears the burden of blame for the ills of modern

Islamic history. This study is a reaction to my trying to understand the role of saints before this dichotomy between "saint" and "reformer" became pervasive and normative.

How did we get to the point where it seems absurd to ask whether saints and reformers have always been incommensurate and opposed? From the point of view of modern experience, reform movements act against "Sufism" and denounce saints. But what if there were Muslim saints who were also Islamic reformers? To even ask this question is to unravel many of the assumptions that undergird modern perceptions of Islam, both among Muslims and Western scholars. To grasp the implications of unraveling these assumptions and discover what conceptual terrain it lays open for us, this study addresses a figure for whom these assumptions did not hold: Ahmad Zarruq, who saw himself as a saint as well as a jurist and reformer.

Acknowledgments

It is with great joy that I acknowledge the many people and institutions that have helped me complete this study. Though I alone must, in the end, take responsibility for its limitations and errors, there are many people who stand behind it and within it: some in the endnotes, some in the shadows, and some between the lines. Carl Ernst, Vincent Cornell, and Bruce Lawrence guided me through the research and writing process with patience, playfulness, and encouragement. Katherine Ewing and David Gilmartin were generous with their insightful suggestions. I am grateful to Rkia Cornell and Miriam Cooke for transforming the complexities of Arabic into the beauties of Arabic.

While I depended on these teachers' personal guidance and inspiration, I have also benefited from financial support. The American Institute of Maghribi Studies, The American Institute of Pakistan Studies, The American Institute of Indian Studies, The Charlotte Newcomb Fellowship, the Mellon Foundation, and Swarthmore College have provided the means for me to carry out archival research and long months of writing. These institutions allowed me to learn from the personal, local knowledge of experts in Morocco, Tunisia, India, and Pakistan. In Fes, those who helped me struggle with language through their own love of words include Kenneth Honerkamp and ᶜAli Filali.

I appreciate the patience and care of Robert Sloan and the editorial staff at Indiana University Press. I would also like to thank the keen eyes and quick wit of Tamara Manik-Perlman for her editorial help when she was my student at Swarthmore College. Tom Paradise lent his professional hand to prepare the maps. Special acknowledgment goes to the directors and staff of the archives where I worked, who facilitated access to rare manuscripts: these include Ahmed Toufiq, Muhammad Binbin, and Mustafa Naji in Rabat, Muhammad al-Dabbagh in Fes, and the Directorate of Khizana al-Zaytuna Archives in Tunis. Such a wide network of support for such a humble product! May it be worth the commitment you have all entrusted to me along the way.

Notes on Transliteration

THE TRANSLITERATION SYSTEM used throughout this book to represent the sounds of the Arabic alphabet is as follows: ʾ (hamza), b, t, th, j, ḥ, kh, d, dh, r, z, ṣ, ḍ, ṭ, ẓ, ʿ (ayn), gh, f, q, k, l, m, n, h, w, y.

The short vowels are represented as: a (fatha), i (kasra), u (dumma).

The long vowels are represented as: ā, ī, ū.

Diphthongs are represented as *ay* and *aw*, as in the common words *khayr* and *yawm*.

The definite article *al-* is not changed according to pronunciation, for ease of visual recognition; for instance "the sun" is *al-shams* rather than *ash-shams*.

The *tāʾ marbūṭa* is represented as pronounced: as a final *-a*, unless the word is part of an *iḍāfa* phrase, in which case it is represented as *-at*.

In translations of Arabic texts, terms are given in (parentheses) for accuracy, while explanations of the translator are given in [brackets] for clarity.

Transliterations of words from Persian are given as they are spelled in letters derived from the Arabic alphabet; for consistency, they follow the same transliteration system as for Arabic rather than a system that represents how the words are actually pronounced.

Abbreviations

Manuscript Libraries and Archives

Azad	Maulana Abul Kalam Azad Library, Aligarh Muslim University (Uttar Pradesh, India)
BL	British Library in London
KhA	al-Khizāna al-ᶜĀmma (formerly Bibliotheque General) in Rabat (Morocco)
KhM	al-Khizāna al-Malakīyya al-Ḥasanīyya (Bibliotheque Royale) in Rabat (Morocco)
KhQ	Khizāna al-Qarawiyyīn in Fes (Morocco)
KhZ	Khizāna al-Zaytūna in Tunis (Tunisia)
RL	Reza Library in Rampur (Uttar Pradesh, India)

List of Abbreviations of Reference Terminology

Ar.	Arabic, classical
diss.	dissertation
ed.	edited by
Fr.	French
lith.	lithograph print
mss.	manuscript
Pr.	Persian
Pt.	Portuguese
Sp.	Spanish
trans.	translated by

REBEL
BETWEEN
SPIRIT AND LAW

Introduction

THIS BOOK ADDRESSES the issue of religious authority in Islamic societies, specifically the authority generated by the overlapping fields of spirituality and law. Political crises and social tensions in fifteenth-century North Africa raised the issue of authority, as have contemporary tensions after the September 11, 2001, attacks, in different but comparable ways. This book explores what comparative insights into our present might be gained from a detailed study of a creative life in the past. It will explore the question of religious authority in the interstices between spirit and law through the intriguing figure of Shaykh Aḥmad Zarrūq, a Sufi jurist from late medieval Morocco. Though his reformist aspirations failed in his immediate historical context, Zarruq's ideas resound through the present and echo through the discourse of Sufi leaders who are taking on an increasingly vocal role as social critics and religious reformers in the contemporary situation after September 11, 2001, in Islamic communities, even in North America.

By focusing on Zarruq, this book addresses a particular kind of religious authority, the authority of saints and their ability to build communities among Muslims in North Africa. It analyzes the power generated in religious communities through their allegiance to saints, a power usually identified with the term "Sufism." It analyzes the special power generated in religious communities through their allegiance to saints, and how this religious authority supports more mundane exercises of social and political power. This inquiry will take us on a journey with many resting places: tombs of saints, institutes of religious learning, courts of law, marketplaces in popular rebellion, and even trenches in the midst of military conflict. At times the journey will take on the expectant color of a pilgrimage, at others the bitter taste of exile, and occasionally it will adopt the heady fragrance of an interior journey through spiritual disclosures.

More specifically, this book is about a distinct concept of juridical sainthood that fuses Islamic legal rectitude and devotional piety. A community of Sufis in Fes, Morocco, advocated this particular paradigm of sainthood (along with colleagues in a network of juridical Sufis in other urban centers across North Africa) at a time of intense political and religious crisis in the late fifteenth century C.E. Juridical sainthood was the center of their reformist agenda; it was also a form of social critique against other Sufi communities whose rhetoric of jihad encouraged their active participation in military and political struggles. For this reason, the figure of the jurist saint stirred great controversy in its time; the ideal of the jurist saint raised powerful questions of political loyalty and dynastic legitimacy, even though on the surface it might appear concerned mainly with legal training and religious values.

The life story of one such reformist saint, Zarruq, offers a way to answer the question of how reform movements operate within Sufi communities, with saints as the primary agents of reform. Shaykh Zarruq was a late medieval Moroccan intellectual, jurist, and Sufi who devoted his life to spiritual cultivation, juridical reasoning, and social critique. His exile from Fes spread his teachings, writings, and followers widely over North Africa from Morocco to Libya, and in Arabia from Cairo to Mecca. More impressive than the geographic range of his peregrinations is the intellectual depth of his reflection on the complex interplay between sainthood and law in Islamic society. He has not yet received scholarly attention in proportion to his importance in the Islamic disciplines of knowledge.

Shaykh Zarruq lived through the end of the fifteenth century C.E., the transitional period in Islamic society from the late medieval era to the early modern. In this period, the comparatively secure world of Fes and northern Morocco began to crack under increasingly complex changes. The early modern period begins in 1492 C.E., a date marking not just the fateful Atlantic crossing of Columbus but also the fall of Granada, the last haven for Islamicate civilization (shared by Jews and many Christians) in Iberia. These events would shatter the Mediterranean world, deeply shake the Islamic societies that formed its southern shore, and remake patterns of world trade and currency flow. These events would place Europe at the center of a new map of the emerging early modern world.

In those uncertain, shifting times, Ahmad Zarruq was a saint who did not take the institution of sainthood for granted. Rather he saw it as his mission to fuse sainthood with juridical and scriptural scholarship, within the conditions of his Islamic, Arab, and African society. The stakes of his project were not just personal but also political, for he felt that the social welfare of Islamic societies rested on the centrality of jurist-saints like him. Zarruq's ideals alienated him from the early modern sharifian dynasty that was gaining ascendancy in his home region. Such alienation made him feel that the fabric of Islamic society was threatened with dissolution.

Zarruq endeavored to create a new devotional order, a reformist Sufi community with himself as the guiding saint at its center, that might fuse the projects of Islamic law and Sufi devotion. Jurists, as religious authorities specializing in Islamic law, advocate regulating the behavior of individuals and social groups. They look to the external actions of Muslims and elaborate the teachings of the Prophet Muhammad into customs and rules that give Muslims a clear basis for establishing interpersonal justice in their dealings and defining a communal path toward salvation in their dealings with God. Sufis, as religious authorities specializing in devotional practices, advocate cultivating a deep spiritual awareness, conscientious scrupulousness against selfishness, and inner reliance upon God over and against all other material, social, or power relations. Sufis look to the inner virtues and attitudes of the Prophet Muhammad (which cannot be codified in law) and search for devotional, meditative, and ascetic practices that could help people to embody them.

The two Islamic disciplines, law and Sufi devotion, seem divided by a distinction between the public and the private. Law is meant to regulate society and evaluates actions that are manifest in social interactions; devotional practice is meant to inculcate inward sincerity and purify intentions that are not directly manifest in visible actions. One metaphor that Muslims use to understand this distinction is anatomical: law judges the actions of the limbs while devotion purifies the inclinations of the heart, yet both are integral to the body. Each religious discipline is derived from the conduct of the Prophet Muhammad (*sunna*) and inspired by the message he communicated (*qurʾān*). Jurists and Sufis might argue about which dimension of the Islamic message is primary, the inner or the outer. Each group has generally insisted that its own tradition is what promotes goodness in Islamic society and keeps Islam alive as a faith. Yet both Islamic law and Sufi devotion are potentially in balance and are ideally complementary, even if in practice the representatives of these disciplines quarrel over aims, priorities, and limitations. Those religious authorities with deep experience in both Islamic law and Sufi devotion assert that both disciplines, law and devotion, are disciplines of knowledge. They are to be controlled and calibrated by *uṣūl al-fiqh*, or the principles of reasoning.

Ahmad Zarruq was one such religious authority who dedicated his life to balancing Islamic law and Sufi devotion. His paradigm of the juridical saint was his way of ensuring this balance between religious disciplines of knowledge, which he perceived as having become fragmented and dispersed. He argued that the juridical saint, by juxtaposing devotion and law, sincerity and rectitude, had an intensified authority, as if he were the human embodiment of *uṣūl al-fiqh*, the master discipline of diverse types of Islamic knowledge. In claiming to be a juridical saint, Zarruq endeavored to reconcile these disciplines of knowledge, and on a deeper psychological level he also tried to reconcile the dispersed pieces of his past and present.[1]

The life and teachings of Zarruq are still useful for Muslims in the contemporary world. In bringing Zarruq's writings and narratives into the present and into English, this study has a wider aim. It strives to show how Zarruq's personality and writings are themselves pieces of the past that contemporary Muslim thinkers are rediscovering and redeploying to reconcile the past Islamic tradition with the exigencies of its troubled postcolonial present. Some Muslim authorities still use Zarruq's legacy to reconcile difficult ethical issues in the present. Muslim leaders with Sufi loyalties, like Shaykh Hamza Yusuf, a Muslim thinker and Sufi community leader from California, are engaged in a project to reconstruct an "integral Islam," with explicit reference to Ahmad Zarruq's authority and textual legacy.[2]

The plan of this book is to begin in the present, for only through the present can we access the past. We begin by listening intently to the protest of Sufi leaders against the "hijacking of Islam" by Islamist extremists. Westerners are hearing them more vocally and explicitly after September 11, 2001, but they have been speaking out long before. They are arguing for an "integral Islam" with a humanist vision very different from Islamists, whom the Western media labels as fundamentalists. As we listen to their protests, we can hear not just political themes, but also ethical grace notes and theological harmonies with resonance deep in the past of Islamic societies. In particular, we can hear echoes of Ahmad Zarruq's personality and variations of his ideas, which provide a foundation for this reformist movement.

Therefore, a deep understanding of the present leads us back in to the more remote past. We will find not only that Ahmad Zarruq's ideas are important, but also that his life story is intriguing in itself, especially for the issues it raises about religious authority among Muslims generated by the fusion between spiritual cultivation and legal rectitude. For Zarruq was a rebel against the emerging religio-political consensus of his time and place; in rebellion, he looked to salvage from his immediate past ideals that aimed to fuse the pursuit of Islamic law and spirituality. His life ended in some bitterness, as his ideals did not take root among many of his contemporaries. However, in the immediate present, Muslim leaders with Sufi allegiances are finding inspiration in his role as a rebel between spirit and law.

PART I. SUFISM

The root principle of being a Sufi is the dimension of virtue.... Therefore, the discipline of being a Sufi is one of the integral parts of Muslim moral obligation.[1]

THE PAST IS present. It is impossible to access the past except through the portal of the present. Likewise, it is impossible to act in the present unconstrained by the ramifications of the past, as they ripple through the present into the future. We can chart time on a linear scale, giving days numbers in a series and imagining years to progress sequentially. Yet time is always multiple, with each moment staring in contradictory directions: back to the horizon of what is completed and toward the horizon of the future of what is unknown and yet undefined. The Prophet Muhammad has said: "Each person is suspended between two dreads: an eternity that has already passed of which he doesn't know what Allah will make, and an eternity yet to come in which he doesn't know what Allah has decreed. So let every person prepare himself as provision for himself. Let every person prepare this world as provision for the next world. Let every person prepare life as provision for death. By that power that holds the soul of Muhammad, after death there is no way to ask Allah's favor and after this world there is no abode except the garden of paradise or the fire of hell!"[2] To cut through this existential dread, Sufis have cultivated the wise saying, "be a child of your own moment (*kun ibn waqtika*)," encouraging us to be absorbed in the demands and opportunities of the moment without care for what has passed or what is yet to come. This is hard advice to live by, for most of us habitually slip (for lack of spiritual discipline or mental concentration) into preoccupied worrying about the past or fretful brooding about the future. It is a person's relationship to time that sets some people apart as saints, claims the Moroccan Sufi author Ibn ᶜAjība.

> People react to actions in the past, present and future in one of four ways. There are some people overwhelmed by fear of actions that are already completed. Others are terrified by the results that are yet to come. Yet others are

> preoccupied with acting in the moment to fill all their time with what they are obliged by duty so that, to the extent that they stay busy in the moment, they are distracted from worrying about past actions or present events; these are the sincere worshipers and severe ascetics. Finally there are others who are immersed in undistracted witness to the actual author of all action who chooses what happens to them; in this witnessing they pass away from themselves, unconcerned for their own existence, and concentrating only on the existence of their object of worship. Not a worry crosses their minds about the actions of the past or the results of events occurring in the present, since they have resigned themselves to their master in everything that has been commanded and decreed. These are the people who truly know Allah.[3]

To be absorbed in the moment without care for past or future may be the quality of saints "who truly know Allah," but it is a quality that is especially hard to achieve for scholars and revolutionaries. Scholars sift the past to establish a firmer sense of order in the present, while revolutionaries imagine the future to free the present of an entirely unsatisfactory order. Both remind us that the past and the future are each bound up in the present: it is the fleeting moment that gives these vast expanses form and meaning.

If anyone is still under the illusion that history consists of facts arranged in chronological order, not based on the more speculative investigations of religion, philosophy, or anthropology, then just listen to Ibn Khaldūn, the historian *par excellence* of medieval North Africa. "On the surface, history is no more than information about political events, dynasties and occurrences of the remote past.... The inner meaning of history, on the other hand, involves speculation and an attempt to get at the truth, subtle explanation of the causes and origins of existing things, and deep knowledge of the how and why of events. History, therefore, is firmly rooted in philosophy."[4] Ibn Khaldūn integrated historical writing with religious, sociological, and philosophical inquiry. Following his lead, this study will examine a historical subject in early modern North Africa. It will do so in ways that make us see with new clarity the "how and why of events" involving authority in Islam, events in which revolutionaries are certainly also involved. It will also address the role of Sufism in recalibrating authority in Islam, primarily in early modern North Africa. However, we can only reach back into the past through the present. Let us begin, then, in 2001, in contemporary North America. Let us juxtapose two snapshots revealing different dimensions of Islamic religious authority. The contrast between them will provide us a bridge for reaching back into the more remote past in hopes of making more meaningful sense of the present—a bridge from 2001 to 1492.

1 Integral Islam

In October 2001, an American-born Muslim leader, Hamza Yusuf, sat in the White House. President Bush had called upon Hamza Yusuf to discuss the possible Muslim reactions to an American "war against terrorism." This leader had leapt into media attention when he pronounced that "Islam has been hijacked" by the perpetrators of the attacks of September 11. Hamza Yusuf advised the president that calling the impending military action against terrorists Operation Infinite Justice would be perceived as "blasphemous" by Muslims worldwide, for infinite justice is a quality of Allah that can be claimed by no military operation, militant organization, or government. The president listened and changed the name of the operation to Operation Enduring Freedom before it was launched.

In August 1998, Hamza Yusuf sat in a different sort of institution. He sat in the congregational mosque of al-Qarawiyyīn in the heart of the walled medieval city of Fes, Morocco, which has served as an Islamic university since the medieval age. Each evening Hamza Yusuf would sit with more than a hundred Muslims from North America and Europe, in the role of a traditional teacher, sitting on the floor with his pupils and reading aloud from a medieval text on the purification of the heart, while weaving his own commentary around its words. This text was *Aid to the Needy who Turn toward the Path of Empowerment and Success*, written by Shaykh Ahmad Zarruq, a Moroccan Sufi, jurist, and saint who had studied at al-Qarawiyyīn more than 500 years before.[1]

These two sittings may seem disconnected. They are separated by continents and by centuries. They are separated by furnishings, for there are no seats in the mosque-university and one must sit in a chair in an interview with the president. They are separated by the political and religious crisis of September 11 that has radically changed the relationship between Muslims and Americans, even for American Muslims. Yet as we juxtapose these two snapshots we notice that the sittings are, in fact, integrally connected. They are connected by Hamza Yusuf himself and his search for a voice of Islamic authority that is both effective in contemporary contexts and authentic to tradition. As he speaks out against the authoritarian voices of Muslim extremists and radicals, he is forced to creatively reconstruct the nature of authority in Islamic societies, which has been fragmented into decentered dimensions of legal, scriptural, political, and saintly authority. The need to reconstruct authority is the subject of this study.

Hamza Yusuf bases his authority on the precedence of the past as well as political clout in the present. His project is haunted by a specter of the past, for behind him in these two snapshots lingers the figure of Ahmad Zarruq, the fifteenth-century Moroccan intellectual whom Hamza Yusuf quotes, not only in his teaching lessons at al-Qarawiyyīn but also in his public speeches to American audiences. Ahmad Zarruq is Hamza Yusuf's primary anchor in the Islamic past. Five centuries earlier, Zarruq wrestled with many of the same problems of constructing an authoritative voice of "integral Islam" in which Islamic law was balanced with the cultivation of virtue. Zarruq's goal was, like Hamza Yusuf's goal is, to limit opportunistic rhetoric of jihad and prevent Muslims from making scapegoats of other communities in order to increase their own communal strength.

Who is Ahmad Zarruq? Why does his name echo thorough the discourse of contemporary Sufi leaders who are increasingly intervening in political discussion and social criticism? Why should he be mentioned as the proponent of ideas of critical importance in the post–September 11 scenario, in the troubled fissures between American policies and Muslim communities? This book will answer these questions, for investigating the life of Zarruq will provide us an insightful lens for looking at the issue of authority in Islamic societies. A detailed study of a fifteenth-century Moroccan leader will allow us to understand in greater depth the struggles of a twenty-first-century American Muslim leader with spiritual links to North Africa.

A short biographical sketch of Ahmad Zarruq is necessary to understand why he echoes through the present (while the details of his life will be clarified more fully in chapters 3 and 4). Zarruq was born in 1442 C.E. and grew up in Fes. Though an orphan, he escaped poverty by working as an apprentice cobbler, then found a way out of manual labor by gaining admission to the madrasa as an aspiring jurist. While studying, Zarruq encountered different kinds of Sufi devotion and took initiation from two Sufi masters of very different ideological orientations. Zarruq lived through a political revolution in Fes which drew his two Sufi masters into conflict with each other as spokespersons for opposing forces. Zarruq opposed the revolutionaries on religious, legal, and political grounds; at the age of twenty-four, he became an outspoken critic of "opportunistic jihad," as he called the revolution. Exiled from Fes, Zarruq developed his critical stand and the style of juridical Sufism that he had adopted in the madrasa into a fully developed ideology of reform centered on the reified figure of the jurist-saint. His ideal was to fuse juridical rectitude with sainthood in the hopes of reforming Sufism from within. Precisely because his reform movement was not immediately successful in North Africa, Zarruq committed his incisive ideals to paper with a clarity, vigor, and bitter energy that was rare among late-medieval Sufis. He has left posterity a large corpus of books through which his ideals have survived. One might even say they lay dormant in writing until, in the contemporary period, Muslim scholars and leaders have begun to revive them.

Hamza Yusuf is a powerful example of such a contemporary Muslim leader. His lectures have repositioned Shaykh Zarruq as the key to the reform of Islam in America and the wider world. Zarruq's ideas emerge from Hamza Yusuf's public speaking as the latter seeks to temper fundamentalist extremism and shape Sufism into a force that can mediate between Islam and Americans after September 11, 2001. Hamza Yusuf was born Mark Hanson in California in the late 1950s. After a potentially deadly accident at age seventeen, he adopted Islam as his religious affiliation. He proceeded to study in the United Arab Emirates, Algeria, Morocco, and Mauritania. He holds allegiance to a Sufi community with close historical ties to Morocco, asserting simply that his approach to Sufism is "Shadhili." One Tunisian Sufi teacher specifically charged Hamza Yusuf, in his younger years, to spread the ideas and ideals of Ahmad Zarruq in the West. He is reluctant to discuss publicly his Sufi initiations, cautious that some will misunderstand Sufism as "cultish." Such caution is perhaps justified for one aiming to become a public intellectual and community leader in the United States, since simplistic or antagonistic opinions of Sufism have become rife among Muslims in North America. Returning to the United States, he has served as the preacher at the Muslim Community Association of Santa Clara, California. He has founded, with Dr. Hesham Alalusi, the Zaytuna Institute in Hayward, California, and directs this non-profit educational and cultural institute for the promotion of Islamic learning. His goal is to revive the tradition of "Islamic humanities" by teaching the comprehensiveness of Islamic theology, the rationalism of Islamic law, and the subtleties of Arabic language and poetry.

> His [Hamza Yusuf's] great concern is that Muslim thinking has sunk into theological shallowness that allows violent fundamentalists to fill the vacuum. Colonialism and successor powers, he contends, dismantled the great Islamic learning institutions, leaving a poverty of great scholarship. "We Muslims have lost theologically sound understanding of our teaching," he says. "We are living through a reformation, but without any theologians to guide us through it. Islam has been hijacked by a discourse of anger and the rhetoric of rage. We have lost our bearings because we have lost our theology." He has been examining the backgrounds of the extremists. The consistent feature, he says, is that they have been educated in the sciences rather than the humanities. "So they see things in very simplistic, black-and-white terms. They don't understand the subtleties of the human soul that you get, for example, from poetry. Take the *Iliad*, for example. It is the ultimate text on war, yet you never know whether Homer is really on the side of the Greeks or the Trojans. It helps you understand the moral ambiguities of war."[2]

He clearly points out how ethics, or how one acts, is dependent on epistemology, or how one knows what one claims to know. In this way, the revival of Islamic humanities that he advocates is the basis of Sufi practice through the cultivation of sincerity and moral virtue. In this way, Hamza Yusuf's preaching and public speaking is directly in line with Ahmad Zarruq's project of fusing jurisprudence with Sufi practice.

In contemporary Sufi reformers' discourse, Zarruq's name surfaces with surprising frequency. It is attached to certain ideals: the fusion of Sufi cultivation of virtue with jurists' rectitude to create an integral Islamic ethics that would balance spirit and law. This cluster of ideas is woven together in his ideal of juridical sainthood. If Muslims respected and followed the guidance of a juridical saint, Zarruq argues, their society would achieve an empowering balance of jurisprudence and Sufism, exterior and interior, law and spirit. These are ideals that contemporary Sufi leaders, like Hamza Yusuf, invoke with the slogan of "Islamic humanities" to counter the ideology of extremists who deny the authenticity of Sufi devotion that disciplines the inner life and break with juridical norms that regulate the outer life. To understand from where these ideals emerged and how Zarruq's writings brought them into focus, we must move back in time, from contemporary crises into the late medieval Islamic world. This book will navigate such a move and help to understand the contemporary relevance of Zarruq's ideals by exploring who Zarruq is, how he lived through a revolution, and how his confrontation with authority provoked him to creatively reformulate the role of saints and jurists in Islamic societies.

In his public speeches, Hamza Yusuf makes frequent reference to Shaykh Ahmad Zarruq. In fact, his speeches attempt to mobilize and popularize Zarruq's ideals about the balance between Sufis and jurists in the entirely new context of contemporary Islam. A fine example of this is Hamza Yusuf's public speech at Stanford University (May 4, 1997) that had been sponsored by the Center for American Islamic Relations (CAIR).

> The fundamental and underlying message in the tradition of Islam, I think personally, is that it does not and refuses to create this dialectic in which a person's inward and their outward become split. [In non-Islamic systems] people are either forced to become esoterists or they are forced to become exoterists. In fact what Islam is trying to do, and what most of the other spiritual religions (and in fact from the Muslim perspective all of them) have failed to do, is to join these two elements in a harmonious and balanced way. This is why, in the tradition of Islam, Sufism has always been part of the traditional Islamic curriculum in every single Muslim university. I know of no period in the Islamic tradition in which Sufism was not taught in the universities and not seen as an important and fundamental aspect of the tradition of Islam.
>
> Shaykh Ahmad Zarruq wrote a great book called the *Principles of Sufism* in which he clarified traditional and orthodox Sufism. He says in his principle number 208: "There are five reasons for repudiating the Sufis. The first of these is with reference to the perfection of their path. For if the Sufis latch on

to a special dispensation or if they misbehave or are negligent in a matter or if a fault manifests itself in them, people hasten to repudiate them." Because they are people who have traditionally been the most strongest and fierce adherents to the sacred teaching of Islam and they have been the ones also that have never inclined toward easy ways out in terms of the *sharīᶜa* or the sacred law. They have been the strictest adherents to the sacred law, but they have a wonderful principle: be hard on yourself and be gentle with other people.

Unfortunately, the disease of this age amongst many Muslims is being easy on yourself and being hard on everybody else. So I think this is where the real crisis of rejecting Sufism as one-third of Islam has had really devastating results in much of the modern Islamic phenomenon. [Shaykh Ahmad Zarruq] said, "This is because no servant is free of fault unless he is granted infallibility or protection by God."

In this speech, Hamza Yusuf charges extremists (who go by Wahhabi, Salafi, or other labels) who reject Sufism of "rejecting one-third of Islam." By this, he implies that they ignore the cultivation of *iḥsān,* or virtue through sincerity. This was the explicit aim of the Sufi tradition, and *iḥsān* is one-third of the Prophet Muhammad's description of the moral path (*dīn*) of Muslims, which consists of a balance of three factors: *islām*, or acting in accord with God's will, *īmān*, or having faith in the Prophet's teaching, and *iḥsān*, or sincerely holding virtuous attitudes.

Those who advocate an integral Islam base their vocabulary for describing religion on a crucial hadith report of the Prophet Muhammad, who once explicitly explained to his followers the nature of their *dīn,* or moral obligation. The narration of the hadith is reported in the voice of ᶜUmar ibn al-Khaṭṭāb:

> One day when we were with Allah's messenger, a man with very white clothing and very black hair came up to us. No mark of travel was visible on him and none of us recognized him. Sitting down before the Prophet, leaning his knees against his, and placing his hands on his thighs, he said, "Tell me, Muhammad, about submission (*islām*)." He replied, "Submission means that you should bear witness that there is no god but God and that Muhammad is God's messenger, that you should perform the ritual prayer, pay the alms tax, fast during Ramadan, and make the pilgrimage to the House (the Kaᶜba) if you are able to go there."
>
> The man said, "You have spoken the truth." We were surprised at his questioning him and then declaring that he had spoken the truth. He said, "Now tell me about faith (*īmān*)." He replied, "Faith means that you have faith in God, God's angels, God's books, God's messengers, and the Last Day, and that you have faith in the measuring out, both its good and its evil."
>
> Remarking that he had spoken the truth, he then said, "Now tell me about doing what is beautiful (*iḥsān*)." He replied, "Doing what is beautiful means

> that you should worship God as if you see God, and if you do not see God, God sees you." ...Then the man went away. After I had waited for a long time, the Prophet said to me, "Do you know who the questioner was, ᶜUmar? I replied, "God and God's messenger know best." He said, "He was Gabriel. He came to teach you your religion (*dīn*)."[3]

This is the closest that the Islamic tradition comes to defining "religion" which would correspond to the term *dīn* in this hadith (as in the Qurʾān, where it is used repeatedly). According to this hadith, "Islam" is not a single, sufficient term. Before the modern era, Muslims used a cluster of interrelated terms (all derived from the Qurʾānic source) to describe their "religion." Religion consists of *islām* (outward conformity), *īmān* (inward faith), and *iḥsān* (virtuous excellence). This contrasts pointedly with the custom in the modern period when Western scholars and Salafi extremist have colluded to assert that the term *Islam* exclusively defines "the religion of Muslims."[4] Yet *islām* (meaning submission or coming to accord) is just one of a cluster of Qurʾānic words used to describe the nature of religion: Islam is neither the most general term nor the most frequent.[5]

The dimension of *islām* corresponds to outward actions and rituals located in the body or limbs. The dimension of *īmān* corresponds to beliefs and oral attestations located in the mind or tongue. Finally, the dimension of *iḥsān* corresponds to inward experience and intentionality located in the soul or heart. This multivalent description of "religion" includes three areas to which different classes of religious specialists devote their attention (with their own disciplines of knowledge and their own authorities of power). Jurists are concerned with outward actions; they speak mainly about aspects of *islām*. Theologians, philosophers, and experts in jurisprudence (*uṣulis*) are concerned with the objects of faith, belief, and dogma; they speak mainly about aspects of *īmān*. Sufis and saints are concerned with intent, sincerity, and its expression as virtue; they speak mainly about *iḥsān*. None of these domains excludes the others, but rather each depends on the others.

This is the implicit understanding of religion, religious beings, and religious specialists that pertained to Muslims before the modern period.[6] Ahmad Zarruq was especially clear in explicating this balance of three different terms and the religious disciplines that revolve around them, even if most premodern Muslim intellectuals shared his world-view. In his text *The Principles of Being a Sufi* (the same text cited in the speech by Hamza Yusuf), Zarruq explained: "the root principle of being a Sufi (*taṣawwuf*) is the dimension of virtue (*maqām al-iḥsān*). This is what the Prophet of Allah explicated with his words 'to worship Allah as if you were seeing Allah, for if you cannot see Allah then surely Allah is seeing you.' ... Likewise legal rulings (*fiqh*) centers on the dimension of submission (*maqām al-islām*) while jurisprudence (*uṣūl*) centers on the dimensions of faith (*maqām al-īmān*). Therefore, the discipline of being a Sufi is one of the integral parts of Muslim moral obligation (*dīn*) that Gabriel taught to the Prophet Muhammad (upon him be blessings and peace)."[7]

Restoring an Integral Islam

Hamza Yusuf does not just critique fundamentalists directly. Rather, he does so by citing Zarruq. He does this to show that fundamentalists who condemn Sufism as a religious innovation or deviation and reject sainthood as "un-Islamic" are actually excising one-third of the integral religion of Muslims as taught by the Prophet Muhammad. Zarruq describes this integral relation between being a Sufi and the religion of Islam as analogous to the integral religion between body and spirit in a living being. "Being a Sufi (*tasawwuf*) has an integral relation to religious obligation (*dīn*), just like the spirit (*rūḥ*) has an integral relation to the body (*jasad*). Jurisprudence is the body of religious obligation. Therefore being a Sufi only manifests within adhering to Islamic law and never without it, just as the spirit only appears in its relation to the body and never without it. The Sufi looks into the dimensions of spiritual completion and lack (or perfection and defect). The jurist looks into matters that get rid of aggravation and social conflict (*ḥaraj*), and the Usuli looks into matters that make faith sound and firm."[8] By Usuli, Zarruq refers to religious intellectuals who are trained in law, but delve below the surface of the law into the ethical principles that animate legal rulings. Usulis are reformist thinkers who elucidate the principles of the law, the *uṣūl* or "roots." By explicating the basic principles, they judge whether the law, in practice, maintains connection with the ethical force of scripture, from which Islamic law is ostensibly derived. Jurisprudence is a good English equivalent of Usuli practice: *juris-* relates to the letter of the law and *-prudence* relates to ethical judgment. In Zarruq's pithy formulation, law, spiritual cultivation, and Usuli reformist jurisprudence are all necessary for the religion of Muslims to remain alive.

In fact, in premodern times, many jurists were also practicing Sufis, so that these three categories of religious specialists were often overlapping. Hamza Yusuf highlights this fact as his speech continues to describe how the Sufis' systematic pursuit of moral perfection and the cultivation of virtue earned them wide admiration in premodern Islamic societies. This brings up another prevalent theme of his leadership: to challenge the Wahhabi appropriation of Islam. Hamza Yusuf stresses how those Islamic leaders of the past who are appropriated as revivalist puritans by Wahhabi and Salafi extremists were actually heavily involved in Sufi communities as well. This is the practical illustration of how Sufi devotion was inextricably fused to Islamic jurisprudence and hadith studies.

> The final reason [that people reject Sufism] is the covetousness some people have for the ranks of Sufism. In traditional Muslim society the Sufis were held up as literally the highest people in the society; they were the shaykhs. Imām Nawawī was a great Sufi. [Qāḍī] ᶜIyyāḍ was a great Sufi. Ibn Ḥajar ᶜAsqalānī was a great Sufi, Imām Ibn al-Jawzi was a great Sufi. All of these great imāms were known to be Sufis of great stature. Abū Ḥāmid al Ghazālī, who is given

the title Ḥujjat al-Islām (Proof of the Faith), is probably the greatest example. People wanted to be like them, and the Arabs are notorious in their understanding if you are not like noble people pretend to be like them because even that is a type of nobility.

Finally [Shaykh Ahmad Zarruq] said, "Thus people are inclined to become inflamed with the Sufis, more so than with any other group." People in official positions exert pressure on them more than anybody else. This was a traditional area in which the government would try to influence the Sufis because [government officials] knew that they had such a vast amount of power over the common people. The Sufis were traditionally the most distant and furthest people from the governors or the government, unless they were righteous rulers like Niẓām al-Mulk, whom Imām al-Ghazālī actually helped to build the *Niẓāmiyya* system of teaching. Anyway [Shaykh Ahmad Zarruq] says, "Anyone who falls in any of these categories except for the last is either rewarded or excused and Allah knows best."[9]

This list of *imāms*, or Islamic leaders of the past, is designed to show that even leaders who were known for jurisprudence and hadith studies were also engaged in Sufi devotional activities. These include many Islamic leaders that Salafi and fundamentalist leaders cite as the architects of Islamic revivalism that is antagonistic to Sufis and dismissive of rationalist jurists. Ahmad Zarruq is often compared to Ibn Taymiyya and Ibn al-Jawzī as a social critique and advocate of reform within Sufi communities. Yet the literary historian Abdullah Guennoun notes the similarity between the figures and concludes that Zarruq was actually the more insightful critic of Sufis because he was more deeply involved with Sufi communities.[10]

It is crucial for Hamza Yusuf to cite Zarruq's name frequently in his speeches as a way of deconstructing the binary opposition between Sufism and "orthodox Islam" that is engineered by Wahhabi and Salafi ideology. On the surface, Zarruq is a Sufi leader who is legitimate from the point of view of jurists. On a deeper lever, Zarruq argued for the fusion of Islamic legal reasoning and Sufi spiritual devotion by advocating his ideal of the juridical saint (as will become clear in the second half of this study). By quoting Zarruq as his ideal, Hamza Yusuf makes clear a subtle point: the Wahhabis and Salafis have rejected not only Sufism but also Islamic legal reasoning. If extremists reject one dimension of an integral Islam, the other dimensions become fractured as well. This is where Hamza Yusuf can join the contemporary jurist and scholar Khaled Abou El Fadl, another Muslim social critic based in California. Abou El Fadl documents how Salafi and Wahhabi movements have rejected not just the concrete decisions of Islamic jurisprudence, but the trust in reason that underlies it. Abou El Fadl is not explicit that the revival of Islamic legal reasoning must be fused with Sufi cultivation of virtue. However, he does imply this when he notes that Salafi and Wahhabi ideologues have lost a crucial ethical element of self-restraint and self-reflection, without which jurisprudence collapses into simple rhetoric. "Representing God's law to other human beings is truly an onerous burden. The burden is not simply to represent the evidence of God's particular injunctions, but to also internalize God's goodness and morality within oneself. The burden is one of diligence and honesty, not just with the textual sources, but with oneself—to bring the intellect and conscience to bear upon how we evaluate and understand the evidence."[11] This is the point where, Zarruq argues and Hamza Yusuf iterates, jurists need Sufis and their techniques of spiritual cultivation.

Muslim leaders who are also active Sufis have a new importance in the environment after September 11, 2001. Their voices offer a potent counter-force to critique and contain fundamentalist ideological movements. Sufi communities have the new role of maintaining humanistic values that stress the harmony between reason and revelation and the balance between social activism and internal virtue. This role has become crucial in the contemporary battle over the nature of the Islamic message, as noted by Khaled Abou El Fadl. "[T]here is a battle being waged over the very identity and character of the Islamic message. The battle includes fighting over the normative values, the ethics, and morals that the Islamic message is supposed to represent. There is also a battle over the relevance of the Islamic intellectual heritage, its role and character, and an intense battle over who gets to speak for Islamic law, how and what ought to be said. In many ways, the arguments and struggles that rage in the United States about these issues is but a microcosm of the much larger reality of Islam."[12] In trying to restore an integral balance to the component dimensions of Islam, like law, Sufism, and humanist intellectual rigor, Hamza Yusuf is an active player in the battle being waged over the character of the Islamic message.

Hamza Yusuf's contemporary engagement with Zarruq's ideals is deeper than his rhetorical use of Zarruq in speeches. The community he leads is also building institutions and engaging in education through study and travel. In this sense, his project mirrors that of Shaykh Zarruq five centuries before him. Hamza Yusuf trains his followers and disciples in Zarruq's methodology. He founded the Zaytuna Institute in California based on the ideal of the Islamic university in North Africa. The name of his institute echoes that of Jāmiᶜa al-Zaytūna in Tunisia, one of the major institutes of Islamic learning in North Africa. The curriculum of learning offered by the institute includes all the elements important to the traditional Islamic curriculum: Qur'ān, Prophetic traditions, Arabic language and poetry, and even arts of physical concentration like archery. In reviving this kind of Islamic humanities curriculum, Hamza Yusuf is reviving the methodology through which Zarruq aimed to train reform-oriented Sufi disciples.

This methodology has explicit links to Zarruq, not just through his texts, but also through his personality. In August 1998, Hamza Yusuf conducted a "Rihla Program" for Western students to travel and study about Islam in Morocco. About 120 Muslims from North America and Europe joined the venture, then attended classes at the recently reopened Islamic university at al-Qarawiyyīn in the heart of

Fes, studying Maliki law, doctrinal theology, and Arabic language during the day. In the evenings they sat with Shaykh Hamza to read from *Aid to the Needy* on the purification of the heart, written by Shaykh Ahmad Zarruq, who had studied there more than five centuries before.[13]

This was a fascinating attempt to physically transport contemporary Western Muslims back to the educational, geographic, and aesthetic environment that had shaped Zarruq. This involves the illusion that the Qarawiyyin of today is the same as the Qarawiyyin of Zarruq's time and that Fes in 2002 is "unchanged" from the Fes of 1492 C.E. But it is a strategic illusion that, though not true, is useful. It is useful in pointing out that the bifurcated life of contemporary America fosters a preconscious disposition to accept Wahhabism in North America. Hamza Yusuf's own training North Africa and Mauritania was a way of "recovering" integral Islam far from the prosperity of the modern West and its propensity to warp religion into ideology. He encourages his followers to take his example and move to Mauritania to study Arabic and Qur'anic recitation in the simple (from a Western point of view, impoverished) environment of a *maḥdhara*, the Islamic school of Shaykh Murabit al Hajj. A maḥdhara is literally an "encampment," the Mauritanian nomadic society's equivalent of the madrasa educational establishment. It follows the traditional curriculum of the North African madrasa in the Maliki methodology of jurisprudence, in a format not much different from the time of Zarruq.[14]

The Network of Sufi Reformers

Hamza Yusuf is not a voice in the wilderness, nor is his institute in California isolated from other Muslim leaders, in America or worldwide. Rather, Hamza Yusuf is one of a network of contemporary Sufis who are also political reformers and cultural critics who speak out against Wahhabism, Salafism, and Islamic fundamentalism. Their critique is much subtler than American political denunciations of the same movements. Rather, their critique is based on an insider's view, a participant's perspective, and an emic "thick description" of what constitutes the Islamic religion.

In the United States, Hamza Yusuf is joined by many colleagues, such as Shaykh Muhammad Hisham Kabbani of the Naqshbandi Sufi community, who was born in Lebanon (from a family that includes the grand Mufti of Lebanon) and is now an American citizen based in Michigan. Educated in Beirut and Belgium in the medical sciences and in Damascus in Islamic law (specializing in the Hanafi methodology), Hisham Kabbani settled permanently in the United States in 1991 in order to center the Naqshbandi community in North America, where he has since founded many educational and charitable initiatives.[15] Like Hamza Yusuf, Shaykh Hisham was among the American Muslim leaders called to the White House to confer with President Bush in the aftermath of the September 11 attacks. Several years before then, Shaykh Hisham had raised his voice to protest against the way "religious extremists" (referring to Wahhabi and Salafi groups) have dominated Muslim institutions in North America, and has published a two-volume work to make his point.[16] In this text, he not only defends Sufi practices as authentically Islamic (against allegations to the contrary by Salafis and Wahhabis), but reverses the rhetoric to accuse Salafis of inauthentic innovations (*bidᶜa*) in Islamic devotional practices.[17]

These voices of protest that take up the rhetoric of Ahmad Zarruq are firmly based in North America. Yet they have colleagues in the wider Islamic world who take up their discourse of protest. One of their colleagues, Shaykh Yūsuf al-Rifāᶜi of Kuwait, is an ideological voice for "Sufism against Salafism" in Arab regions. Since he is based in the Persian Gulf region, Shaykh al-Rifāᶜi projects this discourse close to the center of Wahhabi activities in Saudi Arabia. Shaykh al-Rifāᶜi is an Islamic scholar in Shafiᶜi jurisprudence and has served as minister of state, educator, and author. He is a leader in the Rifāᶜiyya Sufi community and has served in high governmental positions in Kuwait. According to an interview, Shaykh al-Rifāᶜi finds that the value of Sufism "is not only a means of spiritual sincerity, but also a powerful force that conveys Islam to non-Muslims and regenerates the religion in the Muslim heart-lands from within."[18] He is a vocal critic of "narrow-minded Muslims whose view of Allah is anthropomorphic," referring to Wahhabis and their literalist insistence on not interpreting Qurᵓanic reference to Allah's hands, face, and throne. "Their [Wahhabis'] view of the Prophet (Allah bless him and give him peace) is that he is over-venerated and loved by Muslims, and their view of Muslims is that they are unbelievers or immersed in unlawful innovations (*bidᶜa*). The unity of the community and its future lie in holding fast to the agreed upon schools of jurisprudence and tenets of faith, directing our efforts to non-Muslims, not in trying to convince Muslims that everything their forefathers believed was a mistake." Like Hamza Yusuf in the United States, Shaykh al-Rifāᶜī stresses the contemporary need to recreate an integral Islam against extremists. This integral Islam would include Sufism as ethical cultivation, Islamic jurisprudence as the means to create consensus, mutual respect for disagreements in ritual and dogma, and restraint in refusing to brand other Muslims as "unbelievers." His speech at a recent conference on "The Power of Sufism in the Modern World" was bolstered by a Moroccan scholar's speech about Ahmad Zarruq, highlighting how Zarruq's words are pulled into polemical discourse about Islamic extremism in the contemporary world.[19]

Of course, Wahhabi extremism is not limited to Saudi Arabia and the Persian Gulf region; it has been exported internationally on a grand scale since the oil boom in the Saudi kingdom. Internationally, the pattern has emerged that wherever Wahhabi or Salafi extremists become institutionally established, Sufi leaders begin to raise their voices to protest their coercive repudiation of Sufism and Islamic law. Another example is Shaykh Fadlalla Haeri, a popular author and community leader based in South Africa, whose Sufi lineage in the Shadhili community leads back to Ahmad Zarruq (through the Shadhili-Darqawi branch). In contrast to Shaykh al-Rifāᶜī, his approach is less ideologically confrontational, but seeks to revive interest in Sufism as the cultural and humanistic dimension of Islamic spiritual life. His definition of Sufism, though phrased in contemporary English through metaphors such as "ecology," is based solidly on the insight that Sufi devotion is balance and Sufism provides balance and harmony between the other Islamic disciples, as argued most forcefully by Ahmad Zarruq, whom Shaykh Fadlalla cites explicitly.

> We define Sufism as the art or the way that leads man to being in full harmony and balance. It is the way which enables him to attain inner perception, understanding and therefore contentment in every situation in which he happens to be. The Sufi's interaction in all circumstances is in such harmony and in such unity with the total ecology that his actions appear as the manifestation of love and contentment in all circumstances.... Occasionally we find some Sufi masters performing all the orthodox functions of the religious scholars, such as, for example, Shaykh Ahmad Zarruq who is buried in Libya. As well as being a great spiritual master, he was very learned in the outer Islamic Law. He defined the Sufi as a jurist who acts by his knowledge, and was highly critical of those people who claim to be Sufis but who do not follow the way of Islam. Numerous Sufi masters have combined the functions of being the spiritual leader of a community as well as being a spiritual master with a circle of close followers ... on the other hand, we also find many religious scholars and judges and other men concerned primarily with the outer Islamic Law, who have strong inclinations towards Sufism.
>
> One requirement of life is to recognize all the aspects of creation within us, and to be in spontaneous awareness of the unitive nature of reality at all times. That is why one is constantly interested in the code of conduct prescribed by the Sufis. Throughout history, we find that every now and then, whenever the outer aspect, the physical and material, has been developed and stabilized, then man's attention has been drawn more towards the inner aspect of life. This is what gives rise to the periodic emergence of the Sufis and their influence in society. Also, when the outer circumstances of a society become intolerable, and its people are in confusion and suffering privation, and are in dire need of understanding the purpose of life, then again, we find man's attention turning towards knowledge and the search for a way out of such an intolerable situation. It is in these situations that the Sufi centers and Sufi masters emerge. When excessive materialism, consumerism and decadence reach their zenith, then the situation demands the need to balance itself by turning towards establishing spiritual awareness and awakening, which is when Sufism begins to rise. Thus it is often the particular quality of life and its specific demands which determine the appropriate counter-balance needed to restore equilibrium.[20]

The need for a new equilibrium is what draws Shaykh Fadlalla's attention to Ahmad Zarruq and his reformist orientation toward Sufi practice.

Shaykh Fadlalla joins Hamza Yusuf and others in leading a movement that is slowly but steadily growing into discursive opposition to fundamentalist extremism. In Hisham Kabbani's words, this is a movement to perpetuate "traditionally moderate" Islamic leadership. This movement constitutes more than a general rehabilitation of Sufism, insisting that Sufism is an integral part of the Islamic tradition, without which jurisprudence and obedience are not complete. This movement is also taking up the rhetorical task of challenging the authority that fundamentalists and political extremists have arrogated for themselves. They arrogate this authority to themselves through their narrowly militant concept of jihad. And it is here that Zarruq's biography and his critical writings about the dangers of opportunistic jihad give a basis for Hamza Yusuf to declare that those who advocate jihad in militant Islamic groups are un-Islamic.

The Critique of Opportunistic Jihad

Hamza Yusuf has deployed Zarruq's ideas on jihad in the context of the post–September 11 United States. This is a vastly different context than the sharifian revolution in Fes in 1465 through which Zarruq lived and which he criticized so outspokenly. However, there are similar features that allow Hamza Yusuf to invoke Zarruq with great force. The teachings and example of Zarruq allow Hamza Yusuf to denounce terrorist jihad with the assurance that he is representing "authentic" Islam that fuses jurisprudence with Sufi cultivation of virtue. "Then, after joining in with *God Bless America*, Yusuf stood outside the White House and delivered an unequivocal message.... 'Islam was hijacked on September 11, 2001, on that plane was an innocent victim.' ... The imam quickly turns to the World Trade Center attack—an act of 'mass murder, pure and simple.' Suicide, he says, is *ḥarām*, prohibited by the Koran, as is the killing of innocent civilians. He quotes Qurʾanic texts demonstrating that the suicide bombers do not qualify as martyrs."[21] This is the Western media's representation of Hamza Yusuf's controversial position directly after the attacks. They portray him as a "moderate Muslim leader," meaning one who appears to support the American government's position against terrorism. However, Yusuf's own words are far more detailed and nuanced, and their detail reveals the deep structural similarities between his arguments and those of Zarruq.

> The points that I made at the White House were four. The first was emphasizing, and it had to be reiterated again and again, that Islam does not have anything to do with this [the attacks of September 11, 2001], that this is not the teaching of Islam. [Islam] is a religion that teaches mercy and compassion, and when it uses martial force, it uses it with just laws, and non-combatants are never involved. It is based on legitimate authority, not on vigilantism. We

> do not believe in vigilantism; we do not believe in outlaws; we do not believe in Robin Hood.... I also spoke about the idea of consensus.... I told them that there should be a summit meeting of the most prominent Muslim *ᶜulamāᵓ* [scholars] in the Muslim world to declare [that] terrorism is inconsistent with the teachings of Islam and that it is prohibited by *ijmāᶜ*, consensus of the scholars. I said the attacks should be just rejected by an *ijmāᶜ*. I also suggested that there be one done by the Abrahamic religions in someplace like Rome or Jerusalem, where there is a declaration that the taking of innocent lives is not consistent with the teachings of the Prophets, whether it is state terrorism or individual terrorism. Both forms of terrorism are rejected by religion. Let them be seen as what they are: as political means to political ends because that is what they are.... Then the last point I made to the President was about oppression. I said that this country [the United States] had a responsibility in creating just regimes because of the power that this country has and that we have to recognize that the oppression and the extreme circumstances in the Muslim world breed the type of extremism that exists in some parts of the Muslim world.[22]

Having criticized both extremist Muslims' use of terrorism and the American government's support of oppressive regimes in the Muslim world, Hamza Yusuf had to dismiss the argument circulating in journalism and government that Islam preaches "holy war" which justifies terrorist actions. Just as he argues for an expanded meaning for the term Islam (beyond ideological and overly politicized reductions of the religion), he argues for an expanded meaning for the term jihad (beyond warfare or the application of violence). In the same speech, he notes that there is no Qurᵓanic verse where jihad is specifically used to refer to war.

> You can look through the entire Qurᵓan. When Allah speaks about war, [Allah] uses the word *qitāl*. Jihad is a general comprehensive term that includes a military endeavor that is for the truth, but it has the broadest meanings in the Qurᵓan. It includes all that Muslims struggle to do. For example, building schools is a jihad, fighting the *nafs* [selfish ego] is a jihad, and so forth. That is why the Qurᵓan does not limit the word. *Juhūd* [the verbal noun of the root letters from which the word jihad is derived] just means struggle.... There are verses where it does refer to martial combat, but it does not specifically limit the term to that one use, and that is why we do not have a "holy war" so to speak. The struggle for the sake of Allah is a high thing.

In an integral Islam, framed by Islamic legal norms and deepened by Sufi cultivation of virtue, jihad would be far more than a permanent call to arms. However, Hamza Yusuf does note that jihad can mean armed struggle in specific circumstances. The issue then is who can declare that such circumstances exist and by what means an armed struggle can be carried out. Hamza Yusuf specifies that only legitimate political leaders of Muslim communities can declare and carry out armed struggle that would qualify as jihad, and that they must do so within the norms laid out by Muslim jurists.

The current application of violence by Osama bin Laden and his allies would not qualify. Hamza Yusuf does not use the term, but opportunistic jihad might describe the phenomenon of fighting in the name of Islam without endorsement and leadership from the legitimate rulers and without following the guidelines of Islamic law. In the same speech, he answered a question from the audience about Osama bin Laden. "According to Islamic law, [Osama bin Laden] does not represent legitimate state authority. He has no authority to declare war on anybody. There are a lot of Muslims around the world that feel this kind of solidarity with him, and I think that this is misplaced emotionalism. It is a romantic type of image of an individual standing up.... However, it is very dangerous for us to say that Osama bin Laden represents Muslim law because he does not. He does not have that authority. The only people who can declare jihad are legitimate rulers, and none of these groups has that legitimacy."[23] This is a powerful argument that Islamic law and ethics requires one to fulfill one's explicit pledge, whether in personal agreements or business contracts. Citizenship is also a contract with a political government. To declare jihad and engage in armed struggle is to break an implicit contract of citizenship between the individual and the state, one that is binding despite whatever moral critiques one might have of the state or its agents. Hamza Yusuf's position is analogous to Ahmad Zarruq's position during the revolution in Fes in 1465 C.E., when in his loyalty to Islamic law he refused to disobey the recognized government or justify armed struggle beyond its purview.

Hamza Yusuf's speech, however, does not address the essential issue in assessing these movements of "opportunistic jihad." Osama bin Laden knows perfectly well that he broke the bond of allegiance (*bay*ᶜ*a*) to the current government (in his case, the kingdom of Saudi Arabia). This is because he does not recognize it as a legitimate government whose command has moral force, despite its alleged commitment to administering Islamic law. This situation is far more complicated in other parts of the Muslim world, where postcolonial nation-states rule without Islamic legitimacy and do not seek popular support through administering Islamic law in its classical form. What Yusuf dismisses as "misplaced emotionalism" is actually the deep-seated discontent among some Muslims with the governments that rule them without ever having asked for or received their citizens' allegiance. They rule by political coercion and economic collaboration with a global economy that does not work to the benefit of the vast majority of their subjects. Many extremist movements among Muslims call for the abolition of postcolonial nation-states and the re-establishment of the caliphate, which would, they imagine, have more direct Islamic legitimacy.

Hamza Yusuf and Ahmad Zarruq might counter, with some historical realism, that the governments of Muslims have not been "Islamic governments" since the early medieval period. Certainly the sultans who ruled during Zarruq's life were more like strongmen who ruled by tribal solidarity, control of trade, and coercive taxation more than by explicit justification in Islamic law or right as vice regent (*khalīfa*) of the Prophet. In this sense, the sultans who ruled Muslims for most of their history are not so different from postcolonial states that currently rule Muslims, though they arose from intra-Muslim political and communal struggles rather than from colonial occupation, nationalist agitation, and global economic convenience. Zarruq had no romantic utopian hopes for Muslim rulers, but he also refused to criticize them for moral lapses. He asserted conservatively that the ruler remains legitimate even if he is a sinner, with the caveat "as long he upholds the ritual prayers." To justify himself, Zarruq quotes the hadith reporting that the Prophet said, "There will be such princes and rulers as practice oppression and corruption." When those present asked the Prophet, "Should we fight against such rulers, O Prophet of God?" he answered, "No, as long as they pray." Zarruq further clarifies that "as long as they pray" does not mean that the rulers themselves pray, but rather "as long as they order others to pray and do not actually forbid prayer in general."[24]

For Hamza Yusuf and Zarruq, the revolutionary romanticism and puritanical idealism that fuel extremist political movements are extremely dangerous. They undermine the crucial Islamic principles of balance, moderation, and respect for legal rights. Upholding these principles tends to make Yusuf politically conservative. Both he and Zarruq could be labeled as "conservative rebels." They rebelled against their colleagues who overwhelmingly pushed for revolutionary change. They rebelled in the present to preserve something of value from the past that they saw as threatened with extinction or irrelevancy. They sought to protect the future by correcting the impulses of the present through returning to ideals of the past.

As noted above, Hamza Yusuf ignores the moral argument of Muslim extremist revolutionaries who argue that it is the duty of Muslims to reject obedience to current governments that rule them and engage in violent jihad to establish a new, just, and Islamic regime. As he cites the routine obligations of Islamic law, Hamza Yusuf, like Zarruq before him, does not acknowledge the moral argument for political urgency of the revolutionaries; if he did, he would undermine his own critique of revolutionary politics. Hamza Yusuf's and Zarruq's critiques, which are structurally very similar, have ethical as well as legal dimensions. In their view, opportunistic jihad is a means through which political discontents revolt against rulers: if they cannot rise up directly through political ideology, they revolt indirectly through religious ideology. By juxtaposing Hamza Yusuf's critique of Osama bin Laden's and his allies' movement with Zarruq's critique of Sufi jihad leaders of the fifteenth century C.E., the structural similarities of their theological, ethical, and political position becomes clear. Zarruq said:

> There is a group of people incited by what they take to be the public good (*al-maṣāliḥ al-ᶜāmma*) who pursue a course to secure their own superiority and political advantage through matters that are not their business. They incline

> toward providing free food to gain the support of common people (*ᶜawwām*), then expend their energy in acts of oppression in opposing oppression. Sometimes they do this by posing as intercessors (*shifāᶜa*) between leaders and commoners; sometimes they do it by breaking from obedience to the ruling government in open rebellion. They think all this to be piety and established religion on the approved moral path. That leads them inevitably to deviate from the truth, trespass beyond their rights and enter into secret plotting that conceals their true intentions to capture political power (*riyāsa*) and suzerainty (*istiẓhār*). In this, they require whatever might establish their social status (*nāmūs*) that will inspire obedience in others. They require the means to make sound the authority of their voices.... In this drive to acquire religious justification, there remains the suspicious whispering of obsession with worldly power. If they take on the pretext that they do all this in order to feed the masses, they should know that giving a bit of charity from the little one owns is better [than stealing from others to give much in public charity]. If they do this under the pretext of preserving their high position, they should know that respecting the sacred dignity (*ḥurma*) of Allah is more profitable for the true believer and more wholesome than perpetrating sinful actions under the guise of piety.[25]

Opportunistic jihad, in Zarruq's pithy definition, is "acts of oppression in opposing oppression." Such jihad focuses violence against innocent people and noncombatants as a way to attack the legitimacy of the state. In the same passage, Zarruq continues to describe how jihad movements strive to delegitimize the ruling state and capture government authority for themselves. "Such movements result in oppositional politics, such as taking recourse to jihad or standing up against alleged injustices or coercively changing perceived practices that are popularly disapproved. Such movements enter into these political actions without legitimate authority as the ruling state and without the apparatus by which it can claim to fulfill the functions of the state according to the norms of the *sharīᶜa*. This illegal political activity opens the gates to social discord, civil strife and the destruction of countless lives of common poor people."[26] The state's legitimacy often rests on guaranteeing protection to civilians. Therefore, to delegitimize the state, jihad movements threaten the lives of civilians to demonstrate the limits of the protective power of the state. Jihad movements often target civilians who are marked as religiously other and are therefore particularly vulnerable.

This dynamic was particularly vivid in the case of Ahmad Zarruq. His youth corresponded to the waning days of the Marinid dynasty, which ruled over northern Morocco from its capital in Fes. The Marinid elite consisted of Muslim Berbers, who lacked any directly "Islamic" legitimacy. Rather they ruled as sultans, military strongmen who commanded an army strong enough to collect taxes and enforce social order. They relied on Muslim jurists to declare their rule legitimate, while buttressing their authority by honoring the Arab clans who were descendents of the Prophet Muhammad (*shurafā*ᵓ) and also, in a pattern common to Muslim rulers, cultivating close ties to the Jewish community. Jews have a long and rich history in the city of Fes, for as the *convivencia* in Andalusia fell bit by bit to the Spanish Catholic *reconquista*, Sephardic Jews (like Andalusian Muslims of Arab, Berber, or Iberian ancestry) took refuge in urban spaces of northern Morocco, particularly in Fes. They brought civic, artistic, administrative, and commercial skills with them, and they were promoted and protected by the Marinid dynasty. During the revolution of the *shurafā*ᵓ, or sharifian clans, Muslim rioters who wished to delegitimize the Marinids attacked the Jewish quarter that was housed in the Marinid garrison next to the royal palace (al-Madīna al-Bayḍāᵓ), now commonly known as "New Fes" (Fās al-Jadīd). Historians have questioned how extensive this attack on the Jewish community actually was, suspecting that beneath the revolutionary rhetoric only those few Jewish leaders who actively participated in the Marinid government of sultan ᶜAbd al-Ḥaqq al-Marīnī were actually assaulted.[27]

What is clear, however, is that the anti-Jewish rhetoric of the revolutionaries was strong enough that anyone who opposed their political agenda of jihad and revolution against the Marinid dynasty was accused of "being a Jew." This accusation was leveled against Ahmad Zarruq in his youth. Zarruq believed that Islamic law required continuity of legitimacy of the government against revolutionary change; he believed it also required the protection of religious minorities (*dhimmī*) living as citizens under such a legitimate Islamic government. When he spoke out openly against the sharifian revolution, even refusing to pray behind its leaders, he was driven from Fes under the shadow of the accusation of "being a Jew" and not a Muslim. Zarruq's personal suffering as a victim of this scapegoating dynamic of revolutionary politics in an opportunistic jihad is one of the most vivid dimensions of his autobiographical account (which will be discussed in detail in chapter 3). It is also strikingly familiar to those who resist contemporary extremist movements, like Hamza Yusuf or Hisham Kabbani.

Creative Conservatives amid Revolutionary Violence

Hamza Yusuf is a conservative rebel, much like Zarruq was in the fifteenth century. He amplifies in the present Zarruq's project of integrating Islamic law, ethics, and Sufi devotion by articulating their common foundational principles. His project is conservative in that it opposes revolutionary idealism and refuses to sanction the application of violence for revolutionary aims. It is conservative in upholding the legality of existing regimes and asserting the duty of Muslims to fulfill their political contracts with such regimes. However, his project is conservative in other, more creative ways. He seeks to preserve the continuity of Islamic disciplines of knowledge and virtue despite the vicissitudes of historical change (even when those vicissitudes are particularly vicious, as was the colonization and loss of sovereignty of Islamic polities in the nineteenth century). Through this preservation, he hopes to unravel the knots of Wahhabi and Salafi ideology, which has reduced Islam from a multidimensional religious culture into a religious ideology defined against Euro-American world hegemony.

Hamza Yusuf's creative conservatism contrasts profoundly with the logic of fundamentalism. Wahhabis and Salafis perceive a radical discontinuity between Muslims in the present and the Islamic past. This discontinuity allows them to assert that their ideological movements restore the "original" Islam of the Prophet Muhammad's age. By eliding history, they adopt the utopian posture that they can build an Islamic state that will revive the original Islamic community as it was in the time of the Prophet. Such an Islamic state would rule Muslims untainted by disappointments of the past, without relying on Islamic disciplines of knowledge like Islamic jurisprudence or Sufi ethical cultivation. It is Hamza's goal to forcefully point out that such ideology betrays the Islamic past instead of redeeming it. It enmeshes Muslims in mimetic reactions to modern Euro-American hegemony rather than freeing them to reconstruct their past to build on the opportunities modernity provides while challenging its moral weakness and cultural hypocrisy.

Supported by the specter of Ahmad Zarruq, Sufi leaders have begun to raise their voices to contribute to the public debate over religion and ideology in North America and the West in general. Ideology certainly seems to have tipped the scales, overwhelming and co-opting non-ideological experiences of religion. Zarruq articulated his position as the one who tests the scales in the marketplace of sincerity, and for this reason he was known to posterity as "the one who calls to account both Sufis and jurists" (*muḥtasib al-ṣūfīya waʾl-faqarāʾ*). He saw himself echoed in the resonance of the Qurʾan's praise of balance in the opening verses of *Surat al-Raḥmān*.

> The compassionate One
> taught the Qurʾan
> created the human being
> taught the human being clear articulation.
> The heavens the compassionate One raised
> and set in place the balance
> that you not disrupt the balance.
> So give just weight to every matter
> and never assert your overweening ego
> to upset the balance.

In North America, Muslim leaders might find new cultural space to reintegrate Sufi devotion and Islamic law in ways Zarruq could not have imagined. Yet Zarruq's profound and incisive ideas are playing a role in such a reconstruction. His role could be crucial, for references to his Sufi writings carry the weight of authority in the eyes of jurists, and his juridical writings are respected by Sufis. Finding new ways to assert the balance between the two (and the very necessity of preserving the two) might open new ways for Muslims to take part in modernity, as currently defined by Euro-American hegemony. It might actually change that hegemony from within by insisting that there is no justice without balance in what has become a very unbalanced world.

Is it possible to be a conservative rebel? Those who currently advocate the reconstruction of an integral Islam fit that description. They rebel against the social and political forces that are seemingly dominant in their community. Yet they rebel by turning to the past, to restore ideals from their community's tradition, ideas that will address their society's current crisis. By standing against the rising floodwaters of revolutionary change, the conservative rebel looks forward while pointing backward. Hamza Yusuf takes this stance in the present, as a critic of Muslim extremism (and also American chauvinism) in the revolution brewing between two Persian Gulf wars and the attacks of September 11 that they frame. In doing so he stands politically, intellectually, and spiritually in the footsteps of Ahmad Zarruq.

Exploring the life and legacy of the earlier conservative rebel is the goal of the remainder of this book. The next chapter will explain Sufism and sainthood in Islamic societies and provide a theoretical framework for understanding more fully the reformist project of Zarruq. This will complete the first section. Chapters 3 and 4 will illuminate Zarruq's coming of age in Fes with his intellectual, spiritual, and political foundations, which led to great promise and bitter exile. Chapters 5 and 6 will portray of Zarruq's mature life through his writings and ideals, through which he transformed exile into a pilgrimage toward greater sincerity. His idealistic principles and the reform of Islamic authority that he advocated clashed with his colleagues and competitors, leading to a confrontation over principles and critique that is the subject of chapters 7 and 8. The conclusion will account for Zarruq's legacy, his short-term failure to achieve his goals, and his long-term success in laying the foundations for reformist Sufi movements. Through this legacy, Zarruq could serve as the model for Hamza Yusuf, a model rebel negotiating the terrain of religious authority between spirit and law.

2 Sainthood

HAMZA YUSUF ENGAGES in politics, but not as a mere politician. He engages politics from his prior commitment to Islamic law and Sufism. Although he speaks explicitly about law and promotes openly the Islamic humanistic intellectual heritage, he refers more subtly to Sufism as an integral part of this heritage. Hamza Yusuf's public discourse does not highlight the integral connection between Sufism and his political critique of extremists; he relies more on legal terminology and *sharīʿa* rhetoric to announce his stance in opposition to them. In the contemporary period, it has become rare for public figures to openly claim allegiance to Sufi communities. However, in the past (arguably until the late nineteenth century C.E.), allegiance to Sufi communities was ubiquitous in Islamic societies. In Ahmad Zarruq's time, it was rare for a Muslim intellectual or public figure not to have explicit ties to Sufi communities or to discuss issues of Islamic identity, loyalty, and authority without recourse to Sufi terminology. For this reason, we need to critically comprehend the concepts of Sufism and sainthood before we can proceed to a detailed exploration of Zarruq's life or come to a fuller understanding of echoes from the past in Hamza Yusuf's voice.

However, sainthood is not a concept that contemporary American and European audiences can approach directly. Like the concept of religion itself, the concept of sainthood has been shaped by modernity. The terms saint and Sufi are central to this study, yet there exists no firm scholarly consensus on their meaning and usage in the modern discipline of Islamic Studies. Therefore this chapter endeavors to orient the reader to how the terms are used in this study.

Saints as Objects of Modern Discourse

Let us begin with what is familiar. In highly modernized societies like the United States, saints are not publicly acknowledged features of the social terrain. Yet modern Western scholars have observed the high profile of saints within the Christian past that formed modernism's immediate foundation in Europe and America, and also within the present of predominantly non-Christian Asian and African societies that formed modernism's outer boundary. In the beginning of the twentieth century, the American psychologist William James (arguably one of the founders of Religious Studies as a modern scholarly discipline) upheld saints as important objects of analysis. He revived the study of saints as holy people, observing that they are common to all traditions, although their roles differ from one religious tradition to another. Within a tradition, their personalities vary from one generation to another, yet they partake of certain durable and persistent patterns. "The man who lives in his religious center of personal energy, and is actuated by spiritual enthusiasms, differs from his previous carnal self in perfectly definite ways.... Magnanimities once impossible are now easy; paltry conventionalities and mean incentives once tyrannical hold no sway. The stone wall inside him has fallen, the hardness in his heart has broken down.... With most of us the customary hardness quickly returns, but not so with saintly persons."[1]

Becoming a saint involves dissolving certain boundaries of routine within a saint's life, what James refers to as the stone wall inside the heart. Such a dissolution, if durable, establishes new boundaries of inviolability between the saint's life and the lives of others who observe her or him. Sanctity is that quality of being different, of being "set apart," which is an irreducible part of the social order of a community and the psychological structure of an individual. "The rest of us can, I think, imagine this by recalling our state of feeling in those temporary 'melting moods' into which either the trials of real life, or the theater, or a novel sometimes throws us. Especially if we weep! For it is then as if our tears broke through an inveterate inner dam, and let all sorts of ancient peccancies and moral stagnancies drain away, leaving us now washed and soft of heart and open to every nobler leading."[2] We will address James's provocative metaphor of the theater below, but for now let us concentrate on how James defines the sanctity of saints as a dual difference: difference from their lives as formerly lived and difference from the lives of their neighbors. In a constructive way, he imagines saints at the intersection of social relations and personal development. As they struggle to overcome the limitations of self, communities elevate them as exemplars.

The analytic category of saint must strike a balance between "saint as person," whose life sets one apart from others, and "saint as social role," whose life is typecast by an expectant public. These two dimensions are certainly in tension. In his study of Buddhist saints, Reginald Ray offers a useful theory about the universal category of the saint. He suggests that three types of forces come into play in "creating a saint": ascetic forces, hagiographic forces, and cultic forces. Ascetic forces inhere in the actual life of a person who engages in practices of social liminality and disengagement from routine life.[3] Hagiographic forces come into play as saints-in-process mold their individual lives to a paradigm (or pervasive pattern) of religious authority based on past models of sainthood.[4] Finally, cultic forces come into play when saints reintegrate into their surrounding society, as "people with a difference" to act as channels for the sacred and give others access to sacred forces.[5] When listed in this order, these ascetic, hagiographic, and cultic forces mark out a process of becoming a saint in stages of alienation, liminality, and reintegration with empowerment. These terms evoke the theoretical constructs of Victor Turner, who described a social process of transformation through liminality.[6] In highlighting how these forces shape a process, we can make sense of the tension between saints as people and saints as social roles in Islamic societies. Both the role and the people emerge from communities of Sufis, whose devotional practice, mystical theology, and social activities provide the fertile ground for the emergence of saints.

Sufis are actual people, whereas sainthood is a remote ideal. Saints are those people from among the Sufis who are believed to have embodied this ideal. For this reason, saints are controversial; they hover between the murk of routine personhood and the brilliant light of an ideal state. They shimmer, providing an image on that vibrant field upon which the trajectory of an individual's life becomes the projected hopes of others who watch. The metaphor used here is of the movie hall or the shadow puppet theater that was its premodern predecessor in the Islamic world. With sainthood, as in cinema or theater, there is a willing suspension of disbelief. An admiring public believes that the human weakness, cupidity, and hypocrisy in which they are mired can actually be overcome. The person who overcomes these vices becomes more than a person, he (or sometimes she, albeit rarely in the Islamic past) becomes semi-transparent; such a person's actions and words reveal the illumination from a source that would remain hidden if not for the reflective screen that their burnished hearts provide.

As in a theater, the interaction between the audience's hopeful expectation, the hidden light source, and the actors' gestures become fused as images on a screen. These images are mythic; they are neither real (in the sense of social-historical fact) nor unreal (in the sense of meaningless lie). The images allow people to live out a drama through which they create meaning in their lives, meaning witnessed as outside the self but which emerges from deep within the self. The difference is that in cinema, the audience can never become the screen. In the theater of Sufism, the audience can become the screen because the medium is not mechanical but rather social, and the driving power is not electricity but the dynamics of human consciousness. Through mystical experience, spiritual discipline, and the social interaction to which it gives rise, Sufis can hope to become realized saints, who are saints-become-real in the eyes of others. At the individual level, achieving recognition as a saint is rare; its causes are subtle and its results are open to contention. However, at the level of society, the presence of saints is common, consistent, and predictable, as observed by William James.

The Cultural Logic of Sanctity

As persons who confront the sacred, saints become sacred persons. Their very persons are considered sacred, inviolable, and set apart from routine social hierarchies and expectations. However, this very act of being set apart becomes the foundation for supporting and replicating the routine social world around them. Saints are the exception that allows the rules to be defined. This paradox allows us to identify the cultural logic of sanctity.

Although saints constitute a "spiritual elite" in society, they are an elite that is woven into society at many levels. In a paradox, their set-apart nature gives them a power that is contagious and overflows all boundaries that demarcate its origins. The most concrete example of the contagious spread of sacredness is in the relics of saints: places they reside, things they touch, clothes they wear, or even parts of their bodies become infused with the sacredness of their inner natures. Paradoxically, these secondary objects (which are not the saint but are pieces of the saint) metonymically stand in for the saint's inaccessible difference and function as tools or conduits that channel sacred power toward more mundane purposes within the framework of routine social relations. Those people who cannot or will not grapple with overcoming the internal boundaries of selfishness (which includes most of us) uphold the outer boundaries that separate and elevate saints above themselves. The public elevates them either to imitate them in whatever limited ways possible or to simply admire them from afar, for the inaccessible qualities that they nonetheless make present in the eyes and ears of others.

When the contagiousness of sacred power and the eagerness to touch, possess, or manipulate the power of saints come together, they provide the force that drives the cultural logic of sanctity. As societies invest those perceived as saints with power (not just supernatural power but also social capital and political authority), the possibility opens for manipulation or abuse of this power. There could be selfish motives to being recognized as selfless! Attention to this contradiction brings up the uncomfortable discussion of temptation, dissimulation, or backsliding among those recognized as saints. In the immediate context of this study, Ahmad Zarruq raised these troubling questions and attempted to define sainthood in ways that might preclude the free operation of the cultural logic of sanctity. From a broader perspective, interregional Sufi communities that engaged Islamic jurisprudence and scriptural studies often opposed regional local cohesions of Sufi communities in order to arrest this cultural logic, as did Zarruq, his followers, and other allied reformist Sufi movements.

This theoretical sketch of saints suggests that they are universal. It suggests that their key role in the cultural logic of sanctity is found in every society, whether they are canonized by a papal bureaucracy, entombed under domes built by their descendants, or embalmed in their Tennessee mansions by fans. There is a great deal of comparative value in seeing examples of saints in different religions and different styles of social organization. However, we must also take great care in using the word "saint." Is it in reality a universal category? What analytical value is lost by using it in this way? How can we differentiate between saints in different religious traditions, or between kinds of saints in any one religious tradition?

To answer these critical questions, let us return to William James. It is he who first postulated the universal character of saints. "The collective name for the ripe fruits of religion in a character is saintliness. The saintly character is the character for which spiritual emotions are the habitual center of the personal energy; and there is a certain composite photograph of universal saintliness, the same in all religions."[7] This simple statement initiated the comparative study of saints, for James states that all saints belong to a universal category, even in their different appearances. This is not an axiom to be accepted, but an open challenge for comparative studies of religion. James describes saintliness as "a character," highlighting its emergence from a personality and its immersion in a communal drama. This very term "character" leads us to acknowledge the importance of communal audience. Saints will be different for different audiences.

Many scholars have risen to William James's challenge. A body of scholarship deals with saints from a comparative perspective, usually rooted in one tradition or region, but seeing a specific kind of saint as one variation of a general class of "saints" or "holy people" that is more universal than the phenomenon of saints in Western Christianity. Scholars must be diligent to take Christianity out of "saint" if the category is to have analytic, cross-cultural validity.[8]

Christian bias could take the dual form of "Protestant" and "Catholic" preconceptions that limit theories of sainthood. Scholars evoke Protestant conceptions when presenting saints as individual seekers, reducing them to "mystics" who are irrelevant to the social structure (though they might be fascinating from the point of view of psychology or literature).[9] Scholars evoke Catholic conceptions when viewing saints in their social or communal roles, reducing them to "the cult of the saints" that builds up around them, often to dismiss them as manipulators, fanatics, or manifestations of superstitious popular religion. The distorting interplay between Protestant and Catholic preconceptions is vivid in the work of J. Spencer Trimingham, which is hailed as an authoritative guide to the history of Islamic saints. He conceives of the history of Sufism as an initial vibrancy in personal experience, an intermediate organization into communal groups, and a final dissipation into socially powerful "cults" devoid of any authentic religious experience.[10] Between mystic and cult, Trimingham does not articulate a theoretical position that makes sense of saints as figures of religious leadership and social importance.[11]

Throughout their history and in every region, Muslims identify specific individuals in their communities as *Awliyāʾ* of God [Arabic, singular *Walī Allah*]. What risks do we take in identifying the *walī* with the English term "saint"? Some scholars of Islam avoid using "saint" because it is already supersaturated with residual Christian meaning; instead they endeavor to preserve the indigenous term *walī* to mean a "holy person" among Muslims. While I respect their desire to prevent indigenous terms from becoming eclipsed by terms that are more familiar in politically dominant cultures, I cannot agree with their logic. One cannot avoid translation on the level of terms or of concepts without abandoning the intellectual work of explanation. One cannot insist that others learn Arabic before discussing Islamic culture (though one can hope that in the process of discussing Islamic culture others will learn to respect and understand terms in Arabic).

Other scholars of Islam prefer a more literal translation of the term *walī:* as "friend of God," "protégé of God," or "ally of God." These more literal translations capture important characteristics of the holy person among Muslims, yet they have conceptual limitations. "Friend of God" indicates the importance of intimacy: a *walī* is someone who is on intimate terms with God, experiencing protection through proximity and self-abandonment through closeness. Yet as a direct translation, "friend" does not make semantic sense. *Walī* in Arabic never conveys the colloquial sense of "friend" as in English. Rather it has taken on a special religious sense that distinguishes it from other terms for companions and intimates, a sense that emphasizes the element of power and authority inherent in the term *walī*. "Protégé of God" points out this dimension of authority more clearly: the *walī* draws near to a source of power, which then protects and empowers him or her as a channel for divine actions among other people.[12] "Ally of God" accents this dimension of authority and social power even more forcefully. As God's ally, the *walī* can demand the allegiance of a community and take decidedly political positions; the *walī* is be not just a gifted favorite of God but also a powerful leader among people.

Any one of these more literal translations into English would capture only a portion of the polysemic resonance of the term *walī*. As a single term, then, "saint" has a great advantage. In English, it already marks a category of holy people who play socially and politically important roles. Saint is a term that makes intellectual sense as long as one insists that Muslim saints are different in many ways from Christian saints, Hindu saints, or Buddhist saints. At present, studies of sainthood in different traditions try to maintain each tradition's distinctiveness from Catholicism even when noting underlying commonalities between saints. However, there is always the danger of slipping back into Catholic models, since these are, for many, the most familiar saints.[13] This study examines the person of saints and the category of sainthood, while avoiding all other terminology that might suggest Christian parallels.[14]

The *walī* as an Islamic saint is directly defined in relation to God, but indirectly defined in relation to communities of disciples, followers, and admirers. The authority of the *awliyāʾ* comes from a relationship to God, but this is only known and mediated through their relation to other people. Indeed, the fact that we know anything about particular *awliyāʾ* depends on others narrating or writing about them during their lifetime or, more often, after their death. Despite the insistence on inner attachment to God or virtues inherent in their character, the *walī* participates in a network of relationships in society. Social expectation and social structure condition the emergence of a *walī* (either partially or totally).

That Islamic society invests hope and wonder in the figure of the saint has been fairly constant from the classical through the early modern periods. However, this expectation changes form and intensity in different social conditions. Because of this continuity, saints may appear stereotyped and idealized. Yet, since the saint is a saint in the eyes of an audience, they are never actually separate from their cultural context or untouched by the forces of historical change or social conflict. Hagiographic literature, even as it presents individual saints as stereotyped personalities, is rife with reports of differences, conflicts, and alliances between saints. As more studies plumb the vast literature of Islamic hagiography (most of which has not been published in original languages, let alone in translation) it becomes possible to see Muslim saints as very much in interaction with their surrounding societies, and even as important agents of social change.

Several recent studies of Muslim saints pay closer attention to the question of authority in sainthood. This is an important advance that brings to light the agency of saints in political events, intellectual debates, and social movements. Most of these recent studies take as their object the development of a certain paradigm of sainthood over a broad period of time.[15] This study builds upon such prior achievements, even though its contours and aims are slightly different. It presents the development of a paradigm of the jurist-saint within a reform movement, as defined against other competing paradigms in the surrounding society. Therefore the element of authority in sainthood is even more pronounced, expressed in competition between different types of saints belonging to different communities. Rather than focusing upon one paradigm of sainthood that developed over a long period in a discrete region, this study will focus on the competition between multiple paradigms of sainthood within a more condensed period of time across linked North African regions.

Sufis before Saints

In early modern Islamic societies, *Awliyā ͗*, or saints, were extraordinary persons who emerged from the wider, more inclusive pool of people known as "Sufis." Western studies often conflate these two terms, "saint" and "Sufi," as upholders of "Islamic mysticism." The *a priori* western category of "mysticism" had created the neologism "Sufi-ism" in European languages.[16] This category obscures more than it illuminates. This study sets aside these abstractions to focus on persons and communities. Its methodology will disaggregate the terms "saint," "Sufi," and "mystic."

In modern Western perceptions of Islam, mystic was the primary category, from which emerged the more indigenous "Sufi" as a Muslim mystic, and later "saint" as an ideal, spiritually realized Sufi. In contrast, this study will invert this series of terms and reverse their importance. The saint is taken as a primary category, for the material evidence of hagiography presents it as such. Hagiographic collections include as "saints" people from different backgrounds, with different practices, in different styles of piety or devotion. Their paths to become saints may be very different and even contradictory, yet they are all included in the textual genre of hagiography. They all "made it" across the boundary of distinction into a category of special, elevated persons known as saints. It is their very distinction (their separation or sanctity) that defines them, rather than some interior, mystical attitude or allegiance to a doctrinal system of mysticism.[17] As Vincent Cornell explains, they are saints because other people recognize them as such—"a saint's reputation for holiness is socially generated: 'to be a saint is to be a saint for others.'"[18]

If saints are defined by the distinction that others perceive in them, then Sufis are the primary audience of saints. Sufis are those who make that perception and distinguish some persons as saints. In this inclusive definition, Sufis are those who self-consciously participate in the social manifestation of sainthood in an Islamic society. The category "Sufi" would include a whole variety of people: a realized saint, the few who aspire to become a realized saint, the some who see themselves as the followers of a saint, and the many who seek to imitate, obey, or revere a saint. In this way, saints emerge from communities of Sufis, while Sufi communities define themselves around saints. This is true whether the saint is living in the present or passed beyond the present, for Islamic saints are not considered "dead" after their deaths, but are considered conscious and active within the grave.

The outer edge of these inclusive and overlapping Sufi communities would be marked by those who only revere saints from a distance as a part of the social-religious landscape. The phrase "self-consciously participates" in the manifestation of sainthood is therefore crucial. Being a Sufi would depend on having a personal relationship with a saint and engaging self-consciously in some devotional practice related to a saint. Such devotional practice could be very intense and elaborate, or it could be occasional and diffuse. As Carl Ernst notes, Sufism is a wide category which includes meditation techniques pursued by only a select few, as well as poetry, music, and dance which occasion community gatherings, in addition to the architecture of tomb-shrines that engages a wide public. We can grasp the diversity of Sufi communities' practices through Vincent Cornell's description of "imitation" and "admiration." The social reception of saintly persons (as recorded in hagiographies) includes seeing the saint as an exemplar, teacher, and guide who demands imitation, as well as seeing the saint as a source of wonder, inspiration, and extraordinary power who evokes admiration.[19] Both these reactions bind the saint to a community that "participates" in the drama of sainthood. Such participation embodied the experience of the "religion" that we denominate as Islam for the vast majority of Muslims from the medieval through the early modern periods, and continues to do so for many through the modern period and into contemporary times. The issue of how religion is defined is of crucial importance in contemporary debates over Islam, as highlighted by Hamza Yusuf's speeches. The ways in which Zarruq's ideas clarify this issue will be addressed in the conclusion of this study.

This definition of how saints relate to Sufis is oriented to the social sciences and avoids theological definitions or idealized pronouncements that riddle most studies of Sufism. It does not take into account the "origins" of Sufism or mysticism among Muslims.[20] This study offers the above definition of terms not as a final judgment, but as a place to begin an inquiry about sainthood as a social institution that is integrated fully into most Muslims' experience of Islam. As a social institution, the Sufi community bridges the considerable distance between the inner experience of a saint, the rituals of a devotional community, and the wider practices of social movements which looked to saints to lead them or justify them. Reform movements within Sufi communities address the contradictions or disjunctures that appear in this ontological expanse. The reform-oriented saint who is the subject of this study turned his attention to all these diverse levels and presented them as interrelated. This definition provides a conceptual framework to allow Zarruq's writings and stories to make sense in a holistic way.

The indigenous term for "Sufism" is *taṣawwuf*, which means literally "being a Sufi."[21] Yet the use of *taṣawwuf* is rare, limited mainly to doctrinal works in defense of saints and their followers or in titles or introductory prefaces of hagiographic collections of the life record of saints. The more common term is *ṭarīqa*, literally "the Way." *Ṭarīqa* is a multivalent term that cannot be reduced to a single translation (much like the English "Way"). It is the name of a spiritual method recommended by a saint and through which the saint himself became a saint. *Ṭarīqa* is also the community that follows a saint; it is a community of people defined by their shared veneration of a lineage of saints known as masters (Ar. *Shaykh* or *Murshid*, and Pr. *Pīr* or *Khwāja*), which leads from a living master back in time through a series of initiations to the Prophet Muḥammad.[22]

Ṭarīqa could point to an actual community of people centered on a saintly guide in a synchronic way, or it could indicate a lineage of saintly exemplars stretching back in the past in a diachronic way. The two are intimately related, for the community respects a present saintly guide who embodies the authority of an entire lineage of saints who inherited the authority of the Prophet. The term *ṭarīqa* is often used synonymously with "the Lineage" (Ar. *silsila*, *sanad*, or *shajara*). Alternatively, the present saintly guide has cultivated his inner life and outer authority in conformity to the example of the past saints of his lineage; through this he becomes the center of a present community. Therefore, this study translates the term *ṭarīqa* in various ways depending on its context: as "community," as "lineage," and also as "spiritual method." Community would be "the way" that people join together around a saint. Spiritual method would be "the way" the saint enjoins others to cultivate virtue. Finally, lineage would be "the way" a saint is positioned in regard to other saints.[23]

This study questions the usefulness of studies that reify the *ṭarīqa* as the basic term of analysis. It suggests that we look at how communities of Sufis formed and operated with *ṭarīqa* loyalties, but often in opposition to other communities within the same *ṭarīqa*. Whether the term of analysis is Qādirī, Shādhilī, or Majdhūbī, this study highlights the multiplicity of communities, styles of devotion, and conceptualization of sainthood that flourished and often sparked competition. At its most basic level, this study asserts that Islamic sainthood in the early modern period, like the modern category of mysticism, "always represents a site of struggle, a conflict for recognition and authority."[24]

The story of Zarruq as a juridical saint reveals the coexistence of competing paradigms of sainthood within an Islamic society. This study offers us a new way of looking at Islamic saints and the Sufi communities that promote them. Western scholars of religion have depicted Sufis as marginal "mystics."[25] Anthropologists have also concentrated on analyzing Sufis and have endeavored to pull saints into social history. This is laudable; however, anthropologists have often portrayed Muslim saints in stereotyped and simplified ways that lack historical depth and are unaccountable to the rich archival record of Arabic manuscripts about the lives of individual saints.[26] In contrast, we must marshal the theological dexterity and phenomenological realism to take saints seriously as agents of historical change; saints were not abstract figures representing culture but rather were agents who made culture. Through the stories of their debate, competition, and struggle, Muslim saints offer us a view of authority in Islamic culture which is always provisional and ever dynamic.

This study, then, returns the stories of Islamic saints to their historical context. Only through this operation can we observe various communities promoting particular paradigms of sainthood that are in competition with and even contradictory to one another. We can do this is by closely following the life story of a particular saint, one at odds with his contemporaries. Ahmad Zarruq is an ideal object for this method. That he was a reformer, scholar, author, and critical intellectual of his time means that the written record of his life richly details the complexity of his interactions with his contemporaries.

Zarruq's role as a critical reformer is distilled into his ideal of the juridical saint, which he tried to embody in his life and promote in his writings. In the figure of the juridical saint, we can observe the powerful dynamic of the cultural logic of sanctity directed against its own foundations. We have seen how Muslim saints emerge from Sufi communities, as leaders in the political sense and as reflections of their religious ideals in the cultural sense. In Zarruq's view, the juridical saint is a type of saint who criticizes the way other saints rise from popular participation in other Sufi communities. He is able to express such criticism because he arises from a distinct kind of Sufi community: the juridical Sufis who thrived in urban conditions within the madrasa system of Islamic colleges. The juridical saint takes it upon himself to regulate the practices of other Sufi communities and criticize their leaders who emerge with competing paradigms of sainthood.

Zarruq himself is the prime exemplar of juridical sainthood. However, his life took shape in a community of juridical Sufis who shared his ideas, and circles of his followers perpetuated his ideals. Therefore, the biographical details of Zarruq's life are woven into the lives of his colleagues; to write about Zarruq is to document the activities of the whole juridical Sufi community around him. Yet Zarruq sharpened their focus. Not only was his life disrupted when their ideals conflicted with the political aspirations of competing local Sufi communities, but he reacted to this trauma with profound thought and incisive writing.

As a juridical saint who took a critical stance against other Sufi communities, Ahmad Zarruq did not take the institution of sainthood for granted. He advocated a movement of reform that sought to reunite saintly authority with scriptural scholarship and juridical rectitude. He saw Sufi communities as the natural vehicle for such reforms, and also as the primary object of reform. He articulated a particular paradigm of saintly authority even as he subjected the institution of sainthood (and other competing paradigms of saintly authority) to vocal criticism. As a reformer, he aimed to refashion the very notion of sainthood into a particular configuration: that of the juridical saint. The community of reform-minded Sufis that gathered around him attempted to build an interregional reform movement. Brought together by the fusion of "saint" and "jurist," devotion and erudition, their movement was an imaginative and political search for social stability and devotional sincerity in a time of revolutionary change.

Their movement challenged other Sufi communities and the paradigms of sainthood upon which they were built. Zarruq boldly asserted that he and his followers were jurist-saints over and against the competing paradigms of other saints who did not share their reformist agenda. In doing so, he generated an acute critique of the institution of sainthood and the actions of others who were socially recognized as saints. He criticized the involvement of other saints and Sufi communities in the rise of new empires and the Mahdist rhetoric that justified them. He launched this critique from the standpoint that he and his followers were not just saints among other saints, but were empowered as reform-oriented juridical saints to define, first for themselves and then for the society as a whole, who a real saint is and who can become one. His critiques incited resistance, as competitors challenged his assertion of unique authority, the terms and conditions of which will be explicated in chapters 7 and 8.

Reflecting this dynamic, this study treats sainthood as an institution of Islamic society, and as an institution it is the site of contest and competition. It reveals opposing ideological currents within and between Sufi communities and the saints at their center. This is the major importance of this story. Beyond the biographical and textual portrait of Zarruq's life, it asserts that Muslim saints like Zarruq were important social actors who shaped ideologies that were harnessed by more explicitly political forces in their society, such as dynastic rulers, tribal leaders, and guild representatives. It highlights not only the wide variety of Muslim saints, but also that they were often in conflict with each other. These conflicts can reveal for us the contours of competing political forces just preceding their emergence into the arena of open political or military contest.

This political edge to the analysis offered here should not cause us to view Muslim saints as *essentially* or *solely* political. In contrast, their aspirations and activities were thoroughly religious, as long as we understand that "religious" does not mean peripheral, private, and narrowly psychological. We must leave aside this modernist (and for many of us habitual) construction of the religious dimension of life as the binary opposite of the political dimension, which is considered central, public, and broadly historical. A cultural history of Muslim saints must explore the interweaving of religious ideals, personal aspirations, and political forces. This study is just such a cultural history that takes Ahmad Zarruq as its focus in the context of North African Islamic societies.

Zarruq and Juridical Sainthood

The contours of Zarruq's life have a theoretical importance beyond their specificity in Moroccan history. He championed the concept of the juridical saint and offered himself as its exemplar. This is an important example of reaction against the "local cohesion" of Sufi communities. One crucial function of Sufi communities was to "root" Islam in the regional particularities of local cultural zones. Traditions of Sufi piety that take on a local color, adopt a local sacred geography, and take an active role in articulating local forms of Islam can be called "local cohesions" of Sufi communities. Many scholars have noted this crucial function of Sufi communities throughout the medieval period in many different Islamic regions. Marshall Hodgson and Richard Eaton, in particular, stress the syncretic nature of local Sufi cohesions that do not deny or suppress local pre-Islamic customs, but rather absorb them and Islamize them.[27] When such local cohesions grow strong, they can form a legitimizing authority for ascendant political regimes that try to justify their local dominance through cooperation with or patronage of the local Sufi cohesions.

Some scholars have focused exclusively on local cohesion of Sufi communities and reduced "Sufism" to this role, ignoring the fact that Sufi communities have always been varied and plural and that the institution of sainthood has always been a site of conflict and competition between different Sufi groups. Cultural anthropologists have been vulnerable to such generalizations. However, while some Sufis who drew on local resources from their particular ethnic, cultural, and devotional geography, others drew on explicitly interregional and universal scriptural or legal discourses for their authority. Individuals or communities that linked Sufi devotion to these more universally Islamic discourses are often termed representatives of "orthodox Sufism." This is a misleading term, as it implies that regional articulations of Sufism are inherently "heterodox" or "un-Islamic." In reality, representatives of local Sufi cohesions and transregional Sufi alliances have always coexisted, usually amicably and often within the same communities.

However, in certain historical situations, the two types of Sufi orientations can come into conflict. If a community allied to transregional Islamic discourses of scriptural studies and legal rectitude gains enough strength, its leaders can take on the role of critics and arbiters of authenticity over and against local Sufi cohesions. Its representatives can pit themselves against local Sufi communities and regional practices, claiming to stand as the norm against which local Sufi communities are measured as "deviations" compromised by acquiescence to local needs. In the city of Fes during Zarruq's lifetime, local Sufi cohesions grew in strength to the point that they served as the logistical support for revolution against the ruling political regime and ideological justification for the emergence of a new one. In reaction, Sufis with transregional allegiance to the discourses of scripture and law came forward as a political counter-force. They criticized the alliance of local Sufis and *shurafāʾ*, the "sharifian clans" who claimed spiritual potency due to their noble descent from the Prophet Muhammad's offspring, as extremist, partisan, and not authentically "Islamic." While this powerful local alliance forged the logistical and ideological basis of new dynastic rule in Morocco, Zarruq as a juridical saint argued that local Sufi communities needed to undergo reform in order to rein in such excesses and restore their practices to "Islamic" principles. Zarruq's life personifies the clash of these forces that are simultaneously religious, political, and cultural. His life and writings give us a clear lens through which to examine these forces in action in during a critical moment when North African polities underwent the painful transition into the early modern period.

In articulating a paradigm of juridical sainthood, Zarruq transcended local regional cohesions of Sufi communities and claimed to represent more universal Islamic norms. In contrast, from the local perspective, Zarruq betrayed these cohesions and the cultural loyalties they enshrined. By claiming a higher authority, he put himself forward as a reformer, able to point out and correct the errors, excesses, or inauthentic practices of local Sufi communities. Zarruq, and others who articulated a higher loyalty to scriptural norms and legal principles, spoke out in a critical counterpoint to local Sufi cohesions and their forceful entry into political activism. They saw themselves as "authentic" with regard to those who deviate from the norm, "lawful" with regard to those who trespass ritual, legal, and moral boundaries, and "sincere" with regard to those who use their status in local Sufi cohesions to gain personal or political power.

In making such bold claims, Zarruq was acting both as an individual and as the representative of a distinctive community of juridical Sufis. He adopted the paradigm of sainthood that emerged from their juridical Sufi community. Their community itself emerged through several generations of Sufi scholars who thrived in the Islamic colleges that the Marinid dynasty set up in urban centers in Morocco. Zarruq adapted their paradigm of sainthood to the crisis of his times by articulating it more forcefully, specifying more exactly its devotional forms and social ramifications, and sharpening its political force by claiming to embody its ideals personally as a juridical saint. His claims to absolute rectitude, selflessness, and sincerity as a juridical saint can be contextualized by analyzing historically how his ideals emerged from a regional Sufi community that was just one among many in Fes and northern Morocco. The analytical framework of regional Sufi cohesions conflicting with supra-regional Sufi alliances is the clearest way of explaining this set of phenomena. It steers clear of theoretical pitfalls that limit so many past analyses of Sufi communities, such as asserting binary oppositions between orthodoxy and heresy or between "official" Islam and "popular" Islam. This analytical framework not only illustrates the widest horizons of Zarruq's claims, but also explains the more limited contingencies of his origins.

Of course, competitors from among Zarruq's contemporaries who did not share his existential commitments heard his claim to sincerity and authenticity as subjectively self-serving, politically conservative, and culturally elitist. However, these claims were crucial to Zarruq and his followers, who felt inwardly and asserted outwardly that they were indeed juridical saints who were more authentically "Islamic" than others. As such, they were empowered to distinguish authentic practices from deviant practices and sincere motives from self-aggrandizing ones. Analyzing these claims cannot tell us who was actually right. But they can inform us about the concept of sainthood as it was contested in Morocco and North Africa and offer us insights into conflicts over authority in Islam that are applicable beyond this limited regional history.

Zarruq's Life within Temporal and Spatial Limits

Before we turn to the next six chapters that document Ahmad Zarruq's life in detail, the time frame and geographic scope of this study must be specified. The scope is firmly rooted in the events of Zarruq's life from 1442 to 1494 C.E. (846–899 Hijri). To contextualize his ideals and the community that shaped them, this study reaches back several generations before his birth to chart the growth of the juridical Sufi community. To analyze the reception and reaction to his life and teachings, it places Zarruq in the wider context of political upheaval and new dynastic formation in Morocco. This period spans from the sharifian revolution in Fes in 1460 C.E. (864 Hijri) to the establishment of the sharifian Saᶜdian dynasty's rule over Fes and northern Morocco in 1580 C.E. (988 Hijri). One can imagine this span of time as a "long sixteenth century" that includes the radical changes in the late fifteenth century C.E.. One can also chart these temporal limits according to the rhythms of the Islamic calendar, corresponding to the end of the ninth through the tenth Islamic century.[28] The inclusion of Hijri dates is more than a technicality; Hijri dates mark the inexorable progression toward the first Islamic millennium. That date, 1 Muḥarram 1000 Hijri (or October 19, 1591 C.E.), acted as an imaginative threshold for many Muslims, whether theologians, saints, or political adventurers. The late ninth and the tenth century after the *Hijra* witnessed an increase in millennial rhetoric about the advent of the Mahdi, both within Sufi communities and among political and social movements that looked to them for leadership or support.[29] Resistance to Mahdist rhetoric and Mahdist movements is a crucial aspect of Zarruq's reform program for Sufi communities.[30]

In a strange paradox, modern historians would label this time span as "early modern" in reference to Europe, but as "medieval" in reference to Islamic societies in Africa and Asia. Such a double standard disguises the intense interactions between European and Islamic states throughout this period and the abiding balance of power between them well into the eighteenth century C.E. In his groundbreaking historiographic revision of Islamic history, Marshall Hodgson addressed the ethical and political assumptions of this division into periods. He renamed this period "the era of gunpowder empires" to take into account the rise of the Sa^cdian, Ottoman, and Mughal empires in the Islamic Afro-Asian world, and to place Islamic polities, if not on par with European polities, then at least in comparison with them. This study follows Hodgson's lead in asserting that this time span falls within the "early modern" history of Islamic societies, for early modern (like the characteristic "gunpowder") places Islamic societies on an equal intellectual and conceptual ground with those in Eurocentric studies of history.

This study will combine these three ways of seeing the passage of time through the life of Ahmad Zarruq and his followers. It will analyze events that occur simultaneously in the long sixteenth century C.E., as the climax of the tenth century Hijri, and as an "early modern" period of increasingly shared complications between European states, Islamic polities, and interregional commerce. Through this complex lens, it is not sufficient to discuss sainthood and Sufism in Morocco as a local phenomenon. This study will examine types of Islamic sainthood that were in competition and conflict, punctuated by the contrapuntal themes of travel, voices of protest, and movements of reform that linked discrete regions and opposed regional hegemonies. Geographically, this study centers on the city of Fes, which was not only the city where Zarruq was born and raised, but was also the capital city of the ruling Marinid dynasty and the intellectual and juristic center of Morocco beyond the limits of Marinid rule. Rooted in Fes, the scope of this study extends across North Africa (along the coastal cities and interior Sahel oases) to Cairo in Egypt and Makka in the Hijāz (the Arabian peninsular area bordering the Red Sea), where Zarruq traveled, studied, lived, and built circles of followers. At its widest, this study takes into account larger forces in the whole Mediterranean basin and Atlantic seaways, where Spanish, Portuguese, and Ottoman expansion shaped Morocco's political, religious, and military history and with it the legacy of Zarruq's teachings.

PART II.
REBEL

I threw myself headlong into the care of the true One in a leap of faith unaccompanied by any trust in my own power and means.... I have found servanthood unadulterated by looking out for myself, and a vision unadulterated by relying on others.[1]

AHMAD ZARRUQ IS one of the most intriguing figures in the religious history of Islamic North Africa in the early modern period. Although he grew into a widely respected jurist and was revered by many as a saint, most of Zarruq's life was lived in loss and conflict, thrown "headlong into the care of the true One." He left his home city of Fes, Morocco, in exile at the tender age of twenty-four. He had displeased his Sufi master, who accused him of acting disrespectfully; as Zarruq was sincerely unrepentant for an offense he insisted he did not commit, he was banished from Fes as an upstart. Let us listen to his own words as he narrates his first exile from Fes after rebelling against his Sufi master. "I was not able to disavow that of which my Shaykh accused me, nor could I believe him because of what I knew myself to be true. I considered it possible that Allah was imposing a trial upon me.... After this conflict, the place that had once welcomed me so comfortably became suddenly cramped and constricted; so I left the city of Fes."[2]

This scene captures the persistent tone of Zarruq's life, a life led under threat by forces beyond his control, which he argued against with all the strength, acuity, and tenacity he could muster. He was exiled from Fes in the midst of social turmoil and political upheaval. Revolutionaries in the city, inspired by religious preachers and aggravated by heavy taxation, had executed the Muslim sultan and his Jewish ministers. The Jewish community in Fes, having thrived under the protection of the sultans of the Marinid dynasty, ducked for cover or fled the city under a threat of violence against them that was unusual in Moroccan history.

The details of this political revolution will become clear later in this chapter. Here, it suffices to note only that Zarruq was a conservative rebel, rejecting a popular revolution that was gaining momentum around him. Rebelling against conformity, Zarruq was forced to flee Fes, was misidentified as a Jew, and had his life placed in peril. Zarruq wavered between having people accuse him of apostasy, of "being a

Jew," and being defended by people who recognized him as a student of Islamic knowledge known in Fes. Later on his journey, which will be discussed in detail in chapter 5, Zarruq found himself utterly isolated, mistakenly in the Jewish quarter, "desolate and depressed."[3] Alone and under threat, Zarruq appears as the quintessential victim in his own autobiography. How did such a pathetic young man, bereft of what little he owned and stripped even of his identity as a Muslim citizen of the Moroccan capital, grow into one of North Africa's premier jurists and saints?

Thirty years later, near the end of the life he had led as an exemplary "jurist-saint," Zarruq could proclaim his status with iconoclastic verve:

> I have circled the east and the west searching for the truth. I have used all my resources in cultivating the self and curing its overweening impulses as far as possible to satisfy the true One.... I have taken refuge in total surrender in tranquility, and for this Allah has removed me from looking after my own existence and my own being, for this is the root cause of all weakness and spiritual ailments. I threw myself headlong into the care of the true One in a leap of faith unaccompanied by any trust in my own power and means. I have truly found that security from all things comes from staying aloof from all things. I have found contentment from all things by returning to Allah in all things, according to my own reserve of wisdom and ability.... I have found servanthood unadulterated by looking out for my self, and a vision [of myself] unadulterated by relying on others.[4]

Between starting off "despondent and depressed," holed up in mosque among hostile strangers, and finishing as a saint who has "circled the east and the west searching for the truth," Zarruq's life unfolds.

In these words, Zarruq claimed to embody the highest religious ideals of Muslims as a seeker who is both a juridical scholar and a saint. Yet he also admits that he has broken away from the well-trodden path and has rejected conformity with those around him who may aspire to the same ultimate goals. "I have found servanthood unadulterated by looking out for my self, and a vision [of myself] unadulterated by relying on others." For a saint, he uses unusually candid prose unashamed of the first-person pronoun "I." For a jurist, he makes extraordinary claims to absolute sincerity and freedom from the impulses of his own ego. The voice that weaves these contradictions together belongs to a person who has carefully crafted his individuality. This tone of voice, the very need to make a claim to individuality, is the result of a complex life and a lifelong quest to understand and practice the authority of Islamic sainthood. Although it involved subtle points of Islamic law and devotional practices, this quest was not esoteric. Rather, his struggle engaged the most acute historical events of his time, events that were ushering in the early modern period, events that would transform Islamic societies in their internal political organization, religious orientation, and relations with newly aggressive European states.

To understand how he transformed a rebel's exile into a search for the truth, we must trace the circle of Zarruq's life ourselves. We have to return to Zarruq's youth in Fes.

3 Promise

AHMAD ZARRUQ GREW up with a tenuous hold on privilege. He was born in 846 Hijri (1442 C.E.), in Fes, the political capital of Morocco under the Marinid dynasty and the center of intellectual and religious life in North Africa's far western reaches (*al-maghrib al-aqṣā*). This city seemed secure in its late-medieval stability. It was a city that prided itself on being one of the most vibrant centers of civilization, not just in North Africa but across the wider Islamic world. Zarruq's family position in Fes granted him the opportunity to study and to gain access to the class of religious notables of the city. Yet his hold on privilege was never firm. He was an orphan, always having to search for patronage and prove himself in the eyes of others. Even more precarious was the whole social structure: the Marinid edifice of political power supported by institutions of religious learning, which seemed so secure in Zarruq's youth, began to show signs of straining and cracking.

This image of a whole and harmonious world that is just out of reach will shape Zarruq's entire life story. He felt entitled to a holistic existence that cracked under his feet and fell into pieces around him just as he stepped into it as a maturing youth. This existential reality forced Zarruq to become resourceful; he searched through the rubble of his world for fragments (in the form of elusive patronage, hard-won knowledge, and spiritual insight) that suggested a possible wholeness. It also drove him toward a conservative creativity, to reconstruct a lost world by exercising authority as a writer, teacher, and spiritual guide.

In this way, Zarruq lived on the cusp of a new era in the Islamic world, the end of late-medieval stability that opened onto the "early modern" era (as we can call it with hindsight). He lived looking backwards in many respects, trying to recapture a world that was lost to him. The frantic activity of his life—combining deep study, long travels, and constant writing—adds a discordant note to the seemingly pensive and bitter tone of his life. It is as though he was trying to retrieve what was most valuable from a past that he imagined should have been his, and to preserve it jealously from the dust and dirt of a world being built around him on a pattern he disowned.

The basic theme in Zarruq's life is the harmony that he perceived between Islamic law and Sufi devotion. It is a balance that once shaped him, and to which he would cling when the world around him began to diverge from the ideal to which he thought it should conform. In the end, this balance is reality-in-the-making for Zarruq. Although he perceived it to be natural in his youth, he would have to fashion it around him in his maturity, in a world which seemed to be moving contrary to his efforts and veering dangerously toward imbalance and chaos.

Education in the madrasa system of Fes first provided Zarruq with this sense of balance. He gained access to this prestigious education through the social connections of his paternal grandmother. She was extraordinarily important for Zarruq, and education at the madrasa must have seemed like a natural extension of the personal training he received at her hands. Zarruq documented his own history, recalling his own childhood and young adulthood, giving us rare specificity in understanding his upbringing and his social connections to different religious authorities in Fes.

Within a week of Zarruq's birth, both his father and mother died of an epidemic that swept through Fes. An only child, he was entrusted to his grandmother, Umm al-Banīn, who raised him.[1] She was an advanced scholar in religious studies and Islamic law, and in Zarruq's estimation she was a saintly woman. She enjoyed social standing as a jurist and religious notary, though she had little material means.[2] Though being orphaned was a great disadvantage, Zarruq later saw it as the beginning of his training as a saint, since his father had entrusted his infant son to God's care as he died. Zarruq counted his upbringing, education, and material welfare as a major miracle. From this impoverished beginning, he supported five wives and many followers in his lifetime. Receiving donations from others, he never suffered from want.

His grandmother began Zarruq's education early. She did not allow him to breastfeed beyond nine months, but rather fed him almonds and figs she had chewed to a paste.[3] Dried fruits and nuts are understood in Morocco to stimulate intellectual prowess. She carried her infant charge into the company of religious scholars. She used to attend the study sessions one of Fes's pre-eminent jurists, ᶜAbdallah al-ᶜAbdūsī, along with her sister and another scholarly woman, with little Ahmad at their side.[4] She taught him to pray at the age of five and sent him off to primary school (*kuttāb*) to memorize scripture. At home, Zarruq's grandmother tried to inculcate in him a sense of belonging to an Islamic elite and consequent mistrust of "the commoners" (whether they were rural folk outside the walls of Fes, or petty merchants and artisans in the marketplaces within the city). She even changed his given name from Muḥammad to Aḥmad, since common people "mispronounced" Muḥammad in various local accents.

While learning the Qurʾān, Zarruq also served as the apprentice of a cobbler. His grandmother encouraged his apprenticeship, to provide for him in case he could not become a professional scholar or because she did not want him to "live off of religion." In either case, it was a wise decision. His protective grandmother died when Zarruq was only ten, and he became an orphan for a second time. By this age, he had memorized the Qurʾān and earned the status of being a *ḥāfiẓ*.

However, he had to work full-time with a cobbler to support himself, as he had no direct protection from his wider family.

Youth in the Madrasa

At age sixteen, Zarruq showed a spark of ambition. He gained admission to the chief Islamic college of Fes, Madrasat al-ᶜAṭṭārīn, while living in the college dormitory at Madrasa Būᶜinānīyya. He must have chafed under the routine of manual labor, having been raised in the aura of juridical scholarship. To obtain admission, he may have fallen back upon his grandmother's connections with the scholarly circles of Fes, for his grandmother's teacher, al-ᶜAbdūsī, was a leading jurist and the preacher at the congregational mosque of al-Qarawiyyīn.[5] Although al-ᶜAbdūsī died when Zarruq was only thirteen or fourteen, their earlier relationship may have gained Zarruq entry among al-ᶜAbdūsī's colleagues. Zarruq recalls him as "the axis of generosity" among the religious notables of Fes. After al-ᶜAbdūsī's death, the leader of that circle was Shaykh al-Qūrī, who became Zarruq's favorite teacher and early mentor. Zarruq pursued scriptural and legal studies for seven years under the guidance of al-Qūrī, who also introduced him to Sufi texts and devotions. In al-Qūrī, Zarruq found the embodiment of the balance between legal rectitude and spiritual potency that infused his early life.[6] He may even have found in his teacher a surrogate father.

In the madrasa, Zarruq concentrated on studying texts in jurisprudence (*uṣūl al-fiqh*). This was the master discipline that regulated and synthesized all the other traditional disciplines of scriptural knowledge, including Sufi devotional practices. As the Marinid dynasty came to power in Morocco (two centuries before Zarruq's birth), it earned the respect of jurists and scholars by patronizing religious colleges; in return, the religious notables grudgingly granted the dynasty legitimacy. The building program began in Fes, and soon the Marinid rulers built colleges (modeled upon Madrasat al-Ṣaffārīn in Fes) in every urban center under their rule. The scholars who taught in these colleges authored commentaries on juridical texts to standardize Islamic education. Zarruq's curriculum in college followed these standard texts closely.[7]

By Zarruq's time, the madrasa was not just a juridical training ground and a passport for government service. It was also a social institution that combined a rich cultural life with strong devotional elements. In the madrasa, Sufi devotions and legal studies thrived side by side, practiced and taught by the very same authorities. Madrasas formed the institutional anchors of a community of religious authorities whom we can call "juridical Sufis."[8] Under al-Qūrī's guidance, Zarruq joined this community and began to read texts by the Shādhilī Sufi master and jurist Ibn ᶜAṭāʾillah al-Iskandarī.[9] Al-Qūrī would have seen this as one step deeper into the roots (*uṣūl*) of Islamic practice. The basic ritual practices can be understood only through their roots in scripture. These can only be understood through reasoned discernment of the life of the Prophet. This can only be understood by spiritual emulation of his example, which necessitates participation in a Sufi community.

Al-Qūrī introduced Zarruq to the disciplines of his Sufi community through Ibn ᶜAṭāʾillah's text *Kitāb al-Tanwīr fi Isqāṭ al-Tadbīr* or *The Book of Illumination*. This text presents a simple argument in a penetrating way: to really believe in the singularity of Allah, one must cease relying on one's own ego, ambition, or planning. It advocates moderate asceticism by earning only from legal means, consuming only what one needs, and attributing all provision to Allah. In this way, *The Book of Illumination* would, with its emphasis on practice (*ᶜamal*), appeal to a student of Maliki jurisprudence. "You should know that your concern and direction of your affairs for your own sake is willful ignorance of how to really look after your own wellbeing. True believers know that when they leave aside anxious concern for themselves in deference to God's caring for them, then they enjoy a more wholesome care.... Their acute self-concern is transformed into dropping self-concern, just as their taking care of themselves aptly transforms into leaving aside looking after their own cares. In this regard, consider the Divine Speech: *enter houses by their proper doors*. Surely, the proper door entering into Allah's oversight of your concerns for you is simply your refusing to be anxiously concerned on your own behalf!"[10]

Despite its deceptively simple appeal to practical reason and juridical norms, *The Book of Illumination* opens a bottomless well of meditational possibilities. For if one abandons self-concern (as the author, Ibn ᶜAṭāʾillah, urges), one in effect abandons the ego as well, and must meditate on the possibilities as well as the limits of selflessness and sainthood. *The Book of Illumination* was only Zarruq's introduction to Sufi practice and spiritual cultivation. It led him to study the central text to Ibn ᶜAṭāʾillah's spiritual method, *al-Ḥikam, The Book of Wisdom Sayings*.

In fact, Ibn ᶜAṭāʾillah had written *The Book of Illumination* as a practical introduction and spiritual training to prepare Sufis to read and meditate upon his more abstract *Ḥikam, The Book of Wisdom Sayings*. Commentaries on the *Ḥikam* make the complementarity of these two texts explicit and illustrate how the *Wisdom Sayings* deepen and refine the basic ethical insights taught by *The Book of Illumination*. The first *Wisdom Sayings* all have to do with learning to be content with Allah's provision for you, rather than taking into your own hands care for yourself. Take, for example, the fourth Wisdom Saying: "Clear yourself of self-direction in everything that another has endeavored to decide for you so that you won't have to suffer exhaustion and endure aggravation." Zarruq would have studied the *Wisdom Sayings* with the aid of Ibn ᶜAbbād's commentary that unpacks the hidden meanings of the pithy saying.

> The self-direction (*tadbīr*) that people exert to control their affairs in the world is, from the Sufi point of view, a blameworthy quality because God has already endeavored to take care of their affairs for them for their own benefit. God has undertaken this so that people might leave their hearts free of self-

> direction's distraction and take up the more challenging task of being true servants.... Self-direction (*tadbīr*) is a person's empowering him or herself with things, decisions and means to reach goals in the world that fulfill desires and appetites. So people plot and plan for themselves in whatever they desire through actions and possessions (*aᶜmāl*) as well as mental and spiritual states (*aḥwāl*).... Abū al-Ḥasan al-Shādhilī has said, "If you must plot and plan for yourself, and how can you not plot and plan, then plan only on ways of not planning!" Finding ways to plan how not to plan for yourself ... is the whole path in general and its deepest fulfillment. To speak of it is a matter deep and wide. I have in brief, mentioning only the most succinct points that call to attention its importance, since Ibn ᶜAṭāʾillah himself has devoted a full text to the topic, called "The Book of Illumination," which is outstanding beyond the bounds of excellence. That little book alone penetrates to the heart of the matter in ways that make it sufficient to replace volumes of texts written by the Sufi community.[11]

These texts influenced Zarruq throughout his life. He would write commentaries upon the *Wisdom Sayings* (perhaps up to twenty commentaries throughout his life), and he integrated insights from Ibn ᶜAṭāʾillah's teachings into his other writings.

Zarruq displays his creative appropriation of Ibn ᶜAbbād when he comments on the Wisdom Saying quoted above, "clear yourself of self-direction." Zarruq writes that "Ibn ᶜAṭāʾillah mentions the verb 'to clear' for a subtle purpose. It implies the exhaustion of carrying a heavy burden and contrasts with the relaxation of comfort during moments cleared of all the anxiety that obscures our true nature. This exhaustion is the result of self-direction and calculation (*tadbīr*). It exhausts us because it places us in murky situations that are polluted (*takdīr*) and urges us to rebel against Divine command and decree (*taqdīr*).... The Prophet Muhammad has said 'Self-direction is half of life' while others have noted that 'Desisting from self-direction is all of life!' because those who stop caring for their own affairs can let themselves be taken care of in full by another who is more able."[12] These texts were the foundation of the method of Sufi cultivation that Zarruq advocated throughout his life. He inherited it from Ibn ᶜAbbād through the agency of Shaykh al-Qūrī.

Zarruq's very first textual production reveals the nature of his juridical Sufi training under the direction of al-Qūrī. Near the end of his school days, a friend asked Zarruq to record what he thought most profound from his wide reading. He produced a notebook of quotations, *Gift of the Disciple*, in answer to this request.[13] In it, the young Zarruq quotes from all these juridical Sufi authors in a way that reveals his teacher's approach of rooting Sufi insights and meditational methods in the canonical Sunni practices so staunchly advocated by Muslim jurists.

He begins by quoting the Sufis' praise of knowledge and reason and their encouragement of study and finely honed discernment. He then discusses the basic rituals of Islam, as laid out in the textbooks of jurisprudence, yet he tries to show the deep symbolic meaning that each basic action had for the Sufis. Washing before one prays, for instance, is not just a series of actions guided by rules and conditioned by legal constraints. In the young Zarruq's treatment, such ritual invites the Sufi to wash away heedlessness by remembering the errors of each part of the body that is washed and to renew one's mindfulness of the divine presence before, during, and after prayer.

His notebook of quotations reveals that Zarruq integrated Sufi practices into his training as a jurist. His mentor, al-Qūrī, introduced him into this world and guided him through his early absorption in its texts and personalities. To understand his world, we have to see al-Qūrī not just as Zarruq's mentor, but as the center of a whole network of juridical Sufis who were elaborating on an older tradition of "*Uṣūlī*" Sufism. Juridical Sufis were active members of the society in Fes and were developing a particular form of sainthood that was suited to their community: the paradigm of the juridical saint. With al-Qūrī at its center, this community engaged in quiet competition with other styles of Sufi devotion and other models of saintly authority.

As he matured, Zarruq would call this particular intellectual style of Shādhilī devotion "the *uṣūlī*'s way of being a Sufi (*taṣawwuf al-uṣūliyyīn*)."[14] An Usuli is a jurist who delves into the principles that lie behind jurisprudence and theology. An Usuli develops a sophisticated reasoning that links a sacred source to a legal decision, rather than relying on imitation of paradigmatic jurists of the past (*taqlīd*). An Usuli style of being a Sufi would similarly sift all Sufi devotions to make sure they were firmly rooted in a sacred source: the Qur'an, the Prophet Muhammad's personal example, or the practices of the early Muslim community. Zarruq would later reflect on his juridical Sufi training with al-Qūrī and systematize how jurists, Sufis, and Usulis were not just compatible but thoroughly interdependent. "Being a Sufi (*tasawwuf*) has an integral relation to religious obligation (*dīn*), just like the spirit (*rūḥ*) has an integral relation to the body (*jasad*).... The Sufi looks into the dimensions of spiritual completion and lack (or perfection and defect). The jurist looks into matters that get rid of aggravation and social conflict (*ḥaraj*), and the Usuli looks into matters that make faith sound and firm."[15]

The tradition of Usuli Sufis had arguably begun with the critical thinking of al-Ghazālī. Juridical Sufis elegantly refined and elaborated upon the path of Usuli Sufis, who cherished al-Ghazālī and traced their practices and philosophy to his critical thinking. The jurist and Sufi ᶜAlī ibn Ḥirzihīm (died 1164 C.E./559 Hijri) had introduced al-Ghazālī's texts and thinking into Morocco against much opposition from traditionalist Maliki jurists. Vincent Cornell has documented the important interactions between Sufis and Usulis; not only were there many prominent Sufis who were also jurists, but many jurists contributed to the preservation of saintly narratives and reputations through the composition of hagiographies. In his study of saintly paradigms in Andalusia and the Maghrib, Cornell has noted that the advent of "*uṣūlī*" methodology in jurisprudence sparked a major florescence of Sufi activities in these regions, a practice at once intellectual and devotional.[16]

Juridical Sufis contributed in important ways to developing paradigms for sainthood in Moroccan urban spaces, as well as in religious institutions in the countryside. From the time of Ibn ᶜAbbād, juridical Sufis had given the texts of al-Ghazālī and al-Muḥāsibī a permanent place in Moroccan Sufi piety, in ways that will be documented in the next section of this chapter. Harmony between jurists and Sufis is not a theme that strikes a resonant chord with scholars who research from an Orientalist orientation. Zarruq's experience among juridical Sufis goes against the grain of a large body of social scientific scholarship about Sufis and jurists in North Africa. One reason to delve into Zarruq's life is to call previous scholarly stereotypes into question.

The Invisibility of Juridical Sufis

As we venture with the young Zarruq into the world of Moroccan Sufis, we enter a world that is already thickly populated with stereotypes about Moroccan saints. Western scholars have already built up a thick literature on Sufis and Muslim saints in Morocco. All this literature is fascinating, but some of it is of doubtful accuracy. Al-Qūrī and the juridical Sufis do not fit the stereotypes that Western scholarship asserts is characteristic of Moroccan saints. This tradition of juridical Sufis has remained invisible to most Western scholars due to the narrowness of their theoretical lenses. For this reason, it is crucial to describe these stereotypes and clear the slate before describing and assessing juridical Sufis and their paradigm of sainthood. Zarruq's early involvement with this juridical Sufi community and his later reassertion of its paradigm of sainthood constitutes an intellectual challenge to the Western tradition of scholarship on Morocco.

This literature is based upon the French scholars Levi-Provençal, Berque, and Bel. Their analytic frameworks were reinforced by Ernest Gellner of Britain and amplified by Clifford Geertz, the most well-known and widely read American scholar on Moroccan Sufism. French studies sponsored by the colonial regime asserted a categorical divide between "rural, uneducated Berber" religious figures who are Sufis (called marabouts) and "urban, literate Arab" religious figures who are jurists (*fuqahāʾ*). Alfred Bel's influential study asserts that the subtle doctrines of Islam as practiced in urban areas degenerated when transferred to the Moroccan countryside. There they were reduced to primordial Berber religious conventions that were simply magic and superstition. "Does not the idea of the tutelary God of Islam—more powerful than demonic spirits—lead to that by which God can transmit to certain men, his friends, a part of his power, his *baraka*? To become one of these men by Sufi exercises, to gather from them human fetishes (*hommes fetiches*) a parcel of their beneficent influence, which chases and destroys the forces of evil, was a perspective well in accord with everyone's aspirations."[17] As exemplified in this passage, French colonial ethnographies reduced Sufi devotional communities to a kind of "primitive religion" that lacked the requisite intellectual sophistication to be a basis for civilization.

In particular, Alfred Bel refurbishes the notion of "fetishes" that characterized "primitive" religion in Western Africa.[18] In his conception, Sufis approached saints as human fetishes that they could manipulate to channel supernatural power to secure their purely practical projects and concerns. Beyond justifying the civilizing mission of French colonization in Africa, these ethnographic representations posited a radical binary division between Arabs who were doctrinaire Muslims and Berbers who were only nominally Islamized while remaining "anthropolatrous" (worshiping other human beings). This agenda, followed to its logical political conclusion, led the French colonial government to enforce the "Berber Decree" in 1930, declaring that Arabs would be ruled by the Moroccan sultan and Islamic law while Berbers would be ruled by their own local councils and customary practice. This bold decree sparked the modern anti-colonial nationalist struggle that led to Moroccan independence. Even after independence, the concepts that grounded colonial-era studies continued to hold sway over Western sociologists and anthropologists, who have built upon them while ignoring or concealing their original political agenda. After the colonial era, social scientific studies describe Sufis as exemplifying "popular religion" rather than the more pejorative "primitive religion." Yet the idea persists that sainthood is "heretical" when juxtaposed with an "orthodox" scripturalist Islam, which jurists are assumed to uphold.[19]

Western scholarship about Sufis and saints in Morocco has been obsessed with "marabouts." This is the supposedly indigenous term that anthropologists have applied to Moroccan saints. The marabout is defined as a holy person who channels blessing and power from God and a supernatural world into the human realm; the marabout is a supposedly indigenous term for the "human fetish" described by Bel. The marabouts, according to anthropologists like Gellner and Geertz, personify a Moroccan Islam that is "activist, rigorous, dogmatic and more than a little anthropolatrous," so the Moroccan saint, in general and apparently without exception, is a "self-made warrior saint" who combines holy man piety with strongman politics.[20] Such holy men thrive on the Moroccans' alleged propensity to worship God through a human form (the meaning of "anthropolatry"), especially in the countryside and far from the influence of jurists who form the foil against marabouts. However, the obsession with marabouts obscures more than it reveals about sainthood in Morocco. It certainly obscures the tradition of juridical Sufis. This might explain why al-Qūrī and others have been largely ignored by historians and scholars in Religious Studies.[21]

As later anthropologists embraced the idea of "historical anthropology," they tried to limit the generalizations about marabouts without, however, questioning their historical validity. Anthropologists assert that a "maraboutic crisis" emerged during the time of Zarruq's life in the late fifteenth century, altering the religious and political terrain of Morocco. If that were so, Zarruq's life story and writings should vividly portray his reaction against these forces. Yet Zarruq never uses the term "marabout" to describe Sufis or saints of any sort. Like Zarruq, other chroniclers of the lives of Sufis and saints from this whole period (fifteenth and sixteenth centuries) who compiled numerous hagiographic collections do not use the term "marabout."[22]

How could scholars have gotten it so wrong? Within a scholarly discipline, concepts can grow with a slow accumulation, gaining legitimacy by dispersal and common use rather than by accuracy. Anthropologists originally picked up the term "marabout" from French ethnographies about local communities in Algeria, who may have used it to describe the holy men in their midst.[23] Anthropologists used the term in an expansive way to mean holy people or saints in general throughout Islamic North Africa. Then they projected the term into the past as a way of conceptualizing "popular religion" and the rise of new dynasties that claimed legitimacy as sharifian clans. The term began to be projected into the past without being limited by reading the rich archival sources that preserve how North African Sufis in that past actually described saints and their relation to law, spirituality, and political power. In the end, the anthropologists have obscured important distinctions between different Sufi communities and diverse types of saints. Zarruq's life story forces us to question the category of marabout and explore what it has obscured.

In questioning the validity of the conceptual category "marabout," this study argues not only that anthropologists got it wrong, but also that anyone who posits that one type of saint is the organic expression of a regional culture would get it wrong. Anthropologists like Geertz depict culture as personality writ large such that a description of one man (whether a king or a saint) can represent "the culture" of an entire region over many centuries.[24] In contrast, this study insists that saints are always of multiple types, even within any one "culture," and that they are often in conflict in any particular historical situation. This is one of the basic insights that the study of Zarruq's life provides us.

Zarruq's teacher, Shaykh al-Qūrī, exemplified one such type with a distinct model of sainthood that was particularly important in the urban areas of northern Morocco in the late medieval period. He and his followers in the juridical Sufi community upheld an ideal type of saint who differs radically from the maraboutic model. However, their ideal was never the only one; it was one of many competing paradigms of sainthood in North Africa. Distinct Sufi communities in specific historic conditions have asserted a paradigm of sainthood that is characterized by the qualities that anthropologists have identified as "maraboutic"; this paradigm came to dominance only gradually with great struggle against competing paradigms of Islamic sainthood. The paradigm of sainthood that contrasts most vividly with what has been called "maraboutic" sainthood is that of the juridical saint. In Zarruq's early life, it was Shaykh al-Qūrī who exemplified this paradigm of the juridical saint.

Al-Qūrī enjoyed a position of social esteem as a teacher in a madrasa, a preacher, and a chief judge of the capital city. Yet many students who gathered around him saw him as more than just a teacher. Some saw him as the center of a Sufi community that overlapped almost fully with his circle of students, fellow jurists, and scholars. In the generations preceding Zarruq, this community of juridical Sufis was especially active in Meknes and Fes among the urban centers of northern Morocco. They developed a devotional style, textual foundations, Sufi lineages, and spiritual affiliations to renowned saints that set them off as a discrete community. Within their community, they also developed a paradigm of sainthood in accord with their needs and aspirations. The type of spiritual master and guide that emerged from their community can be termed a "juridical saint." This term renders into English the Arabic term *al-Walī al-Jāmiᶜ*, which literally means "the comprehensive saint" who joins together jurisprudence and saintly authority.[25]

The primary characteristic of this juridical Sufi community is that its members perceived a harmony between law and devotion under the guidance of a spiritual master. This harmony was not just a rhetorical ideal, but a lived practice in their community. In earlier centuries, Sufis who were trained as jurists often played a leading role in Sufi communities. They put their literary and legal skills as jurists to use in the Sufi communities to which they belonged. They recorded the lives of the saints at their center in hagiographic texts, elaborated theories to explicate sainthood, and defended their communities against critics.

Yet in al-Qūrī's circle, juridical Sufis were moving beyond this participation in wider Sufi communities; they were building a distinctive Sufi community unto themselves. In this context, they defined a type of saint particular to their own community, a saint who not only had jurists as devotees and allies, but a saint who was himself a jurist. This mode of sainthood stood out in particular relief to Zarruq, who perceived in al-Qūrī its zenith. As Zarruq records al-Qūrī's personality, he presents him as more than a highly revered teacher or spiritual mentor. He presents him in the language normally reserved for saints. Al-Qūrī's personality was "illuminating" in all dimensions, spiritually as well as intellectually. Zarruq later would commit to paper the contours of this mode of sainthood in sharply defined ways and commit himself to embodying its ideals. And Zarruq was not alone in perceiving his teacher as a saint.

Juridical Sufis and Saints in Fes

Al-Qūrī commanded the allegiance of a small community of students, scholars, jurists, and preachers in Meknes and Fes. Such a community of juridical Sufis saw the figure of the "juridical saint" as a legacy of Ibn ᶜAbbād al-Rundī and as an authentic expression of the Shādhilī lineage in Morocco. This mode of sainthood functioned to fuse jurists and Sufis into one community. Elevating some of their members as saints represented a powerful commitment to this ideal of community and a way of giving its devotional practices depth and resonance. Juridical Sufis in previous eras showed respect and deference to jurists who defined the outer limit of religiously sanctioned behavior. But they did not claim that legal training is compulsory before one can become a Sufi or that the saint who leads them must be a jurist. In contrast, the juridical Sufi community around al-Qūrī was refining this juridical Sufi practice to claim that one cannot be a saint who is not a jurist. Zarruq himself took many themes of juridical Sufism to an extreme to forge it into a movement of reform in which the jurist becomes a saint.

In this paradigm lies an inherent contradiction. The juridical saint shields himself from public acclaim and popular recognition through his role as jurist, scholar, and preacher. He is an official in a public institution, and that public front prevents him from having recourse, need, or opportunity to perform explicit miracles or build a wide community of followers. It was a way for him to "hide his saintly status" from an expectant public.[26] Therefore, this paradigm of the juridical saint emerges from a very limited community of "insiders" at official religious and educational institutions. Juridical saints interacted with a wider public through their official roles while interacting among students and colleagues as spiritual guides. For this reason, textual records present them with two distinct faces. Most people in the cities respected them as scholars, preachers, and jurists (roles which already gave them a certain valence as "holy men"). However, their community of students and fellow jurists perceived some of them to be saints and described them in terms usually reserved for saints who lead Sufi communities.

This double face of the juridical saint will become clear after an analysis of the personalities who participated in building this paradigm. These include al-Qūrī and those who preceded him (from whom he took on this role). Al-Qūrī was born in Meknes, where he pursued religious studies, including jurisprudence, and qualified for a seat of instruction in Meknes. When al-Qūrī moved to Fes, he gained an appointment as a teacher in the madrasa system, where he gained renown as a teacher of jurisprudence. He joined the circle of juridical teachers who were not mere professors, but a socially powerful group of religious authorities. Al-Qūrī's erudition and eloquence led to his eventual appointment as the preacher at al-Qarawiyyīn, one of the highest religious posts in the Marinid polity. He also served as a jurist and judge.

To this extent, al-Qūrī's life reads like that of a successful jurist and scholar, guided by the social ambition to achieve the high offices available in the Marinid bureaucracy. However, this is but half the story. Sources record that he lived a vivid inner life, free of any ambition for the high posts to which he was appointed. Zarruq notes that some of his companions wrote texts about al-Qūrī's virtues and personality as if he were a saint. Although these texts have not been preserved, Zarruq uses the terms *manāqib* and *shamāʾil* to describe al-Qūrī's qualities; these are terms descriptive of heroic and saintly virtues. The students who rose to fame under al-Qūrī's tutelage preserved his memory. Besides Zarruq himself, they include Ibn Ghāzi, Abū al-Ḥasan al-Zaqqāq, and Aḥmad al-Wansharīsī.[27] Zarruq recounts, "Al-Qūrī was a sign of God's presence in Fes. He was the spiritual leader of the community (*shaykh al-jamāʿa*) due to his knowledge, awareness and perception. He was always prepared to be summoned by the people in case of public disputes and social problems.... Al-Qūrī's teaching sessions were full of benefits and wonderful stories. He had such a strength of presentation and limitless intelligence, mixed with sweet nature and strict piety and manliness (*ḥifẓ al-muruwwa*)."[28] In this intimate description of Zarruq's teacher and exemplar, we have a vivid example of Sufi devotion that pervades scholarship. As a juridical Sufi, al-Qūrī did not publicize his lineage in Sufi initiations, but relied on the transmission of knowledge to spread spiritual insight. Zarruq describes him as not just a juridical Sufi, but as a kind of saint concealed within the demeanor of a jurist. He ascribes to al-Qūrī the multivalent title *Shaykh al-Jamāʿa*. On the surface this was a title befitting the chief judge of an urban community, similar to the more bureaucratic title *Qāḍī al-Jamāʿa*. Yet this title hints at a deeper authority, for Sufis used the term *Shaykh al-Jamāʿa* to describe the person of highest authority within their community, a person considered a saint.[29] Although the general public might comprehend al-Qūrī as the chief jurist, those in his Sufi community around him perceived him to be a saint.

It was typical of this community to describe their leader in such terms, which might be understood in relation to an official position as jurist or in relation to a devotional community, depending on one's own position. Al-Qūrī himself tried to draw these two fields together in his method of teaching. Zarruq highlights how al-Qūrī would seamlessly embroider Sufi insights into discourses on legal and scriptural issues, creating a harmony that Zarruq tried to recreate in his own Sufi notebook as a young man. Zarruq records that al-Qūrī "would recall the words of Sufi masters both old and recent, along with those of the jurists and hadith scholars. He would embroider the text with stories about them, mentioning their times of birth and death and examine in detail reports about them. Then he would conclude the discourse with retelling the hadith reports that they had fought over in trying to secure the victory of their particular school of thought. Indeed, his sittings were endlessly enjoyable for those who would sit listening."[30] Zarruq was not alone in being profoundly moved by Al-Qūrī. Ibn Ghāzī wrote that "al-Qūrī was deeply immersed in knowledge, and this knowledge was saturated with his being a Sufi (*taṣawwuf*)" while Aḥmad al-Wansharīsī noted his "qualities of radiant knowledge."[31] Al-Qūrī shared these qualities with his close friend and fellow jurist Aḥmad ibn ʿAlī al-Fīlālī, who was known as the Sufi exemplar of Fes (*al-qudwa al-ṣūfī*).[32] The titles *Qudwa* and *Shaykh* had deep resonance among Sufis; both were applied to a person who was believed to act as a saint for a particular community that gathered around him for instruction and devotional piety.

However, as a juridical saint, al-Qūrī encountered contradictions while serving in official posts as professor, chief judge, and preacher. The first was the common perception that government service was not a pure way of earning a livelihood. Al-Qūrī would avoid ostentatious living and even refuse to consume his government stipend. Zarruq revealed that he secretly learned that al-Qūrī would seclude himself in private and weave palm-fiber into useful objects without anyone knowing. He would give these to a merchant to sell in exchange for food to eat during the month of Ramaḍān, food that neither government service nor profit from religious guidance had tainted.[33]

Other scholars did not have the same restraint and ethical strength of al-Qūrī, and they used the study of jurisprudence to collect wealth and social capital. Al-Qūrī criticized the age for its corruption, especially as scholars and judges stoked their ambitions to gain high positions. Zarruq recalls that al-Qūrī refused to marry, not wanting to bring a child into the world in such a state of corruption.[34] In this light, Zarruq's comment about his teacher's "preservation of manliness" takes on a new meaning. Even without the security of a wife and children, al-Qūrī was able to maintain his public dignity, simple lifestyle, and ethical integrity in the luxurious Marinid capital. Al-Qūrī represented the mature exemplar of juridical Sufis, who could perceive in this jurist the light of a saint. The distinct type of sainthood advocated by this community originated with the Sufi and jurist Ibn ᶜAbbād al-Rundī (d. 792 Hijri/1390 C.E.). This type of sainthood developed continuously until reaching its culmination almost eighty years later in al-Qūrī.

The example of Ibn ᶜAbbād set the parameters for this mode of sainthood, and the community of juridical Sufis cherished his memory in hagiographies.[35] This narrative reveals the contradictory elements that made up his personality and characterized the sainthood that later juridical Sufis tried to model. "Children loved Ibn ᶜAbbād more than they loved their own fathers and mothers. They would wait outside his house in large numbers, waiting for the moment when he would come out to head to the mosque for prayer.... When they spotted Ibn ᶜAbbād, they would rush forward, jostling for the chance to greet him and kiss his hand."[36] This gentleness and simplicity contrasts with Ibn ᶜAbbād's stern cleverness when facing abuses of power, a quality of exemplary jurists. Ibn ᶜAbbād took up important public positions in government-sponsored religious institutions and served as a teacher in Meknes and as the preacher of the congregational mosque al-Qarawiyyīn in Fes. The same source describes this incident: "Once he was leading Friday congregational prayers [gathering] common people along with the Sultan, his courtiers and followers.... Now, some people had raised complaints that the governor (*walī*) was being oppressive. So Ibn ᶜAbbād ... gave a sermon to the people in the presence of the governor himself and notable witnesses. He said, 'Wouldn't it be better for the people's welfare if the governor were not to remain [in power] for another year?' Without a doubt, that is what became true." Most common people revered him as a preacher, while many students flocked around him as a teacher; still others in this narrow circle of juridical Sufis saw in him a saint.

Born in the Andalusian town of Ronda, Ibn ᶜAbbād received a young scholar's education. For spiritual development, he focused on texts of Ibn ᶜAṭāʾillah, including *The Book of Wisdom Sayings*, *The Book of Illumination,* and *The Subtle Blessings* (*Laṭāʾif al-Minan*).[37] After a period of religious studies in the madrasas of Tilimsan and Fes, Ibn ᶜAbbād moved to Salé where he joined a Sufi community. This circle gathered around the ascetic and scholarly saint Ibn ᶜĀshir, who specialized in the texts upon which juridical Sufis built their method, like those of al-Muḥāsibī, al-Makkī, and al-Ghazālī.[38] This method's formal exterior was illumined from within by the wise probings of the *Ḥikam*. Ibn ᶜAbbād initiated a tradition of teaching the *Wisdom Sayings* (that became a primary tradition of all Sufis in Morocco), authoring an important early commentary on the text and establishing the discussion of it and meditation on it as the central exercise of this juridical type of Sufi training.[39] Upon the death of Ibn ᶜĀshir, Ibn ᶜAbbād moved back to Fes to take up an official position as preacher at the mosque of al-Qarawiyyīn, where he reached out to children and preached out to nobles. He joined a growing community of juridical Sufis who were active in Fes and especially in Meknes (away from the political turmoil of the capital).

This small community grew in the three generations that separated Ibn ᶜAbbād and Ahmad Zarruq, as its members found official support and patronage under Marinid rulers. Ibn ᶜAbbād was joined by his friend Mūsā al-ᶜAbdūsī.[40] Mūsā al-ᶜAbdūsī excelled in the study and explication of the *Mudāwwana*, a massive, four-volume compendium of Prophetic traditions and Maliki commentaries.[41] Juridical Sufis recited and explicated the *Mudāwwana* as a devotional exercise, even though as a juridical text it was of little use as a teaching text in the madrasa syllabus. Rather, juridical Sufis used it as a literary icon that preserved "an image" of the Prophet, and through that image conjured up his presence within the community.[42] Most of the leaders of this community who were described as "saintly" had memorized the entire text and recited it publicly during religious celebrations. Al-ᶜAbdūsī became famous for public recitations of the *Mudāwwana* and found its public, juridical nature to complement the private, contemplative pursuit of the *Ḥikam* and other ethical Sufi treatises. Ibn ᶜAbbād had made this congruence explicit when he said that *Qūt al-Qulūb* was to the interior life what the *Mudāwwana* was to the exterior life of religion, an "all-sufficient and irreplaceable" manual of practice.[43] Ibn ᶜAbbād used to attend al-ᶜAbdūsī's recitations and teaching sessions, in the company many other famous juridical Sufis.[44] Al-ᶜAbdūsī's emphasis on the *Mudāwwana* and Ibn ᶜAbbād's emphasis on the *Wisdom Sayings* set the inner and outer practices of devotion that would mark their colleagues off as a distinct Sufi community.

As this juridical Sufi community grew in numbers and prestige, its members began to find qualities of saints in some of its leading members. These were the initial signs of a distinct mode of sainthood that would only gradually appear fully articulated. In Meknes, a community grew up around Mūsā al-ᶜAbdūsī. One of his followers, ᶜAbdullah ibn Ḥamd, developed a reputation for fusing religious knowledge with ascetic renunciation.[45] Hearing of his reputation, Ibn al-Futūḥ migrated to Meknes to find one who could guide him along the path of spiritual development, and the two became fast friends.[46] Together, they were leaders for the second generation of this juridical Sufi community.

Ibn al-Futūḥ had been a bright and promising young jurist in the educational colleges of Fes, but erotic awakening sparked a crisis in him. After he exchanged glances with a beautiful woman on the streets of Fes, she reproached him and exhorted him to fear God. The following night, he had a dream about a beautiful bride being carried to his home; when she stepped out of the palanquin, he saw that she was "an ugly hag," and recognized his threatening bride as *al-dunyā,* the lower world. He vowed to renounce the world, yet he could not find anyone from his student friends to encourage him along this path of renunciation. Someone advised him that "if you want a friend who combines knowledge with ascetic endeavor, then you must go join Ibn Ḥamd in Meknes." He looked to Ibn Ḥamd as his saintly guide and means of spiritual development. Even after leaving college and the capital city, Ibn al-Futūḥ was active in jurisprudence and teaching.[47] He was buried next to Ibn Ḥamd in Meknes, and their twin tombs became popular points of pilgrimage and visitation.[48]

The reputation of these juridical Sufis across the urban spaces of northern Morocco attracted a younger generation of disciples in Meknes. As they matured, many of them moved to Fes to take up official positions in state-sponsored religious institutions. From this circle, ᶜImrān al-Janātī was famed for having learned the skills of explicating the *Mudāwwana* from Mūsā al-ᶜAbdūsī, and he passed this learning on to the young al-Qūrī.[49] In Fes, this community included ᶜUmar al-Ragrāgī.[50] Ibn Ghāzi praised him as the "best of the ascetics, leader of the worshippers, and saint (*walī allah*)" to sum up his knowledge of jurisprudence, his personal righteousness, and his ability to inspire others. He took up the position as preacher and prayer leader (*imām*) of the congregational mosque of al-Andalus, in the "Andalusian Quarter" in the southern bank of Fes. His student and disciple ᶜIsa ibn ᶜAllāl al-Kattāni al-Maṣmūdī took over that position on his retirement; al-Maṣmūdi had been a disciple of Ibn al-Futūḥ in Meknes, which shows the continuity in this tradition between those two urban communities.[51] From Ibn al-Futūḥ al-Maṣmūdi learned to combine his social role as a jurist and his religious role as a saintly exemplar. Members of this community compared al-Maṣmūdi explicitly with Ibn ᶜAbbād as a saint suited to lead quietist, juridical, and moderate Sufis who served the urban Muslim community from within institutional structures.[52]

Another member of this community, ᶜAbdullah al-ᶜAbdūsī, moved from Meknes to become the sermon deliverer of the congregational mosque of al-Qarawiyyīn, on the other bank of Fes.[53] Zarruq calls him "the jurist, Sufi master, saint and judge (*faqīh*, *shaykh*, *ṣāliḥ*, *muftī*)" in recognition of the many public roles he united in one person. In his time, ᶜAbdullah al-ᶜAbdūsī became a powerful public leader and ethical exemplar. Zarruq recalls that he was "the undisputed leader in giving advice and admonition to the Muslims.... He insisted on having legal limits (*ḥudūd*) obeyed and giving everyone their rights (*ḥuqūq*)." He was a jurist and a professor of scriptural traditions (*fiqh al-hadīth*), who became the preacher at the mosque of al-Qarawiyyīn, following the model of Ibn ᶜAbbād. In acknowledging his role as the upholder of this tradition of juridical Sufi training, Zarruq calls him "the master of Sufis and jurists" (*shaykh al-fuqahā᾽ wa'l-ṣūfiya*).[54]

Zarruq's prime exemplar, al-Qūrī, came to Fes as a member of this spiritual community. ᶜAbdullah al-ᶜAbdūsī helped al-Qūrī to move to Fes from Meknes and promoted him as a protégé. ᶜAbdullah al-ᶜAbdūsi and al-Qūrī became leaders among the generation of juridical Sufis who flourished in Fes. Al-Qūrī had studied in Meknes under Ibn Ḥamd and Ibn al-Futūḥ and had been a devoted disciple of their spiritual method. Ibn Ghāzī relates that even though al-Qūrī had studied with many teachers, he relied on Ibn Ḥamd as his spiritual exemplar. Al-Qūrī himself attracted many disciples to this model of saintly authority.[55]

Al-Qūrī as the Model of Juridical Sufis

There are some particular features that characterize this circle of juridical Sufis. These features are evident in the figure of al-Qūrī, and they link him to the earlier generations of juridical Sufis outlined above. First, they were all jurists, who sought to unite jurists and Sufis together into one community. Mirroring the companionship of Mūsā al-ᶜAbdūsī and Ibn ᶜAbbād, the members of this community centered their devotions around the axis of two texts, the *Mudāwwana* and the *Ḥikam*. They perpetuated the tradition of a public recitation of the *Mudāwwana*. This would be an occasion for public pious celebration, and they tried to graft this ritual onto the long tradition of reciting love poetry, both in popular recitals and in Sufi gatherings. Mūsā al-ᶜAbdūsī used to recite this poem:

> There is nothing written in all the volumes of poetry
> like the *Mudāwwana* that incites a pious swoon.
> Sahnūn fashioned it for those like us who desire:
> Oh Lord who made Sahnūn! Make me like Sahnūn![56]

He lauded the juridical commentary written by Sahnūn as superior to love poetry in the ecstasies it inspires! That was a strategy to call the Sufis and jurists to sit together in one gathering, as one community. For in reciting the whole juridical text, they would interweave it with commentary: legal observations, historical example, and ethical insights. Like love poetry, this juridical performance could have enchanting effects; it was said of one of al-Qūrī's companions, Aḥmad al-Mazgildī, that "[i]f you would sit down to listen to him recite the *Mudāwwana* you would experience white magic for sure."[57] Zarruq praised his master al-Qūrī for being "the last of the scholars to continue the Maliki custom of committing the whole *Mudāwwana* to memory."[58]

If reciting the *Mudāwwana* marked the outer, public face of their teaching, meditating on the *Ḥikam* formed the inner, private source of illumination. They would study intensely these Wisdom Sayings of Ibn Aṭāᵓillah as the form of contemplation and poetic expression most suited to a mind trained in *uṣūli* methodology and a spirit attuned to public service as jurists. From the time of Ibn ᶜAbbād, this community engaged in commentary on the *Ḥikam*. The importance of this genre of spiritual hermeneutics will become clear during the discussion of Zarruq's program of reform in part III.

This fusion of juridical teaching and Sufi training took place in the state-sponsored religious colleges. Members of this community were the agents for the "revival of religious sciences" that historians note during the Marinid reign. They were among the teachers who made commentaries of Maliki juridical texts popular material for study in these colleges. Their public recitations of the *Mudāwwana,* like the public celebration of the Prophet Muḥammad's birthday (*mawlid al-nabī*), were new forms of pious celebration that gained popular acclaim in the Marinid period. They pictured these commentaries as conduits to a heightened religious life. In teaching they were not only transmitting knowledge, but also exercising a form of religious authority that their circle of followers described as the work of saints.

Later hagiographies that self-consciously aimed to preserve the memory of saints do not provide a clear portrait of this community. Rather, such a portrait emerges from the recollections of their juridical students who formed the natural audience for their spiritual potency. These students recorded the character and lineage of their teachers to demonstrate the legitimacy of their own scriptural knowledge.[59] The saintly characteristics of their teachers emerge only from the background of these records. Therefore, it is difficult to trace the concrete Sufi affiliations or rituals of these scholars. They did not distinguish between being a pupil with a teacher and being a disciple with a saint; both relations of discipline were complementary and mutually reinforcing. Leaders in this juridical Sufi community did not publicize their Sufi lineages. They derived their legitimacy from other, scholarly forms as jurists, rather than by cultivating an explicit lineage of Sufi masters.

For this reason, it is difficult to chart the development of initiations among this circle into the Shādhilī Sufi communtiy. From their concentration on the *Ḥikam,* they formed an attachment to the Shādhilī community, though their lineage as Shādhilīs is not clear. Ibn ᶜAbbād himself possessed a document of permission (*ijāza*) to teach and transmit the text of a Shādhilī invocation, but he may not have had a formal initiation into the Shādhilī community.[60] Hagiographic sources gloss over this distinction; they depict him as a Shādhilī due to the reputation of his commentary on the *Ḥikam*. They note that he was surely a Shādhilī by natural inclination rather than by formal affiliation and initiation.[61] Sufi initiations are not usually assumed because of a person's devotion to a particular text, but among juridical Sufis in Morocco, devotion to the *Ḥikam* seemed to grant initiation into the Shādhilī lineage without further formalities.[62]

Despite these ambiguities, members of this juridical Sufi circle experimented with more formal initiations and other rituals that characterized organized Sufi communities. In Meknes, the community of Ibn Ḥamd and Ibn al-Futūḥ were not content with a permission to teach the text of the *Ḥikam*. They desired an initiation that would link them intimately with the author, Ibn ᶜAṭāᵓillah. Beyond scholarly legitimacy, they sought affiliation with a saint. They saw Ibn ᶜAṭāᵓillah not only as an author whose message could be grasped through reason and discussion, but also as a saint whose spiritual potency could be transmitted through a personal connection as initiated disciples, even after the saint's death. Ibn Ḥamd was initiated into the al-Wafāʾīyya community (which was connected to the Egyptian Shādhilī lineage of Ibn ʿAṭāʾillah's followers).[63] This is probably the first such initiation to link a Moroccan Sufi with the Shādhilī lineage of Ibn ʿAṭāʾillah.[64] It is no accident that Ibn Ḥamd and his followers would choose this Egyptian lineage over the geographically and cultural closer lineage of the Tunisian Shādhilīs, for Ibn ʿAṭāʾillah had been both a saint and a jurist. He and his followers enjoyed official positions as judges and jurists in Cairo in addition to their Sufi activities. Intellectual and urbane, they tended to leave aside the charismatic and politically rebellious facets of Shaykh al-Shādhilī's personality.[65]

However, this Wafāʾī connection was tenuous and far-flung. To compensate, this circle in Meknes cultivated quiet or private institutional Sufi rituals. One form of initiation they used was "the spiritual handshake." ʿAbdallah al-ʿAbdūsī would administer a ceremonial handshake, the squeeze of which had been passed down from master to disciple from the Prophet Muḥammad himself. He would explain that the meaning of squeezing the hand was "intensification of your religious responsibility (*dīn*)."[66] The man who seems to have introduced this handshake into juridical Sufi circles was one of the teachers of al-Qūrī, Muḥammad al-Ghassānī (see appendix A).[67] The spiritual handshake was an invisible form of intimate submission to a spiritual guide and an invisible personal connection to the Prophet. It was therefore similar to investment with a Sufi cloak (*khirqa*), but without the display of a social role inherent in wearing distinctive clothing.[68] Like his friend Ibn al-Ghāzī, Zarruq looked upon such Sufi rituals and training with enthusiasm, as a necessary dimension to his training in law and scripture. He criticized jurists who avoided a Sufi orientation; he thought they were ethically lax, hypocritical, or self-interested. The young Zarruq held that only jurists who were fully immersed in Sufi devotions under the guidance of a juridical saint could be just and avoid abusing their power.

This is the community of juridical Sufis that revolved around al-Qūrī, among whom Zarruq hoped to secure a place. It is not clear whether they recited a specific type of prayer (*wird*) or the litanies (*aḥzab*) of al-Shādhilī. Their devotional life centered on the study and contemplation of the *Ḥikam* (along with other texts of Ibn ʿAṭāʾillah). The public dimension of their Sufi devotions was reciting the juridical text of the *Mudāwwana*. In general, this community of juridical Sufis relied on their official positions in the madrasa or mosque to give them status in society. They drew followers and disciples from their wider circle of students. Their leaders did not have to enter a public space of performing dramatic miracles to stake a claim to saintly authority. Rather, their saintly characteristics emerged subtly from their routine activities as teachers, judges, and preachers. Their withdrawal from many dimensions of "common" life in the city was a sign of their sainthood. Yet their public role as teachers, judges, and preachers placed them in a paradox of confronting public admiration with studied aloofness. The figure of Ibn ʿAbbād served as their exemplar. When walking through Fes between his home and the mosque of al-Qarawiyyīn, people would throng around him (from Marinid nobles to commoners) and try to take his hand, kiss his finger, or touch his clothes. Zarruq penned this couplet to praise the way that Ibn ᶜAbbād concealed his saintly power behind a studied veil of modesty:

> His knowledge was such that he never claimed to really know
> His poverty was such that he never claimed to be a renunciant
> His insight led him to blame anyone who witnessed his insight
> He never boasted of meeting God nor complained of separation.[69]

Ibn ᶜAbbād would neither withdraw from anyone nor pay attention to anyone. He was politely curt with political authorities (and gentle with the children who were especially fond of trailing after him as an entourage). Through this behavior, he drew the contours of how to behave like a saint while performing official functions as a jurist and member of the state bureaucracy. Zarruq, like others in this Sufi community, recalled Ibn ᶜAbbād in hagiographic terms, portraying him as the prototype for others who tried to express this emerging and ambiguous mode of saintly authority.

4 Exile

Zarruq's promising youth among the juridical Sufis in Fes was tenuous. He did not spend all his time in the madrasa colleges where these Sufis developed their distinctive concept of juridical sainthood. In his twenties, Zarruq also spent time at Sufi gathering places outside the madrasa. Here he encountered different Sufi communities that advocated competing paradigms of sainthood, and became intimately involved with one of them, the Qādirī Sufis. This involvement led Zarruq into social activism and even political ambitions.

These competing loyalties came to a head when Fes was torn apart by a revolution. Powerful clans within the capital city allied with the Qādirī Sufi community, and together they advocated a revolutionary plot to overthrow the Marinid sultan. Zarruq was caught up in the violence as his teacher, al-Qūrī, was pressured to give a juridical ruling justifying revolution. Zarruq perceived that the revolution and its advocates were undermining the mode of saintly authority, that of the juridical saint, that centered on balancing spiritual cultivation with legal rectitude. The promise of his early youth and his hopes for the future were dashed. In being forced to take unpopular political positions, Zarruq rebelled against his contemporaries. Promise collapsed to be replaced with exile, and his mature life began amid its rubble.

Competing Qādirī Sufis in Fes

Juridical Sufis like Shaykh al-Qūrī were not the only Sufi community in Fes, nor were they the most visible one. The Sufis of the Qādirīyya community played a powerful role in Fes by redressing injustice and maintaining social order, competing with juridical Sufis, and challenging their highly attenuated mode of saintly authority. The Qādirī Sufis commanded a social presence from the zawiya rather than as teachers in the madrasa.[1] Their position as leaders of a zawiya points out two themes that distinguish them from the juridical Sufi community. They built patronage relationships to different social groups, and they exhibited a different paradigm of sainthood that was in many ways more dramatic and socially activist. These Sufis did not rely on official positions or educational institutions for their

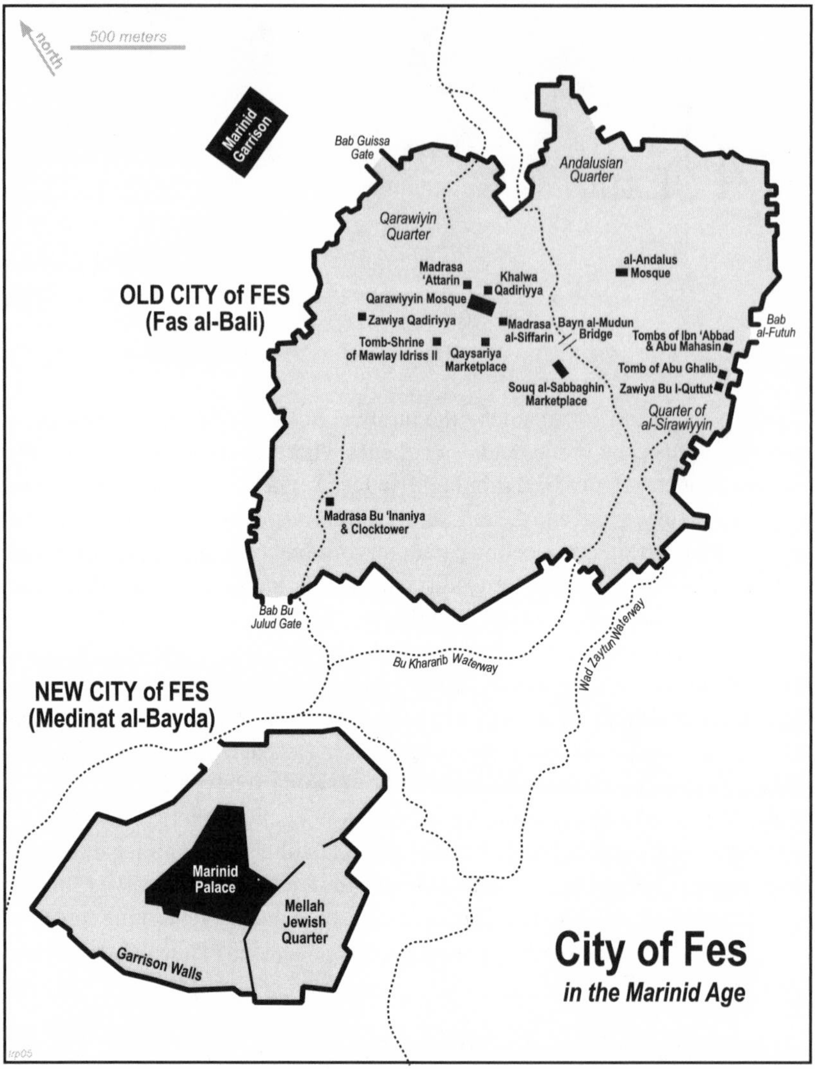

Map A

social clout and constituency of disciples. Instead, their leaders would actively court popular admiration as saints to build up a network of patronage.

Even as Zarruq participated in both the Qādirī and juridical Sufi communities, the previously understated competition between them broke more fiercely into the open. The competition revolved around what type of saint each community projected as truly Islamic. A metaphor from chemistry can help us to see the difference between the type of saint that served these two Sufi communities. The juridical saint was "crystalline"; he did not float freely in society but occupied a position in a structure. His scholarly or juridical constituency formed the community that recognized him as a saint: his relationship with them was already structured by his position as a teacher or judge. In contrast, the Qādirī saint was a "free radical" who moved easily in society with no fixed place. He would gather admirers and build them into a community around himself. Such a "free radical" would often institute a zawiya by transforming a private home, local mosque, or tomb into a meeting place for his Sufi followers and a wider group of admirers. We can roughly term such saints and their Sufi followers as "zawiya-based Sufis" in an effort not to fall into the misleading dichotomies of past scholarship.[2] The zawiya in this era in Fes could be of widely varying scale. It could have been a large institution attached to a mosque or saint's tomb, with provision for numerous visitors and room for permanent ascetics. It could have been an extension of a master's personal home, or just an occasional gathering place for a community devoted to certain rituals or devotional exercises outside the common cycle of canonical prayer. In any case, the zawiya depended on support by a community of admirers for its social status and material prosperity. The leader who garnered such support took an active role in public life by confronting abuses of official authority, championing causes of social justice, or protecting the honor, status, and wealth of the communities from which they drew support, to demonstrate his or her saintly potential.

During his student years, Zarruq nurtured contacts with zawiya-based Sufis even as he was immersed in the world of the madrasa and deeply attached to the juridical Sufi community of al-Qūrī. He met Qādirī Sufis through unofficial relationships. He became the friend of ᶜAbd al-Raḥmān al-Qarmūnī, who was the timekeeper in the clock tower of the dormitory of Madrasa Buᶜinānīyya where Zarruq resided. Al-Qarmūnī held odd jobs; besides calibrating the complicated water clock, he taught children basic literacy at a charity school.[3] Zarruq remembered him as a saintly man who had contacts in the juridical Sufi circles. Al-Qarmūnī (whose family came from the Andalusian town of Carmona) had been a student and disciple of Ibn al-Futūḥ and Ibn Ḥamd in Meknes. After moving to Fes, he studied in the juridical Sufi circles of ᶜUmar al-Ragrāgī (see the previous chapter, n. 44) and then of al-Maṣmūdī (until his death in 864 Hijri/1459–60 C.E.). He enjoyed a moderate level of education but held no post in official educational institutions. In this sense, he was a "dropout" from the juridical Sufi community who did not quite live up to its standards.

Instead, al-Qarmūnī became attracted to the Qādirī saints of Fes. He hosted a gathering of Sufis in the upper room of the clock tower, which became a small and little-known zawiya. The center of this informal devotional group was a man known as Muḥammad al-Amīn "al-ᶜAṭṭār."[4] Zarruq met al-Amīn at these private gatherings and grew to trust him, since he was friend of Zarruq's uncle (the husband of his father's sister). Al-Amīn presents a figure typical of the zawiya-based Sufi. Though literate, al-Amīn was never a student at the madrasa colleges and did not have any formal juridical training. It appears that he worked as a pharmacist or spice merchant (*ᶜaṭṭār*). Al-Amīn was a colorful character who promoted himself openly in society as a saintly person, able to right wrongs and fix injustices without recourse to legal quibbles and official jurists.

Zarruq reports that al-Amīn used to experience frequent and public visions and spiritual disclosures. He used to publicize them as well; Zarruq had heard of them from his uncle and some of al-Amīn's followers. Zarruq admits that "when his spiritual state got flowing, I witnessed with my own eyes what he could do."[5] He recounts how the saint had helped his own aunt and her husband, who had complained to al-Amīn of their neighbor. They shared a common wall between their homes, but the neighbor had taken possession of the area around the wall by force and wanted to tear it down. Al-Amīn told Zarruq's uncle that if the man's allies came to tear down the wall, he should turn toward al-Amīn himself and cry out a particular name to curse any effort to destroy the wall. A long fight ensued, and the neighbors began to demolish the contested wall. As soon as they removed one beam, the neighbor's own house collapsed completely while Zarruq's uncle's home stood undamaged. For the next twenty years, Zarruq attests, the lot "remained a trash heap and sewer, even though the land there was very valuable in the middle of the city," until the oppressive owner died.

This is just one example of how zawiya-based Sufis courted support from the public through rough-and-ready social justice, and thereby build reputations as saints. Al-Amīn's curse never mentioned juridical norms or legal terminology. Zarruq's relative did not need to enter the delicate arena of the court and official arbitrators, who would be scholars (perhaps Sufi scholars) appointed by the Marinid rulers. Of course, the cursed neighbor could not appeal to the court to redress his grievance either. The public did not always appreciate this form of social justice from the hand of a "free radical" saint. The man who eventually came to own the abandoned lot and built a new home there (who had been a servant of the previous, ill-fated owner) met Zarruq one day and asked him, "Why do the saints oppress common people like that by taking their goods and wealth?" Zarruq explained that the results of that curse from al-Amīn were a form of punishment and recompense from Allah, "for my uncle and aunt had pleaded for his help."[6] This explanation reveals that al-Amīn was not just an ambitious holy man or manipulator of magical forces; rather, his social actions and perception were backed by the cultural logic of sanctity. His curse reinforced his own claim to be a socially active saint; those who respected him would receive divine blessing through his patronage, and those who did not would face calamity with no legal recourse. Clearly, al-Amīn appealed to a different model of authority in claiming sainthood than did Zarruq's teachers in the madrasa.

While dispensing his curses, Al-Amīn did not act alone. Rather, he represented an emerging network of zawiyas in Fes. These were associated with the Qādirī lineage, and al-Amīn acted as the patron of those communities that supported them. Their lineage is named after ᶜAbd al-Qādir al-Jīlānī, the eponymous saint whose spiritual reputation spread across the Islamic world. ᶜAbd al-Qādir hailed from Jīlān (Pr. *Gīlān*) on the Caspian Sea, but moved to Baghdād when he was about eighteen years old, where he lived as a scholar and preacher. Before he died in the first half of the sixth century Hijri (twelfth century C.E.), he gained renown in Baghdad as a hadith scholar, Hanbali jurist and popular preacher. He was also an ascetic, and later Sufis have preserved stories of his isolated retreats for contemplation in the wastelands outside the city. It is historically unclear how this jurist, scholar, and popular preacher became transformed into a Sufi and saint (either during his lifetime or after his death). The sharifian family of ᶜAbd al-Qādir was responsible for preserving, amplifying, and spreading the reputation of their forefather. In Morocco, Qādirī Sufis, although not born into a sharifian family, claimed personal absorption in the spirit of ᶜAbd al-Qādir, and thus entered into cooperation with the Qādirī *shurafāʾ*. Under the leadership of such Sufis, the Qādirī community expanded from a closed genealogy to an open, socially active, and politically potent Sufi community. The history of the young Zarruq's interaction with the Qādirīs in Fes demonstrates the unique potency of this Sufi community and its sharifian roots.

The case of al-Amīn's demolishing houses and imposing rough social justice depended upon his spiritual allegiance to ᶜAbd al-Qādir al-Jīlānī. Al-Amīn's flair for the dramatic characterized his Sufi initiation as well. Al-Amīn claimed allegiance to ᶜAbd al-Qādir al-Jilānī directly, through a type of visionary initiation with no living human intermediary (*bi-la wāsiṭa*). Further, he demonstrates that Qādirīs in Fes grafted their lineage onto the local precedent by claiming that the great North African saint, Abū Madyan, was really a Qādirī. These claims shine through al-Amīn's personal story of spiritual crisis and Sufi allegiance. "When I was young, I was a simple ignorant fellow—but I was very determined to strive to be good. When a stranger would come to the mosque, I would always be the first to invite him home as my guest. Every time some guest would come, I would take a thread from his clothing and place it into a small pouch that I kept bound on my arm with an amulet for protection. Then one night I said, 'Look what you have been carrying around with you!' I threw the pouch into the fire, but was amazed to see half of it burn and half of it remain intact with the flames licking at it but not consuming it! This sight disturbed me and moved me to repentance."[7] In this strange confessional tale, al-Amīn recounts his youthful attempts to win salvation through conventionally good actions, like generosity to strangers and travelers. Yet he would calculate and count the number of people he hosted, in an attempt to store up good deeds and win divine protection. This attempt to earn salvation was manifested concretely in the threads he would tie into his amulet.

Al-Amīn does not record what spiritual unrest drove him to question his approach to virtue and look with disgust at his literal attempt to track his good deeds in a balance sheet with God. He threw the amulet into the flames, as if overwhelmed by the thought that his calculated attempts to secure salvation would lead him only to divine wrath. Yet half the amulet did not burn. It was as if some portion of his heart might contain the virtue necessary to escape the flames of hell if he renounced all effort to secure rewards for himself. In Al-Amīn's narrative, "repentance" (*tawba*) means that he renounced routine life and its security in order to join a Sufi community. "I repented with God from what I had done, and said to myself, 'In these days, there is no saintly guide apparent among the living, so take allegiance to ᶜAbd al-Qādir al-Jīlānī and Abū Yiᶜzza as the means to reach God!'"[8] He resolved not only to take allegiance to ᶜAbd al-Qādir, but also to abandon himself in the master's personality and ascribe to the saint any reward he might accrue for pious actions in the future. "Then I thought a minute, and realized that ᶜAbd al-Qādir's tomb [in Baghdād] was so far away, reached by a seldom traversed road. Pilgrimage to there would be impossible. So I resolved to make the pilgrimage to the tomb of Abū Yiᶜzza instead. I vowed to Allah that the reward I would accrue for any act of worship should go to these two great saints rather than to me."[9]

Al-Amīn set out for the tomb of Abū Yiᶜzza, the Berber saint and healer who was the spiritual master of Abū Madyan. Abū Yiᶜzza, known in Berber language as "Possessor of Light" (Yallanūr), is one of the most colorful saints of medieval Morocco, and his tomb at Jabal Taghiya in the Middle Atlas Mountains became a popular pilgrimage place. For three weeks al-Amīn stayed there, engaging in fasting during the day and meditating at night. During a noontime nap, he had a vision. "Suddenly, I saw that the grave opened up, and a man came out of it. Another man with a tall turban came up to him, and said to the one who had come from his grave, 'Give this man whatever he needs!' The first man answered, 'It's not for me to give by myself.' The turbaned man replied, 'Give it to him!' Then I saw the two together give me knowledge. I awoke thrilled with what I had seen in that dream vision. I realized that I had received the blessing of these two great masters combined. Then I saw a Maṣmūda Berber at the doorway of the mosque, who said to me in the language of the Zanāta Berbers, 'Congratulations on getting what you needed!' When I rose to ask him a question, I found nobody there."[10] In this dream initiation, the local saint is Abū Yiᶜzza who rises from his tomb to meet al-Amīn. His partner in the tall turban is ᶜAbd al-Qādir al-Jīlānī, who wore the turban of a jurist and scholar and came to him from afar (from Baghdād in the inaccessible east where he is buried). Al-Amīn received not just initiation but also illuminating spiritual knowledge on the command of ᶜAbd al-Qādir and through the delegated authority of Abū Yiᶜzza.

In al-Amīn's spiritual lineage, both Abū Yiᶜzza and ᶜAbd al-Qādir share the honor of being masters of Abū Madyan. This structure grounded the seemingly "foreign" Qādirī lineage in local Moroccan Sufi lore and provided al-Amīn's colleagues with the foundation for claiming spiritual leadership among Moroccan Sufi communities.[11]

Youth in the Zawiya of al-Zaytūnī

It was al-Amīn who introduced the young Zarruq into the wider world of the Qādirīs. He was one of a community of Qādirī Sufis who gathered in zawiyas in Fes. In the generation before Zarruq, they began to make bold spiritual claims for leadership in the urban centers of northern Morocco. Al-Amīn introduced Zarruq to the zawiya that dominated the Qādirī community at that time, Zāwiya Būʾl-Quṭūṭ, and the

Sufi master who ran the institution, Shaykh Muḥammad al-Zaytūnī. Whether it was through his friendship with al-Amīn or through fascination by their dramatic exercises of saintly power, Zarruq became increasingly involved in the community at this zawiya. In his early twenties, he began to "serve" al-Zaytūnī, along with other spiritual initiates (*fuqarāʾ*) at the zawiya. He participated in the yearly pilgrimages they organized to the tomb of Abū Yiᶜzza, which served as a substitute for visiting ᶜAbd al-Qādir al-Jīlānī.

Muḥammad al-Zaytūnī's spiritual authority was similar to that of al-Amīn, but on a grander scale. Like al-Amīn, he cultivated a spiritual relationship with ᶜAbd al-Qādir al-Jīlānī, though he did not have a living master who trained him and gave him an explicit lineage. All the sources specify that he was a Qādirī, though some qualify that he was "a Qādirī without a known lineage."[12] This clarifies that he was an "*uwaysī*" with all the visionary dexterity and spiritual audacity this term implies.[13] Like al-Amīn, he would not hesitate to wield the social power inherent in his reputation as a saint through dramatic miracles and immediate punishments of those who wronged him or threatened his clients. However, while al-Amīn's zawiya was just an informal meeting room, the zawiya that al-Zaytūnī ran was a powerful institution. It housed resident Sufis and ascetics and received financial support from extensive grants. The key to his social authority was that al-Zaytūnī acted as the patron saint of the lucrative trade routes linking Fes to Cairo.

In order to demonstrate how al-Zaytūnī's saintly authority (that he exercised through his control of a zawiya) directly challenged that of the juridical Sufi community in Fes, this chapter describes the growth of the Qādirīs as a Sufi community. The actual formation of the Qādirīs as a "Sufi lineage" remains unclear. Though this formation is crucial to the history of Sufism and dynastic politics in the Maghrib, it has not yet been adequately researched. This study provides a preliminary foray into the wider topic, for the history of Zāwiya Būʾl-Quṭūṭ's growth and its place in the social structure of Fes provides important clues about the growth of the Qādirī community in northern Morocco.

Most studies approach "Sufism" from the point of view of distinct "orders." Such studies claim that the "Qāḍīri order" is the oldest and most widespread of all. Such bold claims have led some scholars to question not only the early date of the Qādirī organization, but also the identity of ᶜAbd al-Qādir as a saint, or even as a Sufi. It is clear that ᶜAbd al-Qādir did not project himself as a saint in order to establish a Sufi community (*ṭariqa*), in the sense understood in the later medieval period. He did not organize a distinct community of devotees sharing a common set of litanies and recitations, linked by a lineage back to an eponymous axial saint. Such a reality was a later organization projected back into history.

In the earliest evidence of Qādirī communities, it is difficult to differentiate whether "Qādirī" referred a genealogical lineage joined by common ancestry or a devotional community joined by common spiritual aspiration. ᶜAbd al-Qādir hailed from a sharifian family (descended from the lineages of both the Prophet's grandsons, Ḥasan and Ḥusayn). ᶜAbd al-Qādir's descendants spread through the Islamic world after the Mongols sacked Baghdad in 1255 C.E. and gained social respect and religious authority as *shurafā'*. They intensified their genealogical link to the Prophet's descendants with a spiritual devotion to ᶜAbd al-Qādir himself as a saint. Thus, the Qādirī lineage often coalesces around a member of the sharifian Qādirī family, who claimed the role of spiritual patrons and social mediators with the dual appeal to sharifian descent and adherence to the teachings of a saint.[14]

As members of the Qādirī family attracted followers who were not part of the family, the Qādirī community began to take on the characteristics of a systematic devotional method (*ṭarīqa*). Such followers cultivated a nobility of spirit and intimacy to the Prophet through devotional exercises and ascetic endeavors, since they could not gain nobility and intimacy through genealogy itself. Although ᶜAbd al-Qādir's genealogical descendants may have carried the fame of his name, it attracted others who claimed allegiance to ᶜAbd al-Qādir not through blood but through visionary meetings and pure loyalty. Shaykh al-Zaytūnī is an example of such a follower.

The Qādirīs initially came to Morocco as a sharifian family. In the mid-fifteenth century C.E., a Qādirī sharif (named Abū Muḥammad al-Qādirī) led a band of his relatives to Fes from Andalusia.[15] They had left Iraq as refugees from the Mongols' invasion and had come to Spain after experiencing local resistance to their settling in the Hijāz (see appendix B).[16] When the areas near Granada became unstable due to the *reconquista*, they fled to Morocco. The family of Abū Muḥammad al-Qādirī soon grew in wealth and stature to form an influential sharifian clan in Fes. The historian Ibrahim Harakat notes that Abū Muḥammad al-Qādirī also propagated the Qādirī lineage as a Sufi affiliation and devotional method; however, this appears to be an oversimplification of a highly complex process.[17]

The earliest evidence of the Qādirī lineage as a devotional community engaging in distinctive worship practices is architectural. Local lore in Fes preserves the memory of many sites that are considered holy due to ᶜAbd al-Qādir al-Jīlānī's miraculous presence in them. These were gathering places where members of the Qādirī lineage would perform devotions. Such places soon developed a reputation for enabling devotees to meet ᶜAbd al-Qādir in person through dreams or visions. Folk stories circulated to justify these events, claiming that ᶜAbd al-Qādir himself had visited Fes and spent time praying in these locations. Such stories accounted for their holiness by the direct physical presence of the saint, thereby erasing the historical activities of the sharifian Qādirī clan in establishing these holy places.

One such site is the eastern side of the congregational mosque of al-Qarawiyyīn, where a small room above the street has been used for solitary worship. A nineteenth-century collector of local lore, al-Kattānī, preserves this account. "The people of Fes have long named that place after Shaykh ᶜAbd al-Qādir, because some people supposedly saw him in dream visions while praying there.... If people attribute the place to ᶜAbd al-Qādir because of visions of him during worship or sleep, then this is sound.... In reality, however, most people vainly imagine that ᶜAbd al-Qādir actually worshipped in this place, either while he was living or in spectral form after his death, or other such false claims that have no proof."[18] Another site in Fes is known as the *khalwa,* or meditation retreat, of ᶜAbd al-Qādir.[19] Although this building is called a retreat, it is in fact a zawiya built to house the recitation of Qurᵓān. Devotees would publicly recite the Qurᵓān there, completing the scripture once each month over a seven-day period.

The location became associated with ᶜAbd al-Qādir due to the story that some of the shaykh's followers found refuge in Fes and used to recite litanies composed by the saint at this place. Such a story obscures the fact that it was Qādirī sharifian clan who promoted the public recitations. They would devote the day the recitation would come to a close to ᶜAbd al-Qādir. People gathered at this spot to hear the recitation, benefit from the blessing of the saint's presence, and give charitable donations, which the Qādirī *shurafāᵓ* would collect. The poetry of an ᶜImrānī *sharīf* adorns the *qibla* wall of this small shrine. Six couplets laud the visitors who come to this zawiya, saying that they have earned high praise for coming to a zawiya of such lofty stature, the Zawiya of ᶜAbd al-Qādir, the axial saint of all saints, the leader (*imām*) of all those who are wary of God.[20] In such small sacred spaces, we can see the legacy of the Qādirī family in Fes. They carved out devotional niches in the city and gained popular fame in the fifteenth century C.E. The presence of Abū Muḥammad al-Qādirī became transparent in the popular imagination of the people of Fes, who connected through him to the presence of his ancestor, the saint ᶜAbd al-Qādir al-Jīlānī.

Yet the center of his family's religious authority and social power was a different architectural site. His descendants settled a neighborhood in Fes called Ṣirāwiyyīn (in the Andalusian quarter). The center of this neighborhood was the shrine of a posthumously saintly man, Abū Ghālib.[21] The story of Abū Ghālib is crucial, for through it, the Qādirī *shurafāᵓ* allied themselves to Idrīsī *shurafāᵓ* of Fes and wove themselves into the city's power structure. The Idrīsī sharifian clans, especially the five families of the al-Jūṭī clan, were the most powerful clans in Fes. They all traced their descent through Mawlay Idrīs (who founded the city of Fes) back to Imam Ḥasan, the grandson of the Prophet. The Qādirī *shurafāᵓ* also trace their lineage through Ḥasan, through one of his great-grandsons, Mūsā ibn ᶜAbdullah al-Kāmil (rather than through a closely related great-grandson, Idrīs ibn ᶜAbdullah al-Kāmil, through whom the Idrīsī clan traces its descent). The Qādirīs would be seen as distant cousins of the Idrīsī clan, cousins long since separated by geography and culture, with no established status in Morocco. The Qādirīs positioned the tomb of Abū Ghālib to bridge this evident gulf in genealogy and status between themselves and the local elite.

Lore of Fes preserves the story that Abū Ghālib hailed from the Idrīsī family of *shurafāᵓ,* who settled in the neighborhood al-Ṣirāwiyyīn. He developed a reputation for pious ecstasy and generosity to the Sufis, who gathered at his home and eventually transformed it into a zawiya. When he died, Abū Ghālib was buried on the spot and his tomb gained wide renown as a center of healing, especially of open sores or wounds. Its popularity as a devotional center provided the *shurafāʾ* with a platform of power.

The Idrīsī *shurafāʾ* who settled at al-Ṣirāwiyyīn were reinforced by another contingent of *shurafāʾ*, from the al-Ṭālibī clan (a branch of the powerful al-Jūṭī al-ᶜImrānī family). Marinid rulers had forcibly moved them from their ancestral stronghold in the center of Fes,[22] and in recompense, the Marinids decreed that the financial proceeds from Abū Ghālib's tomb and charitable contributions to its founder would go to the coffers of the at-Ṭālibī *shurafāʾ*. Through this arrangement, a branch of the sharifian al-Jūṭī clan became the promoters and caretakers of Abū Ghalib's tomb, and they reinforced the story of his sharifian genealogy.

The Qādirī *shurafāʾ*, once they settled in Fes, became deeply involved in the promotion of the tomb of Abū Ghālib, entering into close relations with the al-Jūṭī al-ᶜImrānī clan. The arrival of the Qādirīs and their alliance with the ᶜImrānī *shurafāʾ* were crucial to the success of Abū Ghālib's tomb. The Qādirī family crafted out of the sketchy biography of Abū Ghālib a mythic saintly story in which Abū Ghālib mirrored the personality of their own pious ancestor, ᶜAbd al-Qādir al-Jīlānī. The reputation of ᶜAbd al-Qādir as a healer (in the Islamic tradition, second only to Jesus) helped to bolster the local efficacy of Abū Ghālib's earthly remains.[23] As the Qādirīs lent the miraculous reputation of their ancestor to Abū Ghālib's tomb, undergirding the biography of the saint with echoes of the life of ᶜAbd al-Qādir, the crowds poured in as did pious contributions. The money enriched the Ṭālibī clan of ᶜImrānī *shurafāʾ*, who may have acted as sponsors for the newly arrived Qādirīs. The same family that composed poems in praise of the saint ᶜAbd al-Qādir composed poems lauding the curing power of Abū Ghālib's tomb.[24] The same al-ᶜImrānī family that promoted the healing power of Abū Ghālib's tomb was also patronizing the newly found Qādirī shrines in Fes.

The first mention of the site as a zawiya comes in the generation of Ahmad Zarruq. The zawiya consisted of a set of buildings near the tomb that housed devotees, giving them space for occasional devotional gatherings, cells for isolated retreats, or even permanent residence as caretakers. Al-Zaytūnī is the first Sufi master mentioned as director of the zawiya. He may even have been its founder, for he enlarged the compound with money extracted from the Marinid rulers. It became known as Zāwiya Bū'l-Quṭūṭ, "The Devotional Center of Cats," due to the many cats that lived on the premises (that charitable donations may have fed). There is still a proverb current in Fes: "Whoever loves Sīdī Bū Ghālib loves him by loving his cats" [Moroccan dialect, *illī kayuḥibb sīdī Bū Ghālib yuḥibbū bi-quṭūṭū*]. The proverb is used to communicate the folk wisdom that you express your love for a man by showering love on his children (as if the cats at the zawiya were the children of Abū Ghālib).[25]

The later story of Abū Ghālib having instituted a zawiya at his home is most likely a retroactive explanation of the institution's origins. The story should not be discarded as apocryphal, though, for it paints a lively picture of the devotional practice at the Zāwiya Būʾl-Quṭūṭ. "Abū Ghālib would keep company with the

Sufis, and come to be their guest uninvited, and attend with them sessions of devotional music and poetry (*samāᶜ*) whenever he had time. Listening, he would sway in a trance and dance in ecstasy. Then he began to practice such sessions at his home, with whomever would follow him there … and he grew famous in Fes for these devotions. His state of ecstasy would flood over into others, and many people would become his disciples. Slowly, his home grew into a zawiya where they would live together."[26] The story attributes ecstatic devotions to Abū Ghālib himself. Such devotions characterized the zawiya in its heyday under al-Zaytūnī. Attributing them to the legendary figure of Abū Ghālib may have been a way to defend these practices from vocal critics. What is fascinating about this story is how the uninvited guest, Abū Ghālib, eventually set himself up as the keeper of the zawiya and dispenser of hospitality to other Sufis. In this story, we can discern traces of the Qādirī *shurafāʾ* themselves. They came to Fes uninvited as refugees. However, by building alliances with more established Idrīsī *shurafāʾ*, they were able to found devotional centers across the city.

The story also preserves echoes of ecstatic saints like al-Zaytūnī and al-Amīn. Although not born into a sharifian family, they claimed to have been personally absorbed into the spirit of ᶜAbd al-Qādir al-Jīlānī, and thus made a bid for support from the Qādirī *shurafāʾ*. Under their leadership, the Qādirī community expanded from a closed genealogy to an open, socially active, and politically potent Sufi community. By allowing al-Zaytūnī to command the zawiya, the Qādirī *shurafāʾ* could count on a source of wealth from the caravans he protected. Along the caravan routes the Qādirī network expanded rapidly, until "the Qādirī lineage spread throughout northern Africa during the reign of the Marinid sultans, and even reached the areas of Tuwat and the Sudan long before the arrival of the Turks in those regions."[27] The early Qādirī *shurafāʾ* may have preserved certain prayers or litanies ascribed to their saintly ancestor. Yet it is not until the ninth century Hijri (fifteenth century C.E.) that one can discern distinctive devotional practices and institutional settings of a Sufi community in the Maghrib built around the person of ᶜAbd al-Qādir.[28]

These innovations must be attributed to al-Zaytūnī and the community he led. None of them seems to have had a living Sufi master who passed down these institutions to them from an earlier time.[29] The Qādirīs quickly became dedicated advocates of the local lore surrounding Abū Yiᶜzza as the founding saint of a distinctly Moroccan Sufi community. They drew from the stories about Abū Madyan having met ᶜAbd al-Qādir and taken initiation from him to argue that Abū Madyan's two masters, Abū Yiᶜzza and ᶜAbd al-Qādir, were spiritually contiguous.[30] In their mythological world, ᶜAbd al-Qādir is the master of masters of transregional scope and Arab pedigree, while Abū Yiᶜzza is his Maghribi manifestation in distinctly Moroccan and Berber form.

The Qādirīs embodied these community-origin myths in ritual. They popularized the pilgrimage (*ziyāra*) to the tomb-shrine of Abū Yiᶜzza in the Middle Atlas Mountains just south of Fes, presenting it as a Moroccan counterpoint to the tomb of ᶜAbd al-Qādir in Baghdad. This pilgrimage gave the Qādirīs' sense of sacred geography a local anchor. The regional devotional figure of Abū Madyan, an Andalusian Sufi who reputedly met ᶜAbd al-Qādir in Mecca and took initiation from him, served to mythologically link the distant ᶜAbd al-Qādir with the local Berber, Abū Yiᶜzza. Each figure in this story represents a place that was a stopping point for the Qādirī family in their progress toward the Maghrib: Baghdad, Makka, Andalusia, and finally Fes. The Qādirī Sufi community drew even more concrete analogies between ᶜAbd al-Qādir and their newly acquired local patrons; they used soil from the tomb of Abū Yiᶜzza in healing and advocated the same use for that of Abū Ghālib in Fes.[31] Finally, the stories about Abū Madyan meeting ᶜAbd al-Qādir helped the Qādirī Sufis justify their daring "*uwaysī*" initiations. Ambitious Sufis like al-Zaytūnī claimed allegiance to ᶜAbd al-Qādir and aimed to take a leadership role among the Qādirī *shurafā*ᵓ even though he had no sharifian descent. Their personal absorption in ᶜAbd al-Qādir had to be more demonstrably intense to outshine the genealogical pride of the saint's sharifian descendants. They publicized the story of the North African saint, Abū Madyan, claiming that he met ᶜAbd al-Qādir in a vision or in astral travel in order to offer him allegiance. This narrative bolstered the legitimacy of those non-sharifian Qādirī Sufis who also claimed intimacy to ᶜAbd al-Qādir. Despite this potential for competition, the Qādirīs whose affiliation was spiritual worked in close cooperation in Fes with those Qādirīs whose affiliation was genealogical as well. The visionary saints may have looked upon the Qādirī family as their patrons and protégés, while the Qādirī family used the saints' reputation for miracles to boost the status of their family name.

The emergence of al-Zaytūnī and his visionary Qādirī colleagues transformed the Qādirī lineage from a family genealogy into a wider Sufi community. Al-Zaytūnī himself was responsible for converting the healing tomb of Abū Ghālib into a Sufi zawiya. He personally expanded the architectural scope of the complex. Zarruq records that al-Zaytūnī took advantage of an opportunity to "construct the zawiya." He spoke with a courtier of the sultan and persuaded him to give him a document of financial support. The courtiers were able to advocate his case and advanced al-Zaytūnī an amount sufficient to support the building project.[32] Al-Zaytuni's personality and reputation were so powerful that Zarruq was attracted to serve him and ask for his hand in initiation as a saintly guide, beyond his previous allegiance to al-Qūrī.

Al-Zaytūnī's family origins or educational background are obscure, as they were to his contemporaries.[33] Hagiographies are clear, however, about his character. He was a strong-willed, even vindictive saint who coupled spiritual training with building a strong social patronage network. Although he was blind, he traveled far beyond Fes on the trade routes to the east. Along these desert paths, he enforced treaties with the various Arab tribes who threatened the caravans, robbed them, or extorted protection money. Al-Zaytūnī's many miracles preserve the traces of his political brokering in the countryside and desert where government control did not extend. "Those Sufis who were known to affect the affairs of this world would call al-Zaytūnī 'the Blind Viper' because of the stinging bite of his words, since whatever he prayed for would be quickly enacted. He would transport caravans from the Maghrib for the pilgrimage to Makka and Madīna. The Arab tribes ...would never molest his caravans due to what they had witnessed of the miraculous events that Allah let loose from al-Zaytūnī's hands."[34] Al-Zaytūnī cultivated his reputation for vindictiveness and revenge to establish his authority over the tribes who lived in the vast and danger-filled territories that caravans had to cross.[35] As a caravan would prepare to depart from Fes toward the east, the captain would invite al-Zaytūnī to circle around it, reciting the Qur'ānic verses of *Sūrat al-Qadr*, until he completed a full circuit. He would then declare the caravan immune from thieves and plunderers, invoking Allah to maintain an unbreakable wall of protection around it. Arab tribes who had tried to plunder such caravans reported finding it surrounded by a high wall that none could climb or breach.[36]

Others were not so lucky. A pilgrim who traveled with one of the caravans with Shaykh al-Zaytūnī reported, "We camped in al-Zāb when suddenly a tribe of corrupt Arabs surrounded us on all sides, intending to loot the caravan. We ran to the master and told him what was happening. He asked us from what direction the plundering Arabs were approaching [because he was blind]. 'From every side!' we answered. He picked up a pinch of dust and threw it to his right, then another to his left, then in front of him, then behind. The dust flew out from his hand in a flood of bees that swarmed over the Arab encampments, driving them away until not one was left to be seen.... Later that day, the Arabs returned, humble and on foot, with offerings of cattle and sheep, bringing along their families and children to stand before al-Zaytūnī to receive his pardon and blessing. Each man mentioned his mighty terror when confronted by the bees."[37]

Policing the caravan routes was crucial to the Qādirī Sufi community's rise to prominence, especially since it was not "native" to Morocco. This activity connected the zawiya in Fes with other centers in North Africa and eventually with Cairo, where the Qādirīs had previously built a strong presence and maintained a large zawiya at al-Qarāfa cemetery.[38] The legends they spread about ᶜAbd al-Qādir traveling from the east to visit the Maghrib were veiled allusions to the Qādirī saint's social role in promoting travel, trade and pilgrimage from the Maghrib to the centers of urban civilization to the east.

This role must also have secured for the Qādirīs an influence in the Marinid court. The Marinid rulers were eager to secure any legitimacy they could for their rule; to this end they promoted the institutions of Sunni piety, including madrasa colleges, celebrations of the Prophet's birthday, and government-sponsored Hajj caravans. They contributed money to the sharifian rulers of the *Ḥijāz* who controlled Makka and Madina to elicit their recognition and raise their prestige in the eyes of scholars and pilgrims returning from the Hajj. Qādirī leaders organized and protected official caravans that were vulnerable to plunder, serving a function that the Marinid state itself was too weak to perform. The Marinids relied upon the

Qādirīs to maintain interregional trade, which gave Qādirī saints more clout in Fes. Al-Zaytūnī's transregional role as the mediator between the Marinid dynasty and the Arab tribes, combined with his metropolitan role as the patron of the Qādirī *shurafā*ᵓ, made him a politically powerful player in Fes. Al-Zaytūnī had found it easy to secure money from the royal coffers to expand the zawiya compound at Bū'l-Quṭūṭ.

Other Sufis in Fes may have seen al-Zaytūnī as an upstart. Certainly his lack of a clear spiritual lineage must have caused some to question his legitimacy. Hagiographic records contain traces of argument over this issue. One author titled al-Zaytūnī "One of the *Abdāl*," meaning those saints who play a crucial role in upholding the order of the cosmos.[39] In the saintly hierarchy as imagined by Sufis, the *Abdāl* are highly mobile figures; their title means "those who exchange places." When one of the *Abdāl* passes away, another saint will move instantaneously, perhaps from obscurity or from a vast distance, to take his or her place and keep holding the cosmos in order. Although not literally a part of the definition, *Abdāl* saints suggest a constant motion and circulation. To call a living figure "One of the *Abdāl*" would be a way to explain his or her legitimacy as a saint even if he or she suddenly appeared in a region without known provenance. Including him the company of the *Abdāl* may have been a strategy by al-Zaytūnī's followers to cover his rise from obscurity with a positive veneer. During his lifetime, however, al-Zaytūnī did not have to rely on such props of oral history. Instead, he demonstrated his saintly power directly through miracles and indirectly through the social network maintained by his patronage. Every hagiographic record notes that "strange and wonderful tales are told" of the miracles he produced.[40]

We must be careful not to conclude that, because of this reputation for miracles and political ambition, al-Zaytūnī's Qādirī community represents "popular Sufism." That term itself is fraught with ambiguities, yet it persists in scholarly literature.[41] It suggests an absolute dichotomy between educated, urban elite Sufis and illiterate, rural Sufis. The evidence of this Qādirī community challenges the validity of this easy dichotomy. They were a very urban community, yet with important activities in the rural areas who even acted as the agents of urban political power among the rural tribes. The miracles of al-Zaytūnī (and to a lesser extent his followers like al-Amīn and others) were not manifestations of a "popular Sufism" that panders to the superstitious masses. Rather it is evidence of his social activism, in actively injecting his own saintly personality into society, both urban and rural, to carve out a niche for himself and his lineage among competing models of saintly authority.[42]

Zarruq is reserved about recording what kind of Sufi devotions he encountered at Zāwiya Bū'l-Quṭūṭ. Zarruq does not cite any books he studied there. However, literate persons were active in the zawiya, which may also have served as a study circle. He does mention a "teacher," Shaykh ibn Zimām al-Rakāᶜ, who was a disciple of al-Amīn and may have taught texts at the zawiya. There were many learned persons who participated in the community at Bū'l-Quṭūṭ.[43] However, the kinds of texts they discussed were beyond the boundaries maintained by juridical Sufis like al-Qūrī. Zarruq had definitely heard the theories of Ibn al-ᶜArabī during these early years and probably read some texts by him or summaries of his texts.[44] In his youth, Zarruq asked al-Qūrī whether the controversial Ibn al-ᶜArabī should be considered a saint or an infidel, since there was such difference of opinion about him. Zarruq heard discussions about Ibn al-ᶜArabī's ideas in circles outside the juridical Sufi community of al-Qūrī, then returned to him for a juridical assessment. This suggests that Zarruq came across his texts and theories among the Qādirīs at Zawiya Bū'l-Quṭūṭ.[45] The Qādirī method of Sufi training, then, cannot be dismissed as a type of "popular Sufism." Rather, it was a method of urban and literate Sufi training that rested on a particular model of saintly authority. This quality brought it into increasing competition with the tradition of juridical sainthood in Fes. This competition over the role of saints in society would break into violence as the society itself experienced a revolution.

Accelerating Competition and Jihad

Based in the zawiya, the authority of Qādirī saints spilled over into the wider spaces of urban life and even beyond the city walls. The Qādirī saints were socially active and politically ambitious, and they openly demonstrated miraculous deeds to back up their claim of visionary initiation with a saint. This is a model in contrast to the model of saintly authority advocated by juridical Sufis. Also urban and literate, they were based in the bureaucratic institutions of the mosque and madrasa, and their leaders were seen as saints by students and intimate colleagues while they maintained an institutional facade as jurists, preachers, and teachers to the wider public. These two models existed in the same social space, and in many ways they vied for the patronage of the Marinid dynasty. In Zarruq's generation, the two groups engaged in more open confrontations, disputing over issues of texts and training as well as over issues of social order. Zarruq himself was in the middle of this growing conflict. Intimately involved with both groups, he had difficulty deciding with whom his true loyalties resided.

One confrontation was over the validity of texts of speculative Sufis, such as Ibn al-ᶜArabī. Unlike some jurists, al-Qūrī refused to condemn Ibn al-ᶜArabī's texts or his personality. When Zarruq asked al-Qūrī about his opinion of Ibn al-ᶜArabī, he replied, "I know of each art through the expert practitioners of that art." Zarruq protested, "That's not what I'm asking you about!" Then al-Qūrī said, "Those in authority have differing assessments of him, ranging from claiming he is an infidel to claiming that he is the axial saint (*min al-kufr ilā al-quṭbāniyya*)." "So which opinion is considered most correct?" he was asked persistently. Al-Qūrī answered, "Being equivocal (*taslīm*)."[46] He advised Zarruq not to openly advocate Ibn al-ᶜArabī's ideas, but not to come out in opposition to them either; the extremes on both sides are dangerous, and any discussion of his ideas will distract from the more immediate ethical concerns of self-purification. Al-Qūrī and his circle of juridical Sufis, however, clearly discouraged the textual exploration of more speculative writers and theorists.

There are shadowy clues that the Qādirīs may have been exploring texts considered beyond the pale by the more skeptical juridical Sufis, such as the texts of Aḥmad al-Būnī, who probed the murky boundary between the efficacy of prayer and the manipulation of magic.[47] Zarruq notes that he knew a Qādirī named Abū Zakariyā Yaḥyā, who was a famous Sufi personality of his time. He was a follower of al-Zaytūnī and, like him, performed many miracles in public. Yaḥya comes across as a typical *majdhūb*, or holy madman whose reason has been disjointed by the force of divine attraction that pulled him out of his routine personality (chapter 8 will discuss *majdhūbs* in more detail). He shared in a characteristic common to the Qādirīs of Fes: people had reason to fear his anger. Zarruq paints a portrait of him with these words. "Most of the time he was not conscious of what he was doing or saying. He wore commoners' clothes, and ate any food given to him. People would give him food, but he would take from them whatever he might need. People would give whatever he asked for, since they were afraid of him: he had the reputation that whatever he prayed for would inevitably happen."[48] Up to this point, Yaḥya appears as a standard *majdhūb*: he ignores clothing and home, he does not work but rather begs, and his actions are erratic "beyond his own conscious control." However, later in the narrative, Yaḥya can read, studies texts, and actively challenges the authority of juridical Sufis. Zarruq tells the story of Yaḥya's fight with a certain jurist named ᶜAlī ibn Yūnus, who appears to be a scholar or judge in the circle of al-Qūrī. The cause of their fight is unspecified, but in the heat of argument, Yaḥya curses the jurist, saying, "May your [faculty of] discrimination be destroyed!" Zarruq notes that nobody ever accepted ᶜAlī ibn Yūnus's decisions and opinions after that, which would certainly destroy the career of a judge or scholar.

More suggestively, Zarruq notes that one of his teachers from the madrasa once caught this Qādirī saint, Yaḥya, reading the texts of the speculative Sufi al-Būnī and denounced him for this. Al-Būnī's texts had the reputation of being manuals of sorcery, giving detailed instructions on how to make invocations that would realign the cosmos to one's own will.[49] Yaḥya cursed the scholarly Sufi who denounced him, saying, "May Allah afflict you because of that!" The very fact that Zarruq does not specify the name of this scholarly Sufi in this narrative leads one to believe that it might have been al-Qūrī himself. Zarruq would certainly not want to implicate his master in a squabble with other Sufis, yet he would be eager to record his master's juridical decision against al-Būnī's texts and his courage in confronting those who seem to transgress the limits of religious law and endanger the social order.

A member of al-Qūrī's circle of juridical Sufis had accused al-Zaytūnī's more charismatic followers of magic and sorcery, as shown by their use of al-Būnī's texts. Al-Zaytūnī's followers, in return, were cursing the jurists, causing them to apparently lose their reason and face other afflictions that called their public role as the upholders of social order into question. This rivalry between religious groups in the capital appeared at a time of disturbing signs of unrest, dissatisfaction with existing political structures, and a shifting of alliances into new configurations. These were the local manifestations of larger conflicts caused by interregional and interconfessional warfare between the north and south shores of the Mediterranean basin.

During the mid-fifteenth century C.E. (mid-ninth century Hijri), crusading attacks of the Spanish and Portuguese against Morocco's coastal cities made clear the internal weakness of Marinid rule. Iberian crusades were part of a larger campaign to cut off support for the last remaining Muslim strongholds in Iberia (especially Granada) and to channel the trade of gold and spices into Iberian hands. The campaigns began with the surprise assault on Sebta (Ceuta) organized in 1415 C.E. by Prince Henry the Navigator. Within a week, Iberian forces captured the port city, killing or expelling all its inhabitants. But the conquest of Sebta did not provide the means of dominating trade routes from interior Africa and India, as the Portuguese had hoped. Muslim merchants boycotted Sebta, and local tribal rulers joined by Muslim "irregulars" (called *mujāhidīn* by those who supported their cause) tried to retake the city. Faced with such resistance, the Portuguese were compelled to conquer all the ports on the Moroccan coasts, both Mediterranean and Atlantic. Within a century, all the major ports with the exception of Salé had fallen to Portuguese control. The response of the Marinid dynasty to such novel assaults by Iberian forces was weak. Muslim "irregulars" had put up a defense of Sebta without Marinid support, but failed to retake the city. The regent minister, Abū Zakariyā Yaḥyā al-Waṭṭāsī, supported the defense of Tangier against the Portuguese in 841 Hijri (1437 C.E.), but he failed to commit military forces to a sustained defensive campaign. The Marinid forces were busy with internal conflicts in the countryside, attempting to pacify Arab tribes that revolted against their control and slowly reduced the size of their domains. The Marinid state was inclined to make a show of symbolic resistance to the Portuguese while negotiating for a peace that would allow them to quell internal dissent and prop up their state.[50]

Such an opportunistic policy led to increasing discontent among Moroccan political thinkers, including jurists and Sufis. Moroccans had grown used to seeing Iberia itself as a zone of war and conflict, but the southern shore of the Mediterranean had seemed like an inviolable zone of safety, symbolized by the term *Dār al-Islām*. The fall of Sebta sparked a widespread call for *jihād*. The Marinid state itself was incapable of organizing such campaigns, so the responsibility for *jihād* devolved onto the sharifian clans and Sufi communities. The call for *jihād* against Iberians therefore became an indirect call to oust the Marinids.

The Qādirīyya community in Fes participated in this political response. In addition to advocating a new model of saintly authority within Fes, they also preached the necessity of *jihād* against the Spanish and Portuguese invaders. The clearest example of this is the poetry of Muḥammad ibn Yaggabsh al-Tāzī, who urged his fellow Muslims to join in the fight against the Iberian incursions along the coasts of Morocco. In his *Kitāb al-Jihād,* he echoes Ibn Khaldūn's remarks that insecurity "has led to the loosening of social bonds and the erosion of trust and solidarity."[51]

The internal weakness of Muslim society aided the external threat of invasion from Portugal and Spain. Al-Tāzī played off the mounting panic resulting from the *reconquista*, which was resulting in more expulsions of Andalusian Muslims, who came as refugees to the urban centers of northern Morocco. "Are you not aware that your enemies are investigating you and are employing every stratagem in order to get at you? They have gathered together in numbers too large to count and have sent their spies and scouts to every land in order to inform them of what your numbers are, as well as your strength and convictions."[52] The list of moral faults that al-Tāzī constructs to explain this decay is generic, including greed, adultery, wine drinking, and other stock moralisms. What is unusual is that at the head of the list he blames "the tyrannical ruler" (*al-sulṭān al-jā'ir*) for causing such internal weakness.[53] In this way, his moral criticism of common Muslims led to a tirade against the Marinid rulers and their Waṭṭāsid ministers, and he urged the Muslims to rise up against them. If the present rulers were not able to protect their Muslim subjects from conquest and enslavement, the people should cast them off in favor of others who can organize a collective defense through *jihād*. Such a person would be both a worldly and religious leader (*amīr* and *imām*). According to al-Tāzi, the Marinid and Waṭṭāsid families had no direct claim to religious legitimacy for their rule.

There is earlier evidence of Qādirī agitation in favor of *jihād* from within the capital of Fes beyond the eloquent and fiery poetry of al-Tāzī. In addition to dispensing quick, miraculous vigilante justice, Zarruq's friend Al-Amīn stirred up the public against the Iberian incursions on the Moroccan coast and preached for *jihād*. Zarruq tells how al-Amīn generated a public uproar about a Spanish (Andalusī) spy in the midst of Fes around 865 Hijri (1461–62 C.E.). Al-Amīn confronted an Andalusian in Fes who was presumably a refugee from the *reconquista* and claimed descent from the Prophet's family. He said, "You are not satisfied with just being a Muslim, but go about claiming a noble genealogy, when in fact most likely you are a spy [for the Spanish or Portuguese]!"[54]

By making such an accusation, al-Amīn was playing with fire. Many people in Fes were suspicious of the Andalusian refugees and questioned the depth of their sincerity as converts to Islam. Many also resented the technical skills of these refugees and their success in finding patronage from the Marinid court.[55] The denunciation and squabble escalated until the minister of state, ᶜAlī ibn Yūsuf al-Waṭṭāsī, interceded to end the affair. He favored the Andalusian and came down hard on al-Amīn; he insisted that the Sufi appear in court and submit to an investigation of his "religious beliefs about Muhammad's Prophethood."[56] Al-Amīn publicly prayed that Allah would not let him meet the minister and that the minister would never meet him, and al-Amīn died the next day before any summons could be carried out (inciting gossip that he had committed suicide). The Andalusian returned suddenly to Spanish soil, and some of his associates leaked the information that he really had been spying for the Christians. By then, al-Amīn had already died, a "martyr" (*shahīd*) for the cause of resentment against the Marinid rulers and public frenzy over the need to protect Morocco against Iberian invasion. This was also the first moment when the Qādirīs in Fes openly, though obliquely, protested against Marinid rule. By advocating *jihād* against the Iberians and questioning the legitimacy of Marinid rule, the Qādirīs allied with other Sufi movements outside Fes. The strongest of these was the movement headed by the charismatic Sufi leader Muḥammad ibn Sulaymān al-Jazūlī.[57] Al-Jazūlī combined rural traditions of Sufi activism with urban traditions of learned piety to fashion a new kind of spiritual path. This path set up the "axial saint" as the leader of a mass movement which aimed at the reform of rural life and the exercise of political power. Al-Jazūlī accepted disciples in vast numbers, without educational conditions and without insisting on a long period of personal training under his supervision.[58] In contrast to the Qādirī Sufis, al-Jazūlī encouraged his followers to visit the tombs of Moroccan saints only, rather than to travel east toward Cairo and the *Ḥijāz*. In cultivating a sense of local allegiance and cultural particularity, al-Jazūlī put himself forward as the saintly leader of Morocco, and he used the term *imām* to describe his authority.

Al-Jazūlī was allegedly a *sharīf*, and his method of contemplation focused heavily upon blessing the spirit of the Prophet, his own purported ancestor.[59] Indeed, he claimed that nobility resided in the descendants of the Prophet, implying that political authority should reside in them as well, for the most noble should naturally rule. "One is great because of the greatness of nobility and lineage. I am noble in lineage. My ancestor is the Messenger of God (may God bless and preserve him) and I am nearer to him than all of God's creation. My reputation is eternal, dyed in gold and silver. Oh you who desire gold and silver, follow us, for he who follows us dwells in the heights of *ᶜIliyyin* in this world and the hereafter!"[60] Al-Jazūlī used terms reminiscent of Shiᶜi thought to describe himself as an inerrant spiritual guide, "an intermediary between yourselves and True One."[61] He often referred to himself as *khalīfa*, exciting millenarian hopes among his listeners who may have expected him to lead a political revolution from his position of spiritual authority.[62]

Al-Jazūlī clearly saw political discontent as the fuel that kept his claim to spiritual leadership of all of Morocco burning bright. Yet he tried to focus this discontent into constructive channels: the reform of rural society, the spread of basic literacy and religious education, and the military defense of Moroccan ports against Iberian incursions. Al-Jazūlī was one of the strongest preachers of *jihād* in the countryside and coastal areas. His own aspiration to become a socially active and politically potent saint seems to have come into sharp focus as he participated in the *jihād* to defend Tangier (along with other Sufi colleagues and sharifian nobles) in 841 Hijri (1437–38 C.E.). Later, he encouraged his body of 12,000 followers not only to engage in spiritual devotions, but also to form an irregular army to assist in the *jihād* to compensate for lack of government campaigns.

Cornell cites fascinating evidence to illustrate how al-Jazūlī combined elements of Qādirī devotions in building an ostensibly Shādhilī community. He seems to have kept company with Qādirī Sufis in Egypt and learned from them some forms of invoking blessing upon the Prophet. After his return to Morocco, he does not seem to have had intimate contact with the Qādirīs of Fes. Nevertheless, the Qādirīyya community in Fes and the movement headed by al-Jazūlī outside the capital converged, for both preached the need for *jihād* against the Iberians. Both elevated the prestige of sharifian families as political actors and leaned toward rising up against the Marinid state if it opposed the social mobilization of *jihād*.

However, the question of the relationship between the Qādirīs in urban northern Morocco and the followers of al-Jazūlī is open to speculation. Some historians argue that followers of al-Jazūlī were involved in political activities against the Marinids in Fes itself.[63] However, evidence for this strong thesis is lacking. There was no zawiya affiliated with the Jazūlī community in Fes until after the revolution and the death of al-Jazūlī, when his primary successor, ᶜAbd al-ᶜAzīz al-Tabbāᶜ, founded a zawiya there.[64] Others speculate about the possibility of "a doctrinal influence" of al-Jazūlī upon Qādirīs in this period.[65] Such an influence did not come into play before the revolution, before which there is no direct evidence of Jazūlī community activities in Fes or doctrinal influence upon the Qādirīs. Yet it did come into play in the ensuing decade after the revolution.

A more cautious thesis is in greater accord with the known facts. An open partnership between Qādirīs and followers of al-Jazūlī should not be projected back in time to a period when the Marinid hold on power would have made such open associations dangerous. It is more accurate to assert that different Sufi communities shared the common hope that a sharifian leader would capture power through *jihād* propaganda. The Qādirīyya community in the urban centers (especially in Fes) entertained this hope, as did the Jazūlīyya in rural centers (especially in southern Morocco). The commonality of certain rhetoric or doctrines arose due to the congruent political aspirations of these groups. This commonality does not prove the existence of a formal political alliance or even sustained personal contact between these Sufi communities. It is not clear that the Qādirīs developed any complex ideology of religious leadership comparable to that developed by al-Jazūlī and elaborated by his later followers. The Qādirīs may have felt that any just ruler, especially from among the *shurafā*ʾ, should replace the corrupt Marinid dynasty and reunite the Muslims of Morocco in a *jihād*. When al-Jazūlī's followers came to Fes, they naturally gravitated toward the Qādirī zawiya as a meeting place, since they had no opportunity to build their own zawiya in this period. The first mention of al-Jazūlī's followers in Fes occurred after his death, when Ahmad Zarruq met two prominent followers of al-Jazūli who visited Zawiya Bū'l-Quṭūṭ.[66]

It is crucial to note the relation of the Qādirī Sufis with other Sufi movements that advocated *jihād* and open opposition to the Marinid sultan. Zarruq's precarious position in Fes is intimately connected to the activities of the Qādirīs. The balance Zarruq enjoyed in his youth (between spiritual cultivation with juridical Sufis and spiritual exploration with Qādirī Sufis) was toppled when Qādirī saints supported a sharifian revolution. This crucial event in Zarruq's life can only be understood if the Qādirī community's political agenda is carefully distinguished from that of the Jazūlīyya movement that was to dominate Morocco in later periods.

Revolution against Legal Rule

During his youth, Zarruq enjoyed education, patronage by a stable authority figure in al-Qūrī, and wider adventures among more speculative and activist Sufis in the circle of al-Zaytūnī. Although he experienced tension between the different modes of saintly authority projected by al-Qūrī and al-Zaytūnī, these tensions may not have seemed irreconcilable or mutually contradictory to him. The fault lines between these foundations of his world grew volatile as he reached maturity. They ruptured in the year 869 Hijri (1465 C.E.), when Zarruq was twenty-three years old. In that year, his world seemed to fall apart, both in its intimate dimensions and its wider structural dimensions. The mounting pressures of political discontent in Morocco reached a threshold point. Contesting modes of saintly authority became congruent with political factions that erupted into violence. These events threatened Zarruq's life and turned his world and its assumed values upside down in a literal revolution.

In 869 Hijri (1465 C.E.), certain religious leaders in Fes allied with the leader of the *shurafā'* in the city to overthrow the Marinid sultan, ʿAbd al-Ḥaqq. They mobilized the commoners of Fes and some underclass elements around a cluster of ideological themes: the corruption of the Marinid regime, the nobility of sharifian genealogy, resentment against the Jews of Fes, and the need for *jihād* against the Iberians. In one day, in what seemed to be a spontaneous popular uprising, political fault lines that had been bearing increasing tension suddenly broke. This created a truly revolutionary situation. The sultan was killed, the Marinid dynasty came to an end, and a new ideology of rule triumphed. These events called into question previously respected religious authorities, such as those Sufis who had held posts in Marinid-sponsored institutions. The Qādirī Sufis of Fes played an active role in the revolution and helped to catalyze popular support for the sharifian revolutionaries.

These events trapped Aḥmad Zarruq in a contest of loyalties and religious authorities. Because of certain legal points, ethical principles, assumptions about legitimacy, and suspicion of radical change, he threw his lot in with the losing side, al-Qūrī and his circle of juridical Sufis. The results of his decision were catastrophic for him. The rest of Zarruq's life was a quest to recover the stability and equilibrium lost in these events. First he needed to avoid threats to his safety and welfare. Then he had to recover his sense of legitimacy by finding his own basis of authority as a maturing jurist and aspiring saint.

To understand these radical changes that overwhelmed Zarruq in a single year, we have to analyze the revolution in Fes. Such an analysis will revisit many of the themes mentioned in the previous section in greater detail to demonstrate the political collision of the competing models of Sufi training and saintly authority. Such an analysis must begin with a pair of themes: the increasing strength of sharifian political clout in Fes and the decreasing strength of Marinid rule. The Marinid dynasty had come to power without a coherent ideology of religious legitimacy to justify their rule. They developed many strategies to compensate for this lack, patronizing many religious institutions in a bid for legitimacy from religious notables, including scholars, jurists, Sufis, and the *shurafāʾ*. Such state patronage of jurists and Sufis established the very possibility for a juridical Sufi community to develop around saints like al-Qūrī.

The Marinid rulers also extended patronage to the *shurafāʾ*, who played an increasingly dominant role in the civic life of Fes during the final period of Marinid rule. They put themselves forward as the natural leaders of the people of Fes, sometimes in vocal competition with jurists, who also saw themselves in that role. The historian al-Nāṣiri has summarized this dynamic. "The Marinid rulers would praise these sharifian families and pay deference to them. The rulers would claim pious benefit from raising the social station of the *shurafāʾ* and indulging their every need, since the Marinids themselves lacked any rightful claim to religious legitimacy (*ratbat al-khilāfa*) which might accrue to them through religious law and custom. Thus when they turned to religious institutions and rituals [to justify their rule] they saw themselves as having taken power through conquest, even though these *shurafāʾ* had more right to rule. For this reason, the Marinid rulers showed humility and deference toward the *shurafāʾ*, taking guidance and advice from them as far as possible."[67] A story illustrates this deference and the resentment it sparked in other religious leaders. In the court of the Marinid sultan Abū ʿInān al-Marīnī in the fourteenth century C.E., even the sultan would stand up in deference to the head of the sharifian clans (*naqīb al-shurafāʾ*) when he entered the court. Only the scholar and jurist Abū ʿAbdullah al-Muqrī refused to stand in honor of the *sharīf*. "He justified this violation of protocol to the outraged *sharīf* by declaring: 'I carry in myself my *sharaf* [honor or nobility]: it is the knowledge that I dispense around me and that no one can doubt. As for your [honor], it is subject to doubt. Who can guarantee its authenticity [of genealogical descent] after over seven hundred years? Anyway, if we were really convinced of it, we would have removed this one (pointing to the non-sharifian Marinid sultan) and put you in his place.'"[68] This confrontation sparked a feud between the descendant of the Prophet and the scholar of scripture, a clash which foreshadows the fault lines which would rupture during the revolution in Fes a century later.[69]

The Marinid rulers recognized a single person as *naqīb al-shurafāʾ*, "the representative of the descendants of the Prophet," and gave him an official administrative role. The Marinid ruler invested the leader of the sharifian al-Jūṭī clan with this position, and this clan played the leading role in the rising political power of the *shurafāʾ* through this period.[70] The al-ᶜImrānī family was dominant in Fes in Marinid times and led the *shurafāʾ* to take leading roles in many other official rituals and new religious celebrations patronized by the court, like the birthday of the Prophet (*mawlid al-nabī*).[71] Not all religious authorities recognized this practice as an authentic holiday; some thought it a "religious innovation" unknown in earlier times. Slowly, however, skepticism fell away and the celebration gained widespread acceptance, by both Sufis and jurists. It was the occasion for grand ceremonial processions, in which the *shurafāʾ* played a leading role. They used this occasion to raise their social status considerably throughout the period of Marinid rule.[72]

Only a few years before Zarruq's birth, a major event further secured the institutional power of this branch of the al-Jūṭī clan and launched them into political prominence. In 841 Hijri (1438 C.E.) the lost tomb of their saintly ancestor, Mawlay Idrīs II, was "rediscovered" in the center of Fes. The Marinid rulers were quickly enjoined to support the building of a proper shrine (housing a mosque and tomb) for the site. In deference to its holiness, the entire area surrounding the tomb was designated as a "sanctuary" in the care of sharifian protectors. This area included one of the most important marketplaces of Fes (the Qayṣarīyya, in which gold, spices, and other valuable commodities were traded). By a trump of sacred geography, the market was cleared of Jewish merchants and landowners who had grown in power over several generations and was arrogated to the al-ᶜImrānī family. By this move, the *shurafāʾ* claimed a central role as the social axis of Fes in control of the overlapping arenas of sacred sites, urban space, and economic networks. This new shrine also provided the *shurafāʾ* a platform from which they would shortly launch their new political role.[73]

The story of the "rediscovery" of the tomb reveals a potent bid for power by the al-Jūṭī *shurafāʾ*. An anonymous author of the time frames this uncovering of the bones of Mawlay Idrīs as a miracle, "a sign of compassion and grace to this divinely appointed community of faith."[74] It was certainly a time when a miracle was needed. The Portuguese were assaulting the port of Tangier while the Marinid sultan appeared unwilling or unable to lead its defense; it was left to various Sufi groups and *shurafāʾ* to lead troops in the city's defense. Uncovering the body of the saintly ancestor of the *shurafāʾ* in the center of Fes seemed to confirm the victory of the *mujāhidīn* along the Mediterranean coast, led by Sufis and *shurafāʾ* (and saintly *shurafāʾ* like al-Jazūlī, who participated in this campaign).

Upon finding a body, the "representative of the descendants of the Prophet," ᶜAlī al-ᶜImrānī, head of the al-Jūṭī clan in Fes, immediately called upon the chief minister, Abū Zakariyā Yaḥyā al-Waṭṭāsī.[75] They called upon the prayer leader of the congregational mosque of al-Qarawiyyīn, who was none other than ᶜAbdallah al-ᶜAbdūsi (the juridical Sufi teacher of Zarruq's grandmother). The three authorities (political, religious by genealogy, and religious by juridical and Sufi authority) conferred to decide how to preserve the site.

The overwhelming popularity of this rediscovery of Mawlay Idrīs II's tomb, in the midst of a military crisis in the north, forced the Marinid rulers and the juridical Sufis to acknowledge sharifian political might. The refurbished tomb-shrine gave the *shurafāʾ* a new architectural symbol of their religious legitimacy as leaders of the people of Fes. The rulers were coerced into giving the *shurafāʾ* increasing political power as they themselves lost public credibility. As he stood over the site of Mawlay Idrīs's body to grant money for the reconstruction of a tomb, the minister of state was hailed as "the preserver of love for the *shurafāʾ*, ever ready to show forth their exalted status and establish their glory, always desiring to revive the sunna of their glorious ancestor [the Prophet Muḥammad]."[76] In previous generations, the Marinid sultans and their Wattasid ministers of state gained political legitimacy from such dramatic acknowledgment of the *shurafāʾ*. That was possible if the *shurafāʾ* were content with public acclaim, ceremonial deference ,and tax exemptions. However, after the founding of the tomb of Mawlay Idrīs II, the *shurafāʾ* acquired an economic and political power base totally independent of the Marinid regime. Only twenty-five years after the Marinid officials lauded and graced the Idrīsī *shurafāʾ* with a grand tomb-shrine, the same *shurafāʾ* revolted openly against their rule.

The *shurafāʾ* threw caution to the wind and courted accusations of betrayal because, in the intervening quarter-century, the Marinid administration fell to new depths of ineptitude and violent coercion. Many historical factors combined to ensure this decline: infighting between the sultan and his ministers, increasing assault of coastal areas by the Portuguese, popular resentment against increasing taxation, and the incursion of Arab Banū Maᶜqil tribes (who resisted allegiance to the Marinid state) into the broad plain that stretches from Tilimsan to Taza, Fes, and Meknes. The Waṭṭāsī family, who served as ministers of state, undermined the authority of the Marinid sultan from within. Abū Zakariyā Yaḥyā al-Waṭṭāsī held the sultan as a puppet ruler and wielded power himself. He introduced ᶜAbd al-Ḥaqq al-Marīnī, a seven-year-old boy, into Fes as the rightful sultan under his protection, and proceeded to keep him locked up in the palace. This arrangement worked well for the minister as he negotiated a balance of power with the *shurafāʾ*, and for his son who became minister of state after him. Historians blame these ministers for tinkering with offices and administration, demobilizing key components of the army, and treating the peasantry with coercive violence. He also dismissed the Qāḍī of Fes, Muḥammad al-Maṣmūdī, who had been a popular figure known for upholding justice and protecting the rights of the peasants and common people.[77]

However, as sultan ᶜAbd al-Ḥaqq grew up, he plotted to recapture power. In 863 Hijri (1458–59 C.E.) he took advantage of discontent with the Waṭṭāsid ministers and engineered a coup that murdered most leading members of the Waṭṭāsī family. He thought he had rid himself of the yoke of the Waṭṭāsī family for good, but he still decided not to appoint ministers out of fear of being dominated by them again. Many notables in Fes supported the Waṭṭāsī family and may even have helped some of them escape during the coup to the safety of Asila.[78] As an act of revenge, ᶜAbd al-Ḥaqq appointed two men from the Jewish community to act as ministers to collect tax revenue and spite the leaders of Fes for their support of the Waṭṭāsī family. Through these Jewish ministers, the sultan unleashed violence and coercion against the people of Fes. Popular accounts cite beatings of the *shurafāʾ*, scholars, and jurists, and appropriation of their property.[79] The tax burden on Fes rose considerably in these years, for the Marinid dynasty's control of the countryside was reduced to the outlying areas of Fes. Resentment against the state and its chosen ministers rose to feverish levels, combining anti-taxation slogans with rhetoric that was anti-Jewish, anti-Marinid, and pro-sharifian.

The situation in the countryside was no better than that within the capital. The activist Sufi movement that looked to al-Jazūlī as its saintly leader had gained a wide following after he participated in the defense of Tangier against the Portuguese in 841 Hijri (1437–38 C.E.). Al-Jazūlī developed his doctrine of an ideal sharifian-Sufi ruler, and through his leadership forged a Sufi community into a mass movement that threatened the ruling dynasty. His followers had numbered up to 12,000, including Sufis training in fighting in the *jihād* and restive Arab tribes who had been fighting against Marinid control. To those in power, this movement looked like a revolt in the making. In Āṣafī, traders who profited from relations with the Portuguese feared that al-Jazūlī's *jihād* rhetoric might lead his followers camped outside the city to take control of the city itself. They pressured the Marinid governor of Āṣafī to exile al-Jazūlī and his camp in 863 Hijri (1458–59 C.E.). Such discontent in the countryside around a major port like Āṣafī must have threatened the Marinid sultan even as far away as Fes.

Rebel against Revolution

Although no textual evidence demonstrates that the sultan ᶜAbd al-Ḥaqq directly opposed al-Jazūlī and his movement or ordered the governor of Āsafī to exile them, news from the countryside must have filtered into the capital city, sparking revolutionary fervor.[80] Against this backdrop of political intrigue and administrative decay, one can understand the popular uprising against the Marinid sultan. This study will present these events to highlight the role of Zarruq in these events and their consequences in his life.

Despite disagreements between the earliest sources, a basic narrative of the events of the revolution exists.[81] The sultan ᶜAbd al-Ḥaqq left Fes to fight against the Waṭṭāsid forces that had taken over areas of the northern countryside around Tangier and Taza. While he was away, certain communities in Fes rose up against the Jewish administrators whom he had left in charge of collecting taxes and keeping order in the city. Al-Waryāghalī, the preacher of the congregational mosque of al-Qarawiyyīn, began delivering fiery sermons denouncing the Jews in general, and these administrators in particular.[82] Issues included the high rates of taxation, the coercive means of extracting them, and the withdrawal of tax exemptions and charitable donations to the *shurafā*ʾ. Al-Waryāghalī stirred popular resentment by spreading allegations that ᶜAbd al-Ḥaqq's administrators were transferring these charitable funds to the poor in the Jewish community. He also spread the story that a certain Jew, who had been appointed as police chief, had beaten a sharifian woman in Fes; he used this event (whether factual or rumored) to galvanize a violent riot for the purpose of *jihād*. The broad front of this *jihād* would include the Jews in Fes, the Marinid administration of ᶜAbd al-Ḥaqq, and eventually the Spaniards (who had recently taken Gibraltar) and the Portuguese (who had taken Tangier).

Al-Waryāghalī struck the pose of a religious authority who spoke the will of the common people. He was known as "the thunderbolt of his age" because of his ability to motivate the crowd. In his youth, he had taken part in the *jihād* against the Portuguese at Tangier and Asila, working as a teacher and jurist in the ribats and encampments.[83] Zarruq remarks that he was "eloquent and outspoken as a preacher, and threw himself headlong into matters of public dispute without hesitating."[84] On the 27th of Ramadan, 869 Hijri, he declared that the people no longer owed their allegiance to the sultan ᶜAbd al-Ḥaqq and transferred his allegiance to the head of the *shurafā*ʾ, Muḥammad al-ᶜImrānī al-Jūṭī. This date marked the "Night of Power" (*laylat al-qadr*), an important night of ceremonial worship for Muslims. It would have been a ripe time for al-Waryāghalī to mobilize a vast mob as people gathered for all-night devotions in the mosque. Historical sources describe this mob as *wakkāra*, *zu*ᶜ*ār*, or *qalqalīyyūn* (organized gangs of ruffians) from the margins of society who nonetheless played important roles as popular protectors of specified quarters or guilds. The term might even apply to a "young men's brotherhood" (*futuwwa*) which owed allegiance to Sufi communities, and it suggests that the Qādirī Sufi community may have directly participated in the revolution.

Through the mediation of al-Waryāghalī, the mob pledged allegiance to the head of the sharifian clans, Muḥammad al-ᶜImrānī. He secured two juridical decisions that sanctioned violence against the Jews and revolution against the sultan. The earliest accounts of the revolution place responsibility for the uprising upon the preacher and the mob, who asked the *sharīf* al-ᶜImrānī to accept political allegiance. In these records, al-ᶜImrānī joins the revolution only after securing juridical permission. Yet al-ᶜImrānī's followers probably wrote these accounts once they came to power, and they would naturally shy away from depicting al-ᶜImrānī as the instigator of the revolution. In all likelihood, al-ᶜImrānī was a major force behind it. For several decades prior, he had engineered a dominant role for himself and the *shurafā*ʾ he led, against the financial power of the Jews in Fes and the authority of the sultan himself. Al-ᶜImrānī may have played a central role in advancing al-Waryāghalī as a juridical authority in Fes, in competition with others who owed traditional allegiance to the Marinid authorities, like al-Qūrī and his juridical Sufi colleagues.[85]

This transfer of political authority onto the *sharīf* sparked two further acts of public violence that tore at the fabric of civil order in Fes. The sultan ᶜAbd al-Ḥaqq returned to Fes; at the news of the revolution, his army abandoned him and joined the mob. Sources display the mob, led by al-ᶜImrānī, confronting the sultan outside of Fes with shouts of "*Jihād, Jihād*!"[86] Al-ᶜImrānī stripped the sultan of his royal regalia, paraded him before the people and nobles of Fes on a donkey, then executed him.[87] The second act of violence was directed against the Jews of Fes. The center of Jewish life in Fes had moved to quarters within the garrison town that held Marinid military forces, administrative buildings, and the palace (al-Madīna al-Bayḍā). By overrunning the Jewish quarter, therefore, the revolutionary forces were also storming the sultan's palace and administration. Sources record that these forces killed every man in the Jewish quarter and confiscated all their property.[88]

The *sharīf* al-ᶜImrānī proceeded to set up a new "republic" in which the *shurafāʾ* ruled as the rightful and just leaders of the Muslim community. Although we do not possess written records of their new ideology of political power, it seems that they dispensed with the position of sultan and minister of state.[89] The strength of their new ideology is evident in the aftermath of the revolution. On hearing of the overthrow of the Marinid sultan, the Waṭṭāsī family sought to return to Fes as its rightful rulers. They expected the *sharīf* and his supporters to welcome them back, since they had previously championed themselves as ruling on behalf of the *shurafāʾ* as their patrons and protectors. However, the *sharīf* refused the Waṭṭāsī family and their military forces entry into the city; after a tussle, the Waṭṭāsī family ensconced their forces in the garrison town just beyond the city walls and cut off the small sharifian republic from access to the countryside.

Within Fes, the *sharīf* and his son ruled for six years, showing that he controlled a following of religious notables and Sufis who rallied the people to his cause. In this support, the Qādirī community played a major role. The Qādirī saints were involved in the intrigue that marked the beginning phases of the revolution. As mentioned above, al-Amīn rose to public controversy by denouncing a man (who was evidently close to the Waṭṭāsī minister) as a Spanish spy within Fes. In addition, Zarruq reports that al-Zaytūnī predicted the downfall of ᶜAbd al-Ḥaqq's Jewish administrators before the revolution got underway. The very fact that the revolution broke out on the "Night of Power" suggests that al-Zaytūnī played a role in inciting it, for his protective powers were put into force by reciting *Surat al-Qadr* (verses from the Qurʾan which describe this "Night of Power"). The Qādirīs also articulated a basis of legitimacy for the sharif's rule. They had already been experimenting with visionary initiations and the idea of total absorption in the personality of ᶜAbd al-Qādir al-Jīlānī, a saint who was a *sharīf*. In addition, they cultivated a spiritual connection directly to the Prophet himself while garnering patronage from the Qādirī family of *shurafāʾ*. This mode of spiritual authority shared a reciprocal affinity with the al-Jūṭī sharif's claim to political authority based on genealogical descent from the Prophet. This claim was that the descendants carried the Prophet's own personal virtues, sense of justice, and right to rule. Qādirī leaders forged this Sufi-sharifian alliance in Fes, in a similar way that the Jazūlīyya community forged an alliance with the Saᶜdian family of *shurafāᵓ* outside of Fes.

The events of the revolution in Fes thrust the young Zarruq into the midst of intrigue and public debate in a way that threatened to destroy his future in Fes. His ideals clashed with political expediency. His budding maturity rested on a delicate balance of patronage and juridical training in the madrasa and exploration of Sufi devotions and exercises under the care of two spirituals guides: al-Qūrī and al-Zaytūnī. The revolution destroyed any semblance of balance between these various forces and institutions. The revolution ruptured the cultural consensus over political rule and its religious legitimacy that had been in force since the beginning of Marinid rule, over two centuries before.

The revolution pitted Zarruq's two patrons, both of whom he looked to as saints, against each other in a moment of political danger. His loyalty to one could only be seen as betrayal of the other. In the months preceding the actual revolution, Zarruq's colleagues in the Qādirī community began to intrigue against Marinid rule. Zarruq records that he accompanied al-Zaytūnī and others on their yearly pilgrimage to the tomb of Abū Yiᶜzza. The Qādirīs had already established this pilgrimage as the site of important visionary encounters with the spirit of ᶜAbd al-Qādir (as shown in the narrative of al-Amīn). There, al-Zaytūnī experienced a disclosure that was a spiritual precursor to a declaration of revolution against Marinid rule. In his autobiography, Zarruq records: "That year, I visited [the tomb of] Abū Yiᶜzza with our Shaykh al-Zaytūnī and a group of his disciples (*fuqarāᵓ*). Intimate secrets were revealed to us, while illuminations and blessings came to us that could never be surpassed.... One day al-Zaytūnī said something about the two new servants of the sultan and commanded me to keep this secret for some days; and I did keep silent."[90]

In manuscript copies of Zarruq's autobiography, this crucial phrase recording al-Zaytuni's prediction about "two new servants of the sultan" is obscured.[91] An unexplored historiographic source, *Kitab al-Muᶜza*, offers an account of this incident that renders the event more explicit and more intelligible than previously thought. "We all returned [from the pilgrimage to Abū Yiᶜzza] with the blessings of the Shaykh. Brilliant lights were illumining us from above and secrets were revealed to the Shaykh during this journey. It was revealed to al-Zaytūnī who from among the kings would be stripped of power and killed and who would take control of the government. Therefore, al-Zaytūnī turned to me and said, 'Hey Aḥmad!' I answered, 'Yes?' He said, 'Listen, it is two new servants of the sultan.' Then he swore me to secrecy regarding this information. So I kept quiet and did not divulge this secret to anyone."[92] Al-Zaytūnī's statement about "two new servants of the sultan" is the secret content of his prediction of who would be stripped of power and killed in the future. This is an example of foreknowledge (*firāsa*) that is characteristic of al-Zaytūnī's politically potent miracles, predicting the imminent downfall of sultan ᶜAbd al-Ḥaqq's two new Jewish administrators. As word of this miracle foretelling the success of the coming revolution spread in Fes, it must have considerably buoyed the confidence of the revolutionaries and may have further specified that the head *sharīf*, Muḥammad al-ᶜImrānī, was to come to power. Just as al-Waryāghalī played the role of the populist jurist who urged a revolution, so al-Zaytūnī played the role of a populist saint who did the same.

Upon the return of the pilgrims to Fes, rumor of al-Zaytūnī's vision and political foreknowledge ran rampant through Fes. Zarruq's account insists that he maintained secrecy, even when al-Zaytūnī confronted him and accused him of having betrayed the revolutionary cause by divulging this slogan and its origins. "Then Shaykh al-Zaytūnī told me, 'I heard you revealing this secret to so-and-so!' I swore with my fullest sincerity that I had told this secret to nobody, but he did not accept my oath. I was not able to disavow that of which he accused me, nor could I believe him because of what I know myself to be true."[93] This dispute may have erupted before, during, or just after the revolution in Fes. In any case, political alliances were polarizing quickly, and Zarruq was trapped in the middle. Al-Zaytūnī may have intimated this secret knowledge to Zarruq to lure him to the side of the revolutionaries, or at least to test his loyalty. Clearly he felt that Zarruq owed a prior and weightier loyalty to his first Sufi exemplar, al-Qūrī.

Al-Qūrī himself was trapped in a losing situation as the chief jurist of Fes. Upon taking the helm of the revolutionary forces, al-ᶜImrānī came to al-Qūrī requesting one judicial sanction (*fatwā*) for his uprising against the sultan and another sanction justifying violence against the Jews. Al-Qūrī refused to furnish such judicial sanctions for actions that he saw as clearly contravening Islamic law.[94] In his view, ᶜAbd al-Ḥaqq might be an incompetent and ruthless sultan, but he was nonetheless a legal sultan. Al-Qūrī's loyalty was not to the person of the sultan but to the legal principle of orderly succession, which formed a bulwark against civic unrest and mob violence. In addition, he saw that Islamic law upheld the rights of religious minorities like the Jews, who could not be deprived of life or property while under the protection of an Islamic government.

In the face of this refusal, the *sharīf* al-ᶜImrānī coerced al-Qūrī into issuing the demanded fatwas, with threats of violence from him and the mob.[95] Al-Qūrī evidently provided the necessary documents in order to save his life. Under the shadow of such threats, the three most authoritative juridical notables in Fes left their official posts and went into hiding: al-Qūrī, al-Miknāsī (the prayer leader of the congregational mosque of al-Andalus) and Qāḍī al-Fakhkhārī. These last two may have left their posts in a protest of sympathy with al-Qūrī or to protect themselves from similar coercion. The people of his constituency requested al-Miknāsī to return to his post, but he refused, saying, "I left due to an injury (*jarḥa*) that I suffered. My coming forward now will not make matters lawful for you. Even if I had not stepped down from injury, my accepting this position now would show weak resolve (*qillat al-himma*)."[96] Resignation was the only response possible for these jurists and representatives of the official establishment when faced with a revolutionary mob demanding that they declare lawful something to which they could not conscientiously accede.

At this point, Zarruq stepped in to protect the safety and reputation of his teacher and spiritual master, al-Qūrī. Zarruq's autobiography omits mention of the revolution and its violent aftermath. However, other sources record him as opposing the revolution at those points where the popular movement transgressed legal norms. He is known to have declared the "*jihād*" against the Jews of Fes to be illegal and their blood and property protected. Clearly, the tide of popular sentiment was against Zarruq's position. However, with al-Qūrī driven into hiding or public shame, Zarruq became the most public voice denouncing the leaders.[97] Since al-Waryāghalī supported the revolution, Zarruq refused to pray behind his leadership, saying "I don't entrust my prayers to an arrogant and conceited show-off, since my prayers might become as hollow as he is." He also accused al-Waryāghalī of being a *ghandūr*, "a pretender of most audacious boldness."[98]

Zarruq protested that al-Waryāghalī was not the legitimate juridical spokesman for the Muslims of Fes. He held that al-Waryāghalī had appropriated that position from al-Qūrī at the inception of the revolution. Only al-Qūrī could issue an authoritative legal decision, while the words of al-Waryāghalī were only a *mushāwara,* or "a consultation" with no binding authority. By resisting the coercive power of the mob, al-Qūrī could only have incurred his own death, but by giving in he relegated himself to irrelevance. Religious authority in Fes passed into the hands of al-Waryāghalī and those scholars, saints, and Sufis who supported him. The issue for Zarruq in this public protest was not just political power or a legal principle. In seeing al-Qūrī pushed aside, he perceived that the revolution and its advocates were undermining the mode of saintly authority that centered on balancing spiritual cultivation with legal rectitude. Zarruq had seen al-Qūrī as a distinctive type of juridical saint who played a special role in society. In witnessing al-Qūrī exit the public stage in shame, Zarruq saw his cherished model of the juridical saint thrust aside, not only in its personal embodiment in al-Qūrī, but also as a publicly acclaimed ideal.

This paradigm of sainthood was eclipsed by a competing one, of socially activist saintly power that relied on the political dominance of the *shurafāʾ* to secure its social position. Within Fes, the leaders of the Qādirī community advocated this paradigm, while the Jazūlīyya community leaders outside Fes would soon raise it to unprecedented dominance. Zarruq's protest failed to win over his contemporaries in Fes. Al-Qūrī never recuperated his lost authority against the coup of al-Waryāghalī. The *shurafāʾ* set up an independent republic that did not rely on jurists and educators for its political legitimacy. The two Jewish ministers were punished for having held administrative positions in the Marinid state, and the wider Jewish community was possibly attacked, while Zarruq was held in suspicion as a "defender of Jews" or as a clandestine Jew himself. His Sufi master, al-Zaytūnī, denounced him as having betrayed his oath of allegiance, throwing his character into disrepute. In his autobiography, Zarruq very carefully avoids mentioning this period, saying only that "after this conflict, the place that had once welcomed me so comfortably became suddenly cramped and constricted; so I left the city of Fes intending to visit [the tomb of] Abū Madyan."[99] In fact, Zarruq seems to have barely escaped Fes with his life.

PART III.
SPIRIT

> There is no spiritual knowledge except what is learned through a discipline from the giver of scripture (*shāri*ᶜ), or from one who is delegated to represent the giver of scripture in later times.[1]

ZARRUQ INSISTED THAT all the disciplines of Islamic knowledge come from the same source, "the giver of scripture." Zarruq explains that "[i]t is just as the Prophet Muhammad said, 'Knowledge only comes from the discipline of learning just as patience comes from the discipline of restraint in the face of provocation. [With such discipline] whoever seeks benefit will surely find it and whoever is wary of harm will be protected from it.' … What leads to such enlightened wariness? Understanding that is in accord with scriptural principles, that opens tranquility in the heart and expands the bounds of reasoning."[2] Whether the knowledge is of Islamic law, Qur'anic exegesis, or Sufi devotion, each is derived from the same scriptural sources by recognized authorities through carefully reasoned principles. No single discipline has ontological or epistemological priority or originality; none can stand independent of the others. This was the basic message of Zarruq's reform program, and he insisted that principles, when applied to scripture, give rise to multiple disciplines of religious knowledge. In this section, chapters 5 and 6 will analyze Zarruq's passage to maturity, in which he advocated a reform of Sufi spiritual discipline and embodied the spirit of reform.

The term "reform" is rampant in Islamic Studies and is often used in contradictory ways, for scholars have not delimited its meaning with consensus. Many scholars portray reform as a characteristic of modern Islam and a response to European colonialism in Islamic lands; in this view, reformers are religious authorities who reject Sufi communities and Muslim saints. Such a deployment of reform that forecloses Sufi devotion is too narrow a conception of reform.[3] It certainly makes the life of Zarruq seem anachronistic, for Zarruq was a scripturalist reformer who was also a saint before mature European colonization. Scripture, reasoning, and spiritual insight were not at odds for Zarruq. The roles of jurist, scholar, and saint were not incompatible—in fact they were indivisible.

Zarruq advocated a movement of reform as a bulwark against what he felt was the impending dissolution of Islamic society in Morocco. He sought to reunite saintly authority with scriptural scholarship and juridical rectitude not just in his personality, but in a wider movement of reform based on Sufi devotional practices. He saw Sufi communities as the natural vehicle for such reforms, and also as the primary object of reform. He aimed to refashion the core concept of sainthood into a particular configuration, which would be the center of a reform of Islamic society as a whole. In such a reform movement, the juridical saint was the primary agent of reform, which would radiate out into society through Sufi communities. The community of reform-minded Sufi scholars that gathered around the juridical saint attempted to build an interregional reform movement based on the fusion of saint and jurist, devotion and erudition.

The disaster in Zarruq's early life touched off a series of events that pushed him into a lifelong struggle to live as a juridical saint and recover the lost ideals of al-Qūrī. After the revolution in Fes, Zarruq could only live as a juridical saint by living as a reformist saint. Sincerity (*ṣidq*) is the key that summarizes a cluster of virtues that Zarruq held dear as the foundation of his sainthood: *taqwā* (mindfulness), *war*ᶜ (caution), and *muḥāsaba* (self-scrutiny). Taken together, these virtues form a larger figure of the reformist saint, a figure that the mature Zarruq claimed to embody in himself. Obsessive attention to sincerity emerges as a dominant theme in Zarruq's life that conditioned his psychological and social reactions to his surroundings, first in Fes and later in his exile. Zarruq claimed to have achieved a form of selfless sincerity, which he felt is the foundational principle of sainthood. Zarruq experienced the passage into this state, through exile and reform, as a quest for sincerity.

In rejecting the alliance of the mob, the socially active Sufis, and the emerging political power of sharifian clans, Zarruq rebelled against the social and ethical consensus of his time. He was launched, against his will, into a search for sincerity that would force him into the role of reformer and social critic. For Zarruq, self-alienation was a positive experience, for it led to a confrontation with death. It heightened one's awareness of sincerity and refined one's ability to perform legal obligations. In Zarruq's view, the selfish and limited ego could be transcended. The saint who experienced such transcendence could become the perfect vehicle for embodying the sacred law and restoring social order.

His passage to maturity did not provide Zarruq with tranquil repose. The crisis in authority and political action documented in the last chapter threw him onto a difficult path. He spent the rest of his life wrestling with the terms of sincerity, authority, and sainthood. His own experience of sainthood and his attempt to formulate principles that would define its limits and foundations caused him to question the accepted economy of authority between master and disciple in Sufi training. He emerged as a dissident individual who condemned many of the Sufi practices of his contemporaries in Morocco. He advocated reform in Sufi training which, he felt, would redefine the cultural logic of sanctity and lead, he hoped, to a new depth of sincerity and social cohesion.

5 Pilgrimage

As Zarruq's youthful world collapsed around him, he left Fes on a series of exile journeys, each growing more extended. Through them, he began to understand that he could not lead his mature life in Fes. The sharifian revolution shattered his hopes and his identity, displacing the center of his world. His passage to maturity would be a geographic journey as well as a spiritual one, one that would threaten his physical well-being and tax his intellectual and imaginative resources. Through these journeys, he forged his sense of alienation into an ideal of reform; his growing sense that he was a juridical saint required that he articulate a program for the reform of Sufi communities. In short, he transformed his exile into a pilgrimage toward spiritual maturity.

In his reform program, Zarruq tried to systematically limit a saint's exercise of charisma, which gets to the very heart of the cultural logic of sanctity. Since Weber introduced the term "charisma" into the intellectual discipline of Sociology of Religion, it has become much used and much abused.[1] Weber distinguished between three basic kinds of social authority: traditional, rational-legal, and charismatic. In his definition, "charisma" is a religious leader's claim to authority, preeminence, and obedience due to his singular interface with and personal perception of the divine power. The claim is beyond the purview of holding an office or inheriting a social position.[2] In Zarruq's view, what makes a person a saint is not "charisma" (a quality one possesses) but rather the singular and ineffable "turning to face Allah in all sincerity" (an action that one does). In this sense, all saints inherit their spiritual power from the Prophet Muhammad, while Muhammad's sincerity in facing Allah was what allowed him to receive revelation. However, in Zarruq's reformist vision, no saint should claim authority on the basis of charisma; their claim to authority must come only from the more "rational-legal" dimension of holding an office as a jurist, scholar, or teacher. For this reason, he balked at accepting al-Zaytūnī's visions and the bid for authority inherent in them.

Zarruq offers an insightful exception to the use of the Arabic term *baraka* to mean "charisma." Such usage has become standard in anthropological and sociological studies of Islamic North Africa. Zarruq does not often use the term *baraka* to describe the spiritual authority of the saint, in the sense used in such studies. Rather, Zarruq uses the Arabic term *ḥurma,* which literally means "forbiddenness" or "inviolability." This term is popularly applied to the precinct of shrines in Morocco (such as the area around the tomb of Mawlay Idrīs II in Fes, discussed in the previous chapter); the term is universally applied by Arabic speakers to the *Kaᶜba* in Makka (which is known as *al-Ḥaram al-Sharīf* or the Noble Sanctuary, formed from the same linguistic root as *ḥurma*). When applied to a saint, *ḥurma* denotes the reciprocal relation of respect and deference between saint and disciple. *Ḥurma* is not a quality possessed by an individual, it is rather a quality granted to an individual by others. It is a recognition, a relation based on sincerity. To explain this concept, Zarruq quoted the famous Sufi scholar Abū al-Qāsim Naṣrābādī: "The foundational principle of being a Sufi is obeying the Book (Qurᵓān) and conforming to the Prophet's example (*sunna*). It requires leaving your own selfish cravings (*hawā*) and all inauthentic religious practices (*bidᶜa*). One must magnify the sanctity of spiritual masters (*ḥurmat al-mashāyikh*), guard the rights of others over one, and remain constant in meditation while desisting from making any excuses or exceptions for oneself."[3] In affirming this quotation, Zarruq commented, "Indeed, this is the primary and indispensable principle for being a Sufi. Whoever neglects it is prohibited from reaching the ultimate goal of intimacy with Allah. Most people in the present neglect it, except for those whom Allah has protected from error. And how few they are!"[4]

Ḥurma is recognition by others and must be "preserved" through one's relation to others (*ḥifẓ al-ḥurma*). Zarruq's conception of saintly authority is, ironically, more sociologically subtle than that of contemporary anthropologists. In Zarruq's treatment of spiritual authority, the notion of "supernatural power" is absent. Supernatural power is what anthropologists equate with the term *baraka.* For example, Geertz defines *baraka* as both "religious power" and "supernatural power."[5] In his treatment, *baraka* is the way that the sacred manifests in the world through an individual's capacity, endowment, or special ability. In calling *baraka* an ability that comes as a "gift," Geertz mirrors the word "charisma" in its Christian theological meaning.[6] This term is so central to Geertz's analysis that he defines sainthood as "the possession of baraka."[7]

The way Geertz phrases this definition is crucial, for the religious authority of a saint comes from something that the individual "possesses." Geertz sees two dimensions to a saint's authority: legitimacy and miraculousness, which he often conflates with genealogical descent or genetic inheritance.[8] However, in Zarruq's view, authority cannot be "possessed" either through legitimacy or through genealogy. In Zarruq's writings, *baraka* means "blessing" which comes from Allah and is never an individual's possession or endowment. Rather it must be earned through sincerity. Sincerity demands recognition but can never become a possession.

Like Geertz, Zarruq certainly sees a double dimension to authority. However, Zarruq identifies the two dimensions as sincerity and legitimacy, rather than as miraculous power and legitimacy. Sincerity and legitimacy represent two complementary dimensions of authority. Sincerity is internal to the personality, displayed in virtues, struggles, and personal sacrifices; through these means, sincerity can generate a certain kind of authority that is always interpersonal and not invested in rank, status, or material symbols. In contrast, legitimacy is that authority which is external to a person and is inherent in a person's social network.[9] A saint's legitimacy inheres in his submission to his own masters and his control over his own disciples. Such legitimacy is inherent in formal markers of authority (such as lineages of initiation linked to renowned saints of the past, relics from past masters, distinctive clothes or mannerisms). It is also positioned in sites of devotion (such as schools, mosques, Sufi hospices, or saints' tombs). Sincerity, on the other hand, is not outwardly evident in these institutional sites of social power. Rather, it is inherent in virtuous actions, displays of knowledge, and narratives about experiences of growth and struggle.

The contrast between sincerity and legitimacy that Zarruq highlights is parallel to a contrast inherent in the authority of the saint or *walī*. The very term *walī* in Arabic means a person characterized by two qualities derived from an identical linguistic root with but subtly different meanings: *walāya* and *wilāya*, intimacy and authority.[10] *Walāya* connotes intimacy with Allah, which is a relation inherent in a person's character (and in an Islamic understanding it cannot pass on to followers of a saint). *Wilāya* denotes authority from Allah that makes a person into a certain character, giving him or her a powerful social role.

The *walī*, as a Muslim saint, is the character who embodies both qualities. "Character" is a term in English that can help us see the relation between these distinct qualities.[11] Intimacy and sincerity are expressions of "character as personality," while authority and legitimacy derive from "character as role." The renowned Indian Sufi master Niẓām al-Dīn Awliyāʾ (died 1325 C.E./725 Hijri) once explained to his followers this dual dimension to a saint's authority. The master explained: "The saint possesses both *walāya* and *wilāya* at the same time. *Walāya* is that which masters impart to disciples about God, just as they teach them about the etiquette of the Way … but that which takes place between the Shaykh and God is called *wilāya*. That is a special kind of love, and when the Shaykh leaves the world, he takes his *wilāya* with him."[12] By positioning "sincerity" as the key term in sainthood, Zarruq was making a complex argument. His emphasis on sincerity both necessitated his reformist program and gave it authority. However, before we can examine his reformist program, we have to trace his journey to maturity.

Departing from Oneself

Before Zarruq could announce this reformist vision with any authority, he had to first grasp a firm sense of sincerity, which required "leaving one's own selfish cravings." Zarruq's first journey allowed him to play out this tension between his legitimacy in question and his authoritative sincerity that had not yet emerged. His first journey was an escape from danger in Fes and a turning point in his life. It was a forty-day journey to Tilimsān (Fr. Tlemcen) to visit the tomb-shrine of Abū Madyan, as displayed in Map B. This journey provided him far more than refuge; it provided him with the seeds of new paradigm for his future life. His journey would be "a departure from one's place and oneself," in the phrase Pandolfo uses to describe the theme of Moroccan journey (*riḥla*).[13] It is as if Zarruq experienced a form of death in leaving Fes (a death of his hopes and what he could assume as stable in his life). In the passage to Tilimsān and back, he encountered a rebirth, through exile, liminality, and pilgrimage. This would establish a pattern of achievement for Zarruq that rested not on the fixed horizons and cherished social institutions of Fes, but on recognition by strangers in the flexibility of the open road.

As Zarruq portrays his forty-day journey in his autobiography, he dwells on his pilgrimage in minute detail, as if his life began in earnest only on the road to Tilimsān. In this journey he was transformed, without ambition and without expectation, from a student of scriptural knowledge (*ṭālib*) into a saint with intuitive insight (*walī*).[14] This transformation, hidden from the sight of his former colleagues or competitors, vindicated his rebellious ethical stance during the revolution in Fes. His autobiography almost completely obliterates mention of the revolution (except for some murky references to "the year the Jews were killed"). In this way, this exile journey was transformed into a pilgrimage that restored to Zarruq his sense of religious authority. Though he left Fes as a failed jurist, he returned as a jurist bolstered from within by a sense of inner power as a realized saint. Beyond the sociological transformation of death and adopting a new identity, Zarruq also experienced a more spiritual death and rebirth. He experimented with devotional exercises that deliberately pushed him to the edge of his self-consciousness and (if we believe his prose) transcended it entirely. The death of his self-will, he explained, opened a passage to rebirth as a saint whose actions were directed more by the will of Allah than by his own powers of self-concern and calculation.

However, before he could articulate either his own sense of sanctity or his social role as a reformer, Zarruq had to pass through the terrors of liminality. His narrative reads like a picaresque Wild West film script, a sequence of threatening encounters with strangers. Yet beneath this seemingly haphazard series of encounters is a deeply structured passage. Zarruq passes from Fes through the danger posed by his past ambitions and expectations. On the road outside his home city, Zarruq enters a foreign territory of shifting alliances and uncertain partnerships; he persists through a state of liminality and misrecognition. Finally, he finds a safe haven and temporary rest at the tomb of Abū Madyan. Although this fulfills his vow and is the natural climax of the pilgrimage, it is only the midpoint in the ritual structure. Zarruq then heads back "home" to Fes. During his return, he is transformed in ways that he could not have foreseen, that only become apparent to him through the eyes of others. As he returns to Fes, he is not the same Zarruq, and Fes is no longer "home." This narrative involves tropes of inversion, transformation,

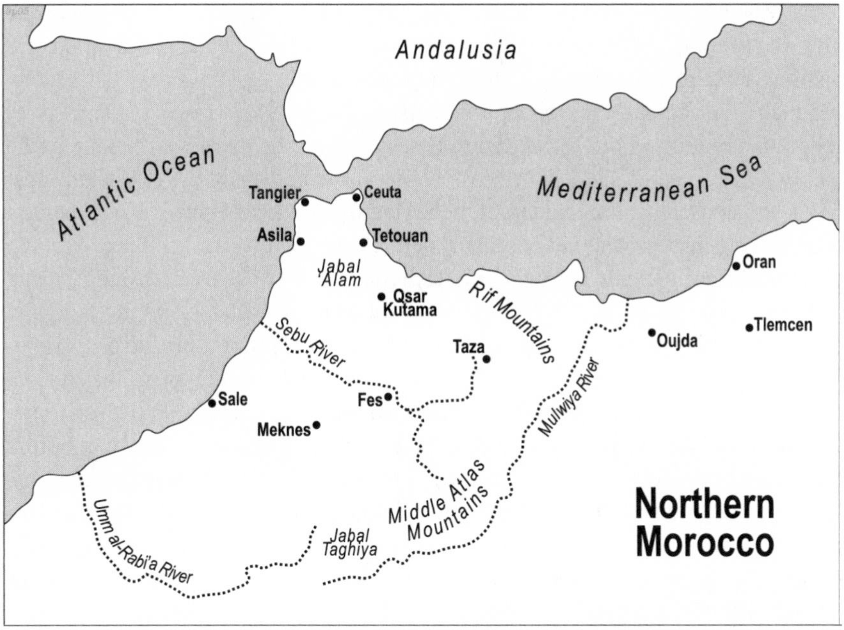

Map B

and achievement without the will to achieve, through which he is finally granted a sense of sincerity.

The narrative begins as Zarruq stepped outside the gates of Fes. He never mentioned the background of the revolution, al-Qūrī's dismissal, or his own confrontations with the supporters of the sharifian republic. However, the scent of danger hung in the air. These were not just the danger of an urbanite in the uncertainty of rural areas, with clashing armies, foreign tribes, ambushing brigands, and suspicious locals. The danger came from the conflict he was fleeing, for the accusation that "Zarruq is a Jew" had hung over him since he had denounced al-Waryāghilī and defended al-Qūrī.

"As I set out from Fes, a man from another region declared 'This is one of the Jews of Fes!' [Another person] increased his suspicion of me and swore by the month of fasting in Ramaḍān [that I was a Jew]. However, a student [from the madrasa college] who knew me overheard the two of them accusing me and challenged their assertions."[15] Zarruq took refuge from such accusations by relying on his past identity as a student in the madrasa network. This position had given him his social identity, his livelihood, and his ambition to become a respected jurist. Even though the situation in Fes had completely changed, eliminating his chances to follow his former career path with all its certainties and advantages, the young Zarruq still sought shelter in the identity of being a pious student (*ṭālib*).

Being a Jew would not only jeopardize his life (in the context of the revolution in Fes) but would also throw Zarruq's religious convictions in grave doubt. That accusation was a cipher for his having betrayed his religious loyalties to his master, al-Zaytūnī, who espoused *jihād*. "As night fell, [our party] entered a mosque after the evening prayer to spend the night there. Without delay, that man's companions set about discussing us, believing vehemently that I was Jewish. But an old man from among their group knew us, and said 'This is really a student of religious sciences whom I know from Fes.' Later on the journey, we came to the city of Bādis ...when suddenly two royal servants came out of the Palace and spat on us and abused us with contempt, believing that I was Jewish.... Later, while I was walking through another neighborhood, a man addressed me without warning or provocation, 'Seize it from them today, you Jew!'"[16] The man accused Zarruq of having protected "the Jewish ministers" of Marinid sultan ᶜAbd al-Ḥaqq and defending their practice of "seizing it from them" by appropriating the property of Muslims (especially the *shurafāʾ*). In a surreal way, this scene repeats the story of the revolution in Fes in inverted form: the two ministers come from the royal palace and abuse Zarruq as "a Jew" just as the two "Jewish ministers" had come from the palace in Fes to abuse "the *shurafāʾ*." The accusation of Zarruq's enemies, his former companions, followed Zarruq even into the countryside and distant towns. However it must be remembered that these roads toward the east were al-Zaytūnī's territory, as he protected the caravans and pilgrims who traveled east from Fes toward Tilimsān and beyond.

According to the cultural logic of sanctity, saints were not just religious leaders of communities but were also the spiritual governors of territories. The term *walī* by itself could mean "governor" who is appointed to a position of power due to his intimacy with the sultan. The term *walī allah,* or friend of Allah, means "a saint" who is appointed to a position of power due to his intimacy with Allah. Socially recognized saints are understood to protect or govern discrete territories, above and beyond the parallel operation of political governors.[17] For Zarruq to travel these routes without al-Zaytūnī's protection was to court disaster at the hand of strangers. These accusations from strangers undercut Zarruq's previous identity in which he had been so secure in Fes. As the gates of Fes closed behind him, the personality formed in Fes was vehemently denied to him.

Zarruq recorded the details of his pilgrimage with a subtle narrative strategy. To read them as an initiatic process, we need the insightful work of the symbolic anthropologist Victor Turner. Pilgrimages often embody the same three stages as rites of passage, according to Turner: expulsion from structure, escape into liminality, and rebirth into a transformed structure. Zarruq left the densely structured environment of Fes and took refuge in the liminal condition of the open road leading to a holy shrine; this passage marks a symbolic death and subsequent rebirth. Turner's distinction between the social activities of structured life with all its legal norms, political struggles, and binary thinking is particularly suited to describing the world from which Zarruq was ejected. "Men who are heavily involved in jural-political, overt, and conscious structure are not free to meditate and speculate on the combinations and oppositions of thought; they are themselves too crucially involved in the combinations and oppositions of social and political structure and stratification.... But in ritual liminality they are placed, so to speak, outside the total system and its conflicts; transiently, they become men apart."[18] The liminality of pilgrimage allowed Zarruq to feel "set apart" or sacred. Yet this same liminality was terrifying, for initiates or pilgrims often experience liminality as humiliation or social leveling.

Zarruq's autobiographical narrative documents this painful erasure of markers of social distinction, status, and ultimately even personal identity. He initially understands his pilgrimage as an exile in its punitive and expiatory senses, yet he eventually comprehends its deeper therapeutic, purifying, and transformative dimensions. Eventually, Zarruq must return from his pilgrimage and re-enter the structured world, but he will re-enter it transformed. "The process and state of liminality represents at once a negation of many, though not all, of the features of pre-liminal social structure and an affirmation of another order of things and relations."[19] Zarruq will re-enter Islamic society as a reform-oriented saint. His reform program becomes the vehicle through which he can affirm "another order of things and relations."

Rejoining Zarruq's journey, we find him separated from his traveling companion, a fellow student and the last protector who could shield him from the accusation of being a Jew. He continued alone eastward toward Tilimsān. "I set out heading up from the river. To my surprise, I found that all along this route were the houses of Jews. When the inhabitants saw me, they began to say amongst themselves, 'Isn't this the son of the Jewish leader (*shaykh* or *bashḥ*) of the city of Tāza?' It seems they had heard news that this man had fled Tāza, frightened of being captured and arrested. So they sent the son of one of their elders to meet me. When he drew close and saw me clearly, he said to his people, 'It looked as if it were him, but really he is nobody!'"[20] Ironically, it was the Jews in this town who recognized Zarruq for who he was, while his own people, the Muslims, misrecognized him. The Jews could see that "really he is nobody," stripped of identity, patronage, and protection. Zarruq walked alone through the Jewish quarter and began to understand the immense alienation into which he had plunged. In a vain attempt to regain his composure and reassert his identity as a Muslim student, he took refuge in a mosque.

But that refuge was a dead end for him. "All of the Jews stood at the doorways, men and women, young and old, watching me. They were completely startled when I entered a mosque, for then a great clamor and heated debate rose up among them. I stayed holed up in the mosque for some days, until I grew desolate and depressed."[21] Having left the assumed safety of the mosque and finally acknowledging his own grief and loss, Zarruq began to find some human company that signaled hope. He began to understand that his current alienation was a curse from al-Zaytūnī.

This insight came to him while he was in the company of a holy man (*faqīr*) who helped Zarruq cross the river Mulwīya. "The *faqīr* had just recently renounced worldly ambitions and was remarkably sincere with a wholesome spiritual state.

We stayed there with him for some days, because I had suffered a wound to my foot. There my Shaykh, al-Zaytūnī, appeared to me in a dream; he said to me 'You are imprisoned for forty days, after which Allah will ease your travel once again with a safe caravan.'"[22] Zarruq's wounded foot and his inability to cross the river were symptomatic of his deeper quandary. Al-Zaytūnī had cursed him with "imprisonment" in this state of accusation and alienation. The dream vision of al-Zaytūnī offered this explanation: the young Zarruq was punished for his betrayal of loyalty, but could return to Fes if he accepted his punishment with humility. The announcement of his punishment also contained a promise of forgiveness and a resumption of patronage and protection, in the form of "a safe caravan" to ease his return journey.

Zarruq refused al-Zaytūnī's offer of clemency in return for submission. A transformation was happening deep within him, and his own sense of spiritual power was taking root, beyond the patronage of either the humiliated al-Qūrī or the accusatory al-Zaytūnī. Zarruq's narrative displays this growing confidence in subtle ways. He attracted the help of strangers who possess spiritual virtues. "We took heart and gained courage enough to be borne across the river, myself and another man. We walked together until we arrived at Aghyāl, where some kind people warned us, 'Night is drawing close—go spend the night at the home of someone called Uncle Mūsā, for he is virtuous, handsome and strong.' … He welcomed us warmly and treated us with the utmost generosity. When morning dawned, Uncle Mūsā sent us on our way and sent a young man with us, counseling him to take care of us and lead us to a further destination."[23]

Even as care descends upon him, Zarruq incurred increasing pressure from the threatening forces. He was no longer seen as only "a Jew" that threatened his reputation, but also as "an Andalusian" in a territory wracked by wars against Iberian invaders, which threatened his life. He and his young guide ran across an armed band that stopped them with threats of violence. "It became clear to us that they were [gesturing at me and] yelling 'This man is an Andalusian! We have the right of vengeance over the life of an Andalusian! We are going to slay him right here and now, and you are free to take his clothes and belongings!' The youth defended us, saying 'By Allah, over my dead body! Uncle Mūsā entrusted him to me, and I'll never be lax in my duty!' … They said, 'We won't leave well enough alone until we see two witnesses who can testify that this man is really from Fes [and not from Andalusia]!' … It was said to me, 'If you are really who you say, then Sīdī Yūsuf, who was a holy man (*ṣāliḥ*) who lived among them, will recognize you, and if not, then there is no saving you!' … No sooner had [Sīdī Yūsuf] laid eyes on me than he could not restrain himself from rushing over to greet me warmly. Safety came to me at last."[24] When Zarruq took refuge in his former identity as a juridical student of Fes, he was misrecognized and threatened. Having let go of that brittle identity and its reliance on patrons, a holy man recognized him as himself. Sīdī Yūsuf rushed over to greet him, not because Zarruq was a student from Fes as he had been claiming all along, but because he shared in some faint way the aura of holiness that set Sīdī Yūsuf apart from the others in the village.

Safety had come to him at last, in a form he still could not totally recognize himself. "I arrived [at Tilimsān] on the thirty-ninth day since setting out from Fes.... However, I was unable to complete my pilgrimage until the following day, the last remaining day of forty days. I visited Abū Madyan, and Allah inspired me with what was revealed."[25] In the formalities of a pilgrimage, this was the climax. Zarruq reached the destination, entered the shrine of Abū Madyan, and communed with the presence of the saint to achieve some intimacy with Allah. One author who retells this story adds that Zarruq received consolation and divine mercy: "as he felt an outpouring of divine presence, Abū Madyan actually spoke to Zarruq from the grave."[26] One would expect Zarruq to have atoned for his sin of disobedience to al-Zaytūnī, accept his offer of continued patronage, and return to Fes with the "caravan of safety" that he had promised in the dream. This solution would restore the equilibrium of the master-disciple relationship, as Zarruq acknowledged the eclipse of al-Qūrī and the path for future with al-Zaytūnī.

However, Zarruq did not choose this path. It would have required him to abandon his burgeoning sense of saintly sincerity in his own right and to disavow his sense of ethical loyalty to the principles represented by al-Qūrī, however outmoded they appeared in revolutionary Fes. Zarruq missed the caravan of safety that would have brought him back along the well-trodden path to Fes. In doing so, he struck out alone, along a new path, full of danger and also, possibly, of great rewards.

Although al-Zaytūnī asserted that Zarruq's pilgrimage to Tilimsān was to make penance for his disobedience, Zarruq began to see it differently. His arrival at Tilimsān represented a way for Zarruq to reassert his loyalty to the saintly authority of al-Qūrī. The madrasa and congregational mosque that amplified the tomb enclosure of Abū Madyan had been built by the Marinid dynasty. It was a symbol of their institution building that survived the fall of their dynasty. Zarruq's own path as a saint would try to recover the ideal of the juridical saint that had thrived in such Marinid institutions, even after their collapse.

While at Tilimsān, Zarruq stayed with a local saint, Aḥmad ibn al-Ḥasan al-Ghumārī. He even took initiation from him, announcing that he had moved beyond the narrow horizons of allegiance to al-Zaytūnī. Al-Zaytūnī had demanded that Zarruq give him unquestioned obedience, but Zarruq responded (after forty days of "imprisonment") by seeking alternative allegiances. This initiated a pattern that was to structure Zarruq's later life: he searched for masters and teachers in "the east" to offset his youthful disaster under masters in "the west." The figure of Abū Madyan was particularly potent as a pivot that joined Maghribī "western" Sufi lineages to Mashriqī "eastern" ones. It was fitting, therefore, that Abū Madyan's tomb was the stage upon which Zarruq played out this youthful rejection of Moroccan realities in favor of some hope of eastern alternatives. It was his friendship with al-Ghumārī which kept Zarruq from departing in the safety of the promised caravan: "I went to meet the Shaykh al-Ghumārī to say good-bye, but he would not let me leave his house until it was noon. As I left him, I found that a caravan had just departed. I hurried out of the city but I could not catch sight of the caravan. I walked on all by myself."[27]

Reintegration through the Other

As Zarruq headed out alone and unprotected, it became evident that he would never be alone. Divine protection hovered over him, first in the form of benevolent strangers, or protective holy men, and finally of miraculous events without human intermediary. At this point, Zarruq learned not to rely upon his own ego to save him from impending harm. He learned to float on the currents of others' benevolence and leave matters up to Allah. He never stated this in prose, but the details of his travel weave into a drama of *tawakkul ᶜalā Allah*, reliance only upon God. He reveled in his own helplessness and was carried along by others in a state of tranquillity.

Zarruq's new resilience seemed to surprise even him, while his surroundings grew still more threatening. After crossing back over the Mulwīya River, he entered a war zone where Portuguese (or possibly Spanish) soldiers had been battling Muslims in a local *jihād*. Again, he found himself alone at the most dangerous passage. "The local people caught sight of me and cried out 'He's a spy of the marauding Christians!' My companions spoke to these people in their own incomprehensible babble, and vouched for me. I went with them through the battle trenches—I swear there were one hundred trenches and then another trench! The place was dangerous, and the path was prone to being ambushed by wild lions, Christian soldiers, or Berber brigands."[28]

One of these brigands, brandishing a club, accosted Zarruq. "He reached out and grabbed my cloak and snatched it away from me. He turned and fled, but just a little way until he stopped abruptly. He called out to me, 'Here, take your cloak back! Between me and you is Allah—this is protecting you while you are traveling alone!' I took back my cloak saying, 'Allah is mighty and glorious.' Then the man with the club took off, and I noticed that he was crippled with a limp. He had not been crippled when I first saw him."[29] As his weapon morphed into a crutch, the brigand departs. This episode began a series of misadventures with Zarruq's cloak, which is symbolic of his spiritual perplexity. People tried to steal it in many ways, even though it was his last means of protection. The cloak was also the symbol of one's initiation into a Sufi lineage. Zarruq found himself able to relinquish even this, just as he relinquished relying on his status as a student of scriptural studies.

Zarruq may have found a parallel between his life story and a teaching attributed to the Prophet Muhammad, both centering on the importance of cloaks to saints as symbols of abandoning self-concern and trusting only in Allah. It is reported that one of the early Muslims, Abū Saᶜīd al-Khudrī, spoke with the Prophet Muhammad while undergoing a period of personal trial. "I said, 'O Prophet of

Allah, who are the people who have undergone the most intense trials and tribulations?' Muhammad answered, 'The Prophets.' So I asked, 'O Prophet of Allah, and after them?' He answered, 'After the Prophets, the Righteous Ones (*ṣāliḥūn*) have undergone the most intense trials. Some of them are afflicted with poverty to the point that they own nothing but their cloaks (*ᶜabāᵓa*) and yet they take delight in this trial (*balāᵓ*) like some of you take delight in luxury (*rakhāᵓ*).'" Sufis imagine the Prophet to have received such a cloak of poverty during his ascension (*miᶜrāj*) after which he passed it on to some of his closest companions; from this derives the Sufi tradition of initiation with a cloak.[30]

Weaned from relying on external means of protection, Zarruq learned to rely on his intimate and innate relationship to Allah as his sole means of protection and provision. By telling in detail the story of how he lost and regained his cloak, Zarruq cautiously put forward the claim that he had joined the righteous saints by undergoing trials as arduous as theirs. As a saint-in-the-making, his previously surreal and threatening environment began to transform into an environment potent with subtle miracles. At one point, a man acting as Zarruq's guide tries to mug him. "It struck me that his facial expression was alternating between malicious thoughts and cowardly ones. We arrived at a steep gorge that dropped down between rocky outcroppings. Here he stopped and demanded, 'Hand over everything you have!' I told him, 'I swear by Allah, I have nothing.' He searched me over. In the end, he settled on my cloak, 'I'll take it by force if you don't hand it over!' I warned him, 'Hasn't Allah forbidden you from plundering people by force?'"[31]

Zarruq eventually relinquished his cloak with resignation. He later came to a village where some people knew him. "A woman joked with me, 'Where's your cloak? It was your only shelter!' I told her that someone from that particular tribe took it from me. After a little while, her husband came home; his name was Aḥmad ibn Khalīfa al-Asjāᶜī, a trustworthy and holy man (*faqīr*) who had just recently repented of his sins and renounced the cares of the world. [When he heard my story] he began to weep profusely and wipe his wet face with his prayer beads. He cried out 'O Allah provide, Allah provide! Who will find a brother on judgment day? He will reap what he sows! The people of that tribe, what can they do? There is no escaping it, there is no escape!'"[32] Faqīr Aḥmad took Zarruq back to the village that had hosted him the previous night, to which the thief belonged. He exhorted the people of the village to return his cloak or give Zarruq gold coins in reimbursement for his loss. They claimed to not know where the lad was, so Faqīr Aḥmad caused another young man of the tribe to fall unconscious, in rigor mortis. He refused to restore the man until the tribe had taken responsibility for its thieving member. They gave Zarruq some gold, and in return the holy man restored the young man from his paralysis. In this way, Faqīr Aḥmad played a role similar to that of al-Zaytūnī in subjugating highway robbers; however, instead of turning such miracles to political advantage, he channeled them into fulfilling the norms of Islamic law and getting Zarruq payment for his stolen cloak.

Zarruq must have been heartened by such support from saintly power that had previously victimized him. He soon found the voice to express for himself his emerging identity as a saint. Along the road, one man suspiciously asked him, "'Where are you coming from?' 'Tilimsān,' I told him. 'By yourself?' he asked. 'Yes,' I said. He asked, 'Aren't you afraid?' 'Afraid of what?' I asked. 'Of lions …' 'No,' I told him firmly. 'Of other men …' 'Allah protects me from their harm,' I told him. He exclaimed, 'I've never seen anything like this seeker!' then sighed with amazement."[33] The stranger enunciates for Zarruq that his personality has been pared down to his primary identity as a spiritual seeker (*sālik*). One must pass through the trials of being a seeker before becoming either a jurist or a saint. The quest for sincerity can make one a true seeker, who can then fuse the distinct roles of jurist and saint into a new and powerful religious authority.

Even as he enjoyed this recognition, Zarruq's courage and self-awareness were still provisional. He still feared the curse of al-Zaytūnī and the threat of misrecognition. Even in a town where he was familiar with some inhabitants, he balked at eating some unknown type of meat they had prepared. Fearing they would take him for "a Jew" as on his outward journey, he ate the meat but became sick with stomach cramps and diarrhea until he soiled his clothes. Zarruq's fear took a palpable physical form in sickness and pollution, which, through no agency of his own, could be miraculously washed away. "I sat there disgusted at my pollution and confused as to what to do. I began walking outside the village and found a wild grove with a spring of running water, so I washed myself and my clothing. Then I recalled this incident to someone I was staying with, and he told me there is no such grove. I contradicted him and began to quarrel. He said quietly, 'This is truly the care of Allah watching over you intimately.' After this, I passed by that same place again and again, and I never once found a single trace of that grove or that spring. Praise be to the generous One, the One of infinite compassion!"[34]

The details of this narrative make plain that Zarruq's new identity as Muslim saint came to him as an ascription by others whom he encountered, rather than as possession or a claim. This is extraordinarily important, for it allowed Zarruq to claim an experience of divine solicitousness (*ᶜināya*) that lifted him from his own self-concern. In his own telling, his claim to sainthood could not be criticized by others as mere self-aggrandizement or ambition. This would be a grave danger in the context of his having fled Fes in a conflict with the Qādirī saints who claimed him as a disciple, as if his claim to saintly experiences caused his rebelliousness against al-Zaytūnī. Rather, Zarruq presented himself only as a renunciant (*faqīr*). His earliest inklings of saintly power came through his gestures of renunciation: his leaving aside his identity as a student, his abandoning ambitions to become a jurist in Fes, and his renouncing the safety of being a citizen of Fes itself. That others recognized him as a saint to his evident surprise is an illustration of the paradox of intentionality.

The paradox of intentionality was the subject of the first Sufi work Zarruq studied, *The Book of Illumination*. Its basic argument is this: the harder one tries to achieve something of ultimate worth, the less likely one is to achieve it. This radically inverts the practical logic of the "ethic of attainment" in religious traditions. The experiences of submission to transcendental authority, submersion of ego in the presence of a greater "other," and even selflessness offer an "ethic of consolation" that confronts and contradicts conventional notions that people can attain worth and status through their own efforts.[35] These consoling experiences are often labeled "mysticism," but Zarruq's case makes clear that they are not just subjective and psychological, as modern constructs of mysticism imply. In his case, these experiences were social manifestations and had political ramifications.

The pastiche of details that make up this narrative covers up the fact that Zarruq's forty-day journey marks a rupture in his apprenticeship in Fes and an eruption of Zarruq's personal sense of authority. Such a rupture is potentially very dangerous. The anthropologist Abdullah Hammoudi has analyzed the power relations inherent in the dangerous balance between submitting to a master's authority and asserting one's own authority among Moroccan Sufis.[36] He argues that rebellion against authority is necessary if disciples are to assert their own spiritual potential as masters. Yet overt rebellions are very dangerous for the disciple, since becoming a disciple inverts most social norms (especially in regard to getting married, heading a household, or building a worldly career). Zarruq had moved beyond the protection of his masters (both al-Qūrī and al-Zaytūnī) without overtly asserting a counter-claim to authority. He could only take reassurance in a personal quest for sincerity and scrupulously safeguarding the rights of himself and others. These were the very qualities through which others begin to recognize in him the glow of sanctity. "I came upon a whole group of men clad in battle armor. One of them began to talk to me, asking, 'Are you traveling alone?' 'No,' I answered, 'I travel with Allah, the singular One, the One who overpowers.' He uttered not a single word to me after that, and left me in peace."[37] In this way, without effort or self-promotion, Zarruq gained a reputation among strangers for subtle miracles. They were not miracles that generated political power for his advantage like those of al-Zaytūnī, but rather miracles that quietly confirmed him as a "sincere seeker." When Zarruq reached Miknāsa [Meknes], soldiers accosted him as a spy and stripped all his belongings from him. However, in patiently allowing them to take everything, he lulled their suspicions, and noted simply that "Allah protected me from their designs." The narrative comes full circle as Zarruq approached Fes once more. He met a wandering group of religious students, like he had been when he left only forty days before, of which he had tried to so hard to convince others. At this point, having passed through the dangers of self-alienation and into the fullness of selflessness, he did not even try to protect himself with such a social identity.

Further adventures taught the young Zarruq not to ask for food or hospitality, but to wait until others gave it to him without his having to ask. People began to call him "a holy man" (*rajul ṣāliḥ*) which he outwardly denied. With these auspicious encounters, Zarruq returned to Fes. He was sure that religious students would accept him as a pious upholder of religious law, and that saints and Sufis would accept him as a sincere seeker whom Allah protected due to his sincerity. He conceived of himself as *al-Walī al-Jāmi*ᶜ, one who joins the outer rectitude of being a jurist with the inner illumination of being a saint, a juridical saint.

The details of this initiatic journey are unusual; yet beyond this, the very textual existence of these details is unusual. Zarruq authored an autobiographical narrative, but precious few premodern intellectual figures have done so. Scholars and Sufis occasionally wrote short biographical statements on their lives, call a *fihris*. They wrote in order to register their genealogy, their teachers, their intellectual lineage, and the texts that their teachers had "permitted them" to teach (with an *ijāza*). However, Zarruq wrote his narrative on a different order, including stories of his childhood, personal accounts of his teachers' lives, and the tale of his journey from Fes to Tilimsān. The narrative is included in his *al-Kunnāsh fī ᶜIlm Āsh*, a notebook "on knowledge of whatever," jotted down at the end of his life. His autobiography is incomplete (and ends with the events of this pilgrimage when he was twenty-four), yet its very existence is rare. Its plot involves tropes that are deeper than the events that they claim to portray, for Zarruq arranged them to reveal a rite of passage in his coming of age.

Death of Self-Will

Reading *al-Kunnāsh* as a rite of passage brings out its deep ritual meaning and highlights why this initial journey dominated his imagination and demanded this detailed treatment. It tells of the solidification of Zarruq's personal identity, rather than just the events of a journey. From the vantage point of the elderly Zarruq (who wrote in retrospect about events that had happened thirty years before), the real purpose of the autobiography was to display these structural tropes to dramatize his coming to maturity.[38] How can we imagine the process of "fixation" that plays beneath the surface of an autobiography, especially a premodern autobiography that lacks the confessional tone or documentary ethos of modern works? In premodern autobiographies, the author tries to craft the fluidity of life facts into a paradigmatic life story. By highlighting those elements of his pilgrimage that evoked the ritual structure of an initiatic journey, Zarruq crafted a paradigmatic personality from his life story.

The story of Zarruq's pilgrimage to the tomb of Abū Madyan does far more than answer the biographical question of how Zarruq escaped imminent danger due to his ardent support of al-Qūrī and the legal loyalists during the sharifian revolution in Fes. It sets up a paradigm for the rest of his life path. In its forty days of details, Zarruq marked out the future parameters of his mature life. The very description of a journey of forty days is so symbolically charged that it is of questionable autobiographical accuracy. Forty is an initiatic number implying spiritual trial, transformation, and coming to completion.[39]

The underlying structure of a forty-day passage reminds the reader that Zarruq's autobiography has a ritual dimension. This narrative displays the sociological elements of Zarruq's shift of identity through the tropes of death and rebirth in a spiritual initiation. Zarruq also experimented with spiritual death more directly, in a psychological and devotional dimension, in a ritual practice that also required forty days of his struggle and trial. He claimed to have acted directly on the Sufi advice to desist from selfish concern and calculation. He achieved the "death of his self-will" through simple and direct action. "Once a person was walking along the road and resolved to choose the death of his will (*al-mawt al-ikhtiyārī*). So he laid down right there in the middle of the road and extended his limbs as if he were the body of a dead man. After just an hour had passed, the heat of the sun became unbearable and his self-will demanded that he move into the shade. He answered his self-will that a dead man does not need any shade.... Everything his self-will demanded of him, he refused on the grounds that he had already died, until he passed beyond consciousness. When he awoke after three days, he found that he had already arrived at the goal he had set for himself."[40] Zarruq writes about this experiment in the death of self-will in the passive voice, leaving ambiguous who this bold "someone" might really be. The person who awoke was really himself.

Throughout his lonely journey, Zarruq had ample time to reflect on the *Book of Illumination*, which formed the basic spiritual training bequeathed to him by al-Qūrī. Even though al-Qūrī was now an absent master in public shame, Zarruq searched in the very core of his being for a direct method of realizing this book's advice. He found nothing direct enough in the bewildering array of Sufi devotional exercises. In a burst of aspiration fueled by desperation, he lay down in the road, resolving not to rise until he "already arrived at the goal he had set for himself." This experience provided Zarruq the foundation to make a claim that must have seemed audacious to his contemporaries: to have reached the spiritual goal of true sincerity and selflessness without the mediation of a spiritual guide. "I found that the principles [on which the path of spiritual cultivation is founded] were all dependent on a single principle: to give one's life for Allah. It is said in the proverb: The surest path to Allah trusted by the early companions and those who follow is sacrificing one's life before it wears out and becomes hollow. This is exactly the meaning of the saying 'Die before you die' and 'leave your self and arise' and others like them. The person who 'dies' before death is one who makes all personal qualities and states to be like those of someone who has already died, totally surrendered to the fate decreed by Allah."[41]

It is not just the passive voice, hiding his identity as the advocate of this radical experiment in practical mysticism, that made his audacious claim more acceptable. Zarruq claimed that this method could be implemented by anyone and should be implemented by everyone who finds value in Sufi communities and the ethical ideals they cherish. "Remind yourself constantly of death.... Every time you lay down to sleep imagine this person's sheet to be a shroud, his bed to be a coffin, and his house to be a tomb.... If one wakes up after such a sleep, one should say, 'Praise be to Allah who gives us life after causing us to die and resurrects us for Allah's purposes.'"[42] This method was the spiritual path "trusted by the early companions and those who follow" (*al-salaf waʾl-khalaf*). Their willingness to sacrifice their lives, Zarruq claimed, was not a result of their martial prowess or eagerness for *jihād*. Rather, it was merely the surface expression of their spiritual cultivation: to struggle to limit their self-concern and selfish will or to transcend it completely.

This was "the greater jihad" that the Prophet Muhammad advocated, in contrast to "the lesser jihad" of military action or political activism.[43] Zarruq may have been inspired by a story told of the Prophet Muhammad in which he practically illustrates the necessity of the "greater jihad." That story is told by the Indian Sufi master Niẓām al-Dīn Awliyāʾ in this way: "In the Battle of Uḥud, many companions of the Prophet—may Allah be pleased with him—were slain. When the fighting was over, Gabriel—peace be upon him—came and said, 'O Muhammad, you too lie down with your slain companions, until the heat of anger has passed from you.'"[44] By laying down in the road to quell his selfish passions, Zarruq claimed to follow the Prophet and his exemplary companions more faithfully and more authentically than his contemporary Sufi masters, especially those, like al-Zaytūnī, who advocated revolution in the name of *jihād*.

This method of spiritual cultivation could be followed by anyone with a lofty aspiration and a healthy suspicion of others' authority. "If you persist with these rituals for a time and the least possible time is forty days, then there is hope that Allah will grant you the death of your self-will and ennoble you with everlasting life." Yet it was best followed by Zarruq himself, who presented himself, later in his life, as its exemplar. His forty-day exile from Fes was his forty-day experiment with the death of self-will. These experiments in the death of self-will allowed Zarruq to conceive of himself as a saint not beholden to saintly master. Freed from subservience to the trappings of external legitimacy, he claimed to hold authority through his interior quality of "turning to Allah in sincerity." In his view, this authority was the criterion that could allow him to distinguish sincere Sufi practices from inauthentic innovations. Zarruq tried to deconstruct a *ṭarīqa* (as a rarefied Sufi lineage) to reveal its underlying force as a *ṭarīq*, a dynamic movement toward utter sincerity. With this subtle shift of terms, Zarruq engineered a shift in emphasis that was the crux of his reformist vision. He wanted to disaggregate the distinct community that cohered around a single spiritual method (*ṭarīqa*) and reveal how each method depended on principles of sincerity that propelled a saint along the path (*ṭarīq*) toward the presence of Allah. By weakening the link between the disciple and any particular ritualized method, Zarruq hoped to institute a new form of Sufi community, in which spiritual training would be fused with legal rectitude, and legal training would be infused with spiritual insight.

This is the key to understanding Zarruq's program of reform for Sufi devotional life. However, this program would only unfold later in his life, as shown in chapter 6. Upon returning to Fes, Zarruq was still in a precarious position. According to Zarruq's autobiography, Shaykh al-Zaytūnī welcomed him back, thereby denying any dangerous rupture of authority in Zarruq's master/disciple relationship. In Zarruq's account, his personal trial of exile from Fes led to redemptive healing at the shrine of a higher master, Abū Madyan, which granted him a safe return home and reconciliation with al-Zaytūnī.[45] As a reward for his patient endurance, Zarruq claimed that al-Zaytūnī encouraged him to travel east again, for the *ḥajj* pilgrimage to Makka. He left with al-Zaytūnī's financial support and spiritual blessing. In this way, Zarruq erased the crisis of revolution in Fes that had originally set him upon the pilgrimage in the first place.

However, few people in Fes accepted Zarruq's own version of events. He stayed in Fes for at least a year before leaving for Makka, during which time he could not have rejoined the Qādirī community at Zāwiya Bū'l-Quṭūṭ without seriously jeopardizing his own sincerity as a jurist. He may have lived in quiet retreat, like al-Qūrī. During this period, Zarruq began to write his famous commentaries on the *Ḥikam*, which implies continuity and continued contact with al-Qūrī's circle.[46] The year after al-Qūrī died, Zarruq left Fes for Makka. This suggests that al-Qūrī's continued presence, even if in disgrace and withdrawal from public life, gave Zarruq some shelter. Other sources note that despite his pilgrimage to Abū Madyan's tomb, Zarruq was still persecuted under the accusation of religious hypocrisy or blasphemy (*zandaqa*), especially that he had taken on a secret allegiance to the Jews or Christians (*tahayyud wa tanaṣṣur*).[47]

This scenario contradicts the autobiography of Zarruq. The autobiography is a strange document: it devotes pages to the description of his pilgrimage to Tilimsān, but only a few lines to his reception and "vindication" in Fes. In Zarruq's mind, the events of the pilgrimage outweighed in importance the events of the revolution and his return to Fes. No other source recalls Zarruq as having been vindicated by his trip to Tilimsān in this way; most hagiographies omit mentioning it altogether. Rather, they preserve a sort of "public memory" of the people of Fes about Zarruq. They remember him as the one who questioned al-Zaytūnī's authority in a clear betrayal of his allegiance to a Sufi master. They remember Zarruq's further travels to Cairo and Makka not as a reward for having patiently endured the wrath of al-Zaytūnī, but as the result of being totally banished by al-Zaytūnī from Fes. This collective memory will be discussed in detail in chapter 8. Such collective memory, inscribed in hagiographic accounts in Morocco, forms a later judgment about Zarruq, condemning him for questioning the kind of sharifian-Sufi authority that would rise to dominance in Morocco.[48]

Discovering the Center

Whether it was with Shaykh al-Zaytūnī's blessing or not, Zarruq prepared for his pilgrimage to Makka, for the *ḥajj*. This was a more permanent journey into exile, following his temporary return to Fes and unsuccessful reintegration there while

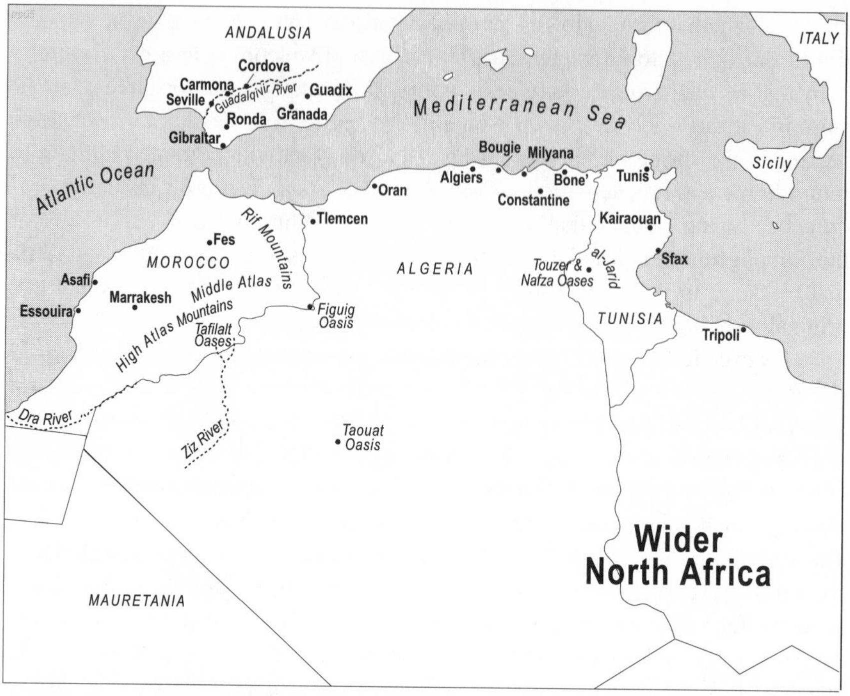

Map C

the sharifian-Sufi revolution still reigned. Zarruq turned his travels to Egypt and Makka to a positive end; in his view he was journeying to the center of the Islamic world, geographically and intellectually. Within his own spiritual imagination, he was searching for his own personal center, a point of equilibrium in the form of a new spiritual teacher and Sufi guide. His travels gave him an opportunity to rebuild the shattered outer dimensions of his life, not only through physical traveling, but also through imaginary traveling in writing. At this point be began to write in earnest, and he never flagged until his death.

His traveling was integrally related to his writing. At each point of rest and settlement, he embarked on a new writing project, often at the insistence of scholars or Sufis in the communities around him. He often wrote variations on the same theme, variations suitable for a new audience even if the message was similar to a prior work. He even wrote the same book multiple times, as exemplified by his commentaries on the *Wisdom Sayings* of Ibn ᶜAṭāʾillah. He wrote approximately twenty commentaries on this single source for the different urban communities with whom he stayed temporarily.[49] In addition, traveling to Egypt and the holy cities of Makka and Madīna allowed him to establish his authority through renowned teachers. Without such authority, he could never have embarked on the bold reform project that fueled his research and writing. His reform project depended on the dual foundation of scholarly teachers and a saintly patron. In Cairo, Zarruq would find both.

Zarruq never felt compelled to leave a complete diary of his wider travels. It is as if the forty-day journey was the paradigm of all his travels; the personal transformation he recorded during that journey eclipsed all other transformations on his subsequent travels. In reality, his personal development was probably spread out over years of travel rather than condensed into a single climactic period (as he later would recall it). He left Fes after 870 Hijri (1465–66 C.E.) and traveled to Cairo by the overland route: through Tilimsān, Bijāya [Bougie], Tūnis, and Tarābulus [Tripoli].[50] In each urban center, Zarruq studied under scholarly teachers, rebuilding his reputation as a jurist and a commentator on the *Ḥikam*. His scholarly reputation was his passport to each new location that compensated for the loss of his reputation as a Sufi in the Maghrib.

In Cairo, Zarruq transformed his social estrangement into scholarly acumen. Between 874 and 876 Hijri (1469–71 C.E.), he spent about a year in Cairo studying under prestigious scholars. Through his learning and skills, he gained access to teachers at the most prestigious religious college, al-Azhar.[51] He found favor with the scholars Muḥammad al-Sakhāwī (in hadith studies) and al-Jawjarī (in jurisprudence), gaining expertise in the full range of disciplines required as a jurist.[52] His intimacy with al-Sakhāwī was crucial, for he cast a long shadow over contemporary scholars and Sufis, who respected his name from North Africa through the central Islamic lands. Zarruq collected his notes from classes with al-Sakhāwī in hadith studies and published them as a commentary on *Ṣaḥīḥ al-Bukhārī*.[53] Al-Sakhāwī also recorded his intimacy with Zarruq and his respect for his student: "He settled in Cairo for about a year, studying Arabic grammar and jurisprudence intensely…. He was my companion in certain affairs and I benefited [through his contacts] from a group of his fellow Moroccans."[54]

So deeply did Zarruq plunge into juridical studies that some early modern biographers have posited that he left the Maghrib for the sole purpose of pursuing studies at the colleges of Cairo, thereby erasing the whole incident of the revolution in Fes and its consequences for his youthful ambitions. Aḥmad Bābā al-Timbūktī portrays Zarruq's travels as a straightforward quest for knowledge; it took Zarruq logically and inexorably beyond his boyhood home and the Sufi master of his adolescence, just as it had for countless young scholars before him. The modern biographer ᶜAbdullah Guennoun follows Aḥmad Bābā in this conclusion.[55] Yet neither of them accounts for the rhetorical complexity of Zarruq's claim to be a saint or the textual uniqueness of his writings that deliberately interweave legal and spiritual topics.

Writing from firsthand experience, Zarruq's teacher, al-Sakhāwī, was more insightful. He noted that Zarruq pursued the scriptural disciplines while simultaneously being deeply immersed in Sufi devotion. Although Zarruq was intensely engaged in juridical training to restore his broken life, he sought ways to renew his spiritual life as well. Al-Sakhāwī was a member of the Qādirī Sufi community in Cairo, despite being publicly known as a scripturalist teacher, and would have been at least conversant with experiences cultivated by Sufi disciples. Whether in classes or in private conversation, the inner meaning of religious experiences must have come up for discussion between them. It could be that Zarruq even looked to al-Sakhāwī as a Sufi guide concealed within his outer edifice of legalistic learning, much as Zarruq had previously looked to al-Qūrī. However, al-Sakhāwī did not engage Zarruq as a disciple.[56]

In this state of tension, Zarruq spent a year in Cairo, then continued east to make the pilgrimage to Makka and the reverential visit to the Prophet's tomb in Madīna. Only upon returning to Cairo did he meet the unlikely man who would take up the role as Zarruq's Sufi master. This man was an obscure spiritual guide who lived in Cairo but was not of Cairo. Little is known of Aḥmad ibn ᶜUqba al-Ḥaḍramī beyond what Zarruq and al-Sakhāwī recorded of his life and sayings. Yet he impressed Zarruq as a deeply spiritual man who was destined to guide him on his path into the future. Al-Ḥaḍramī's crusty, sarcastic personality moved Zarruq, scarred though he was by past traumas. Al-Ḥaḍramī allowed Zarruq to engage him informally as an equal (as gauged by the tone of their conversations and letters), yet al-Ḥaḍramī never agreed with Zarruq. Rather, he always sought to baffle his disciple's assertive will and sense of intellectual acumen. He never lessened the pressure on Zarruq and always sought to divert him from the path of his own volition. This was clear from their very first meeting, when Zarruq arrived back in Cairo from his pilgrimage to Makka in the year 876 Hijri (1471–72 C.E.), eager to resume his comfortable life studying and teaching. Zarruq records, "the first words he ever spoke to me were 'Get out of this country, for it saps you of the light of faith!'"[57]

Aḥmad ibn ᶜUqba al-Ḥaḍramī was born in Yemen, in the mountains of al-Ḥaḍramawt, in 824 Hijri (1421 C.E.). He lived there until he passed the age of twenty, when he moved to the Ḥijāz and lived in Makka for twenty more years. He said that he met his own master in the Ḥijāz, though he was very reticent to provide his name or lineage.[58] He traveled to Jerusalem to visit the Dome of the Rock (Bayt al-Maqdis), then came to Cairo in the middle or late 860s (late 1460s C.E.), where he lived until his death. Although compilers of saintly biographies have preserved little of his personality, al-Sakhāwī notes that in his time, al-Ḥaḍramī was well-known in Cairo as a saint. "He is someone in whom many people believe and on whom many people rely."[59] Yet he lived a marginal life in Cairo and could boast neither of a secure role in a Sufi hospice (*khānqāh*) nor an esteemed position as a teacher or jurist. It is not clear whether he pursued some other profession for his livelihood. It appears that he strove to be a spiritual guide in a rarefied form, without any financial, institutional, or community supports to buoy him up.

Al-Ḥaḍramī was a clever spiritual guide who did not rely on institutional signs of authority and openly contradicted those saints who did. He did not encourage heroic asceticism or renunciation of worldly means, but rather urged his disciples to treat the world with skillful means for a higher goal. He said to Zarruq, "The real man [*rajul*, meaning the "real saint"] is not the one who shuns the world and keeps separate from worldly life, but rather the one who knows how to grasp the world and keeps holding it tight!" Zarruq tried to explain this apparent contradiction of ascetic common sense: "This is because the world is like a snake—it is no great feat to [kill it] and pick it up, but it is a great deed to pick up snake while alive and hold it firmly."[60] In fact, al-Ḥaḍramī actively subverted moments when the social world offered him opportunities to display his authority as a saint. Zarruq recounts that "al-Ḥaḍramī once asked me, 'If someone you know intimately came to you asking for you to pray for him, would you treat him just like you treat a stranger who comes to you asking for the same?' I replied, 'Good council would demand that one treat them equally.' The Shaykh answered, 'No, rather you must treat each according to his place in life (*unzil al-nās manāzilahum*).' A few moments later, a man came up to the Shaykh and sat with him and began to request that the Shaykh pray for him. The Shaykh told him that he was not in need of any such prayers, and with kindness diverted him away from his intention."[61] This is a subtle and revealing episode. Al-Ḥaḍramī at first played into Zarruq's perception of himself as a jurist, trained to discriminate on issues and treat them fairly. He then immediately contradicted Zarruq's juridical opinion, but in a way that might lead him to a deeper kind of comprehension. Al-Ḥaḍramī's actions showed that "treating them equally" or "treating them unequally" was not the issue at all. Instead, with kind words al-Ḥaḍramī diverted the petitioner away from the goal he had formulated in his own will.

By persuading the petitioner that he did not need any prayer, al-Ḥaḍramī subverted his own social role as a saint (the least level of which is to pray on behalf of others). He did not do this with a display of self-abnegation or by fleeing his petitioner, which would have only increased his potency in the cultural logic of sanctity.[62] Rather he left his own status hovering in ambiguity by simply persuading the man that he was in no need of a saint's prayers. Al-Ḥaḍramī demonstrated his own powers only in their barest negative form: as the power to lead someone away from what he thinks he needs. Al-Ḥaḍramī once asked a disciple, "Do you want to take initiation from the hand of Allah directly, or through the mediation of one of the saints?" The disciple said, "Through the mediation of a saint." The shaykh asked, "Why is that better?" The disciple replied, "I don't know." The shaykh said, "It is better because a saint knows what you need and asks Allah to stay with you in the way that you need it, whereas you yourself don't [know what is best for you]."[63]

Al-Ḥaḍramī enacted this self-effacement in an intense form in his personal relationship with Zarruq. He often treated Zarruq as if he were a disciple without a living master, although Zarruq looked to al-Ḥaḍramī as his living master. Al-Ḥaḍramī wrote this advice to Zarruq when they parted for the first time: "You must engage in meditation at all times, and often invoke praise and blessings on the Prophet, for these are a ladder of ascent (*miʿrāj*) and a way of spiritual training (*sulūk*) for a disciple who does not have a master to guide him."[64] Instead of accenting his own authority as a guide who could be present with the disciple at all times or to whom the disciple could turn for aid or focus of concentration, al-Ḥaḍramī attributed all spiritual power to divine providence and the care of destiny.

This devious frankness pierced Zarruq's defensive shell and opened him to the vulnerability of accepting a new master. With a poem, al-Ḥaḍramī counseled Zarruq to embark on life without concern for means, instrumentality, or provision. This implied that Zarruq was even allowed to leave al-Ḥaḍramī's own counsel in an unusual act of self-effacement.

> The world is like the vast expanse of the wild sea,
> each new comer finds sheltered springs and treacherous slopes.
> So leave your strategies and plunge in without worry
> just roll and tumble in the currents of destiny.[65]

By seeming to erase his own presence, al-Ḥaḍramī confirmed the narrative strategy that Zarruq would later employ to record his transformative journey to Tilimsān, when he presented the account of his questioning of al-Zaytūnī, and his punishment as a narrative of his own trust in Allah alone. His transformation from a juridical student into a saint lacked the dramatic mediation of a spiritual guide or initiation from a master. Rather, the agent of his transformation (at least in his retrospective narrative) is only the rigor of the journey, his own desperate confusion, and the providence of Allah.

Al-Ḥaḍramī intentionally minimized his practices to return to the simpler practices of the earliest Muslims (*al-salaf al-ṣāliḥ*) and leave the complex devotions that had evolved among saints and disciples. He felt such practices to be wearying and burdensome. He said to Zarruq's companion, "If you had stayed with some of my brothers, the other saints, you would have grown weary and could not succeed, but Allah is looking after you and has mercy upon you [and sent you to me]."[66] He said, "All I ask of a disciple is sincerity and I can allow him to reach the presence of Allah, even if he never fasts and never stays up all night praying."[67] He advised his disciples to take the simplest prayers and litanies as spiritual training. These simple rituals allowed them to persist with their habitual lives and prior professions, without dramatic displays of renunciation or outward transformation. Zarruq later explained the importance of this simplicity: it keeps the disciple close to his or her original nature (*fiṭra*) and demands only sincerity. "Whoever journeys to Allah through his own nature, his arrival to Allah is closer to him than his own nature. Whoever journeys to Allah through abandoning his own nature, his arrival to Allah is dependent on his distance from his own nature. But attaining distance from one's own nature is difficult indeed."[68]

Despite this minimalism in the outer form of devotions, al-Ḥaḍramī displayed a rich understanding of the movements of spiritual perception and the depths of existential insight. He did not denounce the Sufis' reverence for saints and theories of selflessness as "religious innovation." Rather, his written works reflect a deep engagement with cosmological speculation of the type that would become known as *waḥdat al-wujūd* (or *al-tawḥīd al-muṭlaq*) and is attributed to the writings of Ibn al-ᶜArabī. Ibn ᶜAṭāʾillah al-Iskandarī tried to harness the power of these ideas and images in his *Wisdom Sayings* (*Ḥikam*), to spark the spiritual insight of his followers. This treatment contrasted with other direct followers of Ibn al-ᶜArabī who sought to write systematic treatises of scriptural exegesis or philosophical explication to prove the correctness of his vision. Although al-Ḥaḍramī belonged to the Shādhilī lineage that traced its authority through Ibn ᶜAṭāʾillah, his written works are full prose expositions of the cosmic reality of the existential world.

Books of this genre are known as "books of cosmic realities and spiritual subtleties" (*ḥaqāʾiq wa raqāʾiq*). They addressed the issue of cosmic order: how a singular unique Allah relates to a universe of multiplicity and bewildering diversity. If Allah were the One ultimate being, then how did contingent beings like us and the world we sense exist? Were we creations to be judged, reflections to be gazed upon, or emanations to be recalled to our source? The authors of such texts felt that knowing the order of the world was the key to behaving ethically in it and attaining salvation through it. Such authors used Qurʾānic terms as key words in a philosophical exposition or used Qurʾānic images in an allegorical story of alienation and union. Because of the difficulty of such texts, they were intended for only very advanced disciples in Sufi circles, those who had already mastered the scholarly and doctrinal training needed to read them and who could be trusted not to divulge their contents to scriptural literalists.[69]

Al-Ḥaḍramī wrote at least four texts, each in this genre of subtle cosmic realities.[70] In them, he penned a fine line between bold speculation and scrupulous caution. He notes that his approach stresses "the unity of intuitive insight" (*al-tawḥīd al-ᶜirfānī*) rather than the more assertive "unity of being" or "absolute unity" (*al-tawḥīd al-wujūdī or al-tawḥīd al-muṭlaq*) of others who might have more trust in philosophy and cosmology. This caveat aside, al-Ḥaḍramī writes in the speculative mode that makes this genre so vivid. In his text *The Emergence of Levels and the Fulfillment of Desires*, al-Ḥaḍramī employs the image of letters from the Arabic alphabet to evoke the various stages of emanation of the One original being into the world of perceptible beings. Through this device, he mirrors the way the letters of the Qurʾān as scripture can lead the believer back (through rituals of worship and limits of legal behavior) to the luminous presence of their original divine source.[71]

All people witnessed this divine source in their innermost being before they entered the world of discrete existence and sensory perception. This was the Day of the Covenant when Allah removed all the souls from the loins of Adam and asked, "Am I not your Lord?" This primordial covenant, states al-Ḥaḍramī, actualizes the judgment on the Day of Reckoning. Glimmers of this vision persist in this world, giving people hope of singling out the eternal and unique One from amid the illusory and ephemeral experiences of sensory being. "After revealing the luminous sun of reality, Allah made the progeny of Adam emerge into the unfolding realm of willful caprice and vain thoughts that lodge in the human imagination and in outward sensible forms. This is so that Allah might distinguish the rotten from the wholesome [through their living] in the world."[72] Al-Ḥaḍramī explains that acting ethically in the world (to be judged wholesome) depends not just on acting according to the law, but also on being in accord with one's insight and intuition.

However, the closing section of this book includes al-Ḥaḍramī's advice and admonition to follow the commands of scripture and the limits of religious custom and be wary of those Sufis who claim any existential unity with Allah or emphasize intuition over scriptural knowledge. Al-Ḥaḍramī advised his readers to stick to the letter of revelation and the outward consensus of the Muslim community; he saw no contradiction between this and his exposition of cosmic realities. Zarruq was more attentive to the possible contradiction posed by these two approaches. His commentary on this work is both a tribute to his master and a means of interpreting the text away from rash conclusions that might lead some people to exaggerate his insights or denounce them. "I mention [in this commentary] what I myself understand as I regard al-Ḥaḍramī's lofty spiritual aspiration, and what I am able to grasp of the meaning of his allusions. Indeed, he is like a wide ocean that is never still. You can take water from the ocean to your heart's content, and it will remain as full as it was no matter if you sip it or gulp it down.... But we can comprehend only as much as we are able until, in panic, we accuse him of error for we ventured beyond our limits. How well a poet expressed this with a couplet: how many people confront a truth by reprimanding, when they are at fault with defective understanding."[73]

Zarruq's commentary aimed to shield his master from potential misunderstanding or denunciation. In it, Zarruq interprets al-Ḥaḍramī's expressions through reference to the writings of Ibn ᶜAṭāᵓillah, especially the *Book of Illumination* and the *Wisdom Sayings*. He tries to include al-Ḥaḍramī in the sober and intellectual tradition of Ibn ᶜAṭāᵓillah, whose writings never sparked jurists or literalists to denounce them. Zarruq asserts, "Our intellects can take from this discourse according to their level of comprehension and understanding. Those who may denounce it are excused from blame, since they are ignorant of what they denounce. Those who act partisan in asserting its truth are also excused, since they claim possession of that of which they are not worthy."[74]

Al-Ḥaḍramī's oral teachings display his ambiguous relation to Ibn al-ᶜArabī and other great figures of speculative cosmology (which is sometimes termed "theoretical Sufism"). He showed loyalty to Ibn al-ᶜArabī's ideas but not to his person, for his posthumous reputation had made him a figure of controversy. Al-Ḥaḍramī taught that a common Sufi who has realized Ibn al-ᶜArabī's ideas through illumination and ethical virtue is far superior to Ibn al-ᶜArabī himself, who remained at the level of a philosopher (at least in his mode of expression). Al-Ḥaḍramī considered himself one of these illuminated ones, whose understanding of existential unity was ethical, not just theoretical or intellectual. Still, al-Ḥaḍramī pronounced openly that Ibn al-ᶜArabī should not be subjected to the critiques of literalist jurists, who would not only deny Ibn al-ᶜArabī but also the whole experience of illumination and the social role of saints. When Zarruq complained to al-Ḥaḍramī that people denounce Ibn al-ᶜArabī, he answered, "Ibn al-ᶜArabī certainly deserves to be denounced! But by those have surpassed him, not by those who are living in luxury wearing silk brocades [meaning the jurists who live a worldly life] and do not engage in Sufi [practices]."[75] Al-Ḥaḍramī's tense relationship with Ibn al-ᶜArabī reflects his tense relationship with his contemporary Sufi colleagues. He carefully disentangled the ideals to which Sufis aspire from the practices of Sufis. He wrote on "subtle cosmic realities" for a very limited and select audience of his closest disciples. In contrast, he kept silent about these topics in his oral teachings.

These oral teachings reveal his deep suspicion of other Sufis' practices and show a reformist frame of mind. He claimed the age of freedom for saints was over. "Spiritual training is no longer valid in the sense commonly understood, and all that is left is to benefit from the Shaykh's own aspiration and state (*al-ifāda bi-himma wa ḥāl*)."[76] One can benefit by being in the saint's company, by learning from him as an exemplar and a model of ethical behavior, rather than by seeing the saint as a mediator who can give one access to a higher power. "As for benefiting from a spiritual leader by [being close to] his aspiration and inner state, Anas [a companion of the Prophet] refers to this phenomenon when he said, 'We had barely shaken the dirt off our hands after burying the Prophet when our hearts seemed to not recognize us.' He makes clear that just seeing the Prophet in person was a profound benefit to the early Muslims, since whoever became realized under the influence of the Prophet's spiritual state remained in his presence through that state. For this reason, the Prophet ordered us to stay in the company of righteous people."[77] Zarruq clarified this point, explaining that the early Muslims realized sainthood by simply following the Prophet; this was their "first principle." Likewise, his Sufi colleagues must return to that first principle even after the medieval period when a bewildering variety of Sufi movements and techniques flourished. "Like the first generations, you must embody the Prophet's example (*sunna*) and follow the main trodden path." This means approaching the saint as a model of *sharᶜī* behavior, regardless of the formalities of taking allegiance or accepting ritual tokens of submission.

Reforming Sufi Devotion

Al-Ḥaḍramī's devotional minimalism was one facet of a wider project for the internal reform of Sufi communities. In his view, the social world was full of temptations for the would-be saint, and many of the rituals and institutions of Sufis only intensified temptations for ambition rather than offering correctives to worldly ambition. In this vein, he said to his followers, "The real saint (*rajul*) is not the one who simply enters into a darkened world bravely, or the one who enters a darkened world with more darkness, but rather the one who enters a darkened world bearing light."[78] In this saying, he likens the whole pallet of spiritual practices, litanies, rituals, and networks of initiations that Sufi practice had come to comprise as simply "more darkness" which cannot help one grope through the already darkened world.

This bitter view of the world came into sharp focus when Zarruq asked al-Ḥaḍramī about finding a true saint on whom one can rely for guidance. Al-Ḥaḍramī replied, "Spiritual training as currently understood is no longer valid. In this time, there only remains spiritual assistance through the Shaykh's lofty aspiration and inner state. Therefore, you are obliged to follow the book [the Qur'ān] and the example [of the Prophet's guidance], without adding any practices or subtracting any."[79] Spiritual training in its current meaning consisted of taking initiation from a master, being granted a litany or method of recitation, entering seclusion to practice that method, and abasing one's self-will to the order of the master no matter what form that order might take. Obedience to the master was seen to engender obedience to Allah and embody a connection (though mediated) to the spiritual presence of the Prophet Muhammad. These practices depended on the social manifestation of powerful saints who had the freedom to invent methods to attract disciples and link them to the Prophet. However, in al-Ḥaḍramī's view, this whole edifice of Islamic sainthood, in ritual practice and the social power that undergirded it, was no longer valid. It no longer served as a source of spiritual illumination, since it obscured wisdom and spiritual guidance.

Instead, al-Ḥaḍramī proposed that disciples should simply study the scriptural sources that remained as the legacy of the Prophet Muhammad. In studying, disciples would learn to act within the limits of the law, as derived from these scriptural sources. By acting within the law, they will enact goodness within society, without recourse to Sufi institutions. However, they must pursue this study, legal understanding, and social action in the company of a saintly guide. The guide will direct their actions, not through discrete rituals or through charismatic authority, but simply through the spiritual power of his attention and concentration.

Al-Ḥaḍramī did not enunciate these reformist ideals in an explicit program. Rather, he expressed them in a negative form, through warnings, cautions, and advice on what not to do. He warned against relying on any institution to exercise power in society, in a pessimistic assessment that all power corrupts. "In dealing with other people, the disciple must hold his behavior under the following three conditions: give others their full rights, withdraw from whatever others possess, and flee from whatever causes jealousy in their hearts (except for those matters that are incumbent upon him as obligatory religious duties, for there is no turning away from those). Each disciple [should be careful since] he may be inclined to ride a horse [live a life of public authority] or to influence public affairs, or to engage in changing the forbidden practices circulating among the common people, or to take up *jihād*, or other such activities that seem virtuous."[80] Al-Ḥaḍramī points out that although the intention of these activities may seem virtuous, they will lead to corruption. The corruption he warns against is not just the moral state of an individual, but the corruption of the whole institution of Sufi devotions.

> When the opportunity presents itself, the disciple may think he has the chance to bring such "virtuous activity" to its full completion. Yet he may subsequently scrutinize the faults of his brothers and other people. He may become weakened by living in isolation and refusing to work, or by listening to music and poetry continuously, or by staying too long in the company of others for reasons other than teaching and learning. The disciple may be tempted to seek favor with the lords of worldly power, to the detriment of his piety. He may try to learn the subtle points of Sufi thought without performing the basic deeds of religion and obscuring his own faults. The disciple may put himself forward as advanced in spiritual training without submission to a master, guide or teacher.[81]

In this long list of potential spiritual calamities, al-Ḥaḍramī catalogues most of the "heretical tendencies" that jurists and dogmatists have long accused Sufis of fostering: listening to music, reciting love poetry, holding gatherings for spiritual training that bring different classes of people together, and interpreting scripture allegorically. Yet he also includes in this list spiritual calamities of the opposite, dogmatic nature: numb literalism, satisfaction with routine custom, condemning co-religionists, and self-righteousness. The faults of both sides result from disciples straying from the founding principle of spiritual practice, which is a principle of balance.

In this way, al-Ḥaḍramī endeavored to express an Islamic middle way between extremes. "In short, the disciple may become satisfied with knowledge and lose sight of action, or emphasize action and lose insight into spiritual state or knowledge. [Worse yet] he may become absorbed in his own spiritual state and ignore both knowledge and action! He may become one of those with no principle on which to base any knowledge, action or spiritual state."[82] This oral teaching was al-Ḥaḍramī's most important gift to Zarruq. He emphasized that Sufi practices must be based on principles derived from scripture and must not be allowed to grow freely from one's personal religious experience. To Zarruq, this teaching reconciled the conflicting forces that had shaped his life until that point. In his subsequent writings, Zarruq set about explicating the implicit force of this teaching, rendering it in advisories, expositions, arguments, poetic laments, and even harsh condemnations.

The importance of this inspiration becomes even more dramatic when juxtaposed with what al-Ḥaḍramī did not give to Zarruq. He did not provide Zarruq with a clear lineage of initiation or a discrete litany (*wird*) to characterize his meditative practice. He did not offer Zarruq a dramatic period of spiritual training. He did not give Zarruq any socially recognized signs of power as a disciple and representative of a popular saint.

In training his disciples, al-Ḥaḍramī deliberately obscured his lineage of initiation. He refused to tell even his disciples to what lineage he belonged. Zarruq asked him to confer to him the list of past masters who defined his own spiritual authority (and therefore defined Zarruq's lineage as well), but al-Ḥaḍramī answered in irritation, "I know nothing about all that! Very simply, the Way practiced by my mother and her ancestors has come to us from the Way of Abū Madyan."[83] Al-Ḥaḍramī evidently held a compound allegiance to three lineages: the Qādirī, the Madyanī, and the Shādhilī.[84] Although a Sufi *ṭarīqa* is often understood as a discrete entity, al-Ḥaḍramī did not distinguish between these three lineages. He appears to have taken initiation into all three at once from a single master; yet he refused to name that master. To justify his practices, he would say, "I heard a certain saint in Makka in the year 846 Hijri recite this advice to me, on the authority of a master who was sincere with Allah; both of them are well known as saints, and I met them both face to face." In relating this oral justification, Zarruq writes that "Allah alone knows best," meaning the matter is in doubt, but he had to trust his master.[85]

Al-Ḥaḍramī came from Yemen, where there was a tradition of fusing the Madyanī lineage and the Qādirī lineage. Yemenis apprehended the Madyanī lineage as a branch of the Qādirī lineage that came from the Maghrib to Yemen and was superimposed upon the older Qādirī lineage there.[86] Al-Ḥaḍramī cited this tradition when he claimed that the spiritual method of his mother and his Yemeni ancestors was the way of Abū Madyan.[87] When he moved to Cairo, al-Ḥaḍramī came into contact with the Shādhilī lineage, with its sophisticated urban blend of juridical prestige and literary elegance. Since the Shādhilī lineage was also seen as an extension of the lineage of Abū Madyan, it was easy for al-Ḥaḍramī to combine it with the former two lineages.[88] It was even easier for him to suppress any reference to three lineages at all and apprehend them as fused into one spiritual method, though on the surface they may appear as three distinct lineages.

Al-Ḥaḍramī did not forge this fusion of three lineages into one initiatory bundle himself. Rather, he shared this "triple allegiance through one initiation" with a wider community of Sufis in Egypt and Makka. Al-Ḥaḍramī had a Sufi master by the name of Yaḥyā al-Qādirī. As evident from his name, Yaḥyā was a Qādirī in his affiliation (and he may have been a descendant of the Prophet Muḥammad through the genealogical line of ᶜAbd al-Qādir al-Jīlānī). This is how Zarruq's early followers understood al-Ḥaḍramī to have been "a Qādirī" even as they acknowledged that there were many ambiguities in his lineage.[89] Yaḥyā al-Qādirī also insisted that he had an initiation leading back to Ibn ᶜAṭāᵓillah in the Shādhilī lineage.[90] And although Yaḥyā al-Qādirī is the pivotal link from al-Ḥaḍramī to all of these lineages, al-Ḥaḍramī never specified that Yaḥyā al-Qādirī was his primary Sufi master.[91] Although he inherited this potent cocktail of initiatory lineages, al-Ḥaḍramī systematically downplayed his master, his lineages, and his connections to powerful saints of the past. There is no evidence that he ever specified for Zarruq the discrete links in his lineage, leaving Zarruq with an ambiguous hold on legitimacy.

In addition, al-Ḥaḍramī did not bequeath to Zarruq a formal scholarly permission (*ijāza*) to teach Sufi texts. Zarruq records that he took his *ijāza* in Sufi devotional texts, like those of hadith and jurisprudence, from scholarly teachers in Egypt.[92] Most importantly, he took an *ijāza* for the full set of books of Ibn ᶜAṭāʾillah from al-Sakhāwī.[93] These are all the texts that al-Ḥaḍramī recommended for training his disciples. For inner light, he recommends the books of Ibn ᶜAṭāʾillah, especially the *Book of Illumination*. For outer rectitude, he recommends the *Madkhal* of Ibn al-Ḥājj and the books of Ibn al-Ḥājj's teacher, Ibn Abī Jamra.[94] By studying these texts, Zarruq followed the method of spiritual training that al-Ḥaḍramī advocated; yet al-Ḥaḍramī gave him no formal training in these texts. Most likely, they read and discussed these texts together as part of Zarruq's disciplinary training. However, Zarruq could not rely on al-Ḥaḍramī as a textual-scholarly authority, whose *ijāza* would be respected by other Sufis and scholars, either in Egypt or beyond.

Finally, al-Ḥaḍramī did not give Zarruq the psychological security of a stable social life. He did not allow Zarruq to live tranquilly with a community of fellow disciples or with the prestigious routine of teaching at al-Azhar.[95] Rather, al-Ḥaḍramī deliberately shook him up by telling him, "I've heard that the soil of the Maghrib is good fertile soil: if you would return there your heart would grow healthy and wholesome."[96] After al-Ḥaḍramī recognized that Zarruq's experiences opened him to al-Ḥaḍramī's own reformist urges (which were acute if still not systematically or formally articulated), he encouraged Zarruq to return to the Maghrib. Al-Ḥaḍramī may have harbored ambitions that Zarruq would spread these ideas in his own homeland. He may have felt this necessary in the face of his own perceived failure to secure any significant recognition or following for these ideas in Egypt. In addition to his concern for reforming Sufi communities from within, al-Ḥaḍramī wanted to directly confront Zarruq with his worst fear, returning to Fes.

While his reliance on al-Ḥaḍramī seems like a disadvantage from the outside, Zarruq perceived its inner dimensions that answered his own needs. Zarruq turned his initiation with al-Ḥaḍramī from a disadvantage into an asset. On the surface, Zarruq could claim no firm lineage from al-Ḥaḍramī that he could easily convey to disciples (who would memorize its chain of names as a spiritual lineage, write it out as a devotional exercise and display of authority, or versify it to recite in social contexts). Certainly, all later hagiographers were at a loss to draw up Zarruq's lineage in a neat, unambiguous list.[97] Yet Zarruq himself saw this ambiguity as a resource. His initiation into a Sufi community that fused three lineages into one provided Zarruq with a tool for reform. He saw adherence to this triply compounded lineage as a method of sifting each spiritual method for the clearest principles of Sufi piety and saintly comportment. In addition, fusing three lineages into one was a method of guarding against partisanship or extremism. Initiation into this triple lineage would not force a disciple to surrender the discerning power of reason to absolute devotion to a single master or lineage. In Zarruq's hands, this triple lineage set up a structure in which a disciple could search for the underlying principles of being a Sufi. This was a topic he would elaborate in writing and a structure he would try to actualize in his community of disciples.

Zarruq was not evasive and provocative like al-Ḥaḍramī when challenged to define his lineage. Instead, he tried to clarify the ambiguity in a systematic way. His teachings are reflected in the writings of al-Ṣumāᶜī, who was a fourth-generation follower of Zarruq. Al-Ṣumāᶜī took initiation into the triple *ṭarīqa*, describing it as "three apparently distinct lineages that lead back to a single root, the powerful and enabling Path (*tarīq qadīr*) which is the path of the Prophet."[98] In fusing three lineages, Zarruq claimed to return each to its original practice, the embodiment of the example of the Prophet. In this way, he turned an apparent weakness in his background into a wild card highlighting his own special role as a saintly reformer. Al-Ṣumāᶜī explained, "In reality these three methods (*ṭarīqa*), the Shādhilī, Madyanī and Qādirī, are one single path (*tarīq*), for they are continuously fused and interconnected between themselves."[99] He echoes the formulation of one of Zarruq's direct disciples, Ṭāhir ibn Zayyān, who analyzed the nature of the initiation he received from Shaykh Zarruq.

> This is the authentic chain of blessed transmission of the noble triple *khirqa* [initiatory cloak] which comes from separate initiations representing the Way of Sīdī Abū Madyan, the Way of Sīdī Abū al-Ḥasan al-Shādhilī, and the Way of Sīdī ᶜAbd al-Qādir al-Jīlānī. I have received all three together from my Shaykh Aḥmad al-Burnūsi known as Zarrūq.... In reality, all of these lineages represent one single Way, since the lineage of Shaykh al-Shādhilī grows out of the lineage of Shaykh Abū Madyan, and his lineage grows out of the lineage of Shaykh ᶜAbd al-Qādir. Therefore, my Shaykh, Aḥmad Zarrūq, is a Shādhilī in his outward affiliation to a lineage (*ṭarīqa*), yet is a Madyanī in his method of following the path (*sulūk*), and yet further is a Qādirī in his innermost spiritual reality (*ḥaqīqa*).[100]

This explanation reveals how Zarruq tried to deconstruct a *ṭarīqa* to reveal its underlying force as a *ṭarīq*, a dynamic movement toward sincerity. Through his allegiance to the "triple initiation" he de-emphasized any distinct spiritual method (*ṭarīqa*) or social community that bonded through it. Instead, he emphasized how each method depended on principles of sincerity that propelled a practitioner along the path (*ṭarīq*) toward the presence of Allah. In this way, spiritual training would be fused with legal rectitude and legal training would be infused with spiritual insight.

Zarruq's initiation into this triple lineage allowed him to enunciate a solution to a deep and profound problem: how to insure that saints who claim social status as selfless people actually act without self-aggrandizement and without ambition. Zarruq's goal was to prevent Muslim saints from becoming the center of social movements (through the force of their own ambition or the distorting force of others' devotion to them). He hoped to force saints to act as the symbolic centers of a social order constituted already in the rulings of Islamic law. The solution Zarruq proposed was not new, but he enunciated it in new terms that were subtle and forceful.

He set about answering this problem with an old argument. Both Sufi devotion (*ṭarīqa*) and law (*sharīᶜa*) are reactions to the challenge of Qurʾānic revelation and the Prophet Muḥammad's bringing this revelation into society. They are two different but compatible responses, claimed Zarruq, and each needs the other for completion. Neither the exponents of sainthood nor the upholders of legal rectitude can claim precedence in historical development or dogmatic authority. However, spirituality and law are not equal; they have very different natures, applications, and limits in social function. Law is universal and must apply to each responsible individual. Sufi practices are a specialized provenance of a few, who are selected by aptitude or by experience for its subtleties. Jurisprudence (*fiqh*), as the means to articulate and enact the goals of law, must necessarily be prior to and more comprehensive than Sufi loyalty to a saint as the means to practice and realize the goals of spiritual cultivation.

From this argument, Zarruq made a claim that startled his Sufi colleagues in its wide-ranging ramifications. He asserted that a person must be trained as a jurist first, and only then seek spiritual growth as a Sufi. As a corollary, anyone who does not undergo the intellectual and moral rigors of legal training is unqualified for Sufi practices, especially for the higher levels of spiritual experience through which one lays claim to moments of selflessness, or further, to persisting sainthood. Those who fail to do so are not just unqualified for what they claim for themselves. They are actually dangerous, first to their own spiritual state and second to those who follow them. Zarruq reduces this complex argument down to the pithy recommendation: "Be a jurist first then a Sufi; don't be a Sufi first then a jurist." From his troubled journey as a youth who "departed from himself," Zarruq arrived at a point from which he felt he could judge how well others were progressing on the road of selflessness.

6 Sincerity

"BE A JURIST first then a Sufi; don't be a Sufi first then a jurist." This argument is present, in some form, in almost every page that Zarruq wrote. He articulated its ramifications in many different genres, disciplines, and styles. To take this recommendation seriously as a foundational principle of being a Sufi has far-reaching consequences. Zarruq's injunction was not just a matter of paying lip service to the rhetoric of law in order to pursue spiritual experience free of public scrutiny and juridical condemnation. Nor was it a matter of keeping one's loyalties clear: primarily to law (with its far horizon of Islamic social order) and only secondarily to Sufi piety (with its intimate boundaries of personal, interior experience). Rather, Zarruq aimed to reform how saints behave, how Sufis who follow them exercise their authority in society, and how disciples approached training and education.

His argument resounds on many levels. In it, one can hear his admiration of the tradition of juridical Sufis from Meknes and Fes, who seemed to fluently combine the practical attention to legal rights with the penetrating insights of contemplation and ascetic renunciation. One can see the image of al-Qūrī, who as a juridical saint was careful not to distinguish between his students in scriptural studies and disciples in spiritual training. One can also discern Zarruq as a young man, wonder-struck but also intimidated by the powerful display of saintly miracles, and horrified by the political uses to which some saints put them. It was as if such a reform program would right the injustices he perceived as marring his past. The more impossible that wish became, the more stridently he forged his ideal and articulated the limits to saintly action.

Such a program of reform was possible to imagine only in a liminal space. Certainly, Zarruq personally experienced Egypt and the Ḥijāz as liminal spaces, though he was in no way marginalized by them. He was a new migrant, but he possessed the scholarly and rhetorical skills to access the highest levels of institutional authority. In this way, Egypt and the Ḥijāz constituted a liminal space, but one charged with potential for Zarruq to rebuild his own sense of authority and to acquire his own distinct voice as an author.

In Cairo and Makka, Zarruq found the keys to establishing his own voice of authority, in teachers of scriptural and legal disciples and in saintly guides of Sufi communities. These authoritative figures thrived in religious institutions that were in a relative political vacuum. In this period, Sufis and jurists in these central lands played no role in the dramatic rise of a new dynastic power. They were neither advocates of a new political force nor did any such force coerce them into granting that force legitimacy through their religious sanction. Further, these very authorities in the central lands were perceived as especially prestigious due to their proximity to the holy sites of the Ḥijāz and their location in historically revered institutions of learning and piety. It was this historical condition that allowed Zarruq to imagine a reform program that would limit the social actions of saints and disconnect Sufi communities from patronage networks that rising dynasties could manipulate.

Roots of Sufism

Through articulating the principles of spiritual development, Zarruq combined the intellectual training and textual genres of jurisprudence and Sufi devotion. This was a unique approach to the problem of defining Islamic sainthood as a social institution. He offers his argument in its most succinct form in *Qawāʿid al-Taṣawwuf* (*The Principles of Becoming a Sufi*). The twenty-sixth principle clearly illustrates Zarruq's proposal to limit the scope of sainthood. "The authority of jurisprudence is universal and applies to every Muslim, since its goal is to establish the formal structure of religion, to raise its standard high, and to articulate its pronouncements. In contrast, the authority of being a Sufi (*taṣawwuf*) is specialized and applies to only some, since it deals with the relation between a person and the Lord, and beyond that has no applicability."[1] The issue is not simply which discipline has pre-eminence, but rather how each discipline is applicable for the common good. His principle continues: "To be a Sufi, one must turn to jurisprudence for guidance, for jurisprudence is sufficient for a Muslim without being a Sufi. In contrast, Sufis cannot exist independently without jurisprudence; indeed their practices are not sound without jurisprudence. It is not permissible to turn from jurisprudence to being a Sufi except through jurisprudence itself. Although being a Sufi has a greater pre-eminence than jurisprudence, jurisprudence is safer and more applicable for the public good (*maṣlaḥa*). For this reason, it is said, Be a jurist first then a Sufi; don't be a Sufi first then a jurist." The issue at stake is balance. If Sufis and jurists are to come together into one community, they must be trained as jurists first and only then turn to spiritual cultivation. This community should be delimited by juridical training and then empowered by Sufi training. "The Sufi from among the jurists is more complete and more sound than a jurist from among the Sufis.... A person is not safe relying on Sufi practices without jurisprudence or jurisprudence without Sufi practices. It is like maintaining your health: what good is taking medicine only, without also carefully watching your daily habits?"[2]

Throughout his writings, Zarruq offered many metaphors to illustrate the fusion of sainthood and jurisprudence that he advocated, such as this example of brothers who enact the commands of a single father. "You must know that jurisprudence and Sufi devotion are like two brothers. They both give reliable indication of the commands of Allah. This is because the true reality of being a Sufi depends on one's sincerity in turning to Allah in ways that satisfy Allah through means that satisfy Allah."[3] Although Islamic theology avoided explicitly imagining Allah as "father" in the way that Christian theology did, the patriarchal society that he lived in provided easy examples of the continuity in power between Allah, king, father, and sons. In Zarruq's imagination, shared with most in his society, the image of two sons of one father helped to explain how Sufis and jurists were both equally legitimate and necessary social extensions of the Prophet Muhammad's authority and presence.

Zarruq approached this projected balance and complementarity between Sufis and jurists slowly in his career as an author. He began his career writing commentaries, for this was the most accepted strategy of writing in the madrasa educational system in which he was reared. His earliest commentaries were on the *Wisdom Sayings*; after his period of studies in Cairo, he also began to write commentaries on the primary legal texts of Maliki jurisprudence.[4] These he would use in teaching students, and through them he earned a wide reputation as a legal scholar.

Unlike his juridical colleagues, Zarruq was not content to write commentaries on legal manuals alone. He began to experiment with a new genre, *naṣīḥa* or "advice," that would apply legal boundaries to particular dimensions of social action. Through this genre, he tried to move beyond the specialist's absorption in the details of the law and to interpret the Prophet's example in a general way applicable to the common Muslim. While in Cairo, he wrote *The Sufficient Advice* in 878 Hijri (1473 C.E.).[5] He rewrote this text the following year while on the road back toward Morocco; he condensed it with a new, more pointed title: *The Bringer-Together of Beneficial and Advantageous Pronouncements*.[6] The term *al-jāmiᶜ*, "the one who brings together" what had been dissipated and scattered, is a crucial term in Zarruq's developing Sufi vocabulary. He used it here to describe the goal of his advice: to bring together disparate traditions into a common code of behavior based on the Prophet's example. He wrote these texts to make the norms of the *sharīᶜa* explicit for Sufi disciples and juridical students together. However, the term *al-walī al-jāmiᶜ* would apply especially to himself, as the saint who brings together the formerly disparate disciplines of jurisprudence and spiritual cultivation.[7] He enacted this role as an author by superimposing genres that were normally distinct. In his commentary on the juridical treatise of al-Waghlīsī, for instance, he discusses issues of Sufi practice.[8]

After approaching the question of social action from the angle of jurisprudence, Zarruq approached it from the angle of Sufi training. He wrote a commentary on a text that disciples in zawiyas in Morocco commonly read, *The Original Sources*, by Ibn al-Banāᵓ al-Sarquṣṭī.[9] This didactic poem laid out ethical rules and guidelines for the newly initiated to follow, set to rhyme to facilitate its memorization and daily application. In his commentary on this work, Zarruq claimed that Sufi devotion is dead and those who claim title to it are impostors. A couplet of the original poem is followed by Zarruq's prose.

> You ask me of what is beyond me to express
> if you ask me how to behave like a *faqīr*
> You'll not even find a trace of the path
> yet you crave to establish signposts clear

> [Zarruq comments] "How to behave" on a certain path denotes those guidelines that show one how to travel to reach the destination. "A *Faqīr*" is a person who turns to Allah with full sincerity. The author [al-Sarqusṭī] refers to those behaviors through which the *faqīr* can become fully realized in spiritual poverty and dependence (*faqr*) on Allah alone. This dependence is the highest level of being a Sufi.... When he says that such behaviors are "beyond me to express" he means that they are too difficult to write down and define carefully so that one can achieve the desired results. This is because such behaviors have become so madly disordered and mixed with impurities by the hidden actions of people who claim outward allegiance to this path (*ahl al-tarassum*) in this age. These people have rushed forward greedily to possess this path and have erased all sign of it, to the point that nobody knows where it is to be found anymore! ...They have ruined its appearance and caused its demise, its virtual obliteration, until ...its fragments have become ground into the dirt, as if it were itself nothing but dirt, and it were impossible to release it from the dirt [and restore it] pure and whole.... The signposts that had shown the direction of the path are gone because of the immoral ignorance (*jahl*) of the people. Those who claim to know the way only incite people to accept their own egotistical inventions and evil practices, claiming that these are the very essence of the path.[10]

In his view, the only way to revive the Sufi path is through knowledge of the scriptural sources and the example of the Prophet. The only way to achieve that is to respect scholars and study with them. Yet, Zarruq laments, the Sufis of his time dismiss scholarly knowledge and even attack scholars.

In general, this is an old complaint. Ever since intellectual Sufis tried to systematize Sufi practices and present them in a form acceptable to conservative and literalist scholars, it has been a favored strategy to uphold Sufi ideals while despairing of contemporary practices.[11] In the eleventh century C.E., ᶜAlī Hujwīrī lamented, "Being a Sufi was a reality without a name, but now it has become a name without a reality." In a similar spirit, al-Qushayrī wrote, "Most of the realized Sufis have faded away, and in this time there remains only the barest traces of their having passed." In North Africa, Abū Madyan perpetuated this rhetoric in his poem, the *Qaṣīda in Ra*ᵓ: "Know that the Path of the Sufis has fallen into decline, and the sorry state of those who claim allegiance to it today is as you can see."[12] Yet Zarruq does not use this only as a rhetorical strategy. He is more vehement than others in his lament. His project was not to prune a few wild growths from an otherwise healthy vine, but to cut the vine back to its very roots if there were to be any hope of obtaining good fruit in the distant future.

His despair drove him to a deep level of introspection and a new creative synthesis of genres in his next major work, *Qawāʿid al-Taṣawwuf* (*The Principles of Being a Sufi*). He saw a new potential in the terms "root," or authentic source (*aṣl*), and "principle," or systematic guideline (*qāʿida*). He borrowed these terms from juridical scholarship and applied them to Sufi practice in an exposition at once philosophically acute and intellectually exacting. As described in chapter 1, the study of jurisprudence (*uṣūl al-fiqh*) had a profound impact on Islamic society in the Maghrib. The spread of this discipline broke the hegemonic power of Maliki jurists (who had been hostile to the rational thinking that characterized the Usuli method) by forcing them to become Usulis themselves. This contributed to the fall of the al-Murābiṭīn (Almoravid) dynasty, which based its political legitimacy upon the "old school" of Maliki exclusivists. Usuli scholarship in the Maghrib went hand-in-hand with organized Sufi communities, similar to how the text that became emblematic of the Usuli orientation, the *Iḥyāʾ ʿUlūm al-Dīn* of Abū Ḥāmid al-Ghazālī, enshrined Sufi devotion and religious scholarship.

Just as Usuli scholarship had provoked a major intellectual florescence in the Maghrib (in both juridical and Sufi spheres) and inspired a politically potent movement of reform in the early sixth century Hijri (mid-twelfth century C.E.), Zarruq hoped that its resources had not yet been exhausted. He turned to the tradition of Usuli scholarship and mined it for terms and concepts through which to reform Sufi communities from within. What he brought forth was the "principle" and the "root." Early legal methods were content to base legal decisions upon the custom of a local community or the prudent common sense of the judge. The Usuli legal method differed in insisting that every juridical decision and judicial action be based on a "root" source in scripture. Through analogy or deductive reasoning, the jurist would extend the ruling of a source to cover and justify the decision in question. In the quest to rationalize and regularize the way scripture could be extended into juridical decisions, Usuli authors explicated a whole set of "principles" that would guide jurists in making just decisions. The principles of the Usuli method involved deciding how the mandate of the "root" should be extended (as specific or general, limited or absolute, conditional or unconditioned). Soon Usuli jurists created a new genre of texts to elucidate the principles that would guide the legal extension of scriptural commandments and prohibitions to cover a host of complicated and ambiguous practical situations.[13] Zarruq's legal scholarship included intensive study of these principles, and he even authored commentaries on the genre, which was well-established by his time.[14]

In practice, the principles of jurisprudence restricted the freedom of jurists and forced them to base their practice explicitly on Prophetic sources. Yet in theory, these principles also justified the overall body of legal decisions, securing for them the canopy of sacredness by linking them back to a scriptural "root." Usuli jurists had successfully reformed Islamic law from within by articulating governing principles and writing them out as guidance for jurists. Zarruq strived to achieve a similar reform within Sufi communities by articulating the roots and principles of their practices. The terms "root" and "principle" were also used in other disciplines of knowledge, including grammar and theology. Yet Zarruq applied not only the terms, but also the conceptual structure of juridical principles to Sufi practice in a unique way.[15]

Zarruq applied this structure of juridical reasoning to the subject of Sufi practice. He hoped to articulate the principles of spiritual cultivation under the guidance of a saint, just as jurists had explicated the principles of jurisprudence. This involved a bold but delicate extension of Usuli scholarship into the field of Sufi practice. Zarruq asserted that both were to be guided by principles, reasoned discrimination, and specialized authorities. In this project, Zarruq followed the earlier guidance of the jurist Abū Isḥāq al-Shāṭibī, who insisted that Sufis, like jurists, must establish the principles of their every practice.[16] Although jurisprudence inspired the method of Zarruq's new genre, the *Wisdom Sayings* of classical Sufi authors inspired its form and timbre. He presented each principle in a condensed form, in a chiseled crystal of assertion and example. He employed prose so rarefied and abstract that it attained the intensity of poetry.

Zarruq hoped that his own "principles" would come to guide the outer actions of Sufis that fell under the jurisdiction of law and legal sanction, just as the *Wisdom Sayings* of Ibn ᶜAṭāʾillah had come to guide their inner lives. His principles would both limit their actions and link them to "root" behaviors sanctified by scripture and Prophetic example. Just as *Wisdom Sayings* employed the vocabulary of "cosmic realities and spiritual subtleties" in a new form to spark spiritual insight, so the principles of being a Sufi would employ the vocabulary of jurisprudence in a new form to channel spiritual insight. If *Wisdom Sayings* were designed to illumine the spirit, the principles of being a Sufi were meant to channel that light through the discrimination of reason and focus its energy upon the actions of the physical body and the comportment of the social body.

The profundity and uniqueness of this authorial strategy explains why *The Principles of Being a Sufi* been constantly reprinted from the time lithography was introduced in the Islamic world until the present. It not only limits the range of behavior that Sufis and saints can claim to be "authentic," but also establishes the most articulate defense of Sufis and sainthood against those who claim that it suffices to read scripture literally and apply it legally (and therefore denounce Sufis as an "un-Islamic" deviants from the Prophet's example). Yet Zarruq does not present his argument in prosaic, discursive form. He hides the full scope of the argument from view by breaking the discourse into discrete pieces. He presents each piece as a principle, with examples of how to apply it. In this way, Zarruq subverts the resistance of his readers to his argument from both extremes: jurists who would resist the idea that Sufis share the same sacred sources and rational principles as law, and Sufis who would resist the idea that jurisprudence limits spiritual practice and defines its authentic expressions. This strategy makes reading the *Principles* a difficult task; its cubist style breaks up its argument into discrete angles and planes, thereby almost obscuring its original subject matter. This study will try to reconstruct the basic argument of Zarruq to show its relevance for his reform project.[17]

Fusing Sufism and Jurisprudence

Zarruq is quite explicit that he takes an Usuli approach to Sufi practice. The opening section delves to the heart of the question. What does it mean to be a Sufi? What is its essential feature, and how can it be defined? There have been thousands of definitions of Sufism, and each saint has offered a definition based on his own spiritual insight. "Difference of opinion concerning a single reality proves the difficulty of comprehending that reality's total nature. Since all opinions refer back to one original source (*aṣl*), the reality of the phenomenon encompasses everything that might be said about it. People express that reality in accord with what they understand of it.... There is such a difference of opinion about how to be a Sufi (*taṣawwuf*) ... yet I feel that whoever has a measure of sincerity in turning attention towards Allah (*ṣidq al-tawajjuh*) is a Sufi to a certain extent, and that each individual's way of being a Sufi is the sincerity of that person's turning toward Allah. Try to comprehend this!"[18]

From this basic definition, Zarruq presents a series of principles to demonstrate that the essence of being a Sufi and the essence of jurisprudence are in reality the same. Sincerity toward Allah is the root of both, and that root is subject to conditions that govern any act of sincerity and ensure its authenticity. A practice of sincerity in the field of outward action is considered juridical. A practice of sincerity in the field of inward attitude and intentionality is considered "Sufi" or spiritual. Both share a root and parallel principles; both are compatible, both depend upon each other, and indeed each are invalid without the other. "A person's sincerity in turning towards Allah is conditioned by its being pleasing to Allah in its essence and its coming about by means that are pleasing to Allah. That which is conditioned is not acceptable without its condition.... Therefore realizing faith (*imān*) is a condition that must be fulfilled, and submission to the Prophet's directives (*islām*) is a condition that must be fulfilled. Thus, nobody can be a Sufi without jurisprudence, because divine orders can be known only through jurisprudence. Nor is jurisprudence sound without Sufis, for action cannot be carried out without sincerity and turning towards Allah.... Sufi practice and jurisprudence are integral to each other in principle, just as souls are integral to bodies [and the existence of a living body implies a soul]."[19] Zarruq perceives this illustration to be not just an example following his own principle, but also a commentary on the pivotal report of the Prophet's conversation with the angel Gabriel. The angel asked the Prophet to explain the three components of religious, *imān*, *islām*, and *iḥsān*, as discussed in chapter 1. Zarruq perceived Sufi practices to unfold from the component of *iḥsān*: to worship God as if you were seeing God, and if you cannot see God then knowing that God sees you, in the words of the Prophet Muhammad. Zarruq elaborates, "The legitimacy of a thing depends on its 'root.' It must be based upon its root in such a way as to explicitly display its essential connection to that root, so that nobody can deny its partaking in the reality of that root. The root foundation of being a Sufi is the station of spiritual virtue (*iḥsān*).... That is because the various meanings of sincerely turning to Allah are based on this station and revolve around it.... Similarly, jurisprudence revolves around the station of submission to the Prophet's commands and prohibitions (*islām*), while the discipline of doctrinal theology (*uṣūl al-dīn*) revolves around the station of faith (*imān*).... Sufi practice is one part of the religion that the Prophet explicated to Gabriel, so his companions might learn of its totality."[20]

Of course, the word "Sufi" and the abstract noun "being a Sufi" (*taṣawwuf*, which in English is usually translated as Sufism) did not exist in the time of the Prophet, as critics of saints and Sufis are quick to point out. Zarruq counters that the terms "jurisprudence" or "doctrinal theology" also did not exist in the earliest generations of Muslims. All three terms arose independently to name separate discourses that intended to explicate something essential about the religion introduced by Muhammad. Each discourse operates on a different level, with different principles and different fields of action. Zarruq insists that they are all complementary and integral. To justify his assertions, Zarruq highlights the saying of Mālik ibn Anas, the most authoritative early jurist and founder of the school of law that predominates in the Maghrib. "One who follows the Sufi path while neglecting jurisprudence is a heretic, while one who learns jurisprudence while neglecting the Sufi path commits transgression. However, one who combines both has attained realization of the Truth."[21]

Zarruq's Usuli approach tries to find unity in the multiple definitions of being a Sufi and the complex variety of practices associated with Sufi communities. He brushes aside the long dispute about the linguistic origin of the term "Sufi," as well as the objection that "Sufi" was adopted from non-Muslims and has no place in Islam. "The technical term denoting a thing is that which indicates clearly the essence of that thing. It must be appropriate the thing to which it is affixed, and it must specify clearly that which it indicates, without obscuring its essential meaning, transgressing any legal norms or violating any customs, and without annulling any other legal terminology or customary terms.... The term *taṣawwuf* [being a Sufi] is a technical term that fits these conditions."[22] Sufis are those who try "purify their awareness in each moment (*hāl*) of everything other than the Truth (*ḥaqq*)." Such purification expresses their sincerity in turning toward Allah in every moment and under every external condition. There may appear to be a multitude of ways and means to achieve this, Zarruq notes, and the fact that people argue over which is more original or more effective is bewildering, even disturbing. However, he defines the problem with another general principle: "Multiplicity and contradiction in ways and means (*masālik*) does not necessarily mean that each has a different goal (*maqṣad*). A great variety of means and methods could be united in seeking a single goal."[23] Sufis adopted three basic ways to approach sincerity with Allah: scrupulous attention to ritual norms (*ʿibāda*), ascetic renunciation (*zahāda*), or contemplative insight (*maʿrifa*). These broad means are interdependent and intertwined. One takes the name "ascetic," for instance, by the predominance of renunciation, which does not preclude or contradict the other methods. Therefore, being a Sufi is suitable for a wide variety of temperaments.[24]

One only engages in the difficulties of a discipline hoping for some benefit, and one attains that benefit only by maintaining the true standard of that discipline. With such an analysis, Zarruq tries to cut through the mystique of being a Sufi, which by his time had accrued a thick patina of social status to the extent that Zarruq feared that most people had forgotten the original goal and its benefits. "The advantage of something is that which was intended by its very existence.... Sufi training is a discipline of knowledge and practice that intends to purify and restore the heart, devoting the heart to Allah alone and isolating it from anything other than Allah. In a parallel way, jurisprudence is the discipline of purifying one's actions, of preserving order, and showing the wisdom of clear rules. Likewise, theology is the discipline of investigating levels of faith with rational proofs, thereby embellishing faith with certainty."[25]

The benefit of being a Sufi is very powerful, for without a sound heart one can never achieve the goal, no matter what one believes with the mind or acts upon with the limbs. Zarruq asserts that one should be dedicated to Sufi practice because nothing is nobler, in its essence and in its benefit. "The worthiness of something demands that one should sacrifice everything to acquire it, if one is suited to the effort. If so, one evaluates the worth of the goal by its true value and sets it in its proper context. If not, then one is unsuited to the task and wastes the effort and spoils the goal. This is usually the case."[26] It is fascinating to see how Hamza Yusuf, in the early twenty-first century, articulates this same point by quoting Zarruq's principles, as illustrated in chapter 1. Many people respect being a Sufi because of its tremendous worth once its goals are actualized or its evident status once others recognize in one the saintly qualities it confers. This worth and status make it crucial to establish the criteria to distinguish between those who are sincere and those who are not. This is why Zarruq insists on integrating jurisprudence with Sufi practice, maintaining a careful balance between being a Sufi and following juridical norms.

Restricting Access to Sufi Authority

Zarruq insisted that his disciples be jurists first, then Sufis (rather than Sufis first, then jurists), in accord with the principle that "the mark of those who are sincere is that they evaluate what is most important and place the most important point foremost."[27] Reform-oriented saints should emphasize the general rules and ritual observances as primary, and delve after esoteric truths or spiritual experiences as a subsidiary enterprise. This is to establish a community of followers who will keep this balance, not just among themselves but in society as a whole. Rules are for the general public, while Sufi practices are specific for a smaller group that accepts what is required for the public but goes beyond it. "To establish prohibitions against forbidden actions, it is necessary to specify legal rulings among the general population. That is more important than Sufis' protecting themselves from denunciation on account of their practices.... Legal and pious actions (*aʿmāl*) are for the believers in general; spiritual states (*aḥwāl*) are for the initiates, virtuous benefits are for the steadfast worshippers, and subtle insights are for the contemplatives. Each of these expressions is nourishment for the group of people who can listen and understand them. Why lay claim to something you cannot possibly digest?"[28]

Zarruq means to limit who can claim access to Sufi devotional practices. Just as the domain of jurisprudence is wider than Sufi practice and more general, so the training of jurists must take precedence over the particular training of Sufis. Further, Sufis must engage in juridical training first and only subsequently engage in devotional practices. In this way can those few Sufis who achieve recognition as saints enact their role in a way that is socially useful and spiritually insulated against corruption. "It is a principle that sharing in a common *root* necessitates sharing in a common *ruling*. Jurisprudence and Sufi practice are intimate partners. Both point to the regulations commanded by Allah and the rights Allah asserts over creatures. Both derive from a single root cause, and both are subject to the ruling of the same principle in determining their completeness or incompleteness. Neither one is worthier than the other in regards to their goal."[29] The two disciplines may be equivalent with regard to their "root" but they are not equal in their scope. Jurisprudence must take precedence. Even though being a Sufi is more demanding and in many ways more rewarding, jurisprudence is more socially useful and more universally applicable.

Zarruq concludes that the juridical saint should keep this distinction explicit. He should not expect to directly influence issues of public order as a saint. Jurisprudence is pursued to establish legislation, while being a Sufi is the search for inner completion. One should never use the claim to inner perfection as a way to claim a position of social standing. This tendency is what makes sainthood a dangerous institution. Although Sufi devotion is an authentic expression of Islam, people's adherence to it can and will introduce inauthentic innovations (*bidʿa*). "No true claim has ever come into existence without being confronted with an opposing false claim, or without being infiltrated by inauthentic elements, or without its being made to seem like a falsehood. All of these [subsequent deviations] serve the purpose of manifesting the truth of the original and the power of its exclusive claim to reality ... for all who inherit a spiritual truth are tried by the truth they inherit.... The followers of the path [Sufis] are burdened first with common people exerting power over them, and second with the honor that common people confer on them, and then by both together! ... So if you desire to follow this path, get used to ardor and trials."[30] It is precisely in expectation of such trials and false claims to sanctity that Zarruq urges his fellows to be clear about roots and principles. They can regulate the practices of the Sufi communities and set a standard for judging its practitioners as authentic or misled. "It is crucial to govern a discipline strictly by its principles, because they control its controversial points, explain its meanings, make known its foundations, and refute errors arising from those who claim to represent it illegitimately. The principles guide those who consider it deeply, appoint truth to those who dispute about it, and support the proof of those who debate its truth.... Anyone can deduce the principles of any discipline from the various practices that comprise it."[31]

At this point, Zarruq subtly justifies his whole project of reform. He is the anonymous "anyone" of his own text, who takes great pains to deduce the principles of being a Sufi in an innovative form. Although "anyone" can do this, Zarruq notes that earlier generations of Sufis did not bother to do so. Only later generations perceived the need to explicitly enunciate the principles. In later generations, the branches of practice have become more elaborate and more distanced from their source of inspiration, leading to shallowness of understanding. To sharpen again the keen edge of perception within a discipline, later generations need to extract its principles and write them out explicitly. Just as Usuli jurists turned to this project in the medieval period, Zarruq affirms that saints and the Sufis who follow them must engage in self-correction and renewal in the early modern period.

Zarruq proposed an intellectual upheaval among Sufis. He urged his contemporaries to discard spiriteÈl *taqlīd*, or imitation of past customs, even those instituted by respected teachers and revered spiritual guides. All must now be subject to the scrutiny of intellectual discrimination and measured by explicit principles. Aware that he is calling for an overturning of accepted notions and that he is courting strong opposition, Zarruq summoned Imām Mālik to justify his claims. "By Allah, how excellent is Imām Mālik when he said, 'Since the disciplines of knowledge are truly gifts bestowed by the divine One, given freely to those with God-given capabilities, it is likely that Allah saved up for later generations issues that were difficult for the earlier scholars. I seek refuge in Allah from those who are jealous and slam closed the doors of justice, averting their gaze from virtuous qualities!' How amazing is [Imām Mālik's] exposition!"[32] Zarruq took refuge behind the unassailable reputation of Imām Mālik to divert the accusation that his attention to principles is itself a "misleading innovation." He buttressed his position by recommending that the Sufi practice emulation (*iqidāʾ*) of a saintly guide only after examining his method of training and testing his reputation. This contrasts with blind obedience (*taqlīd*) of a spiritual guide regardless of principles and their criteria of authenticity.

In this project of reform, Zarruq claimed to emulate the example of Shaykh Abū al-Ḥasan al-Shādhilī, for his spiritual style is especially suitable for the devotion of an Usuli. In Zarruq's imagination, the Usuli is someone who is especially bold and restless, who insists on apprehending even the subtlest spiritual truth through the intellect. "The Usuli concentrates on analyzing faith through the instrument of reliable knowledge and thereby realizing certainty, until he can see the truth with his own eyes. By these means, realization of the ultimate reality arises within himself from his own deep comprehension. In this way, he advances or holds back according to the measure of reality that he really grasps. He never hesitates, for he is trained spiritually by that which he firmly comprehends in himself. For that reason, he is at ease from the beginning of his training until the end, and arrives at spiritual realization in the shortest stretch of time."[33]

The Usuli never has to reject the intellect, for he is trained by what he knows and knowing more means being trained more in spiritual humility. The Usuli never has to accept practices on the authority of someone else's experience, for he refers the practices back to their principles and understands them at the root source. Zarruq claims that the Shādhilī method is exceptional, for it is founded on one single source (*aṣl*), while other methods rely on multiple sources. The Shādhilī root source is "abandoning of selfish calculation in deference to the true One" (*isqāṭ al-tadbīr ma*ᶜ *al-ḥaqq*).[34] All the sources of Sufi training actually trace back to this single source, but only the Shādhilī community (especially that of Ibn ᶜAṭāʾillah and those who follow him) insists on the uniqueness and fundamental irreducibility of this source. Just as Zarruq claims that all definitions of "being a Sufi" trace back to sincerity, so he asserts that all spiritual methods can be reduced to this single source, abandoning selfish calculation.

This assertion allows Zarruq to describe the variety of Sufi methods and to explain them away. There are different styles of Sufi practice suitable for different classes of people; the cause of this variation is that there are different kinds of virtuous people who advocate different types of commendable actions.[35] Zarruq explicates this variation with a Qurʾānic verse that lists the nine types of virtuous person and assigns a special name to each type.[36] Yet this broad list of spiritual methods does not mean that Zarruq accepts the diversity that jostled around him. Even of those Sufis who practiced with sincerity and behaved without the norms of legal rectitude, Zarruq insisted that an Usuli spirituality was the purest and most effective. The era made a reformist return to principles necessary, and in Zarruq's analysis it was the Shādhilī method that embodied that return.

This return was effected through texts, through spiritual training, and through a personal orientation toward scholarship and learning. Zarruq insists that the sincere disciple read al-Ghazālī's *Iḥyā*ʾ and al-Makki's *Qūt al-Qulūb*, for they contain an approach that tempers Sufi devotion with juridical concern for outer rectitude. They are suitable for "a jurist who is concerned with the extended and profound meaning of words [of divine commands]," which Zarruq felt the real saint should be.[37] However, these texts were not helpful when read without a saintly guide who could teach them. The way of al-Ghazālī tends to stress pious works too much. To stress worship and asceticism is to seek to realize *iḥsān* through the second half of the Prophet's answer to Gabriel ("to worship God as if God sees you"), rather than the more direct way through illumination ("to worship God as if you see God"). This second way is the method of the Shādhilī community, especially those who follow Ibn ᶜAṭāʾillah with an Usuli orientation.

Taking initiation with such a saintly guide, Zarruq argued, was crucial to reforming Sufi devotion on a society-wide scale. "To subdue and control the self by means of a single root source, to which one can always refer in knowledge and action, is necessary to check the urge toward diversity and disintegration."[38] Initiation with a guide and training under his guidance prevents the disintegration of the self. Further, disintegration of society is prevented by insistence on a saintly guide who is "ruled by principle" and himself refers to one source: the revelatory word as brought by the Prophet. Such a reform of Sufi practices is necessary, Zarruq argues, because "preserving public order is obligatory, and protecting the common good in society is necessary."[39]

Zarruq admitted that mild variation in Sufi practice was natural and even beneficial. Yet he judged the variation in his time as discord and disintegration. By advocating a return to "principles" in Sufi practice, he hoped to unify Sufis within a single spiritual method. If that was not possible, he hoped to reform a single Sufi community by curbing of "excesses" in their particular practices. Toward that lesser goal, the second half of *The Principles of Being a Sufi* identifies practices that have only ambiguous legitimacy and thus bring harm, although their practitioners imagine them to be virtuous. These include any type of ascetic piety that involves excessive opposition to the self, leading to opposition to the intellect and the pursuit of knowledge.[40] On the other hand, he condemns Sufi practices that rely on speculation, such as alchemy, numerology, astrology, or philosophy.[41] He questions all practices that place the saint in a position of public accolade and prominence. From this point of view, Zarruq is skeptical of public recitations of poetry and music, insisting that they follow strict guidelines that would eliminate public display of piety or ecstasy.[42] He is very subtle in criticizing any saint's bid for religious leadership or a saint's speaking out openly on issues of public politics. "Anything that is praised can be rightly blamed and anything that is blamed can be rightly praised; the key is balance and not transgressing appropriate limits…. Taking upon oneself leadership (*riyāsa*) has been praised as a virtuous quality when it leads to preserving order …but it has been blamed when it leads to personal pride and suppressing the rights of others. Similarly hunger has been praised when it leads to inner purity, but is has been blamed when it obscures clear thinking…. The key is balance and moderation."[43] From these broad issues, Zarruq narrows his scope to address minute details of Sufi practice, such as the conditions of group worship, methods of meditation, and style of vocal recitation. However, every detail comes up as an example to illustrate an abstract principle, true to his essay's initial premise.

Zarruq's essay on *The Principles of Being a Sufi* is not easy reading. It demands an intricate knowledge of juridical terminology and assumes that the reader will recognize established patterns of legal reasoning. Further, the form of presenting each principle as an independent guideline disguises Zarruq's overall argument. Rather, Zarruq's reformist argument is present in each principle, in an abstract and decentralized presentation. He relates intellectual principles to one's internal orientation rather than providing concrete rules to follow. Therefore, Zarruq saw the need to translate his principles in a more concrete form, in very specific guidelines that would be suitable for disciples whom his reform orientation attracted.

For this purpose, Zarruq wrote a simpler treatise that became far more popular among his followers than the hyperborean principles. *The Sources of the Way* answered the need of average disciples, and Hamza Yusuf has recently translated it into English. Yet it still demanded a fairly high level of intellectual sophistication from beginning disciples, showing that Zarruq meant his disciples to have already studied the basics of law and scriptural disciplines before even considering entrance into this reformist Sufi orientation.[44] His primary follower, Muḥammad al-Kharrūbī, explains the purpose of the sources in his commentary that helped to spread this text. "Shaykh Zarruq has said, 'there are five basic sources of our way.' By 'sources' (*uṣūl*) he means foundational sources, upon which he bases the building of his spiritual method. No building is set up before the foundation is laid, for that reason [he specifies the sources] so that the Sufis can train themselves by them and progress with them until they comprehend the presence of the generous One. By 'our way' he indicates the soundness of his spiritual method and the verifiability of his lineage. This is a Shādhilī method, and there is no doubt that his lineage is Shādhilī. By 'five basic sources' he specifics the five sources that are most basic and common to all Sufi methods."[45]

In Zarruq's exposition, the five foundational sources of the Sufi Way are: staying conscious of Allah inwardly and outwardly (*taqwā*), following the example of the Prophet in word and deed (*itbāᶜ al-sunna*), turning away from people and things (*al-iᶜrāḍ ᶜan al-khalq*), being content with Allah despite changes in your condition (*al-riḍāʾ*), and referring all affairs back to Allah (*al-rujūᶜ ilā Allah*). Each of these five sources is an expression of sincerity in facing Allah, yet their description is far more concrete and direct than in *The Principles of Being a Sufi*. Each of these five sources unfolds into a number of recommendations, prohibitions, and warnings that should shape the disciple's actions in the world. These include not only guidelines for "right conduct" but also guidelines for suspicion and investigation. Zarruq offers five conditions by which one should reject a supposed saintly guide and judge him as a hypocrite. In his way, Zarruq tried to write his reformist orientation into even the simplest guidelines for basic behavior.

These five foundational sources were the subject of many letters that Zarruq addressed to his various communities of disciples in urban centers across North Africa.[46] He restated their content in various permutations and urged his followers to read *The Sources* at least once a day until they imprinted the treatise's contents firmly on the surface of their selves. His followers gathered these various letters together and circulated them with Zarruq's *The Sources* as a text and commentary by the very author.[47] These guidelines would hold the disciple within the basic framework of his reformist Sufi method until the time when they could read *The Principles* and ground their behaviors in the intellectual certainty he promises.

Grounding Principles in Spiritual Empowerment

In his innovative use of principles, Zarruq tried to evaluate inner religious experience through external, intellectually knowable standards. He defined sincerity by its external signs. He also tried to translate these principles into a less intellectual form by giving his disciples and followers guidelines to follow in their behavior, both in finding a spiritual master, studying with him, and engaging in devotional exercises at his hand. He approached these themes in terms of "employment" by suggesting how sincere disciples should turn their time to good use. Zarruq wrote about inner transformations that a disciple should expect while employing one's time in devotion in his reformist spiritual method. He promises that employment will lead to empowerment. If one accepts his discipline as a juridical Sufi, one can achieve a level of integral sainthood embodied in a life of teaching, judging, and guiding in a reform-oriented Sufi community.

To this end, one year after writing *The Principles of Being a Sufi,* Zarruq completed the text *Aid to the Needy who Turn to toward the Path of Empowerment and Success*.[48] In this text, he reverses the terms of his prior analysis: instead of writing on the principles of being a Sufi, he writes about the process of becoming a principled Sufi. He tries to illustrate what a spiritual life ruled by his principles would look like from the inside. In other words, he argued that a life ruled by his principles would affect not only the outward aspect of religious behavior governed by legality, but would also revive authentic spiritual experience. Zarruq's followers gave this work an alternative title that reveals the intimate relation between this work and the one that immediately preceded it: *Grounding the Principles and Founding Sources for Achieving the Benefits of One who has Arrived at Realization*.[49] If the first work describes the outward appearance of the principles, the second describes how Sufi disciples can make their hearts receptive to the principles, and illustrates what devotional exercises may become once these principles are firmly grounded in the soil of the heart.

This work consists of guidance for the inner life of the disciple, so that the outer life can fully embody the principles Zarruq had enunciated. Anyone who plants the principles in the heart will "grow empowered and be granted success" as a saint who joins the outer structure of religious law and custom with inner illumination of insight into ultimate reality. The introduction to this text reveals its basic outline: "There is no true reality except Allah … and no guidance except to one who takes shelter in the gracious proximity of Allah. Such a person conjoins legitimate religious custom with realizing ultimate reality, after purifying the self of all ugliness and meanness, opening a safe and secure path to follow. Such a person stands with the true One on the wide comfortable expanse of personal realization, with an intellect keen and aware, with a heart clear-sighted and repentant toward its Lord. Such a person puts each phenomenon in its rightful place, realizing knowledge and executing action on their firm foundations. Such an achievement is so rare in these times, especially in certain places among particular communities!"[50] As the introduction proceeds, Zarruq pictures the heart as the center of the human being, as the organ of insight and discernment. If fully realized, it is tranquil with "clear sight," illumined by the light of a keen intellect and resting on the firm foundation of personal experience. It is like rich soil from which fruitful plants may grow.

The heart is the foundation of good and evil. The life or death of the heart is the key to all benefit or harm that may befall you. Whoever has no life in the heart has no means of warding off harm or grasping benefit. "Some hearts are lifeless, though persons who carry them may move and act in the world until the end of their days. A heart is dead that does not accept warnings and reminders from the signs of Allah in the world. Such a heart cannot see its own nature, let alone follow religious customs or treat others with virtue."[51] On the contrary, if life resides in the heart, life calls the heart to wake up and stay aware with reminders and warnings. "Other hearts are pulsing with life. The owners of a vivacious heart are constantly aware of their own limited and contingent natures; they are prepared for any calamity or blessing, and speak with wisdom (*ḥikma*)."[52] Sufis are those who realize, before it is too late, that their hearts are sick with a deficiency of sincerity. The traditions that have developed around worship, devotion, and meditation that go by the name of Sufi practice are the cures available for such sickness. "Between these extremes are those hearts afflicted by sickness and disease. Their disease progresses with each changing state and condition in life, throwing up obstacles and creating hesitations. Such obstacles in the heart prevent people from achieving their potential. Persons with diseased hearts cringe in pain from the very mention of what ails them! Cures are designed for just such people, who must be prepared for the effort and toil of curing the heart, in hopes that their lives will be firmly established and their illness arrested."[53] A saint is someone whose heart is sound and healthy (either because they were never sick or managed to arrest their disease and recuperate). Such saints can serve as doctors, for only they know what it feels like to have sound hearts, and only they have sufficient experience with the means to treat the heart.

After getting the attention of his readers with this diagnosis, Zarruq tries to lighten the language of his prose. He does not burden his listeners with complex remedies and intricate rituals that set his particular regime off from those of other masters. Rather, his reformist vision guides him to articulate what he has distilled as the essence of all Sufi remedies. As his guide, al-Ḥaḍramī, had taught, the usual remedies of "Sufi training in the current sense of the word" are no longer valid and beneficial. Zarruq tries to avoid the usual remedies by specifying the essential components of any potential remedy. The essential ingredient is sincerity, and it takes three forms depending on one's condition. When reviewing the past, sincerity expresses itself as repentance (*tawba*). When facing the present moment, sincerity expresses itself as steadfastness (*istiqāma*). And when turning toward the future, sincerity is expressed in wariness that realization has not yet fully arrived (*war*^{c}). "Repentance is the key to the cage. Wariness is departing the confinement. Steadfastness is restoration and reconciliation. Stick to practicing the principles and enacting the legal rulings. Don't practice what is based on hearsay, wild tales or fabrications. Pay no attention to stories that others tell, except for what increases your power to achieve what you have intended, so that you do not get caught up in images and self-deception. Be clear that you provide a path that returns to a principle and a root source upon which your spiritual state relies."[54] These three dimensions of sincerity lead one back to the root source of sincerity, allowing one to grasp it and realize it in practice. Zarruq is quick to stress that "practice" is not limited to certain rituals, particular meditations, affiliation with a particular Sufi lineage, or loyalty to an individual saint. "Practice" is much wider than that. It includes forms of worship, examination of habits, nurturing virtuous personal qualities, and all dealings with other people. Practice is an employment, a sincere use of one's time in every circumstance, rather than a ritual that separates one set of actions from another habitual or worldly set of actions.

This is a guidebook that seeks to produce neither saints nor people who are so virtuous that their society can easily single them out as saints. His guidelines point to the conclusion that any such "singling out" of the saint, either by personal attitude or capitulation to the social demands of others, is a sign of insincerity. Full spiritual realization is to be carefully placed in the future tense. This is because the saint, like other people, is not preserved from error (*ma*^{c}*sūm*) as a Prophet is. Therefore, legal rulings and religious customs are the only firm foundation for a saint's social behavior, since they derive by authentic principles from the root source of the Prophet's behavior, which was preserved from error. The saint must have the outward comportment of a jurist and must continually engage in scholarship, teaching, and learning to avoid capitulating to the cultural logic of sanctity.

True to the interior focus of this text, Zarruq does not make these pronouncements explicitly; after all, he had argued these points in exoteric language in his previous writing on *The Principles*. However, this work on sincerity and inward spiritual states points out the need for such principles, which will lead the struggling Sufi back to jurisprudence. Zarruq is content to hint at this balance of scriptural knowledge and personal experience through quoting the early Sufi master Junayd of Baghdad.

> Al-Junayd said, "It is true that there is no spiritual completeness without knowledge, and no efficacy of knowledge except with action. So don't listen to anyone who diverts you from knowledge to action, or claims that one is more important than the other, or that one is independent of the other!" You tell me, by God, if knowledge fills your time and occupies your attention, then when will you ever stand in the presence of God with sincerity and truth? And if you

> devote yourself to action, when will you ever reach the state of perfecting your actions? [As the Prophet Muhammad is reported to have said] "Act toward this world as if you will live forever, and act toward the next world as if you will die tomorrow."[55]

With this quote, Zarruq closes his text, asserting clearly that spirituality must lead to action in the world. However, this must be action that reinforces the logic of juridical decisions, not action that conforms to the cultural logic of sanctity as it proliferates in society.

Employing a Sincere Spirit

The reform program of Ahmad Zarruq had a heavy theoretical dimension to it, but theory did not exhaust his resources. Zarruq also wrote in a practical spirit, to train actual disciples. He wrote a litany of prayers and blessings that he compiled for his own use and for the training of his followers. For his followers, this is the most basic of his writings; it constituted their *waẓīfa*, their "employment." This is the literal meaning of the litany's title, and it reveals its function in the hands of disciples. Reciting the litany was how they occupied their time for beneficial results, the way one might seek employment in a trade or craft.

Composing the litany was no small undertaking in Zarruq's eyes. A litany is the most basic literary and devotional product of a saint; its recitation defines his community of followers, separating them from other Sufis and distinguishing them from other Muslims. Sufi litanies, then, were major sources of "innovation" in religious custom; though they seemed like a pious practice on the surface, they could become the catalyst for partisanship, exaggerated loyalty to a particular saint, or chauvinistic aloofness from other Muslims. Such litanies were also known as *wird* (plural *awrād*) or *ḥizb* (plural *aḥzāb*). Both terms convey the importance of a litany in group formation. *Wird* comes from the word for a spring; it conjures up the image of a source from which inspiration wells up. The saint who invents the *wird* and bestows it to his followers is like a spring of clear water, giving sustenance in the parched world of social intercourse. The litany itself is like a boundless source of inspiration; though recited daily it never exhausts its reservoir of blessing. Just as a village will grow up around a source of water, a devotional community grows up around the *wird* of a saint. Just as water sources are important social resources that can lead to disputes and competition, the recitation of a *wird* creates a distinct social group among Sufis who revere a particular saint. Further, the term *ḥizb* denotes a litany. *Ḥizb* can refer to a long portion of the Qurʾān divided into segments for ease of recitation, but its root meaning is "dividing into factions." The litanies recited by Abū al-Ḥasan al-Shādhilī, for instance, were known as *ḥizb*.

Zarruq points out forcefully in his principles that one of the crises of sainthood among Muslims was the way that factions formed around the allegiance to saints, causing distortions in practice and providing a catalyst for political ambitions. Although the *wird* or *ḥizb* was not in itself forbidden, its recitation could easily lead to practices or attitudes that Zarruq felt were forbidden. For example, love for a saint and loyalty to him, displayed by zealous recitation of his *wird*, could replace the study of religious knowledge. To ward off this impulse, Zarruq did not call his litany by either term. He called it instead a *waẓīfa*, an "employment," meaning something that "fills your time and occupies your attention."[56] In this case, the pursuit of knowledge was also a person's *waẓīfa*; like any employment, it could be profitably beneficial or harmfully distracting.

Zarruq crafted his *waẓīfa* carefully. It had to come from an authentic source and be used under the condition of explicit principles. Zarruq maintained that he "found" his *waẓīfa* rather than authored it. Zarruq argued that just as actions must adhere to the juridical rules based on the actions of the Prophet, one's prayers and litanies must follow the words of the Prophet. The words should not come from one's own inspired imagination and should not express one's saintly authority in that way. Rather, one should simply repeat the prayers and blessings that the Prophet Muhammad said. Zarruq combed through hadith reports, searching for words of prayer that Muhammad had uttered, rather than delving into his own heart for innovative expressions of love and dependence on Allah. He compiled his litany rather than composing it.

Zarruq's attitude toward his *waẓīfa* may appear to repudiate creativity and imagination, which were always prime vehicles for saintly authority. If not an absolute repudiation, it was surely a tight restriction on the operations of imagination. Zarruq felt, however, that such restrictions kept him in close contact with the spirit of the Prophet; he felt it insured a saint's authenticity. He called his litany *The Ark of Deliverance* (*safīnat al-najāt*) in a deliberate invocation of Noah. His nailing together a boat in the face of an impending disaster was not "creative" in any formal or artistic sense. Yet, seen from the perspective of sincerity, wariness, and intuition of social crisis around him, his composition of common planks and beams was a supreme act of craftsmanship. Zarruq's planks were bits of text culled from the vast collection of hadith reports that were as common among scholars as wooden beams were among shipbuilders.

Zarruq insisted that the Prophet Muhammad himself had given this title to his work. During one of his pilgrimages to Makka, Zarruq journeyed to Madīna to visit the Prophet's tomb. Upon arriving, he separated from his companions to take a siesta near the tomb, and he experienced a vision: "I saw the Prophet. I was [at his tomb] when his form appeared to me. So I recited the litany to him, and he said, 'Make this very litany your *waẓīfa*—don't add a single word to it and don't subtract anything' … The Prophet said 'What did you entitle this work?' I said something or other, but the Prophet ordered me, 'Call it *The Ark of Deliverance for One who Takes Refuge with God*.'"[57] When Zarruq woke up, he came running back to his companions, overjoyed. Zarruq's followers told this story of how he managed to finalize the composition of the *waẓīfa* in a way that sealed its authority, from the authority of a vision of the Prophet himself. They say that Zarruq stopped abridging the *waẓīfa* after this visionary conversation with the Prophet, for he had been busy editing it previously, adding and taking away certain expressions. His followers differed over whether this authentication happened in a dream while Zarruq was sleeping or in a vision while he was awake. Yet the story spread among them along with the recitation of the *waẓīfa*.[58]

Zarruq felt that the most sincere way to gain intimacy with the Prophet was to repeat his very words. This was an idea that competed with other more captivating means of gaining proximity with the spirit of the Prophet. In the few generations preceding Zarruq, the importance of reciting blessings and praise upon the spirit of the Prophet gained increasing importance; such recitations became even more popular than a simple *wird*. The basic benediction such as *ṣalāt ʿalā al-nabī* formed the basis for a genre of litany that grew increasingly elaborate and invoked blessings and salvation upon the Prophet in innovative cadences, multiplied by images from the natural world or enmeshed in rhyme. There was a crucial correspondence between this growing genre of litany and the rise of sharifian Sufis who claimed authority as saints based, at least partly, on the fact that they were genealogical descendants of the Prophet's family.[59] Other Sufis, who claimed no such genealogical proximity, saw the invocation of blessings upon the Prophet as a method of spiritual training that could dispense with a living master, since the Prophet's spirit would serve as master and guide.[60]

Zarruq discussed the possibility that invoking blessings upon the Prophet Muhammad was a way to secure spiritual training direb¨ely from the Prophet himself, without a living saintly guide. Al-Ḥaḍramī had recommended this technique, as had one of his masters, Ibn Mūsā al-Musharriʿ al-Yamanī. Zarruq does not contradict his master by denying the technique. However, he defines it in a limiting way. "My masters recommend that 'one who cannot find a master to train him spiritually and advance his state of sanctity and show him the way to reach [the presence of] Allah should constantly invoke blessings and praise upon the Prophet.' What they mean is that such a person should train [him or herself] with the wholesome comportment of the Prophet and through this grow into the noblest of virtues and advance to the loftiest level of completeness until arriving at the most brilliant presence of the great One, the One exalted."[61] In this subtle redefinition, Zarruq steers his disciples away from the idea that a direct connection with the Prophet's spirit is possible and that invoking his blessings is a shortcut to spiritual training or a means to achieve a vision of the Prophet. Instead, invoking blessings is only a way to take on the comportment of the Prophet and to behave as he behaved, that is, in conformity with his example as enshrined in jurisprudence. Conforming to juridical norms, derived as they were from the Prophet's own behavior, was the only way to gain Allah's satisfaction. Love for the Prophet himself should not become so intense that it collapses all concern for the Prophet's example. In contrast, he urged that study of scriptural texts was the primary way to gain intimacy with the Prophet. In this way, Zarruq offered his *waẓīfa* to disciples as a tool for

Sufi training. Not everyone could concentrate upon the hadith texts, with their textual intricacies, obscure meanings, and fragmented narratives. In the form of the *waẓīfa*, disciples could recite those bits from the hadith that the Prophet had recited as prayers to Allah. Again, Zarruq based his authority as a saint on his authenticity as a scholar, a strategy to further his reform agenda.

Zarruq wrote commentaries on other Sufi litanies, such as the litanies (*aḥzāb*) of Shaykh al-Shādhilī, exhibiting his subtle reformist strategy. He could not question the authenticity of these litanies, since they were clearly attributed to al-Shādhilī and had become widespread among his followers. However, Zarruq did question the uses to which his contemporaries put these litanies. He also expressed doubts over the ways they interpreted some of the more obscure phrases and expressions in *The Litany of the Sea* in particular. This litany includes verses from the Qurʾān that voice the detached letters (*muqaṭṭaʿāt*), which have often invited speculative interpretations. In addition, the litany was reputed by many Shādhilīs to have almost magical properties: "It is not recited in any place without security reigning there—if it had been with the inhabitants of Baghdad, the Tartars [Mongols] would not have conquered the city."[62] Zarruq's commentaries on these litanies approved of their originator and cautioned against their unregulated use.[63] He intended his commentaries to act like insulation, protecting the litanies against speculative interpretations and illegitimate uses. Similar magical and protective claims were also made about the famous litany of prayers upon the Prophet Muḥammad by al-Jazūlī. It is conceivable that Zarruq wrote a commentary on al-Jazūlī's *Dalāʾil al-Khayrāt* as a form of "insulation" again its misuse or misunderstanding.[64]

Circles of Reformist Disciples

Although in retrospect it appears that Zarruq's strongest contribution to the reform movement within Sufi communities was contained in his writings, he also strove to create a network of disciples who would embody his reformist teachings. He knew that books without an audience were a waste of effort. He wrote his vast output of texts, often with multiple texts on a single topic, for the use of widely scattered communities of disciples. His disciples regarded him as their saintly guide, the center of their world, and the source of their spiritual development. In turn, Zarruq encouraged them to become centers of their own circle of disciples. After initiating disciples in urban spaces across North Africa, he urged them to stay in their local communities as teachers and jurists. The circle of his disciples would be an expanding circle with many centers, held in focus by his reformist vision rather than by loyalty to his person alone.

As his reformist writings indicate, Zarruq approached the role of "saintly guide" in a significantly different way than many of his contemporaries. His ritual of offering of initiation to disciples tends to downplay the role of the master, just at the moment when the disciple is ostensibly submitting to the master's authority. As Zarruq urged the initiate to repent of past failings, he, as the master, would make his own vow of repentance in parallel with the disciple.[65] This is a firm denial of the ideal of an inerrant master and a repudiation of the charisma that many writers assert is the basis of authority between master and disciple.

Zarruq asserts that his role as saintly guide is more akin to that of a teacher in the scholarly disciplines. His training of disciples is more a matter of advice than command. Training is really a cooperative endeavor between master and disciple, since both share an equal place as subjects of the *sharīᶜa* and the norms of religious law. The disciple should thoroughly examine and test a potential guide before offering allegiance to him, and be on guard for any mistakes or heedlessness in regard to religious custom. He should follow the guidance of a saint, but on the condition that this guidance has a root source in scripture and can be deduced via an intellectual principle from that source. For one cannot trust that one's saintly guide is inerrant. "If one asserts that true completeness (*kamāl*) is a quality of the true One alone, this requires the affirmation that everyone other than Allah is incomplete and imperfect. There cannot exist any completion except that Allah makes it complete through Allah's completeness without necessity or coercion. When regarding people, incompleteness and imperfection are the rule, and [apparent] completeness is the exception. By this principle, anyone who claims to be complete and perfect in himself or herself has made a false claim.... If someday a complete person appears, it is only by Allah's bounty and not by any necessity of that person's being. Until then, the rule is the rule and one should expect incompleteness."[66] In this principle, Zarruq offers a pithy critique of any saint's claim to have absolute authority over his followers or any inerrant insight into the truth. Without demolishing hope in a trustworthy human guide, Zarruq cannot emphasize too strongly the need to uphold the *sharīᶜa*.

As a guide himself, Zarruq tried to unite several distinct roles as a saint acting out the paradigm of *al-Jāmiᶜ*. He welded together scholastic, juridical, and spiritual training. In technical terminology, he tried to be a guide in *taᶜlīm* (teaching knowledge), *tarbiya* (disciplining ethics), and *tarqiya* (cultivating spirituality) all at once, so that these various dimensions of training would not become separated. In this program, he intensified the practices of the juridical saints he had known in Marinid Fes, especially al-Qūrī. The madrasa was the environment in which he would train disciples, as they had. He carefully avoided the style of spiritual training that would uproot disciples from their habitual life, like sending them into isolated retreats or setting them to humbling manual labor. Such approaches did not ignore scholarly training, but downplayed it by distinguishing between basic training (in literacy, scripture, and jurisprudence) and "spiritual opening," which almost never occurred in the context of scholarly endeavor.

Zarruq's training of disciples revolved necessarily around reading and studying books. These included a wide variety of texts, starting with basic scholarship and jurisprudence. He used his own "commentaries" on juridical works as teaching tools and lecture notes. For those students who showed sensitivity to devotional practices and an aptitude for them, he would introduce his own writings on spiritual development. These contain numerous references to other Sufi texts and advice on when and how to study them to reinforce one's allegiance to the outward rule of law as well as to increase one's inward illumination.

These moments of advice on reading are crucial in understanding Zarruq's reformist orientation, for they are rare in the writings of saintly guides. Zarruq admitted that books might, in some cases, even replace a living guide, especially since he felt that authentic saints were so rare in his era. One could rely on books for guidance, especially if one had "a sincere companion" with whom to read and share observations. Such a companion could play the role of a guide, Zarruq felt, by keeping one's interpretations and actions in line with religious custom. Because of the dangers involved in individual practice, Zarruq advised that a fully realized spiritual guide is preferable (if one is to be found).[67] Questioning of the "indispensability" of the saintly guide is rare among Sufis. It led Zarruq to catalogue the various kinds of Sufi texts that were available and to give explicit guidelines about which texts were suitable for what purposes. His writings constitute one of the most detailed descriptions of genres in Sufi literature. "Goodness has many different dimensions. Therefore people by necessity consider many different things, even contradictory things, to be good. Each thing considered good can lead a person to acquire some measure of goodness. From this principle, it is clear why different groups of Sufis have different styles [of devotional texts].... One should evaluate each type of Sufi practice according to its own root source in its own specific context."[68] He then details the different kinds of people who are Sufis and the different texts suitable for them: for the common people, the books of al-Muḥāsibī; for jurists, Ibn al-Ḥājj's *al-Madkhal*; for hadith scholars, Abū Bakr ibn al-ᶜArabī's *al-Sirāj*; for pious worshipers, al-Ghazālī's *Minhāj al-ᶜĀbidīn*; for those given to devotional exercises, al-Qushayrī's *Risāla*; for ascetic renunciants, *Qūt al-Qulūb* and *Iḥyā᾽ ᶜUlūm al-Dīn*; for philosophical sages, the books of Ibn al-ᶜArabī al-Ḥātimī; for logicians, Ibn Sabᶜīn's writings; for naturalists, al-Būnī's book *Asrār*; and for Usulis, "there is a way of being a Sufi that al-Shādhilī established through his own spiritual search."[69]

This catalogue of Sufis and their texts tries to include everyone, and it reveals Zarruq in his broadest and most open-minded outlook. Yet when it came to training his own disciples, he clearly did not approve of all these approaches and the texts upon which they relied. He listed "the Usuli" last. This is because he considered himself to be a juridical saint, dedicated to a method of training to produce only juridical Sufis. He also listed this category last because he felt that the Usuli's approach was the keenest and most authentic. An Usuli approach to being a Sufi would be the most direct path to sincerity and would avoid many of the pitfalls into which he saw Sufis of the other types falling. At other points in his writings, Zarruq warns his disciples against relying on many of the texts in his catalogue. He notes that prudence requires avoiding certain texts that are extreme and warns against "reading both Ibn al-Jawzi's *Talbīs Iblīs* [which attacks Sufi practices] and Ibn al-ᶜArabī al-Ḥātimī's *al-Futūḥāt al-Makkīyya*, and indeed all his writings [which assert a speculative and philosophical Sufi style].... One must be on guard against any anomalous statement in these texts, any exaggeration, any aloofness from the common beliefs, and any opposition to scholarly knowledge. If readers do not possess these three conditional qualities (having a trustworthy innate faculty of discernment, having a sound natural disposition toward the truth, and accepting only what is clear on the surface without accepting anything else) then they will surely come to ruin by examining these texts."[70] He warns his disciples not to read these texts not just because some statements in them may seem heretical, but also because they will become entangled in pointless arguments. They will be tempted to either advocate the ideas of the author or to denounce them. In either case, the disciple will transgress the bounds of juridical rectitude and endanger the delicate scaffolding of reform within Sufi communities that Zarruq has tried to build. He recalls the opinion of al-Qūrī in regards to Ibn al-ᶜArabī: "the best opinion is to assert no opinion."[71]

In cautioning against these texts, Zarruq also recommends others. Besides his own writings, Zarruq urges his disciples to read, memorize, and contemplate the *Wisdom Sayings* of Ibn ᶜAṭāʾillah. The *Wisdom Sayings* would come under his recommended reading for "Usuli" or juridical Sufis who claimed allegiance to al-Shādhilī: "for the Usuli, there is a way of being a Sufi that al-Shādhilī established." As we have seen, this brief collection of Wisdom Sayings was a central text for juridical Sufis, perhaps the central text after al-Ghazālī's *Iḥyāʾ*. The two texts represent different but complementary attempts to reconcile sainthood with the outer rectitude of Islamic law. Both did this by juxtaposing technical Sufi vocabulary with reports of the Prophet's teaching or with Qurʾānic phrases. While al-Ghazālī approached this project from the genre of the systematic theological treatise in discursive prose, Ibn ᶜAṭāʾillah had approached it from the genre of Wisdom Sayings, capturing insights with an almost poetic use of words. While al-Ghazālī produced a monumental opus in many volumes, Ibn ᶜAṭāʾillah produced a slim folio of just 262 minimalist maxims.

Their difference in form stemmed from their difference in intent. Al-Ghazālī intended to demonstrate how Sufi practices were contiguous with the scriptural religious disciplines and was indeed the heart that would revive the disciplines and keep them oriented toward justice and conscience. He wanted jurists and theologians to read his work and recognize that Sufi devotional practices were integral to Islam. In contrast, Ibn ᶜAṭāʾillah chose the genre of the Wisdom Sayings, which grew out of the intimate teachings of saints to their closest disciples. The genre began when disciples began to record the sayings of their masters, sayings that tried to capture the insights or metaphors of scripture in rhyming maxims. The rhyme would serve to ease their memorization and would sharpen the words to help them pierce through one's routine distraction (a bit like the cadences of the Qurʾān itself). By the twelfth century C.E., saintly guides set their sayings down in single volumes, to be circulated among disciples in a form more permanent than oral spontaneity. North Africa and Andalusia were fertile ground for this genre, as

Abū Madyan produced such a collection of Wisdom Sayings, along with Ibn al-ᶜArabī.

It was probably on the Wisdom Sayings of al Ibn al-ᶜArabī that Ibn ᶜAṭāʾillah modeled his composition. In his maxims, Ibn ᶜAṭāʾillah adopts much of the specialized terminology that Ibn al-ᶜArabī had developed and systematized. However, he discards any overt reliance on existential philosophy that Ibn al-ᶜArabī had employed to take this terminology (and the ethical training it was meant to incite) and ground it in a vision of cosmic wholeness. In a discursive introduction to his maxims, Ibn al-ᶜArabī noted that each was an expression of *ḥikma*, or wisdom, in understanding the created universe; this wisdom he equated with philosophy (*falsafa*) and drew a parallel between philosophers and prophets who are united in the quest for wisdom.[72] Ibn ᶜAṭāʾillah, by contrast, sets the wide range of this terminology against metaphors of the Qurʾān or images from the Prophet's teachings, in order to emphasize the ethical element of Sufi training and downplay any reliance on philosophy. He also tried to increase the authenticity of the Sufi tradition by stressing its roots in scriptural sources. Through his *Wisdom Sayings*, Ibn ᶜAṭāʾillah rephrased the intuitions of Ibn al-ᶜArabī in a form that could be accepted by jurists and juridically trained saints (for he himself was both). His composition won many admirers, because of its underlying intention and the beauty of its language.[73] There are many Shādhilīs who feel that these maxims represent the Qurʾān refracted into spiritual guidance, and some claim that if any Arabic verses other than the Qurʾān could be recited during prayer, the maxims of Ibn ᶜAṭāʾillah deserve that honor.[74]

With such rave reviews, the *Wisdom Sayings* rapidly became popular, not just among Egyptian adherents to the Shādhilī lineage, but among other branches of the lineage from Tunis to Morocco. As the text gained popularity as a tool for teaching and meditation, many Sufi scholars began to write commentaries on its maxims. Although Ibn ᶜAbbad was the first, Zarruq was the most prolific, having written approximately twenty distinct commentaries throughout his life on this single, slim text. If Ibn ᶜAbbad's sober commentary were the only commentary, Zarruq probably would have been content to teach through it alone; however, others had approached them from the angle of philosophy or speculative cosmology in ways that were suspicious to Zarruq. He summarizes these previous endeavors in his own commentaries. "The first to write a commentary on the *Ḥikam* [Wisdom Sayings] was Ibn ᶜAbbād. The second was Abū al-Mawāhib ibn Zaghdān who was born in Tunis and made his home in Egypt until he died in 882 [Hijri].[75] He had a great ability to discourse about the Sufis, only he never completed his book on the *Ḥikam*. He wrote about them in the way of subtle philosophical points and difficult expressions; I confess that I do not understand what his purpose was in that endeavor! The third I've heard of was the report that a man named al-Sanūn in Syria had written something about the *Ḥikam* in a manner of doctrinal theologians. That might be of some use, but I have never seen the text in order to assess for myself his style and approach. I have found some people in Bijāya with something they call a commentary, that they claim belongs to this al-Sanūn, but the writing is very weak, without proper Arabic grammar and without the true use of words in their original meaning."[76] Through his commentaries, Zarruq praised Ibn ᶜAbbād's commentary for being in harmony with "juridical Sufi" values. At the same time, he subtly sidelined others who tried to approach the *Ḥikam* from "less proper" angles. Only by keeping the *Ḥikam* tightly within the framework of "juridical Sufi" practice could Zarruq ensure that it would remain the primary teaching text of his reform-minded community.

Once Zarruq settled down permanently, many disciples traveled to gather around him for more intensive and protracted training. At the age of forty, Zarruq halted his peregrinations and settled in Misurāta, Libya, in 886 Hijri (1481 C.E.). This was a small town not far from Tarābulus (Tripoli), just inland from the coast, built up around an oasis and located at a point where caravan routes from the west angled into the Sahara for the arduous desert trek to the Nile valley. Alternatively, Misurāta was one of the first settled locales in Libya where travelers would alight after leaving Egypt on the westward journey. The port that served this town, Qaṣr Aḥmad, was an important point for pilgrims. It was a strategic location, in communication with Morocco and Egypt but distant from both zones. By settling in Misurāta, Zarruq showed that he had learned something from al-Zaytūnī about the importance of pilgrimage networks. Some of his primary disciples joined him at Misurāta, and he also gained followers from the community after marrying two local women.[77] He raised four sons here (curiously each named Aḥmad), and his eldest son was considered his disciple and a teacher in his own right.[78] Zarruq died at Misurāta in the year 899 Hijri (1494 C.E.), at the age of fifty-three.

At Misurāta, Zarruq continued to rebel against the cultural logic of sanctity by refusing to behave like a saint who aspired to lead a local community. He refused to build a *zāwiya* at his residence, although he did establish a madrasa.[79] He avoided acting out the role of administrative authority over his network of disciples. One letter he addressed to followers in a distant town clearly shows his hesitation to act out the role that others expected from a saint. "My brother, you have written requesting that some people be admitted into the circle [of our community]. That is not up to me, and not for me to decide for myself, my stubborn rebellious and overweening self. Rather, say to them, 'You must take refuge with Allah with your stated goals, and pray to Allah to provide some means and power for your goals to come into reality. For there is no refuge from Allah except with Allah. There is no restraining Allah's order except through Allah's compassion.'"[80] Instead of offering the petitioners initiation and entrance into his community of followers, Zarruq advised them to make the five "root sources" obligatory upon themselves. He highlighted certain necessary principles even as he constrained his own performance of authority.

In these many ways Zarruq tried to spark and institute a reform internal to Sufi communities across North Africa: through his writings, his relating the teachings and personality of al-Ḥaḍramī, and through his distinct style of training disciples.

Yet no matter how hard Zarruq tried to make his reform program clear and based on explicit principles, it rested on some inherent ambiguities. It depended on allowing the saint to straddle very different roles, as teacher, jurist, and spiritual guide. It depended on downplaying one's lineage as a source of identity and social prestige to emphasize the acquisition of knowledge. Ultimately, it relied upon the aspiration of the disciple to actually become a sincere and scholarly saint, rather than simply being related to one through affiliation, ritual connections, or simple devoted love. With goals so strident and standards so strict, it is not surprising that Zarruq's reform-oriented juridical Sufi training did not attract a large following. Not all those who were attracted to him personally as a saintly guide lived up to the ideals argued in his reformist writings or even accepted his arguments.

This is because his whole vision of reforming Sufi communities from within implied a biting critique of Zarruq's contemporaries. This critique is implicit in almost every moment of his writing and training, and often comes through quite explicitly. His reformist vision was not just a matter of clarifying Sufi practices from within its existing institutions, but also clarifying it over and against what Zarruq defined as sainthood corrupted by inauthentic religious practices. This element of critique meant questioning not only the practices of others but their underlying sincerity; it placed Zarruq and his followers in a precarious position in the middle of heated social and doctrinal conflict. The next two chapters, which make up Part IV, will document this struggle to assert the veracity of his reformist vision over and against the practices and personages of his contemporaries, especially in his home region of Morocco.

PART IV.
LAW

> You can imagine the jurist as the doorkeeper who guards the doorway to the king's chambers. In contrast, the realized Sufi is like the confidant who knows the king's most intimate secrets.[1]

ZARRUQ'S REFORM OF Sufi training and saintly conduct projected an idealized vision of order, which he thought was realizable. In this ideal, the jurist and Sufi worked in harmony to keep regular the flow of commands and insights from Allah, the king, to the public of the believing community. Zarruq continues his parable quoted above: "Whenever a Sufi begins to speak openly about the secrets of the king's personal chamber, the jurist will call out to him, 'You are nothing but a thief, a liar or an impudent interloper!' Only if the Sufi can then present a token or sign given to him by the king [to show their intimate relation] will the doorkeeper accept him and what he reports as authentic. If not, then the jurist's accusation stands as a sound judgment." Cooperation between the jurist chamberlain and the Sufi confidant ensures that messages from the king's inner chamber reach the assembly square of the public without distortion or manipulation.

However, the world around Zarruq did not conform to this projected harmony. Rulers were dethroned and their dynasties overthrown even though they had ruled on the basis of upholding Islamic law and supporting its protectors, the jurists. Genealogical descendants of the Prophet aspired to replace these rulers, and Sufi communities helped fuel and shape their aspirations. As the roles of religious authorities (jurists, Sufis, and *shurafāʾ*) were blended or their place in the hierarchy changed, Zarruq judged that the world had turned upside down and chaos had broken loose. He felt that religious authorities, even saints, were taking advantage of this changeable situation to act out of ambition and greed. In reaction, he articulated the ideal of the jurist saint who harmonized the roles of jurist and Sufi by fusing them into one personality. Zarruq claimed not only to be a saint among others, but, further, to be a juridical saint. As such, he felt authorized to assess the spiritual sincerity of others and to judge the legal limits of their actions, as though he could judge the authenticity of the "sign or token" given by the king to his confidants. That sign was sincerity.

Fusing the roles of jurist and saint was an extreme reaction to the rapid changes around him, and Zarruq vociferously criticized the agents of these changes for transgressing legal norms and established order. The two chapters in this section will follow the details of his critique in its legal, theological, ethical, and sociological dimensions. Zarruq's claim to religious authority through his status as a juridical saint was highly contestable and his contemporaries rejected his critiques and challenged his claims to unique religious authority. At the most basic level, they found his version of "sincerity" to be an absence of "generosity." Both of these values are central to the saint's personality, and Zarruq's contemporaries found his zealous and acerbic attempts to guard the gates to sainthood to be nothing but miserliness and backbiting. In their eyes and through their pens, they rejected Zarruq's reformist mission as lacking the virtue of generosity, by which they tried to invalidate his very claim to religious authority as a saint.

7 Principles

After a brief period of rapid growth and maturation in the liminal space of Cairo, Zarruq's new master, al-Ḥaḍramī, ordered him to return to Morocco. At this time, Zarruq was thirty-three years old. Al-Ḥaḍramī charged Zarruq to take his reform program back to the crucible that had first forced him to formulate it, and in doing so to confront his past and its deep scars. He returned with new authority and prestige as a master-teacher of Maliki jurisprudence at al-Azhar, a scholar authorized by the most learned teachers, and a Sufi with new and innovative initiations. He also returned armed with critiques of his Moroccan contemporaries from among the Sufis, jurists, and *shurafāʾ*. He may have hoped that Fes would recognize him *al-Walī* as *al-Jāmiʿ*, a juridical saint with multiple roles fused into one personality.

It was natural for Zarruq to initiate his program of reform among the jurists of Fes. Many of them already had Sufi affiliations, and others might, out of respect for Zarruq's ideal of juridical sainthood, begin to cultivate ties to Sufi communities. However, Zarruq's vision of a reform from within Sufi communities implied a biting critique of his contemporaries. Most of his writings on saints and their Sufi followers display a keen intellect sharpened by an irascible spirit, as did many of his verbal interactions. Clearly Zarruq did not convince the jurists in Fes, but instead threatened them with the critical edge to his voice, and Zarruq himself admitted that this censuring personality was part of his innate disposition. Zarruq writes of his personality when he was in his twenties: "In those days, I was of a keenly irascible and vituperative disposition (*ḥidda*). If Shaykh Daqūq [one of my elder companions] perceived this hotly critical behavior from me, he would say, 'Take it easy and watch yourself until you pass your fortieth year; after this, these qualities will not remain in you at all!'"[1] Zarruq's keen observations and his quickness to point out others' faults would get him into trouble. This was especially true in his social environment in Fes, where age and status demanded deference, and in Sufi communities where displays of humility were the norm. His penchant to speak out critically about other people's faults took a tragic turn during the sharifian revolution. That crisis of political and religious authority certainly heightened Zarruq's already deep suspicion of the morality of his fellows.

Yet these factors alone do not fully account for the critical project of the mature Zarruq. His critique of the behavior of his contemporary saints was an integral part of his reformist program. To articulate the "principles of being a Sufi" was to display how others had diverted their attention from a sincere Sufi practice ruled by these principles. Even his insistence that honing the intellect as a tool to advance one's spiritual development was an assertion that many of his Sufi colleagues would distrust or dismiss.

At a deeper level, his critical acumen was part of his holistic response to his historical environment, which he feared was dissolving accepted norms and civilizational standards. Zarruq shared this deep pessimism and critical gaze with other thinkers of his age, and his pessimistic assessment of the state of his civilization mirrors the pensive assessment of Ibn Khaldūn (who died in the early fifteenth century C.E.). That philosopher-historian observed that historical conditions had changed completely and that the age-old rhythms of growth and decay no longer held sway.[2] His political history of North African society highlighted the stable principle of ethical inspiration and tribal solidarity that structured past cycles of political change. However, he observed that he was living at the moment when this civilization was reaching the limit of its continuity; the stable principles that emerged from his historical analysis were no longer operative in his own era. As Ibn Khaldūn looked forward from his present (rather than back into the past) he perceived that the times had completely changed in the Maghrib. As if the present were a new creation, people's situation and reactions had altered irreconcilably. "As for this age [at the end of the eighth century Hijri (fourteenth century C.E.)] the historical condition of the Maghrib has completely changed and inverted before our very eyes.... It is as if an existential voice (*lisān al-kawn*) were calling out over the face of the world, ordering grandeur to contract, shrink away, and disappear into humble anonymity, while the world's civilizations each hasten to answer this call.... When the historical conditions change so completely, it is as if human beings, too, have changed completely from the very core of their being. The world transforms them as if they are bound to the world in captivation, as if they were a new type of human being created anew in an entirely new and changed world."[3]

In this profound passage, Ibn Khaldūn articulates a view of civilization that resonates with Zarruq's view. Although their lives were separated by nearly a century, the two men shared many experiences that brought them to similar conclusions. Their intellectual outlooks were both shaped by Marinid-era institutions. They both tried desperately to escape from the instability of North African polities. And they both found refuge in the institutions of Cairo under Mamluk rule, where Ibn Khaldūn became a famous teacher of Maliki jurisprudence, as did Zarruq after him. Ibn Khaldūn observed the Marinid dynasty as it declined in power and cohesion, while Zarruq lived through its final paroxysm before its collapse. Both intellectuals were social critics who thought their contemporaries stood on the precipice of disaster as the old order crumbled beneath their feet. Most people in this new age were "captivated" by the changes around them in the dual sense of the word. Some were fascinated by the new opportunities for their ambitions, while their exploits of power made others captive. Yet on both sides, opportunists and victims, the old loyalties and honor codes of conduct had peeled away.

Zarruq did not simply react against his experience of revolutionary upheaval in Fes. Rather, he understood his experience to be one particularly galling manifestation of the general upheaval of his times, a time in which justice, order, and propriety were inverted. This comparison with Ibn Khaldūn helps us to keep the details of Zarruq's critiques in a wider perspective. Zarruq's ethical reaction led him to an intellectual and social analysis along lines parallel to Ibn Khaldūn's celebrated history. Ibn Khaldūn analyzed how political dynasties took power and subsequently lost it, in an era when such dynasties were irrevocably collapsing; he presented an "aetiology of decline" that probed history for the symptoms and nature of the ills from which civilization dies.[4] Similarly, Zarruq analyzed how saint-centered religious movements formed, cohered, and went astray, in an era when Islamic authority in general, and sainthood in particular, was in grave crisis.

Through his analysis of saints and Sufi communities, Zarruq tried to recover from the crises of his youth in Fes and account for why he found himself in exile. Yet, under the pressure of his intellect and insight, his analysis went much further than simple self-justification, as revealed in the complex structure of his longest critical work, *Preparing a Sincere Disciple* (*ᶜUddat al-Murīd al-Ṣādiq*). Although his reactions to specifically Moroccan incidents sparked his criticisms, they are relevant to early modern Sufi movements across diverse regions, and they probe the very heart of Islamic sainthood and its relationship to other discourses of religious authority, such as Islamic law. But before we can analyze this long masterwork, we must try to understand the origins and tone of Zarruq's critical voice.

Advice and Admonition

As Zarruq approached his native city, the situation seemed favorable. A contingent of religious notables and jurists from the city had come to meet him at the gates. Zarruq may have perceived them as a welcoming party, but the welcome Zarruq received was not what he expected. The religious notables did not generously lead him into the city as a returning prodigal son. Rather, they set up camp outside the gates and invited Zarruq to sit with them. The invitation turned quickly into a confrontation over the relationship of spiritual cultivation and virtue to legal rectitude and social order. An eyewitness, Qāḍī Abū ᶜAbdullah al-Karrāsī, recorded the startling scene. "When we greeted him and sat down with him in his tent, he began to ask the jurists about their means of livelihood and provision. Some of them answered him, 'Most of our income comes from charitable trusts (*awqāf maḥbūsa*) endowed at the graves of the dead.' Then Shaykh Zarruq replied, 'There is no means and no power except with Allah! You are eating from the flesh of carrion!' Everyone fell silent."[5]

This troubling episode raises many questions. Who were these "jurists," why did Zarruq confront them, and how did they resolve this intense rhetorical joust? We will return to this episode in chapter 8 to fully explore the moral debate about virtue and law inherent in the contested metaphor of "carrion." But for now, we will only note the vigor and speed of Zarruq's critical voice as he cried out, "There is no means and no power except with Allah! You are eating from the flesh of carrion!" Zarruq's voice reveals the suspicion, and even horror, with which he confronted the religious authorities who shared his social world. Upon meeting the party of jurists, Zarruq launched directly into criticizing the legality and morality of their livelihood, directly undermining his commission to return to Fes and spread al-Ḥaḍramī's reformist teachings. Even for the sake of strategy and diplomacy, he could not repress his foreboding that the world had gone terribly wrong.

Zarruq's initial critique of his fellow Sufis was a way of calling others to account for al-Qūrī's travails in Fes as he was deposed and threatened. Zarruq stressed the need for political and social order above all else, even to the point of remaining silent about issues of social justice. In his book of comprehensive juridical "advice" to his fellow Muslims, *al-Naṣīḥa al-Kāfiya*, Zarruq urges them to maintain a legitimate authority in political allegiance and to avoid any rebellion that might call legitimate authority into question. In his advice to "the privileged among the Muslims" (those with education, religious authority, and social standing) he includes three obligations: obeying legitimate authority (whether dynastic, scholarly, or patriarchal), believing in the validity of the pronouncements of scholars and jurists as a class, and respecting the practices of Sufi communities (except for what transgresses the bounds of scriptural or juridical knowledge).[6] He meant these obligations as corrective measures that would have prevented the uprising against al-Qūrī's religious, scholarly, and juridical authority in Fes.

In articulating his principles of being a Sufi, Zarruq further argued that Sufi practices were integral to the preservation of order and the public good.[7] The same juridical limitations that restrain the behavior of common Muslims also rule saints and the Sufis who follow them; neither saints nor Sufis have a special authority to revolt against a sultan. "Preservation of order is obligatory, and guarding carefully over the rights of common people is necessary.... For this reason, jurists have concurred that one must follow the leader (*imām*) without diverging in action or word, whether that leader is righteous or a flagrant sinner, as long as his actions are not clearly corrupt in the very moment of prayer. In the same way, they view *jihād* against Muslim rulers: one cannot disobey him even if he is a sinful person."[8] Zarruq argues that saints have no right to play the role of kingmakers. Similarly, they should never justify the actions of any who rebel against political authority. He does this by deploying traditions that have been attributed to the Prophet Muhammad. "Being subversive and trying to destroy [the ruling authority's] rule is absolutely forbidden. As the Prophet has said, 'Any people that curse their ruler are prevented from getting a better one'.... The Prophet has given a comprehensive statement on this problem: 'One sign of a person's wholesome *islām* is that he does not get involved in what does not concern him.' Surely the Sufis should be the most diligent of all people in keeping away from what does not concern them [especially the conduct of rulers]! God alone knows best."[9]

Because religious leaders in Morocco wedded their call to fight against the Portuguese to the struggle to overthrow the rule of the Marinid dynasty, these criticisms of rebellion are intimately related to Zarruq's criticism of reckless and opportunistic *jihād*. "People have considered what is forbidden to be permissible [by arguing] that it is a means to something greater. For instance, people have lied in order to lead armed struggle to protect Muslims (*al-kadhb fi'l-jihād*), or singled out other Muslims as disbelievers (*takfīr*), or tried to reconcile people in conflict by spreading rumors."[10] Foul means toward a fair goal is the critique that Zarruq levels against those *shurafā'* and Sufis who denounced him in Fes in the name of sparking a popular *jihād*. His explication of this principle does not mention the revolution in Fes, but it does catalogue all the indignities he suffered in those events. To anyone in Fes, his criticism of the politics of *jihād* would be clear. He argues that the means used lead to corruption of the public good, despite the attractiveness of the stated goals. "The corruption of one's underlying integrity is of more consequence than any of these apparent goals.... As a general rule it is far more important to allow those means to protect against the corruption of sincerity and intention than to allow other means to a useful or beneficial result."

In this way, Zarruq explicitly forbade his followers from revolutionary politics or from getting involved in other people's business that does not concern them. "Never get caught up in calls for *jihād* without the expressed consent of the majority of Muslims and without the leadership of their ruler. To do this is to surrender to social discord (*fitna*). Rare is the person who gets involved in such activities and is kept preserved from spiritual perdition. He gets caught up in wrangling with those who oppose him in ways that do not allow reconciliation, or holding a good opinion of other Muslims, or being cautious of getting involved in the projects of others. Therefore, do not accept orders from any [self-appointed leader] who tells you how to dispose of your family, your wealth, and your religion except if you have tested him thousands of times and found him sincerely fearful of God and wary of God's commands. He should treat you as if you were a treasure yourself, and not eat off your wealth and waste your resources."[11] Zarruq's criticisms clearly fueled his reformist orientation. Following the teachings of al-Ḥaḍramī, Zarruq described his own spiritual method as the training of "the sincere ones" from among the saints. Saints who focus intently on sincerity are attentive to "political rights, preserving legitimate authority, standing up with advice and warnings to others against every bad quality or sinful activity in others."[12]

In Zarruq's formulation, sincerity is the fundamental principle of sanctity, and sincerity requires advice and admonition to others. In this way, he justifies his vocal critiques and their sharpness: "Al-Ḥaḍramī used to teach, 'Sincerity with

God is the conditioning principle of everything good.' … Sincerity is the blade of truth that Allah has lifted through the lords of truth: it cuts whatever it falls upon, for nothing in the universe can stand up against sincerity."[13] It should be no surprise that sincere saints cut through the hypocrisy or bad faith of others around them, laying their faults bare. With such vociferous critiques of his contemporaries, Zarruq earned the title *Muḥtasib al-Ṣūfīya wa'l-Fuqahā'*, "the watchman calling Sufis and jurists to account."[14] This unique title characterizes this critical dimension of Zarruq's mission. It complements his other title that characterizes the reformist dimension of his mission: *al-Jāmiʿ*, the one who rejoins what became divided by consolidating jurisprudence and spiritual cultivation.

The Trials of Time

In the cosmopolitan environment of Cairo, whose inhabitants held the belief that their city was the navel of the civilized world, Zarruq gained a tentative hold on the balance that had collapsed in Fes. For eight precious months he felt reintegrated, and he grew in confidence that he was, indeed, one who rejoins what had been broken apart. His studies allowed him to rise to the level of an authoritative jurist, while his new Sufi master reinforced his intuition that spiritual experience must be cultivated within the framework of a juridically rectified life. During these blissful months, Zarruq must have felt that the wounds of his youth in Fes had finally healed without any lingering pain or disfiguring scars. Suddenly, al-Ḥaḍramī challenged Zarruq to return to Fes, to carry their community's reformist program back to his home region of the far Maghrib.

It must have been incredibly difficult for Zarruq to face returning to Fes, the crucible of his early confrontation with authority. Zarruq does not record his reaction to al-Ḥaḍramī's order or detail the latter's rationale for charging him with this undesired mission. He may have felt that Zarruq needed to confront and ultimately overcome his having challenged the authority of his early master, al-Zaytūnī. Zarruq proved himself a true disciple this time and accepted al-Ḥaḍramī's order, even though it meant sacrificing his comfortable life in Cairo. Al-Ḥaḍramī may have had deeper concerns. He clearly felt that Egypt and the central Islamic lands were not receptive to his particular style of Sufi practice. Such ideas went against Zarruq's own intuition, and he asked al-Ḥaḍramī why all the Prophets appeared in these central lands, if not because they were most blessed and most holy. Al-Ḥaḍramī answered caustically, "the Prophets are like spiritual doctors, and doctors attend only the sick."

Al-Ḥaḍramī never stated his reason for compelling Zarruq to return to Fes. Yet it seems clear that he sent him on a mission, perhaps as his representative (*khalīfa*) to give initiations in his name and build a distinctive community centered around the devotional method that al-Ḥaḍramī advocated. There were good reasons for Zarruq to be optimistic that he would be received well in Fes. By this time, the sharifian rulers of Fes had succumbed to the outside military pressure of the Waṭṭāsī clan (who had served as ministers of state in the Marinid dynasty and claimed the right to rule for themselves). In 875 Hijri (1472 C.E.) the Waṭṭāsid leader, Muḥammad al-Shaykh, gathered his forces to converge on Fes. He had escaped ᶜAbd al-Ḥaqq al-Marīnī's purge of his family six years earlier and had secured time and opportunity by signing the port of Asila over to the Portuguese.[15] Under his leadership, Waṭṭāsid forces reconquered Fes and exiled the sharifian revolutionaries from the al-Jūṭī clan to Tunis.[16] They restored the sultanate on the model of the Marinid polity (as opposed to the brief sharifian regime, which designated the ruler as *imām*, not *sulṭān*). Muḥammad al-Shaykh al-Waṭṭāsī ruled for another twenty-five years. Meanwhile, the Portuguese took full advantage of this internal turmoil; they reconquered Tangier and sealed their success by pressuring the Waṭṭāsī ruler into a twenty-year truce. Waṭṭāsid rule was reasonably competent, but the centripetal forces of disintegration were stronger, fed as they were by internal revolt and the pressures of Iberian economic and military invasions.

The return of Waṭṭāsid rule to Fes meant that it would be safe for Zarruq to return there. With this poetic couplet, al-Ḥaḍramī urged Zarruq accept returning to Fes as riding the current of his particular fate. "Resign yourself to Salmā and go wherever she takes you—Follow the wind of fate and face wherever it turns you."[17] Accompanied by his friend and fellow disciple, Muḥammad al-Khaṣṣāṣī, Zarruq journeyed back overland toward Morocco with reason to be optimistic. He had kept in contact with many of the top scholars and jurists of Fes and had mediated on their behalf with scholars in Cairo. Jurists in Fes held in high regard *ijāza* documents from Cairo and the Ḥijāz, for such documents sealed their credentials and earned them a good reputation locally. However, because the journey to Cairo was difficult, Zarruq secured *ijāza* documents for them by personally vouching for the status of their learning back in Fes (in a sort of late medieval "distance education" project).[18] It was part of Zarruq's reform program to sponsor scholarship and raise the standard of Moroccan scholars, and he desired to win back allies in Fes by being of service.

His early texts on advice and admonition reveal Zarruq's burgeoning sense of authority and his keen eye for critique. With these inner convictions welded to his reformist project, Zarruq made his way back to Fes. Zarruq's call to order and obedience coincided with the Waṭṭāsid attempt to re-establish Marinid rule under their own control. On the surface, many notable families of scholars and religious leaders of the city appeared to support the Waṭṭāsid restoration. Zarruq may have suspected that the people of Fes would accept his admonitions, repent of their former rebellion and dismissal of al-Qūrī as a juridical saint, and uphold Zarruq as the sincere exemplar of sainthood.

Before he even passed through the gates of the city, as he woke from his shocked faint, Zarruq realized that his mission was doomed. His contemporaries in Fes did not embrace his advice or accept his admonitions. Most did not appreciate his nuanced paradigm of sainthood fused with jurisprudence. Zarruq lived in Fes for four years in very adverse conditions. In response, he wrote his longest work to account for why his society failed to recognize the type of saint he respected, the ideals of which he felt he himself embodied. His proposition was that in the historical development of his society, sainthood had gone awry. His complex work, entitled *ᶜUddat al-Murīd al-Ṣādiq*, constituted his most piercing critique of his fellow saints and the Sufis who followed them, who he felt had become ensnared in "inauthentic" religious practices.

The full title of this work explains his purpose: *Preparing the Sincere Disciple against the Causes of Loathing, to show the True Path and mention the Trials of Time.*[19] The "causes of loathing" are Sufi practices that take people beyond the bounds of religious custom and law. The "trials of time" has a double meaning in Zarruq's text. Through the vicissitudes of generational changes, these corrupting practices had slowly inveigled their way into religious practice: the passage of time is itself a trial to religious purity. However, these small changes have worked their way deep into the very foundation of belief, such that those people who led social movements based on their role as saints (in Zarruq's view) were the cause of innumerable social calamities. In this way, his time was a time of trials.

This complex work is rooted in a detailed discussion of the concept of religious change (*bidᶜa*). Zarruq had ventured to discuss *bidᶜa* in his *Principles,* and the concept lies implicit in many of the examples he cites in that work.[20] In addition, he had written at least two other texts that sketched out these ideas. He bluntly entitled the first one *Denunciation of Those who Practice Bidᶜa* and documented the practices of the early Jazūlīyya community.[21] This text was completed in year 886 Hijri (1481 C.E.) and served as a draft for his longer critique, *ᶜUddat al-Murīd*. It contains many of the same arguments on how the ambition of saints and the partisanship of their followers allow inauthentic religious practices to corrupt Sufi devotional life. In this initial treatise, though, Zarruq's criticism is personal and directed against a specific community, the early Jazūlīyya (notably of al-Mughīṭī and ᶜAbd al-ᶜAzīz al-Tabbāᶜ).

In his later writings, these critiques are repeated in more general terms, stripped of much of their specific targeting of al-Jazuli and his followers, as if the language of *Denunciation of Those who Practice Bidᶜa* is too dangerously specific to be circulated in Morocco. Indeed, we find no manuscript copies of this text in Morocco; they are found only in Tunisia.[22] Zarruq composed a second initial study, entitled *The Most Advantageous Advice and the Shield for those who seek Shelter from Bidᶜa through the Prophet's Example.*[23] In this text, we observe Zarruq stripping his argument of personal detail and sociological description of a specific community in order to reveal its more universal and abstract core. Together, these two texts laid the groundwork for the complex argument of *ᶜUddat al-Murīd al-Ṣādiq*. This more systematic treatise used *bidᶜa* to strategically join sociological observation about mass movements with juridical rulings condemning them.

"Religious change" or "innovation" is a common term in Islamic heresiography, and scholars use it as a rhetorical denunciation of "heretics" without any formal juridical content. However, Zarruq shies away from this rhetorical tactic, for he perceived that the unrestrained (or unprincipled) use of such rhetoric could lead to a rejection of Sufi practices in their entirety.[24] Instead, he provides a legal definition, "The essence of *bidᶜa* is the appearance of a matter in religious custom that bears some superficial resemblance to religious custom but actually is not of it. This technical definition does not apply absolutely to all new phenomena (*al-muḥdath*). Rather, new phenomena must be incorporated into the *sharīᶜa*, and accepted if they are in accord with the principles of the *sharīᶜa* and in harmony through analogy to its already sanctioned behaviors. For this reason, jurists proclaim that a matter is really *bidᶜa* only if it is ruled as forbidden or disapproved.... The truly accomplished jurists [from among the Usulis] have stated that any new appearance of a religious custom can be sifted into one of the five categories of juridical rulings."[25] Zarruq honed the concept of "religious change" by giving it a definition, intellectual explication, and juridical nuance. Although Zarruq cites two hadith reports in which the Prophet Muhammad appears to denounce all *bidᶜa* as harmful, he specifies that the Prophet did not mean to denounce *bidᶜa* in the technical, juridical sense of "new practices" but only *bidᶜa* in the rhetorical sense of "inauthentic practices."[26] Zarruq's aim was to employ the analysis of *bidᶜa* with analytical subtlety, as one would wield a scalpel rather than an axe.

In a pattern familiar from his *Principles of Being a Sufi*, Zarruq mined the conceptual resources of jurisprudence to offer an *uṣūlī* definition of religious change. *Bidᶜa* is commonly translated into English as "innovation" in religious matters; however, the metaphor in Zarruq's mind was not innovating or inventing, but rather grafting. He defined *bidᶜa* as "adding something new to religious practices that had not existed before" while claiming that it is essential to religiosity. When a new branch is grafted onto an old vine, it appears to be an integral part of that vine, even though it came from elsewhere and is not original to the vine itself. Every vintner knows that grafting is extremely useful. Zarruq as a jurist, like a vintner, admits that "religious changes" are not essentially harmful, but must be judged by their effects.

By its effects, a jurist can classify any "religious change" as one of the five categories of juridical rulings: as forbidden, disapproved, neutral, recommended, or obligatory.[27] Intellectually honest jurists will admit that many religious practices that current Muslims consider "obligatory" or "encouraged" (whether in Zarruq's time or in the twenty-first century) are actually religious changes that were unknown in the early community. Rather, they were grafted on in later times, were found to bear worthy fruit, and were accepted as part of religious custom. As disciplines of knowledge and practice, both jurisprudence and Sufi practices fall under the category of "religious changes."[28]

This introduction aside, Zarruq focused his critical faculties on the negative side of "religious change." Not all grafts are beneficial, and not all are authentic. Some "religious changes" involve practices that are clearly forbidden, but which people have given a religious justification. Other are disapproved, since if accepted as an integral part of religiosity, they could lead to forbidden actions or distract from obligatory actions. "*Bid^ca* usually occurs when a phenomenon is related to something clearly forbidden, or leads directly to something clearly forbidden, or results in it.... *Bidᶜa* [in this negative sense] usually occurs in certain contexts, in phenomena that are strange or exceptional, not in matters that are customary and routine in religion."[29] This is the gray zone that concerns Zarruq, and he wields the concept of *bidᶜa* very deftly to try to draw clear lines of black and white through a haze of gray.

> *Bidᶜa* often occurs in matters relating to the results of authentic religious actions. It occurs in the things that people desire to achieve and that people think will lead to good for themselves (like meditative recitation, reciting scripture, praying, or fasting). People invent new ways to perform these actions or new means of training to perform them. These phenomena of *bidᶜa* usually occur when people claim that such practices are justified by one part of the *sharīᶜa* or another, or by some appeal to ultimate reality [beyond the *sharīᶜa*] that actually conceals a lack of knowledge. For this reason, people are either confused by it, or accept it as being part of religion. Then the phenomena spread among the ignorant people and they consider them to be an authentic part of religion even though they don't have the knowledge to distinguish the truth of the matter.[30]

Sainthood is an especially ambiguous zone that involves exceptional people and extreme experiences. Intensification of worship beyond routine limits, craving personal sincerity, and opposing one's own self-will are the hallmark of saints. Zarruq notes that saints, through these practices, have introduced many "religious changes" into the fabric of Islam. Most are beneficial and in harmony with the original spirit of the Muslim community, while some he finds questionable. Further, the followers of saints have introduced many "religious changes," which are far more suspect than those introduced by saints themselves.

People who desire the good fruits of religious actions are misled by the ambiguity of such phenomena and how they relate to a principle. If people with high social standing accept these phenomena or show ambivalence toward them, then common people can be further misled, despite their good intentions. However, in Zarruq's view, everything can be judged by explicit criteria to determine if it is genuine or false. The scholar (*ᶜālim*) knows for sure what those criteria are, while the ignorant person does not. Therefore, the person of little knowledge gets misled, and he misleads others by claiming that religion justifies his actions. His ignorance cannot excuse him from blame in making such claims, for he did not consider the matter deeply in the light of knowledge. Pondering everything in the light of knowledge (*tabaṣṣur*) is the essential basis of any authentic religion.

Saints and those who follow them in devotional practices can be misled even by their heroic opposition to self-will. They may invent means to act piously, means which were not previously known in religious custom. Others who follow them may accept these as religious obligations. Only scriptural knowledge and juridical principles can establish the criteria to judge whether such means to a good end are in themselves good. Love and devotion, argues Zarruq, must be tempered by knowledge and discretion.

Jurisprudence provided Zarruq with the intellectual procedure for analyzing occurrences of "religious innovation" and the criteria for judging them. He advocates that scholars "examine the phenomenon in the light of juridical categories" and classify it as one of the five categories known in jurisprudence (*uṣūl al-fiqh*).[31] All that fall into the categories of "forbidden" or "discouraged," the jurists should label as *bidᶜa* in its negative, condemned meaning. Even with this procedure, many incidents of *bidᶜa* pass unacknowledged into the field of popular religious practice. This is because, Zarruq clarifies, there are several types of *bidᶜa*, some clearer than others. Absolute *bidᶜa* is clear by its nature. It is a practice that "people establish with no legal source to support it" and displaces another practice supported by a legal source (from among the religious obligations, customs, or allowed actions). "Such clear *bidᶜa* causes authentic religious custom to die out, or alleges that a true command is void."[32] Zarruq asserts that anyone who commands scriptural and juridical knowledge must strive to point out such incidents and oppose them in every way possible. More ambiguous are incidents of *bidᶜa* that arise by contradiction. "These are incidents of inauthentic practice that can be traced back to two different religious sources whose rulings contradict each other. One person could look to the first source and claim that it ruled the phenomenon as an incidence of *bidᶜa*, while another person could look at the second source and claim that it ruled the phenomenon as a part of the *sunna*."[33] Jurists and scholars must oppose such incidents if they arise in the field of religious ritual and worship; however, if they fall in the wider field of habits and daily activities, there is room for disagreement and a scholar should not rush to denounce them. "Even if people claim that certain practices in the field of habit are part of religion which are actually not, one should not contradict them by making judgments against such phenomena."[34] Finally, Zarruq specifies a third class of *bidᶜa* that accounts for the vast majority of cases. These are incident of *bidᶜa* by addition: "an innovation that is added to or compounded upon a matter that has a justified place in religious custom." Because people related these new practices to customary and well-established practices, they consider them part of the *sunna* even though these practices have no justification and are subject to disagreement.

What conditions will keep a saint clear of such ambiguous practices that will lead to *bidᶜa* if practitioners insist that they are part of religious custom and obligation? Zarruq lays out three conditions, each of which leads back to his own reform of Sufi practice. The first is "correcting one's faith" so that it leads to sincerely following the Prophet and upholding the sacredness of the *sharīᶜa*. The second is "researching the scriptural commands and juridical rulings," which requires every Sufi to train as a jurist (or follow the advice of jurists). The third is "knowing and acknowledging the sources of the method of one's Sufi community (*ṭarīqa*)," referring to the principles that Zarruq recorded in his own reformist writings. If Sufis claim the status of sainthood without having adhered to these three conditions, Zarruq asserts, there is a grave risk of their going astray into the mire of *bid^c^a*.

Sainthood's Challenge to Islamic Authority

This is because saints open themselves up to subtle temptations when they accept practices that verge on *bidᶜa*. Zarruq classifies these temptations into three principles of corruption (which reflect the lack of the three conditions listed above). The first is "reduction of faith due to lack of knowledge," for knowledge is light and light is knowledge. For Zarruq, the only light of spiritual guidance is knowledge about the Qurʾān and the Prophet.[35] The second is "ignorance of the sources (*uṣūl*) of the spiritual path" and the concomitant belief that religious custom (*sharīᶜa*) contradicts ultimate spiritual reality (*ḥaqīqa*). This, claims Zarruq, has led many saints and their Sufi communities astray. It is the fundamental principle of hypocrisy, setting the jurists on a stilted path of condemning all the Sufis, and the Sufis on an ignorant path of rejecting the jurists and scholars. The third principle of corruption is "love of worldly power, social prominence, and ambition to lead" while being unsuited to actually act out these roles. This leads saints to stake claims of power, perform miracles, intervene in political issues, and force disciples into positions of absolute submission to their will. Saints who perpetuate such actions, claims Zarruq, are under the fundamental illusion that "they cannot attain the most wondrous station except through miraculous actions." Meanwhile, each action only reinforces the subtle ambition, through "selfish delights" of exercising power over others or attaining physical comforts at the expense of others.[36]

These three principles of corruption are ever-present, if not in the heart of would-be saints, then in the hearts of their followers. In Zarruq's bitter critique of saints, there lurked his fear of their followers. He has no sympathy for uneducated folk who revere saints from afar (without the benefit of proximity, companionship, or training under a saint). Nor does he have patience for educated followers who pander to the needs of less educated ones. In Zarruq's view, the "religious changes" they introduce in their search for relief through saintly intervention are particularly reprehensible and utterly contagious. "In this day, the discipline of Sufi practice seems thoroughly corrupt. Many people at the present time suffer in this state. Some so-called saints have used the knowledge of subtle truths and realities as a ladder to enhance themselves, seducing the hearts of the common people, taking the wealth of the oppressed, despising the unfortunate, and committing acts that are obvious 'religious changes' and are clearly forbidden. Some have gone so far as to depart from [the bounds of] religion altogether. Still, many ignorant people follow these 'saints' because of their customary claims to authority and the privileges they assume in this discipline."[37] Zarruq feels that the institution of sainthood has become so corrupted in its current practice that the Muslim community would be almost better off without it. In such an environment, almost any teaching of Sufis "will have been misinterpreted counter to its aims, and its teacher will be like one who sells a sword to a highway robber."[38] His own reform movement within Sufi communities is the only hope that Zarruq can see to restore to sainthood its prestige.[39]

Zarruq is quick to point out that Sufis have not always been like this. He offers a brief, revisionist history of Sufis to ground his critique and channel it toward his reformist agenda. The earliest Sufis, he claims, had no specialized methods of spiritual training, no hierarchical ranking of masters over disciples, and no specific terminology that set them off from other intellectuals or worshipers. The only method they knew "was companionship and meeting together." One who was of lesser accomplishment would travel to meet one of greater accomplishment and learn directly from observing his spiritual state and imbibing his presence. This method, in its simplicity and directness, did not prevent them from studying scriptural sources or practicing juridical reasoning. They took oaths of allegiance to masters only to confirm their aspiration to be wary and conscious of God.[40] Just as the Prophet had given advice for spiritual training in different forms to his different followers, so early saints gave advice to their younger companions and took pledges of allegiance from them as disciples. Yet they did this only after long observing their disciples and knowing by experience what each needed to overcome her or his willfulness. They did not rely on intricate methods, or oblige everyone to carry out a single ritual form, or try to build up a mass following. Thus each one reached the state of *istiqāma* (bearing one's self according to the ethics of the Qurʾān and the Prophet's example) by the means best suited to each individually, with no room for exaggeration or lack.

However, over time, saints established a social role of their own, and their followers distinguished them from other types of pious Muslims. In Zarruq's vision of history, this development "widened the gate" and allowed people into the social status of sainthood who relied on outer markers of sanctity and may not have known thoroughly what method was best suited to cool down their own particular variety of willfulness. A man could claim to be a saint "while still not knowing if this status was truly suitable to his nature. This allows him to pose as a saint while still hiding inner selfish desires that push him to transgress the proper bounds of behavior here and there. In this, he is aided by special provisions and excuses that he arrogated for himself, and goaded by his own loss of sincere wariness of God."[41] Zarruq blames the social institution of sainthood, the social expectation of and reliance upon saints as the axis of social cohesion, for the inner decay of saints themselves. It is to deny saints this specialized role in society that Zarruq insists that Sufis must be trained as jurists (before identifying as a Sufi or a gaining any reputation for being a saint). Zarruq felt that this firm allegiance to jurists and to scholarly practice would eclipse the distinct social role of the saint in his many guises as political leader, mediator, healer, poet, or divinely distracted madman.

In addition to his revisionist history of Sufi communities, Zarruq based his critique on social observation. Zarruq asserted that in his time, saints allowed certain types of *bid^c^a* (as defined by Zarruq's juridical method) to flourish in their training of disciples. In an attempt to account for this (and, moreover, to excuse past masters from wrongdoing) he notes that saints have been purposefully inattentive to *bid^c^a*. They try to focus on their inner life or train their followers to scrutinize their own inner lives, thereby allowing innovations to serve as "skillful means" to spiritual awakening and ascetic control of the self and selfish desires. Over generations, innovations that a saint may have seen as useful have been accepted by his followers as obligatory. They have lost sight of the original principle of the action and cling to the form of the action instead. In his age, Zarruq lamented, innovations had so thoroughly infiltrated religious practices that some saints claimed: "Nobody in this age can enjoy even a taste of the honey of *sunna*, except by patiently accepting *bid^c^a* [mixed with it]."[42]

In such a lament, Zarruq pictures the special conditions of his age as a crisis of sincerity leading to the promotion of inauthentic religious practices. In Zarruq's concept of "history as decay," a saint's followers and promoters misunderstand his teachings. They take statements out of context, interpret assertions beyond their intent, or apply in a general way suggestions that had specific or limited context. Further, saints themselves have allowed such misunderstandings or even encouraged them. This is the kernel of his sociological observations on sainthood as the basis for a social movement. A saint's lack of vigilance regarding the authenticity of spiritual practices gives rise to apologies for their actions and those of their followers. These apologies fuel partisans to build social movements around a saint's person or teachings. Such partisans cannot accept the critique of jurists against any practices associated with their social movement. Their allegiance to particular saints grows rigid, and they repudiate any critique of a behavior characteristic of their group (let alone a critique of the whole edifice of sainthood).

In this way, saints as spiritual guides can give rise to social movements; in Zarruq's view such movements are very dangerous. Sufi communities grow into social movements when stable political authority breaks down, accompanied by the collapse of the rule of law that depends on political authority. With good intention, saints may strive to fill a vacuum of power, to reform the political-social order, or to console people in troubled times.[43] However, these intentions involve ways and means that take the saint beyond the limits of law and custom. If acted upon, they open a Pandora's box: the spiritual power of saints is countered by the social power of their followers, who perceive a saint according to their own needs and mold him to their own desires. In Zarruq's pessimistic view, common people long for an experience of the strange and exceptional that distracts them from daily routine within legal limits. They bring this longing into the movement with them, and if the saint caters to it, then political ambition, social power, and worldly means seep covertly into a movement ostensibly built on following a saint. Building a movement of mass appeal also involves pandering to popular misconceptions on a grand scale. It could even lead to popular protest against legitimate religious authority of jurists or political authority of rulers. To illustrate this critique, Zarruq returned to the events that initially provoked his critical project, the conjunction of the sharifian revolution in Fes and the ascendance of the Jazūlīyya community.

Critique of the Sharifian-Sufi Alliance

Discussing *bid^c^a* is not simply descriptive of ritual practices or prescriptive in moral denunciation of such practices. Rather, discussing *bid^c^a* is inherently political. To label a community's practices as *bid^c^a* is to attempt to undermine public loyalty and allegiance to such a community. To diffuse the accusation that he was being explicitly political, Zarruq displaced his personal evaluation and denunciation of Sufi communities onto the Prophet Muhammad by citing a hadith report.

> This hadith, reported by al-Bukhārī, preserves the words of the Prophet Muhammad. One of his companions, named Hadhīfa, said "People gathered around the Prophet to ask him about goodness. In contrast, I insisted on asking about evil. I said, 'O Prophet of Allah, we were sunk in ignorance and evil before this goodness [*Islam*] came and transformed us. After this goodness, will there be any evil?' The Prophet said, 'Yes.' So I asked, 'And after that evil will there come a further goodness?' The Prophet said, 'Yes, but the goodness will be degenerating into badness (*dakhan*), like a fire is ruined by too much smoke.' I asked, 'What will make it degenerate?' The Prophet replied, 'A community of people who take as religious practice what is not from my example, and take as religious guidance what is not real guidance. Some of them will be well-respected and others will be little known.' I persisted in asking, 'And after that [mixed and degenerated] goodness, will there come further evil?' The Prophet answered, 'Yes, false claims. And those who respond to the false claims will teeter on the gates of Hell.' I said, "O Prophet of Allah, describe for me these people [who make false claims]!' He said, 'They are from our ancestry and speak in our language.' I asked 'What do you order me to do if I should meet such people?' The Prophet said, 'Adhere diligently to the consensus of the Muslim community and obey their rightful leader (*imām*).' I asked, 'But what if there is no community consensus and no rightful leader at that time?' The Prophet replied, 'Then steer clear of all such people, even if you have to climb the highest tree and stay there until death's appointed day comes and finds you still there.'[44]

In Zarruq's view, his critiques were foreshadowed by the Prophet Muhammad and therefore sanctioned. Zarruq saw himself as simply clarifying the details of how Sufi communities in his own time generated "spiritual murk" that could overwhelm the tentative goodness of their work in cultivating sincere spirits. But rather than avoiding them by climbing a tree or hiding in ascetic isolation, Zarruq's reformist orientation forced him to engage his colleagues in critique and counter-critique.

In the argument of *Preparing the Sincere Disciple*, Zarruq oscillates between an abstract universalism and an observed particularism. He presents an argument based on the sociology of religious change and the formation of factions, yet this veils thinly a particular critique of specific groups of his contemporaries. The kernel of his critique was his opposition to the sharifian-Sufi alliance that had contributed to the revolution in Fes. This alliance included not only the Qādirīyya community with whom Zarruq had clashed in Fes, but also the Jazūlīyya community across Morocco. The Jazūlīyya movement continued to grow even after the revolution in Fes had been suppressed, and saintly leaders of the Jazūlīyya began to build communities even within the city. Both Sufi communities shared a paradigm of socially activist sainthood, yet the Jazūlīyya community would develop this paradigm into its most articulate and politically powerful form. In this paradigm, the saint enjoyed absolute authority in the social realm and projected the *shurafāʾ* as the just and rightful rulers. The Jazūlīyya community was especially strong because their axial saint was also a genealogical descendant of the Prophet. Zarruq's critique argued that such a sharifian-Sufi alliance leads to ethical transgression and theological extremism, especially if the saints who inspire it allow themselves to become the center of social movements. The excesses that Zarruq laments include claims that a saint is the Mahdī, claims that he receives inspiration that subverts the sacredness of Prophetic revelation, and claims that he accesses the Prophet's spirit or personality in ways that marginalize the jurists and scriptural scholars.

Although Zarruq begins his critique with a definition of *bidʿa*, a personal specificity lurks below this "objective" surface, barely suppressed by Zarruq's caution. This explains the strange textual event of a personal object of critique erupting into the otherwise abstract frame of his argument. Almost offhandedly at first, Zarruq mentions "a particular person" who embodies the principles of corruption specified above.[45] Without naming him, Zarruq suggests that he is the saint to whom a particular Sufi community is devoted. Through separate comments interspersed through his argument, the reader learns that these are not historical personages, but Zarruq's own contemporaries in a particular Sufi community. Zarruq attests that he met and "discussed some issues with the earliest members of this community."[46]

This reference leaves little doubt that Zarruq criticized the early followers of al-Jazūlī. Zarruq had never met al-Jazūlī in person. However, he certainly met early followers of al-Jazūlī who came to Fes upon the sudden death of their leader (at his settlement at Āfūghāl in the region of Ḥāḥā). Zarruq carefully recorded the meeting, since it coincided with the events of the revolution in Fes. "I was at that zawiya [Būʾl-Quṭūṭ], serving the devotees there, when there arrived at our door a group of the followers of Sīdī Muḥammad al-Jazūlī. They arrived with al-Ṣughayyir al-Sahlī.[47] They confirmed for us how Shaykh al-Jazūlī had died. Al-Ṣughayyir said to us that he had died [suddenly] during the dawn prayer, either in the second prostration of the first bowing, or in the first prostration of the second bowing."[48] Al-Ṣughayyir al-Sahlī was one of al-Jazūlī's most senior disciples and primary representatives. Zarruq met him and the group of adherents of al-Jazūlī, and they affirmed that al-Jazūlī had died suddenly; some of his followers claimed he had been poisoned. After listening to their reports until evening, Zarruq argued with them over the claims of their saint and the activities of his followers.

Though he avoided accusing al-Jazūlī himself of wrongdoing, Zarruq reacted strongly against the actions of al-Jazūlī's followers. By the time Zarruq had returned to Fes, the sharifian revolution had already sealed an alliance between the Qādirīs who followed al-Zaytūnī and the community that formed around the followers of al-Jazūlī. This alliance excluded Zarruq and the others in the juridical Sufi community. By critiquing "unjustified" attempts to overthrow legal dynastic rulers, Zarruq did not simply lash out at those who had driven him from Fes. Rather, this was part of a complex critique of the grand alliance of Sufis and *shurafā*ᵓ who asserted the rights of the descendants of the Prophet to rule over Morocco. He wrote against the al-ᶜImrānī al-Jūṭī family that seized power temporarily in Fes, and also against the wider coalition of *shurafā*ᵓ, including al-Jazūlī himself, who asserted that just rule was a sharifian prerogative.

In writing a critique of the *shurafā*ᵓ, Zarruq was treading a fine line. He upheld their important role in society, but subjected it to conditions of morality and piety. "It is not permissible for a Muslim to degrade or slur the honor of people about whom God testifies that God has cleansed and removed impurity from them … and al-Ḥātimī has said 'It is believed that God has forgiven all the family of the Prophet of their erroneous ways.' … If some of the family of the Prophet might fall into disobedience, this does not break the bonds of the special relationship they have to the Prophet, so long as the principle of that relationship, which is faith, still remains in them."[49] Having articulated the root principle, faith, that grounds the descendants of the Prophet in their social authority, Zarruq continues this passage by warning them against overstepping the proper bounds of their position. "However, we can ourselves remind them of their duties by the authority of scholarship and jurisprudence. In that case, we are like a servant who disciplines the master's son with the permission of the master. We carry out the wishes of the master without disregarding the superior social status of the master's son." Zarruq censured any *sharīf* who might compete with the scholars for authority or in competition begin to degrade them.

In this bold passage, Zarruq asserts that those with scholarly and juridical authority can and should upbraid the *shurafā*ᵓ and criticize them for any transgressions they may commit. He further discusses how scholars should handle injustice at the hands of descendants of the Prophet. He records how he discussed this issue with al-Qūrī. They both agreed that they should suffer such injustice with patience, as if "it came from a divine decree without reason." Yet al-Qūrī added, "This is with respect to us. However, in respect to the *shurafā*ᵓ, a sin committed by a person close to the Prophet is much weightier than a sin committed by an ordinary person."[50]

Not content to simply criticize what he saw as the misdeeds of the *shurafā*ᵓ, Zarruq questioned the very exclusivity of their claim to spiritual authority. The term for spiritual authority that inheres in saints (*walāya*) depends on their intimacy to the source of power (*wilāya*). Such intimacy to God comes directly from moral virtues that bring one's spiritual life close to the presence of the Prophet. In contrast, such intimacy comes only indirectly from being a genealogical descendant of the Prophet. Spiritual nearness depends on moral virtue; the nearness of being a blood relative can never subsume it. The first is essential nearness, while the second is only accidental nearness. "Affirming the force of a phenomenon's essential property is not like affirming the force of an accidental aspect of its attributes. For instance, the Prophet said, 'Salmān is one of us—one of my family.' This is because Salmān Fārsī shared in all the virtuous qualities that characterized the Prophet's family members [even though he was not related by blood or marriage to the Prophet, and was not even an Arab]. By this analogy, one should consider as spiritual authorities people who are related to the Prophet through their religious and moral qualities exclusively. If a person of excellent moral qualities also happens to be a blood relative of the Prophet, then that reaffirms his or her excellence. However, a blood relative can in no way claim some inner spiritual channel to attaining the status of the Prophet himself."[51] In this way, Zarruq argued that sainthood should be disengaged from descent from the Prophet. Saints achieve intimacy with the Prophet through virtues gained through knowledge of the Prophet's character. This intimacy gives them authority and power. The *shurafā᾿* can claim no exclusive (or even comparable) spiritual authority based on their genealogical descent from the Prophet's family, what Zarruq calls "a fleshly relationship of clay" [*ṭīn*, as opposed to morality, *dīn*].[52]

It was crucial for Zarruq to disengage sharifian descent from saintly authority. Not only did increasing sharifian prestige threaten to overturn dynastic rulers, but it also raised millenarian expectations of the coming of a "rightly guided" Mahdī. The Mahdī is an eschatological figure who combines saintly virtue, sharifian descent, and radical divine justice. The Mahdī represents an almost complete reflection of the Prophet, and his expectation signals a "return to the beginning" for Muslims who yearn for the simple justice of the days when the Prophet was both the ultimate religious authority and the just political leader of the community. The Mahdī will embody the virtues of the Prophet and will be from amongst his descendants. Like the Prophet, divine directives will inspire and guide his every action. The Mahdī represents the final triumph of the *shurafā᾿* in establishing themselves as just political rulers. This explains why expectation of the advent of the Mahdī has been a constant feature of Shiᶜī religious beliefs.

After critiquing the *shurafā᾿* and distinguishing their authority from saints' authority, Zarruq's argument becomes even more vituperative, criticizing those sharifian saints who claim to be the Mahdī (or a figure akin to the Mahdī). Even during Zarruq's lifetime, many Moroccans expected that a descendant of the Prophet would lay claim to political authority and eliminate the perceived inequities of the Marinid dynastic rule. Reference to the Mahdī directly reinforced such expectations. In his oral preaching and his exhortation to Muslims to rise up in *jihād* against the Portuguese (and their "clients," the Marinids), al-Jazūlī veered very close to Mahdīst rhetoric. He claimed spiritual authority due to his intimacy with the spirit of the Prophet. He enjoyed this intimacy due to his genealogical descent from the Prophet's family. He activated this potency through his invocations of blessing upon the Prophet. He further claimed to be "the just Imam" of the community, a subtle reference to the title of ᶜAlī and also of the expected Mahdī. Even further, al-Jazūlī experienced "divine speech" directed to him personally from God; although he termed this inspirational speech *muḥādathāt* (converse with the divine), this phenomenon comes very close to the Prophet Muḥammad's reception of revelation (*waḥy*). After his death, his admirers claimed that he was "conjoined to Prophethood without any intermediary" like none had ever been before his time.[53]

Some of al-Jazūlī's adherents and devotees heard these claims to absolute spiritual authority and affinity with the Prophet as al-Jazūlī's announcement that he was indeed the expected Mahdī. One might distinguish between al-Jazūlī's self-understanding and how his followers may have perceived him, as Vincent Cornell does. Although al-Jazūlī claimed absolute authority as a saint, he did not lead an explicitly "millenarian" social movement or claim to be the Mahdī. Yet al-Jazūlī addressed huge crowds and actively sought disciples from the common people who were not literate, and his finely nuanced teachings could be easily exaggerated by some of his listeners.[54] If some of his followers perceived him to be the Mahdī, they were only drawing a conclusion that appeared obvious to them from his rhetoric, which compounded spiritual leadership, political authority, and descent from the Prophet.

Some of al-Jazuli's followers spread claims that he did embody the figure of the Mahdī. Zarruq heard such claims during his early years in Fes when he met al-Jazūlī's followers, and he argued with al-Ṣughayyir al-Sahlī about whether or not al-Jazūlī's followers had been spreading such claims before and immediately after the shaykh's death. This issue was limited to the realm of rhetoric while al-Jazūlī was still alive, but upon his death, it exploded into social violence and political chaos.

One of al-Jazūlī's followers, ᶜAmr al-Mughīṭī, alleged that the saint died from poisoning, and that certain jurists in the nearby town of Aït Dāwūd had killed him out of jealousy. This follower, known as "al-Sayyāf" [the sword-wielder], rallied the crowds that had gathered around al-Jazūlī and focused their grief into a call for revenge against his murderers. He pursued certain jurists until he killed them, and he may also have terrorized other, more intimate followers of al-Jazūlī into fleeing north. He split al-Jazūlī's community, calling those who supported him "disciples" and those who opposed his actions "infidels." He refused to bury the saint's body, but instead carried it in a wooden coffin at the forefront of his army as a talisman of victory.[55] Military victory was his for the taking, and no other political or tribal force could stand up to him. Al-Mughīṭī consolidated his military victories and political leadership with a bid for religious authority as well. He claimed that he had inherited the authority of the Prophet, and may even have envisioned himself as receiving a sort of divine revelation.[56]

Principles Violated in al-Mughīṭī Uprising

The rampage of al-Mughīṭī against jurists and scholars (as well as against anyone who opposed him even from within the community of al-Jazūlī's own followers) played upon all Zarruq's fears and anxieties and seemed like a living nightmare for Zarruq. He saw in it the inevitable social violence that came from a mass movement built up around a saint who is not careful to uphold legal norms in the pattern required by Zarruq's reform program. Thus Zarruq did not see al-Mughīṭī's violent extremism as an aberration. He saw it as the logical consequence of al-Jazūlī's socially activist and politically ambitious paradigm of saintly authority. Al-Jazūlī had circulated an open letter to "the jurists who pay attention only to the outward appearance of religion," challenging them to accept his leadership as a saint who actualized both the outward appearance and inward reality of religion.[57] Al-Jazūlī probably meant this letter to criticize the jurists of Fes, who supported the Marinid regime because of its customary legitimacy, as Zarruq himself had.[58] He probably knew of al-Jazūlī only by hearing his oral teaching through some of his followers in Fes and hearing them recite the litany of *Dalāʾil al-Khayrāt*.

Zarruq only knew of al-Jazūlī through the actions of the mass movement that had built up around his name. In contrast to researchers in the present, Zarruq had neither the written sources nor the privilege of hindsight to assess al-Jazūlī as a saint. "You should know that everything I have denounced and repudiated in this argument is only according to the knowledge that I have. I have no claim to omniscience. I only give a clear account of what knowledge I have. If I am correct then it is by the grace of God, and if not, then I am only a human being who can err and miss the mark. However, everyone who strives to speak the truth must make clear his argument and its proofs. If he does not make clear his proofs then he is rejected, since there is nobody more ignorant than someone who clings stubbornly to a practice which is invalid and has no proof on which to stand, or someone who denounces a person about whom he knows nothing."[59] This is crucial as we assess his bitter critique of the Jazūlīyya community in the next chapter. Whether Zarruq's critique was accurate or exaggerated by his own fears, it was the movement of al-Mughīṭī that shaped his perception of al-Jazūlī, and al-Mughīṭī rampaged throughout the southern Moroccan countryside for twenty years after the saint's death. Until the end of Zarruq's life, the campaign of al-Mughīṭī completely overshadowed the activities of al-Jazūlī's other followers, such as al-Tabbāᶜ and his theologically astute representative in Fes, ᶜAlī Ṣāliḥ al-Andalusī.

Upon the death of al-Jazūlī, Zarruq discussed the ideology spread by al- Mughīṭī with other followers of al-Jazūlī. He took an accusatory tone with al-Ṣughayyir al-Sahlī as he tried to figure out whether al-Mughīṭī was making claims that al-Jazūlī was the Mahdī, or whether al-Jazūlī himself had made these claims to his closest followers, who kept them secret until the saint's sudden death. "At the end of the night [after lengthy discussion], I said to him [al-Ṣughayyir al-Sahlī], 'Is it true that the people are repeating a rumor spread about you and the issue of the *Fāṭimī*?' or something to that effect. He went out, saying to me 'They are only spreading rumors that will get them killed, and may Allah send someone to exert the power over them to have them killed!' He repeated this prayer many times. ᶜAmr al-Mughīṭī was the one who appeared making his claim."[60] In this argument, the figure of "the *Fāṭimī*" represented the expected Mahdī.[61] The wording of Zarruq is purposefully ambiguous when he says that ᶜAmr al-Mughīṭī was the one who "appeared making his claim." Zarruq does not explicitly say that al-Jazūlī made this claim, yet he opens the possibility that al-Mughīṭī was the one who appeared making al-Jazūlī's claim to be the *Fāṭimī* after the saint's sudden death. On the other hand, Zarruq could be saying that al-Mughīṭī appeared making his own claim that al-Jazūlī was the *Fāṭimī*, a claim not substantiated by the saint's own teachings. Al-Ṣughayyir al-Sahlī's angry response clarifies that he considered al-Mughīṭī to have originated these claims, which multiplied as rumors spread among the expectant public in an environment of impending political and religious change. Al-Sahlī spoke with authority as the eldest of al-Jazūlī's followers.[62] He may even have come to Fes fleeing the mass movement of al-Mughīṭī, which would have threatened him if he had not sided with al-Mughīṭī.[63]

Zarruq's argument with al-Ṣughayyir al-Sahlī was not just doctrinal quibbling. The mass following and twenty-year span of al-Mughīṭī's movement shows that there was enormous potential in the southern countryside of Ḥāḥā and Shyāzma for political and religious uprising against existing social structures and political allegiances. Al-Jazūlī had tapped this discontent in building his own, more moderate and socially activist community. Al-Mughīṭī tapped it through a far more cultic, violent movement. Thirty years later, the sharifian family and their tribal clientele who would later take the name "Saᶜdī" were also tapping this discontent to form a movement of political rebellion against Fes.[64] For this reason, al-Mughīṭī's mass movement seemed like the vanguard of a potential popular revolution against the Marinid state that was centered in Fes, a revolution perpetrated in the name of al-Jazūlī. Whether historians call it "an uprising" or confer on it the status of a "revolution," al-Mughīṭī's movement showed the potential for a religious leader to unify various rival factions under the leadership of a saintly figure and to channel their unrest into a unified political-military force.[65] The movement also represented a new force in Moroccan political history, the "little armies" noted by Weston Cook. The new styles of war that depended on gunpowder and firearms "brought autonomy-minded 'big-men' or communities unusual access to men and material for private forces."[66]

The movement of al-Mughīṭī, then, was a phenomenon of great social importance, even if it appears from hindsight as a singular aberration in the historical development of the Jazūlīyya community. Reports about al-Mughīṭī's actions came to Fes, followed by complaints to the jurists and requests for official rulings against him. Such requests came to al-Qūrī, as Zarruq reports. "Al-Qūrī told me that he received a juridical inquiry about this issue [about al-Mughīṭī or claims that al-Jazūlī was the Mahdī], and he showed me the inquiry. Al-Qūrī said to me, 'This matter is beyond my control.' So I said to him, 'What is the relevant issue?' Al-Qūrī told me, 'It all revolves around the issue that [al-Mughīṭī] is claiming that the commands and rulings of the Qur'ān and the Prophet Muhammad's example are no longer valid, and that all that remains is that his own heart says to him from his Lord.'"[67] Al-Qūrī perceived that the issue went much deeper than a particular follower's claim that his saintly guide was the Mahdī; it involved al-Mughīṭī's ideology that the dispensation of Muhammad's revelation had ended.[68] His own heart "was speaking to him from his Lord," receiving some new revelation that replaced the rulings of the jurists and the interpretations of scholars based on the Qur'ān. Al-Qūrī actually knew al-Mughīṭī personally, for al-Mughīṭī had in his youth been a student of the jurist in Fes. Al-Qūrī remembers that he was already an extremist in his youth, dressed as a devotee, carrying a sword, and making wild religious claims.

Zarruq further explained that "word spread about al-Mughīṭī and he claimed he had 'inherited the spiritual authority of Prophethood (*wārith al-nubuwwa*).' He further claimed that commands and rulings were specified for him [which were deeper than Prophetic revelation] just as in the story of Khiḍr with Mūsā [Moses]. He also claimed that Khiḍr was still alive and that God sent him as a Messenger (*nabī mursal*), and that he had personally met Khiḍr and had taken initiation from him."[69] Zarru comments on this claim:

> There is a Sufi community [whose leaders] claim to see the "men of the unseen" such as al-Khiḍr (upon him be peace) or others like him. They make public messages given to them by these unseen personalities, messages which are either forbidden lies or delusions with which Shayṭān has afflicted them through apparitions. Through such claims they may either come to power as rulers or perhaps be brought to ruin. I have heard that some from this community claim that Khiḍr is a prophetic Messenger (*nabī mursal*) ... and that whoever claims that Khiḍr achieved [only] sainthood has belittled Khiḍr and that belittling a Prophet makes one an infidel. I have heard someone whom I trust describe how members of this community have said this in these exact words. My judgment is to be resigned to his right to claim what he claims, but to never be resigned to his calling others infidels who disbelieve him, because he has no definitive proof for others. If the matter is true for himself, he has no right to make believing it obligatory for others. For this is making an addition to the beliefs of the Islamic faith for which there is no principle (*aṣl*) and no reliable precedent (*mustanad*).[70]

In this way Zarruq widened and deepened his critique of al-Mughīṭī. By spreading rumors that the time of the Mahdī's advent had come and claiming that al-Jazūlī embodied that Mahdī, al-Mughīṭī opened the possibility (even the necessity) of a new Prophetic figure. He stepped into this role; through the visits of Khiḍr with messages from God he claimed revelation that was above mere inspiration. Many Sufis had experienced meetings with the elusive Khiḍr, who represented the force of inner inspiration and closeness to God that complemented Prophetic revelation. Al-Mughīṭī was unique and extreme in claiming to not only have met Khiḍr and taken initiation from him, but also to have received written messages from him as if receiving a new scriptural revelation. "I heard from some reliable and trustworthy people that they observed al-Mughīṭī during the lifetime of Shaykh al-Jazūlī, coming to him with tablets inscribed with a lot of writing that he attributed to Khiḍr. At these times, the Shaykh would not say anything to al-Mughīṭī [in rebuke]. He would only praise him, over and over again."[71] With this report, Zarruq comes very close to laying blame for al-Mughīṭī's extreme doctrines at the feet of al-Jazūlī. Zarruq depicts al-Mughīṭī making such claims even during the lifetime of al-Jazūlī and presenting these "revelations" to him without the "proper response" of rebuke or counseling. Zarruq implies that al-Jazūlī's own claims to spiritual affinity to the Prophet Muḥammad and his publicizing that he heard "divine addresses" (*muḥādathāt*) opened a Pandora's box of potential extremism and exaggeration.

Although it was the mass movement led by al-Mughīṭī that sparked his critical project and colored it thoroughly, Zarruq was far more systematic than to stop with al-Mughīṭī. He expressed ambivalence about al-Jazūlī himself and suspected that his inattention at crucial moments encouraged al-Mughīṭī and his followers. Zarruq's intellectual endeavor to elucidate the principles that drive social action and religious change led him to generalize his critique. Al-Mughīṭī's movement was only the most obvious and dramatic example of a Sufi community gone wrong that gave rise to a social movement. Zarruq's critique embraced the other followers of al-Jazūlī as well.[72]

The movement of al-Mughīṭī illustrates the three "principles of corruption" that Zarruq announced in *ᶜUddat al-Murīd al-Ṣādiq*: ignoring scholarly training, lacking principled practice in devotion, and harboring political ambition. This movement was probably the central event he observed when formulating these principles. Zarruq argued that the subtle forces of these three principles acting over the course of generations allowed *bidᶜa* to manifest itself in religious custom, and the incidence of *bidᶜa* leads a Sufi community to certain negative consequences, the most dramatic of which is partisanship. Al-Mughīṭī provided Zarruq the clearest example of partisanship that can quickly lead to social discord and flagrant disregard for legal principles and authorities. He notes that al-Mughīṭī based his movement on absolute and exaggerated loyalty to the saint whom he followed. "Al-Mughīṭī's schismatic career began when he portrayed himself as the defender of his Shaykh, al-Jazūlī, against those who had poisoned him. For he claimed that some jurists had poisoned al-Jazūlī and did not stop until he had killed them all. Then he began to proselytize among the common people and call them to pray [behind his leadership]. If they resisted, he would fight against them. Then he began to call any who opposed him or denounced him to be an 'infidel' (*jāḥid*) and those who supported him to be a 'disciple' (*murīd*)."[73] Al-Mughīṭī vaulted into a position of leadership due to his excessive loyalty to al-Jazūlī and his call to avenge the saint's death. His "love and loyalty" went to almost insane lengths, as he claimed to be al-Jazūlī's hidden brother and forced the dead shaykh's wife and then his daughter to marry him to seal his close relation. Such loyalty may stem from love for the saint, argues Zarruq, but it must be tempered with knowledge and training in the principles of being a Sufi, or else it becomes a cause of social discord.

This example of an extremist social movement, inspired by love for a saint unhinged from legal principles, was the touchstone for Zarruq's critical writings. As he observed al-Mughīṭī's uprising with horror, he saw behind it principles that were potentially violated by many social movements led by other Sufis among al-Jazūlī's followers who were far more subtle, more authoritative, and more realistically poised to wield political power in Morocco. It is to these Sufi leaders and the social movements they inspired and led that Zarruq turned his legal acumen in a bitter social critique.

8 Critique

ZARRUQ DID NOT limit his critique to the extremist movement of al-Mughīṭī, which has been described in the previous chapter. He did not let his critique of al-Mughīṭī remain personal; rather he pushed its circumference to the limits of a universal critique. He did this by articulating the roots and principles it violated, which other movements might also similarly violate. Zarruq analyzed how al-Mughīṭī's violent movement was fueled by loyalty and partisanship that disguise the ambition for leadership. He argued that these elements incite saints or their followers to construct social movements based on loyalty to a saint. Zarruq labels such devoted followers as *Muḥibbūn*, those ruled by devoted love. By extending this "principle" from the example of al-Mughīṭī into a general ruling, Zarruq extends his critique to the other followers of al-Jazūlī as well, who were clearly not simple loving devotees but were well-educated and had spent years under the close training of al-Jazūlī.

When al-Mughīṭī posed as the true inheritor of al-Jazūlī's spiritual authority, other more senior followers of al-Jazūlī fled. They came to northern Morocco for missionary work and to seek safety from al-Mughīṭī's jealousy and violence. As already noted, al-Ṣughayyir al-Sahlī visited Fes with a group of al-Jazūlī's followers. He did not settle in the city, but instead among the Arabs of the Banū Maᶜqil tribe in the countryside north of Fes.[1] Al-Jazūlī's followers strategically chose to settle among these Arabs to bring their rebelliousness into alliance with their own political vision. Another of al-Jazūlī's senior followers, Aḥmad al-Ḥārithī al-Ṣufyānī, also came north to settle west of Fes, in a primarily Arab tribal area, as did Ḥasan Ajānā.[2] Along with al-Ṣughayyir migrated the young ᶜAbd al-ᶜAzīz al-Tabbāᶜ, who most likely came to Fes under al-Ṣughayyir's care, and thus would have met Zarruq in the group who came to zawiya Būʾl-Quṭūṭ.

At that early stage, Zarruq did not take notice of al-Tabbāᶜ. There is no mention of meeting him (in the record of *al-Kunnāsh*). Yet it was this young man who would later institutionalize the Jazūlīyya community and emerge as the principal leader of al-Jazūlī's followers after the dissipation of al-Mughīṭī's movement. Though he settled in the countryside and sought to attract disciples and admirers from the Arab tribes, al-Tabbāᶜ also maintained contacts in the city of Fes after the

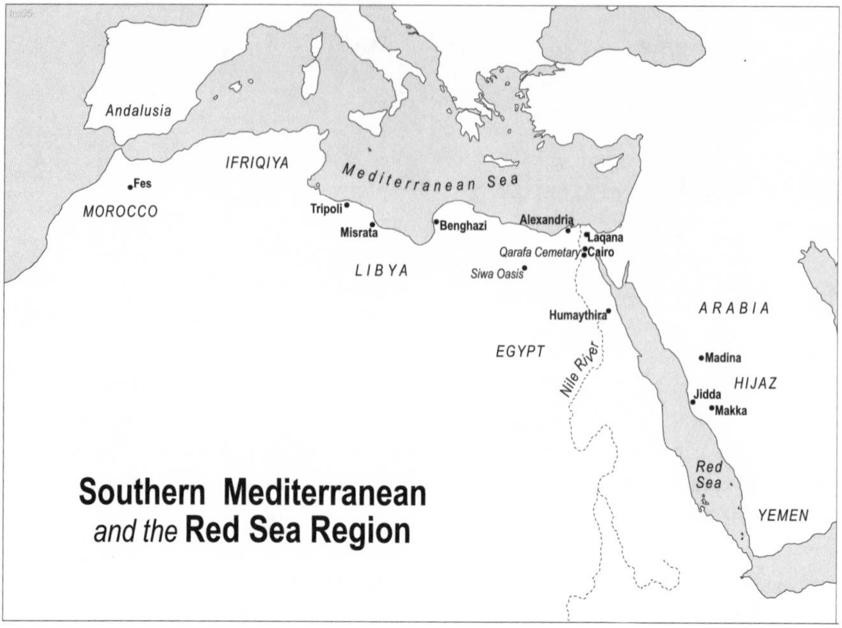

Map D

sharifian revolution opened the city. By 880 Hijri (1475–76 C.E.), he had returned south to his native city of Marrakesh, where he opened the first urban zawiya of the Jazūlīyya community. Even then, he maintained contacts in Fes, where he gave lectures and led sessions of reciting *Dalāʾil al-Khayrāt* in the madrasa al-ᶜAṭṭārīn. In addition, he set up the Jazūlīyya zawiya in Fes under the administration of the scholarly and urbane ᶜAlī Ṣāliḥ al-Andalusī.[3]

While ᶜAlī Ṣāliḥ al-Andalusī began to write texts to systematize the oral and written teachings of al-Jazūlī, al-Tabbāᶜ had other interests. With his forceful personality he excelled in training disciples and gathering followers. Al-Tabbāᶜ and his followers maintained a program of social activism, basic education in the countryside, and roaming missionary work. Zarruq probably observed these rural activities of the Jazūlīyya community rather than their urban institution in Fes. During his four years in Fes, between 879–83 Hijri (1474–79 C.E.), Zarruq observed the Jazūlīyya community in its most active proselytizing phase. Its leaders tried to build a wide social base of support and harness the rebelliousness of Arab tribes for political revolt against central rule in Fes. The story of how ᶜAbdullah al-Ghazwānī (who eventually became the successor to al-Tabbāᶜ) had joined the Jazūlīyya illustrates these activities. He was a Shāwī Arab whose father had sent him from the countryside to the capital for a juridical education. One evening, a group of young devotees (*fuqarāʾ*) saw him standing in the street and cajoled him to join them for a fun evening at the Jazūlīyya zawiya, where the Sufis allowed common people to join their recitation of *Dalāʾil al-Khayrāt* and gave a free banquet. That night, al-Ghazwānī was moved to offer his allegiance to the master of the zawiya, ᶜAlī Ṣāliḥ al-Andalusī.[4]

This story shows the systematic social outreach that the new Jazūlīyya community employed. They not only recruited recent immigrants into the cities from among the students, but they also used their contacts with Arab tribes beyond the cities to cement alliances. Al-Andalusī saw the spiritual potential in his new initiate and, noting his Arab background and ties to the countryside, sent al-Ghazwānī to Marrakesh for training. After ten years of training under al-Tabbāᶜ, al-Ghazwānī would be instrumental in securing the allegiance of many leaders of his Shāwī Arab to the leadership of al-Tabbāᶜ. He then concentrated on securing followers from his own clan, the Banū Ghazwān. This active mission work was a complex phenomenon. On the one hand, allegiance to the Jazūlīyya community meant increasing support for the *jihād* against the Portuguese. Initiates were encouraged to join the military encampments at a series of fortified towns to retake positions from the Portuguese, at Tetuan, Shafshawan, Targha, and al-Kharrub.[5] Beyond defending the Moroccan shores from Iberian marauders, there was a domestic agenda to this *jihād*: cultivating opposition to the Waṭṭāsid rulers, who perpetuated the edifice of the Marinid dynasty after returning to power in Fes in 876 Hijri (1471 C.E.). The initiation offered by the leaders of the Jazūlīyya was a potent blend of spiritual allegiance, military defense, and political rebellion, all revolving around the absolute authority of a saintly leader.

Jurists in Fes noted these developments with alarm, as the Jazūlīyya community assertively recruited common people and tribal groups into their Sufi community. Zarruq recalls that at least thirty-five petitions were received by the jurists of Fes requesting legal decisions on this growing Sufi allegiance in the countryside. He admires the principled stand of his early guide, al-Qūrī, who refused to offer any judgment on these petitions, saying, "I will not answer a single query about them, since they [the leaders of this community] are active in the land of the tribes. That is the region of partisan and fanatical political loyalties (*maḥall al-taᶜassub*). If I would answer in favor of these leaders, then their devoted followers (*muḥibbūn*) would become even more extreme in their loyalty. If I answer against these leaders, then their opponents would become even more extreme in their opposition. In that case, a decision would throw open the door of social discord (*fitna*) between the various tribes, exacerbating a conflict that would last forever. This is something with which God would never charge us [even in speaking the truth]."[6] Zarruq notes, however, that other jurists did not show such restraint and condemned such efforts to build a tribal confederacy around saintly leaders cemented with Sufi initiations. As early as 873 Hijri (1468–69 C.E.), certain jurists went out into the countryside to investigate their activities. They found that "speaking with them [their adherents] rationally was impossible." Jurists and judges in the smaller towns outside Fes found that they were not free to speak at all about this community for fear of reprisals from angered adherents. They had to hold their tongues and say only "that the matter should be carefully examined."[7]

In Fes, some jurists accused the Sufis of the Jazūlīyya of not following any discrete legal method, neither Mālikī nor Shāfiᶜī. Others, like Abū al-Qāsim al-ᶜAbdūsī and Muḥammad ibn Marzūq al-Tilimsānī, leveled more damning decisions against them, accusing these leaders of "being Shiᶜa" (*Rāfiḍīyya*) or of practicing sorcery. Some religious notables in Fes exaggerated these condemnations, pronouncing that "drinking wine and fornication are lighter sins than joining their Sufi community," and even threatened that "their homes should be razed and their assemblies broken up, and they should be individually punished until their activities are eradicated from the land."[8] Zarruq finds such open denunciation to be extreme, but encourages people to examine the community beliefs and practices with a critical eye and skeptical mind before pledging allegiance to a Sufi master.[9] Zarruq's own critique tries to maintain a fine balance between denouncing the practice of al-Tabbāᶜ and his Jazūlīyya colleagues while maintaining the importance of Sufi communities as a whole and the figure of the saint in particular. In this way, Zarruq's program for the internal reform of Sufi practice is the foundation of his rhetoric of critique.

Spirited Critique of Ideology

Zarruq singled out particular practices of "this community" without ever mentioning al-Tabbāᶜ or his colleagues by name. He acknowledges, however, that each detail of their activities reinforces a holistic, almost ideological framework of life. Their dress, their rituals of worship, and their ceremonies of initiation all contribute to their community identity and devotion to the person of the leader. This partisanship, in Zarruq's view, is the fundamental dynamic that links the Jazūlīyya community's style of sainthood with their followers' social practices. His critique therefore focuses on this dynamic of partisanship. "If they protest [that they are doing nothing wrong and nothing against religious custom] I would say to them, 'I repudiate … in particular the evil consequences that come about from your self-aggrandizing claims to pre-eminence in spiritual state and special status in your religious actions, and in your speaking openly to the public and staying in the presence of the common people and ignorant ones.'"[10]

The saints of the Jazūlīyya claimed an absolute authority in the realm of spiritual guidance. Their own paradigm of authority was structurally similar to the Shiᶜī conception of the *Imām*. He would be the singular, living continuation of the Prophet's charismatic personality (even though the Prophet's career, as the bearer of revelation, ended with his death).[11] Explication of this concept of absolute authority is one of the ways that Sufi followers of al-Jazūlī were extraordinarily original in their writings. For instance, ᶜAlī Ṣāliḥ al-Andalusī wrote that the supreme saints act as the "substitutes for God's Prophetic messengers" (*abdāl al-rusūl*) after the period of revelation had ended. They are the vice regents of God on earth (*khalīfat Allah*) and, like the Prophet Muḥammad, they act as the center of both spiritual life and political authority.[12] Especially original is al-Ghazwānī's exposition of the axial saint as "the resounding bell" (*jaras*), who is in himself empty but who vibrates sympathetically with the peal of the Prophet Muhammad's own nature, broadcasting the Prophet's message into his own time.[13] In claiming to be the axial saints of their age and region, al-Tabbā^c and al-Ghazwānī drew a firm boundary around the community of those who held allegiance to them and delineated them from others who did not. Zarruq reacts sharply to "their belief that all other spiritual paths are void or are lesser in comparison with their own."[14]

This claim is the foundation of their building the Jazūlīyya Sufi community into a mass movement. Such absolute authority puts adherents in the role of loving devotees or impassioned partisans, claimed Zarruq. While the Jazūlīyya leaders did not forbid the acquisition of scholarly knowledge (in fact, they encouraged basic literacy in innovative ways), this bond of absolute submission between disciple and saint eclipsed the role of scriptural knowledge and created an environment that devalued learning. An example that would have excited Zarruq's wrath is how ^cAbd al-^cAzīz al-Tabbā^c was reputed to embody the Qur^ān without having "learned it." The story circulated that the young al-Tabbā^c visited the tomb of Abū Yi^czza (after leaving al-Ṣughayyir al-Sahlī en route to beginning his independent career in Marrakesh). He slept by the tomb for the purpose of imploring help in a time of great need and dreamed that Abū Yi^czza opened his chest and inserted a copy of the Qur^ān. When he woke, he found that he knew the whole scripture by heart, though he was "unlearned."[15] This makes Zarruq's insistence of scholarly training more illuminating in comparison to ways other saints "learned" the Qur^ān. They have no standard of knowledge of learning or piety, alleges Zarruq, when they offer initiation to disciples. In fact, they engineer mass initiations of whole towns or whole clans. Such initiations rely on distinct rituals, like shaving the head, to symbolize repentance (*tawba*) and entrance into the community. Yet, Zarruq argues, shaving the head has nothing to do with real repentance and even distracts from the personal relation between master and disciple that alone can foster real repentance. Shaving the head is a custom of the Maṣmūda Berbers, who had been among the first to institute a Sufi community in Morocco.[16] Al-Jazūlī had adopted many of their devotional practices in forging his community into a mass movement, and head shaving was one of the most prominent signs of membership in the movement. Zarruq argued juridically that even if there is some precedent (in the Prophet's having cut the hair of pagan Arabs who joined Islam), the Jazūlīyya community was fostering *bid^ca* by claiming that this practice is integral and indispensable to a Sufi initiation. Similarly, he argued against their practice of wearing distinctive clothes or hanging a prominent string of prayer beads around their necks as signs of membership in the movement. Any outer sign of their populist appeal appeared to Zarruq as a violation of juridical norms and an example of *bid^ca*, insisting that an extraneous practice was integral to religious custom.

It is not just the behavior of adherents that Zarruq criticizes, but also the missionary behavior of the Jazūlīyya community's leaders. He notes that they travel through the countryside for the single purpose of gathering followers.[17] Without limiting initiation to those who have "intellectual and experiential qualification," they encourage everyone to join due to their social activism: illiterate as well as educated, women as well as men, children as well as adults.

> They justify [these mass initiations] saying, "It is to give them [common people] religious guidance." However, in reality guidance (*hidāya*) ... comes from faith and faith alone. In answer to this objection, they say "Then [we do it] to complete their faith with the wariness of God." However, in reality the wariness of God (*taqwā*) comes from giving people exhortation and reminder, not from their taking allegiance to a saint. Then they protest, "The human ego does not accept the truth except in a form which amazes and causes wonder; taking the hand of followers [in initiation] is part of the Prophet's example, and we do this as an authentic way of following his example from which nobody is exempt." However, we maintain that the Prophet took the hand of his companions only as an affirmation of faith and as an aid to their moral rectitude. There is no example of the Prophet taking allegiance like this except from his companions, after they had already realized faith within themselves. We find that you people do it otherwise, not in according with the Prophetic action, nor the Prophet's intention, nor in accord with the truth.[18]

Such mass initiation was crucial to the Jazūlīyya leaders' building their social movement into a political community. Their social activism included promoting libraries, circulating devotional tracts, providing graded initiation in enough levels to make some form of membership open to almost everyone, expressing their devotion through social service, validating contracts, witnessing pledges, giving safe conducts to goods, men, and funds.[19]

Zarruq, however, could see no useful function in this kind of social activism. These are the roles of government and jurists, not the roles of saints. Rather, he links this type of mass initiation to the paradigm of absolute saintly authority that the Jazūlīyya community advocated. "They accept the allegiance of everyone, no matter what kind of people or what they are doing in regards to religious behavior. They do not require initiates to reform their behavior, but only to accept the outer form of this community's practice, most of which is *bidᶜa*.... Further, they believe that repentance is effective only through taking initiation into their own community. If one has taken initiation into a different community and to a different saint, they challenge and discredit this allegiance."[20]

These outer behaviors, which assert the ideological cohesion of the Jazūlīyya community as a social movement, depend on their central conception of the saint's absolute authority. Zarruq swiftly shifts his focus from the level of social practice to the level of doctrinal belief. "They believe that having allegiance to a saint is more sufficient [for salvation] than performing religiously sanctioned deeds. Further, they assert that deeds in fulfillment of religious obligations are not complete without having a saintly master. They make it incumbent upon their disciples to believe in the saint's inerrancy (*ᶜiṣma*), and that everything he does proceeds from God's directive, whether it conforms to the outer appearance of religious custom or not. They treat the disciple after his allegiance as if he were not a full person, as if he were a slave with no will of his own, with no spirit, no soul, no wealth, and no family.... They intend to test the disciple's trust, remove his pride, make sound his spiritual state, and suppress his self-will; but in reality such practices are nothing more than removing their followers' manhood and answering the call of greed—we seek the protection of God from such things."[21] After such a detailed inventory of this community's misdeeds at the level of social practice, juridical justification, and conception of sainthood, Zarruq confronts the key question. What is the use of such a critique?

Combating Partisan Authority

Zarruq's spiritual guide in Fes, al-Qūrī, was faced with the same social phenomena and was asked to give a juridical decision on such practices; he demurred. Zarruq, in blatant contradiction to al-Qūrī's prior example, forges ahead with a detailed and bitter critique. It is not enough to live and let live, or to simply point out the juridical ambiguities in some of their devotional practices. Rather, Zarruq perceives that there are many harmful consequences to this concatenation of inauthentic practices, questionable concept of sainthood, and promotion of a social movement. In his view, the consequences are harmful for followers of the community as well as for the leaders who aspire to be saints. At the level of the common followers, Zarruq perceives partisanship as the major consequence, leading to the division of society into factions. He claims that allegiance to such a community ruins the moral character and virtuous disposition (*malaka*) of the common adherent. "Such beliefs and practices empower their partisanship until it becomes overweening, as they mention their own leaders and their enemies. They come to believe that they prove their own faith in their spiritual master by their constant opposition to whomever their leaders oppose and their loyalty to whomever their leaders support. This leads them into boasting, wrangling and disputing with others, giving little respect to other spiritual masters or to other Muslims in general who are not in their community. One hears from them only a clamor of confused and false claims. One meets only rotten personalities among them. One hears from them only 'us versus you' or 'our master versus your master' or 'our way versus your way.'"[22] In Zarruq's view, members of such a social movement have their egos puffed up rather than tempered with humility. This contradicts the basic principles of Sufi practice and is a sure indicator of this community's inauthenticity.

Of course, such social practices of cohesion are crucial to form a social movement. The ideological distinction between insider and outsider, between a righteous movement and a corrupt society, were crucial in the Jazūlīyya community's attempt to build a movement of social reform and political protest around the nucleus of a Sufi lineage. Zarruq observed this formation of a social movement with the eye of a moralist, not of a historian. He saw this ideological process as evidence of moral decay in the short span of an individual lifetime. Zarruq protested that the formation of a social movement did not establish the virtue of its leaders as saints; rather the rigor of striving to become a saint within the limitation of the law was the only source of virtue.

In contrast, the compromises inherent in building a mass movement around one's assumption of sainthood led to an immediate and dramatic collapse of inner virtue. In this way, Zarruq claimed that the saintly leaders of the Jazūlīyya community were plagued by many moral transgressions latent in their very exercise of political power. "They are plagued with greed and hunger for more followers, until they verily sweep them up and drive them along. They even send their representatives out into the countryside, calling to the common people to become their followers. They coerce them to donate their money and overwhelm them in every way possible."[23] Such is their drive to achieve power through building a mass following that some leaders, claims Zarruq, forced people to take allegiance from them, people who were not only unfit for Sufi practice but uninterested in joining the social movement. Zarruq claims (based on "eyewitness" accounts) that one such leader grabbed the hand of a common man and announced, "There, you have taken initiation from me and owe allegiance to me!"

Such reports sound like caricature, yet Zarruq is responding to very real social pressures from within the Jazūlīyya community to build a mass following. His is a negative assessment of the same missionary tactics that had drawn ᶜAbdallah al-Ghazwānī into the Jazūlīyya zawiya as a youth in Fes. Zarruq feared the self-satisfaction engendered among those saints who led the movement. "They become satisfied with themselves and think themselves somehow better than others, until they are complacent with what they have of spiritual experience, knowledge, and masters."[24] For Zarruq, who spent so much of his life traveling, studying, and searching for spiritual guidance, the comfort of a strong and assertive spiritual community was a certain sign that sincerity is lost. For Zarruq, sincerity comes from internal struggle, not from joining a social movement that advocated a political struggle.

Yet these popular rituals and missionary strategies brought huge numbers of followers into the ranks of the Jazūlīyya community. Zarruq notes sourly that their inauthentic religious practice (*bidᶜa*) secured for their community a devoted following that, in turn, secured for them many worldly benefits: "the world is generous in giving them wealth and means; this is the starting place of every difficulty and social discord."[25] As followers grant them wealth and means, saints accrue the power to spend or consume the money of other people and dispose of their goods.

Such success in worldly affairs condemns these saints and their Sufi followers to a sort of spiritual torpor, thinks Zarruq. The saint should engage the public only through the social roles of teacher or jurist; this acts as to insulate a saint from public expectation and from traces of personal ambition. All other ways of engaging the public will ruin a saint's sincerity and authenticity, whether through giving public speeches, demonstrations of charismatic power or miracles, leading political movements, or building military encampments.

All these types of "public service" involve building a popular following and getting involved with the means of social power. Zarruq's elitist conception of purity and power takes for granted that this mixing of classes causes immorality and extinguishes the light of sainthood. When saintly persons are mixed up in worldly projects, claims Zarruq, the result is torpor, a muddied morality which dulls the spiritual light that is particular to each class of people. What is most evident about the people in this community, alleges Zarruq, is their murkiness (*ghalasa*). "You can hardly find among them a single person who is spiritually illumined: neither by the light of his own inherent nature, like the rest of the common folk, nor by the light of the heart, like the saintly few. Rather, a murky gloom clouds their faces, like a light eclipsed by darkness. Anyone with even a low level of astuteness can perceive this gloom, and by it distinguish [members of this community] from all others. This is the result of their mixing religious truth with baseless falsehood in their practices."[26] The people's urge to be close to a saint and follow his teachings is religious truth, in Zarruq's analysis. However, their propensity for following inauthentic saints alloys this truth with falsehood, as does the propensity for false claimants to sainthood to put themselves forward out of greed, ambition, or ignorance.

After so much denunciatory prose, Zarruq tried to concentrate on what he affirms in Sufi practice, reinforcing the title of his work, *Preparing the Sincere Disciple*. The work was intended to help a neophyte Sufi discriminate between certainty and ambiguity, between practices around sainthood that lead to social discord and practices that lead to social harmony. His piercing critique of others forms the counterpoint to his own reform project, as he points out not only what disciples should not do, but also affirms what they should do. To prepare a disciple for the sincere aspiration to learn from a saint, Zarruq discusses the various kinds of spiritual masters one encounters and gives specific conditions for adhering to each kind.[27]

He counseled that every disciple who aspires to take initiation from a saint should first develop the critical acumen to distinguish between a true saint and a false one. He offers distinct criteria as signs by which a disciple can recognize whether his potential master is firm and sound.[28] Of course, he also offers signs by which a pretender to sainthood can be known. Most of these signs of sincerity or insincerity have to do with a potential saint's involvement in scholarship and jurisprudence. Zarruq's reformist program tries to bring these complementary roles into a firm alliance or, further, to combine the two roles into one. Those who do not combine them to ensure their mutual reciprocity deserve to be condemned, as illustrated by Zarruq's metaphor of the jurist and Sufi who enter the king's inner chamber, as cited on page 157.

In critiquing social movements that were based on belief in the absolute authority of a saint, Zarruq covered a wide range of politically and spiritually potent ideas. He pointed out the propensity of people in the countryside to expect the advent of a Mahdī figure who would exert a radical form of justice in society.

Zarruq noted that a saint claiming absolute authority blended quite easily into a figure of the Mahdī, if not in his own rhetoric then in his reception by a mass audience. His sensitivity to this issue extended well beyond the discrete movement of al-Mughīṭī. In his alarm, Zarruq judged well the tenor of his times. Although Zarruq did not live to see the rise of the Saᶜdian dynasty in Morocco, his critiques would prove farsighted. In the next half-century after he died, many social movements in the Maghrib cohered around a Mahdī figure, including the Saᶜdian movement that established its dynastic rule over Fes and Marrakesh.

The advent of the Mahdī marked a radical departure from the routinized forms of Islam that claimed political legitimacy; its appeal was based on the supposed dawn of a new spiritual dispensation, whether this involved a new scriptural revelation or not. Although later social movements among Muslims tended not to announce a new Prophet, the figure of the Mahdī often verged on taking a quasi-prophetic role. For instance, the *al-Muwaḥḥid* [Sp. Almohad] movement of Ibn Tumart shows the doctrinal variation of movements that appeal to a Mahdī.[29] In Morocco, the Sufi theorist Ibn al-ᶜArabī fused the figures of the ultimate saint with that of the Mahdī. Through his writings and the technical term "the seal of sainthood" (*khātim al-wilāya*) many Sufi communities began to expect the advent of the Mahdī in the form of a saint.[30]

The movement led by al-Mughīṭī displayed many of these same characteristics. His was a political revolt with an implicitly "Khārijī" mode of authority, rejecting rule based on dynastic legitimacy or on juridical rulings in favor of a popular leader who was the "just Imām" of the local community. Al-Jazūlī had himself claimed to be the just Imām of Moroccan society, and al-Mughīṭī elevated him to the rank of the Mahdī to accent the political revolt inherent in his movement. Al-Mughīṭī may have been an anomaly in the doctrinal development of the Jazūlīyya community, but he represented a persistent pattern in the political development of their movement. He insisted that the Jazūlī paradigm of spiritual authority necessitated a political insurrection built around the figure of a just sharifian Imām, the Mahdī. Many admirers of Jazūlīyya among the tribal groupings in Shyāzma and Ḥāḥā found al-Mughīṭī's rhetoric convincing.

In contrast, most of al-Jazūlī's closest followers found al-Mughīṭī to be reckless, if not personally crazed. Although they repudiated al-Mughīṭī, they returned to Mahdist rhetoric when they built their own social movements and entered into the political arena. In this sense, the movement led by al-Mughīṭī raised issues of religio-political ideology that were later used by the Saᶜdian movement. Certain followers of al-Jazūlī who administered rural zawiyas in the Sūs urged local tribal and religious leaders to pledge allegiance to one ruler with both religious and political justification. They further urged the *sharīf* Muḥammad ibn ᶜAbd al-Raḥmān (a jurist and tribal leader from Tagmadert in the fertile oasis region of Zagora) to accept the role of just Imām and step forward as a new political-military leader.[31] He accepted this role and, at the Jazūlīyya zawiya at Tidsī, the Maṣmūda Berber leaders and common people of the Sūs pledged allegiance to him as "The Commander of the Faithful." He took the further title "The One Who Stands with the Command of God" (*al-qā'im bi-ᶜamr Allah*) that evokes the figure of the Mahdī as a proto-messianic figure. The terms *al-Qā'im* and *al-Mahdi* reflect each other and are closely connected in Islamic thought.[32] The *sharīf* Muḥammad ibn ᶜAbd al-Raḥmān took the title *al-Qā'im* while rumor spread that the eldest of his two sons was the expected Mahdī.[33] However, after coming to power in the south of Morocco as a military force and potential dynasty, rivalry arose between the two brothers. The younger and more strategically astute brother, Muḥammad al-Shaykh, wrested power from his older brother, Aḥmad al-Aᶜraj, then appropriated *al-Mahdī* as a formal title for himself. In this way, the leaders of the Saᶜdian movement adopted a Mahdist political ideology as a rhetorical counter to Waṭṭāsid claims of legitimacy by dynastic descent or by appealing to jurists. Such allusions, sometimes suggested and sometimes openly asserted, continued to play an important role in legitimating the Saᶜdian dynasty through the reign of Aḥmad al-Manṣūr.[34]

The leaders of the Jazūlīyya community lent their support to the early Saᶜdian movement, which was fully dependent on the zawiyas for its institutional structure. This alliance shows that the rumors that Aḥmad al-Aᶜraj was the Mahdī were more than just popular expectation. His father deliberately traveled with his son to Āfūghāl to al-Jazūlī's grave.[35] This behavior confirmed the strong link perceived by the educated public between al-Jazūlī and the figure of the Mahdī, as mediated through the talismanic use of the dead saint's body. Al-Mughīṭī had been extraordinarily successful with this strategy, and the Saᶜdian leaders appropriated this element of his ideology. Later, Muḥammad al-Shaykh "al-Mahdī" would confirm this pattern by exhuming al-Jazūlī's body and moving it to Marrakesh, his new capital, where it would support his claim to be the just Imām and rightful sharifian ruler about whom al-Jazūlī had preached.

As it grew, the Saᶜdian dynasty carefully controlled these politically potent symbols of Mahdist ideology. This ideology suited two political purposes: rebellion on moral grounds against a "legitimately constituted" dynasty, and assertion of absolute personal authority by a ruler over other institutions of religious authority. The Saᶜdian regime at different moments in its development would implement both these functions of Mahdist ideology. When Zarruq critiqued al-Mughīṭī at the outset of his insurrection, he could not have foreseen the complicated way in which the Jazūlī legacy would support the rise of a new dynasty. However, his critique did pinpoint many of the elements that the Saᶜdian leaders would weave together in their bid for religious and political power: popular *jihād*, the saint's absolute authority in the social realm, dismissal of jurists who opposed their movement, and the claim that a descendant of Fāṭima has unique religious authority as the Mahdī.

Mahdist rhetoric was instrumental in establishing a new political order based on the ideology of sharifian rule coupled with saintly support. The Saᶜdian claim and its backing by the network of saints of the Jazūlīyya was foreshadowed by the more irrational insurrection of al-Mughīṭī. As the Saᶜdian ruler Muḥammad al-

Shaykh "al-Mahdī" removed al-Jazūlī's body to Marrakesh, he was not just asserting his control over the countryside beyond the city. It was also a defensive move to prevent other Mahdist upstarts from claiming the body for themselves, as al-Mughīṭī had. Once expectations of the advent of the Mahdī arose, various groups laid claim to this status (throughout the decades after Zarruq's death). Many tried to rival the Saᶜdian claim to power, though few met with success against them. The fact that Mahdist rhetoric slipped out of the grasp of the rising Saᶜdian dynasty (to be used forcefully by its detractors) only reveals how powerful Mahdist rhetoric was in their original rise to power.

Legal Contest and Contesting Narratives

Only outside of Morocco could Zarruq write such a detailed and damning critique of his colleagues. He could only write it when safely separated from his former Qādirīyya community that centered on al-Zaytūnī in Fes and the allied Jazūlīyya community that was rising in prominence beyond the walls of Fes. He committed his first tentative critique to paper, in the *Principles of Being a Sufi* he wrote once he returned to Fes from Cairo. After four long and disappointing years in Fes, he left again for Cairo, and en route expanded his critique into its full and vituperative form in *Preparing the Sincere Disciple*. It was during this four-year stay in Fes that Zarruq tried to implement his reform program in his home community and failed miserably, primarily because of the sharp edge of critique that permeated his teachings. This section will illustrate how Zarruq's Moroccan contemporaries received his critique and launched a counter-critique against him.

Zarruq clearly had reservations about the character of those who claimed to be saints in Morocco. He singled out his home region for careful analysis when he wrote his *Principles of Being a Sufi*, asserting that each cultural zone had its own particular moral ethos and its own spiritual tenor. Saints distinguished themselves from the general moral hypocrisy of their fellow countrymen, which allowed others to distinguish them clearly. "Every land has its particular balance of truthfulness and falsehood. If you want [to know how] to find the saint from among a certain land's people, just look for whether he is free of the particular quality of falseness of the general public. If he is free of the bad qualities of those around him, then he is a saint, and if not then not! In the Far West [Morocco], people most respect the quality of unlimited generosity (*sakhā*). If you find this quality in a person, you know him to be a saint, and if not then leave him."[36] Among Moroccans, opines Zarruq, one recognizes the spiritual aristocrats (*sādāt wa qāda*) by their difference from the base and mean characters who surround them, like the stinginess and vicious nastiness of the majority of people.[37] Generosity was the contested moral value in Morocco, around which real virtue or its hypocritical counterpart revolved.

When Zarruq returned to Fes, he was confronted by a drama that confirmed his worst fears, in a story first told in chapter 7. We can return to this episode to understand the counter-critique leveled against Zarruq. As the jurists of Fes came out to meet him, Zarruq fell into a moral duel with them over the virtue of generosity, which was a debate over sainthood in veiled terms. One of the jurists who went out from Fes to meet Zarruq upon his return to the city of his birth recounted: "We greeted Shaykh Zarruq and sat down with him in his tent, he began to ask the jurists about their means of livelihood and provision. Some of them answered him, 'Most of our income comes from charitable trusts (*awqāf maḥbūsa*) endowed at the graves of the dead.' Then Shaykh Zarruq replied, 'There is no means and no power except with Allah! You are eating from the flesh of carrion!' Everyone fell silent. After a time, the jurist Ibn al-Ḥabbāk answered him saying, 'Sir, praise be to God who has made us to take advantage of this opportunity, for eating the flesh of carrion is allowed [in Islamic law] in states of need and duress. By this ruling, God has saved us from eating flesh of the living which is not allowed in the *sharīʿa* under any condition!'"[38] The key to understanding this argument lies in the pollution involved in consuming flesh; the argument was obviously heated and of deep emotional impact, because, as the narrator reports, on hearing the retort that God has saved us from eating flesh of the living, "Shaykh Zarruq let out a cry and fell to the ground unconscious. We left him then and there in that troubled state."

Zarruq charges the jurists with "eating the flesh of carrion" which, in Islamic dietary regulations, is forbidden. By this he means that they eat of the provision left by dead people who had endowed their property as charitable trusts: the wealth that they left was like the flesh left on a dead body. Why would Zarruq criticize the jurists as hypocrites, since they earned their livelihood through legally sanctioned means (such trusts are encouraged in Islamic law)? Through this revolting image, Zarruq meant to shock the jurists and turn them away from the pursuit of jurisprudence for worldly goods. He calls such behavior "eating by means of religion" and says it is like eating food that has been explicitly forbidden, like pork and carrion.[39] He wanted them to be not mere jurists, but Sufi jurists who followed a juridical saint. He judged them according to the example of al-Qūrī, who had not eaten from endowments or stipends even as he held the highest juridical position in Fes.

Zarruq's reform program regarded those trained as jurists as the best potential saints. Through his critique, Zarruq had already dismissed those Sufis who were in Fes, therefore the first stage of building his reform project there was to shake jurists from their ethical distraction and attract them to his brand of Sufi training. For this reason he held up their source of provision as reprehensible. Rather than accepting his words (and his implicit bid to become their juridical saint), the jurists rebuffed him. They answered cleverly that in Islamic law, God established an escape clause that allowed the eating of carrion in case of need.

They countered Zarruq by charging that God had in absolute terms forbidden "the eating of flesh that is still alive." This cryptic rebuttal refers to the Qurʾānic verse that forbids slander and backbiting. *You who believe, avoid holding a bad opinion of others, for some of holding such bad opinion is a moral fault. Likewise, do not examine each other for faults and do not speak about others behind their backs. Is there any of you who like to eat the flesh of your dead brother? No, that is disgusting to you. So stay wary of Allah, for Allah accepts repentance and is merciful.*[40] The Qur'ān asks a rhetorical question in the most alarming terms: "If you would never think of eating the flesh of your dead brother, then why do you so thoughtlessly bite into the flesh of your brother who is still alive? That is what back-biting is like!" The jurists invoked this verse when they accused Zarruq of "eating flesh of the living." They already had a negative perception of him as one who criticizes his own kind through slander and backbiting. Not only was he "eating the flesh" of his own brother's back, but the brother was not even dead yet!

The vivid imagery of this argument reveals how heated the underlying issue of authority was. In Morocco, the authority of sainthood was intimately connected to the virtue of generosity and the accusation of its opposite. The importance of generosity highlights an aspect of *baraka* that is underdeveloped by anthropologists, who treat it as the power of command. Generosity, in contrast, sums up the qualities of abundance, fecundity, and enabling others. Zarruq accused the jurists of hoarding and appropriating wealth: a lack of generosity on the material plane. In rebuttal, the jurists accused Zarruq of being stingy and backbiting against others: a lack of generosity on the social plane. In effect, they were denying Zarruq's authority as a saint, for on the ethical plane the opposite of "generosity" is refusing to give others the credit they deserve, by claiming sincerity only for oneself and denying it to others. By challenging Zarruq's authority, they were obliquely defending the popularly acknowledged saints of Fes from the intellectual and ethical critiques that Zarruq leveled against them. Zarruq tried to bolster his critical apparatus against such accusations when he wrote in his *Principles* that "criticizing others in their absence (*ghība*) is allowable in warning others against bad behavior or in making juridical pronouncements against such behavior, as the exemplary jurists have argued."[41] However, other jurists and Sufis in Fes did not accept Zarruq's critiques as principled.

The narrative of Zarruq's reception in Fes does not provide a clear picture of whom Zarruq was contesting or what alliances existed between local Sufis, saints, and jurists. The one who articulated their opposition to Zarruq was a jurist, hadith scholar, and grammarian named Ibn al-Ḥabbāk.[42] As a student of Aḥmad ibn Ghāzī, he would have known Zarruq and his reputation well. He articulated the challenge to Zarruq, accusing him of criticizing the jurists and scholars of Fes without just cause. In doing so, he defended the privilege of this class of jurists and scholars from a reformist Sufi who alleged that they were distracted by worldly ambitions and power politics. This was also an implicit rejection of Zarruq's claim to be the saintly guide of jurists and scholars, who theoretically would form the vanguard of his reformist Sufi community. Ibn al-Ḥabbāk seems to have voiced the collective opinion of the scholars present, for as a unified group they left Zarruq unconscious on the floor. There may have been other, hidden loyalties at play, for Aḥmad ibn Ḥabbāk had sympathetic relations with the early Jazūlīyya community. His students would include many who would rise to fame as socially activist saints of the Jazūlīyya community.[43]

From his first arrival, Zarruq plunged directly into a vituperative denunciation of religious notables and portrayed himself as the Islamic authority who could point out their ethical weaknesses. Word of this open conflict must have reached al-Ḥaḍramī in Cairo, who wrote to Zarruq and his partner, al-Khaṣṣāṣī, with advice. "Be very careful not to keep the company of people who practice religious innovations (*bidᶜa*) and those who crave for positions of power. Avoid those who use technical terminology in disputing religious points. Beware of sitting with them and listening to them. Avoid them and stay warily away, keeping sensitive to the stratagems of God, lest you be led astray along with them."[44] Initially this advice assumed al-Ḥaḍramī's normal tone. He counseled Zarruq as he always had, to stay aloof from those Sufi groups whom he mistrusts: those who argue in philosophical terms, or claim particular spiritual stations for themselves, or enter into the realm of political power. However, he quickly reversed the tone to throw Zarruq off balance. Zarruq's criticizing such people openly was tantamount to "keeping them company" and Zarruq was well along the path to being led astray with them. "If you despise anyone, do not think yourself better than him, even if you are on the right path. Fear God! Take refuge in God from your self and rely on God to take care of it. You must obey at every moment and in every state, and you must keep your intentions sound and have firm belief in yourself as well as the other Muslims around you. You must be humble."[45] Al-Ḥaḍramī accused Zarruq of arrogance in taking others to task for their ethical faults. Even if Zarruq was right about others, al-Ḥaḍramī warned, he should resist the urge to criticize them harshly, for that is self-indulgent. In addition, he feared that Zarruq would alienate both Sufis and scholars at the outset, ruining any possibility of a reformist Sufi practice taking root in Fes.

This adversarial reception demonstrates that Sufis in Fes had a counter-critique of Zarruq that was persuasive to them. Zarruq represented a challenge to the absolute authority of the Sufi master over his disciples, an authority with deep cultural roots that most Sufis would not question. As a young man, Zarruq had willfully disobeyed his master, al-Zaytūnī, who banished him from Fes as punishment. Now Zarruq had returned, yet he still did not seem penitent or repentant; in fact, he thought that his banishment had led him to a deeper sincerity and higher authority! Clearly, for most Sufis in Fes, Zarruq's example was not about the search for sincerity as a saint, but about the breach of authority as a disciple, created by Zarruq's judgmental lack of generosity.

Few people in Fes accepted Zarruq's autobiographical account of his life. They told his story among themselves in a completely different narrative, one that reflected their own cultural concerns and their suspicions of Zarruq. Their story did not dismiss Zarruq, for he was a powerful figure and an important scholar, but it defused his potency by nullifying his critique of saintly authority as practiced in Morocco during the period of revolt against the Marinids. The prominent hagiographer Ibn ᶜAskar recorded this narrative, which became the most popular retelling of Zarruq's story in Morocco. "Ahmad Zarruq entered deeply and quickly into love for [Shaykh al-Zaytūnī] and claimed that he was the ascendant one. In this way, Zarruq went through a trial in his devotion to this master. [Zarruq] came to visit him and knocked on the door. Hearing a voice giving him leave to enter, he went into the house but found nobody there. So he went up to a room at the top of the house. Here he found the Shaykh [al-Zaytūnī] sitting in the middle of the room, with one beautiful woman on his right side and another on his left side. The Shaykh would turn first to one of them women and then to the other. So Zarruq said, 'This man is a hypocrite and a lapsed saint (*walī rājiᶜ*)!' Then al-Zaytūnī called out to him, 'O Ahmad, you perpetual liar, come back here!' Zarruq returned to him and found no women with him at all; he knew that he had been tried and tested. Then al-Zaytūnī told him, 'That which you saw on my right side was the next world (*ākhira*) and that which you saw on my left side was this world (*dunyā*). You are a liar in what you claim! Don't stay in the Maghrib for even one hour more.'"[46] This narrative, like Zarruq's own autobiography, keeps silent about the events of the revolution in Fes. It also erases Zarruq's relationship with al-Qūrī and the tension he felt between his dual loyalty to jurisprudence and to sainthood. It completely suppresses any mention of Zarruq as a saint who advocated a challenging reform agenda.

Almost every Moroccan hagiographer repeats this as the authoritative version of Zarruq's story. Notable exceptions are the early followers of Zarruq, like Aḥmad Bābā al-Timbuktī and Ibn Maryam al-Tilimsānī, who present Zarruq in the opposite extreme, as primarily a scholar. Modern biographers dismiss this narrative as "legend" without accounting for why it was so pervasive and persuasive to most of Zarruq's contemporaries in Fes. It was persuasive because it reduces his story to a morality play. It presents his character as a caricature of lack of wisdom and hasty judgment, to demonstrate how a Sufi disciple of a saint should not behave. The story continues:

> Zarruq left Fes and headed off toward the east, full of anxiety over himself due to what had befallen him. He headed east until he arrived in Egypt. There on the banks of the Nile, he found a party waiting for him; they were the companions of Ibn ᶜUqba al-Ḥaḍramī. Their master had ordered them to wait there for Zarruq to come, and to inform him of Zarruq's arrival. They greeted Zarruq warmly, welcomed him into their midst and carried him off with them [to Cairo]. When he came into the presence of al-Ḥaḍramī and greeted him, the saint said, "O Ahmad, my son, what has happened between you and that Blind Viper [al-Zaytūnī]? I've taken pity upon you and have been caring for you despite him." He guided Zarruq to a room in his quarters and directed him to take up meditation and invocation. After three days, al-Ḥaḍramī heard a tremendous blow [like a fierce storm wind] and he threw up his hand, crying "O God!" Then he ordered his companions to get up immediately to check on

> Zarruq. They found the house in which he had been in retreat had completely collapsed. Al-Ḥaḍramī ordered them to dig out Zarruq. They found him trapped under the central beam of the house; it had collapsed on top of him, pinning him to the ground but preventing the rubble from crushing him and saving his life. Al-Ḥaḍramī saw him alive and said, "Praise be to God who has kept you safe, Ahmad! This is the last punishment al-Zaytūnī will inflict upon you. He dealt you a crushing blow from the far west of Morocco, but I warded it off with my hand. Here is my hand, smashed from deflecting his blow!" He extended his hand for all to see: it dangled from his wrist, broken.[47]

This story provides a vivid example of how hagiography resolves historic events into mythic patterns. The narrative ignores Zarruq's exile from Fes, his pilgrimage, his search for scholarly legitimacy, and his careful cultivation of new Sufi lineages in Egypt and Arabia. It condenses his story into a titanic struggle between two saintly masters, whose miracles, like stage props, express their bid for loyalty and their anger at betrayal. In such a drama, there is no room for Zarruq's ideals or his critique; the story subverts both.

Clearly, Sufis in Morocco did not value Zarruq's ideals or his critiques. They told his story to reflect their own concern: the authority of the spiritual master over the disciple within the economy of closeness and submission. In this story, Zarruq's quest for the truth was really just a foil for his asserting his own will against his master. His whole juridical critique was summed up in his rash denunciation of al-Zaytūnī, as a "lapsed saint" whose reputation was only a ruse to capture power in this world through the rhetoric of the next world. This narrative quickly established the weakness of Zarruq's critique as al-Zaytūnī reveals the true situation: what Zarruq saw with the power of his observation, reason, and juridical analysis was only a test of his sincerity, a test which found him gravely lacking.

This test of sincerity was also a test of Zarruq's generosity. Rather than material generosity, the test singled out his judgmental generosity: his ability to have patience and forbearance, to allow others to explain their motives without rushing to critique or judge. The narrative deems Zarruq's punishment by al-Zaytūnī to be just retribution for his impetuous trust of his own critical faculties over loyalty to a saint. The punishment is only deflected by the protective intervention of a second, distant master in Cairo. For Zarruq, there is no redemption through his search for sincerity, for the narrative does not mention his pilgrimage to the tomb of Abū Madyan, which played such a central role in Zarruq's own mythic autobiography, as we saw in chapter 5.

The Moroccan narrative erases any possibility of a rupture of authority between master and disciple. The narrative of Zarruq's punishment and flight comes to a resolution in the aggressive combat between two masters. In such a narrative framework, there is no place for the assertion of rival authority by the young disciple, who thought himself more sincere toward God than his master was. This narrative accounts for the outer contours of Zarruq's life as a shift of patronage, not as his questioning the very terms of authority and patronage. Zarruq comes under blame for allowing his scrupulousness to go beyond appropriate bounds. There is no recognition that he was preparing to assert his own authority over against his master, which would impel him to subsequently search for a new model of saintly authority in his reform project.

A Saint Dismissed at Home

These hagiographic accounts rebuff Zarruq's elaborate critique of Moroccan saints indirectly through the practice of storytelling. Their non-confrontational counter-critique was highly effective. However, later Sufi authors rebuffed him directly. They translated these narrative tropes into discursive prose that questioned Zarruq's authenticity and his reformist conception of saintly authority.

Clearly, Zarruq was dismissed as a saint in his home city of Fes. Neither jurists nor Sufis (especially those of the Jazūlīyya movement) accepted Zarruq's reformist vision of himself as a jurist saint. Most Moroccan religious authorities dismissed Zarruq by ignoring him, while some diverted his image into hagiographic narratives that rendered his example harmless and unthreatening to the growing political authority of their ongoing social movements. However, a few Moroccan Sufis directly confronted Zarruq's reformist ideals and their consequent social critique. The clearest example of such a confrontation is in the writings of Aḥmad ibn ᶜAjība. His writings offer a pointed counter-critique against Zarruq's person and ideals.

Ibn ᶜAjība was one of the more productive Sufi authors of the eighteenth century C.E.. He was a proponent of the newly formed Darqāwīyya Sufi community, which led a major upsurge of devotional energy and social organization and northern and eastern Morocco. The paradigmatic saint of this community, Mawlay al-ᶜArabī al-Darqāwī, possessed a lineage leading back to Zarruq. Although ibn ᶜAjība's lineage links him to Zarruq, his temperament and training diverge widely from the ideals set out by Zarruq in his reformist and critical writings. He grew up with a scholar's training, engaged in legal studies, and began to write commentaries on Sufi texts. Upon reading the *Wisdom Sayings* of Ibn ᶜAṭāᵓullah, he decided to devote his life to spiritual training, rejected his scholarly respectability as a teacher, and took on the itinerant poverty exemplified by al-Darqāwī. After suffering persecution and brief imprisonment, he managed to set up many zawiyas of his community in the Jabāla region of northern Morocco.

This missionary work would not require a direct confrontation with the legacy of Zarruq. However, ibn ᶜAjība was also an ambitious author. He wrote commentaries on many of the seminal works of Shādhilī devotion, upon which Zarruq (among others) had long since written authoritative commentaries. Ibn Ajība's dismissal of Zarruq is therefore part of his authorial strategy of clearing a space for his own words on the already congested margins of canonical texts.[48] By contending that Zarruq was "a literalist" who did not comment on the spiritual truths beyond the literal surface of the words of Sufi texts, Ibn ᶜAjība set up his own contrasting authority as a more spiritually realized commentator. Ibn ᶜAjība ran up against Zarruq when he set out to comment on the poetic *Qaṣīda in Nūn* by al-Shushtarī. "Shaykh Zarruq has preceded me in writing a commentary on this *qaṣīda*. However, Zarruq made short shrift of the work, focusing only on explaining the meaning of certain words with a literal approach and going into the deeper meaning of very few terms. He never plunged deeply into the ocean of its secret meanings. He never searched out the deepest of its luminous [pearls]. He never perforated the seal of their secret recesses. He never entered the company of the joyous grooms wedded to these virginal spiritual secrets!"[49] Ibn ᶜAjība moves quickly from dismissing Zarruq's style of analysis to questioning the very basis of Zarruq's authenticity as a saint. By claiming that saintly authority depends on a sudden moment of enlightenment and dramatic display of renunciation, ibn ᶜAjība contends that a person's achieving the status of sainthood can be dated. He continues, "Perhaps Zarruq wrote out his commentary on this poem before he achieved any spiritual opening from the realm of hidden and subtle realities. For our master's master, Sīdī ᶜAlī al-ᶜImrānī, used to say that Zarruq only achieved spiritual awakening at the very end of his life, meaning that he had written all his texts in the period before his real spiritual awakening (but only God knows best). Zarruq's commentary itself supports such a conclusion, since what a man says bears witness to the inner condition of the speaker. When someone utters a word, others can know what condition of life he is in!"

With this contention, Ibn ᶜAjība dismisses most of Zarruq's writings. "Sufis acknowledge Zarruq as an evident leader (*imām*). However, in the dimension of subtle perception and insightful knowledge of spiritual reality, he never earned any ability until the very end of his life. In fact, he almost passed away with his hands yellowed [from the jaundice of a spiteful nature]! For this reason, he piled up criticism upon criticism against people who hold allegiance to saints (*ahl al-nisba*). For this reason he spoke out harshly against them and tried to constrain them."[50] It is clear from this passage that Ibn ᶜAjība's critique of Zarruq pierces deeper than mere reservation about certain of his texts. Rather, he dismisses Zarruq's critical texts by dismissing the basis of authority as "watchman of the saints" that Zarruq had earned for himself. "Some masters among the jurists are fond of saying that 'Zarruq is the watchman (*muḥtasib*) over the Sufis who calls them to account.' He might keep watch over the Sufi-minded of the literalist scholars; he may call to account those who devote themselves to outer acts of pious worship and cling to their outer form. As for the Sufis who engage in real spiritual training and perceive the inner secret dimension of their actions, there is no such accountability over them. No rational knowledge can encompass the meaning of what they do."[51] This is certainly the ultimate dismissal for a juridical saint. But Ibn ᶜAjība delivers a coup de grace by quoting his own Sufi teacher, Shaykh al-Darqāwī, to further dismiss Zarruq. "My master, al-Darqāwī, has said, 'Shaykh Zarruq is a big deal among the literal-minded scholars and jurists (*ahl al-ẓāhir*), but to those who pay attention to interior spiritual realities (*ahl al-bāṭin*) he is insignificant.'" Beyond not being a real saint, he is lumped together with the "literal-minded jurists" who attack Sufi communities and do not recognize the need for saints at all.

Ibn ᶜAjība even mined the autobiographical notes that Zarruq included in his writings to use against him. In doing so, he alleges that Zarruq's reformist method of training disciples is necessarily ineffective. He questions the validity of Zarruq's whole ideological framework that ostensibly unites juridical training with Sufi devotion.

> Because Ahmad Zarruq spent so little time training in the company of his master, al-Ḥaḍramī, he achieved true spiritual opening only late in his life [after he had written most of his texts]. Zarruq admitted himself in his own autobiography that he spent about seven months with al-Ḥaḍramī at first, and then after returning from Madīna he spent another eight months with him. Altogether that amounts to only about fifteen months with a master! Then Zarruq claims "I benefited spiritually from al-Ḥaḍramī in many ways that are very evident." This is much too short a time for a disciple's egoistic nature to be complete stripped away. In such a short time no disciple can be dislodged from his [clinging to] rational knowledge and his habitual states of being in the world, especially a disciple so obsessed with scriptural and rational disciplines. The only thing that can strip these away from him is a long period of intimate contact with his master, with sincere and humble service in complete isolation from the world. Such service is an anathema to Zarruq and others like him. Indeed, his master al-Ḥaḍramī had sent him some texts in which he had written of various subtle spiritual realities and experiences, and Zarruq ignored them since they could not be derived from [scriptural and juridical] knowledge alone.[52] Rather, such subtle experiences are gained from the whole spiritual environment surrounding the master, after realizing sincerity and true belief in him. It is clear that many scholars and jurists have kept the company of known saints for long periods without ever attaining even the smallest measure of this spiritual perception. This is because they were in the saint's company while still looking out for themselves through rational thinking, rather than looking upon the saints as saints. If the saint would order them to do something or forbid them from doing something, they would weigh these words in the balance of their discrimination to see if it accords with their [interpretation of the] *sharīᶜa*. What in their narrow vision they find in accord with religious custom they accept, and what seems to them to contradict it they reject. These scholarly and juridical disciples therefore remain entrenched in their egos. They never dive into the ocean of secrets and sink deep. Only God knows best.[53]

This passage reveals the most basic level of Ibn ᶜAjība's disagreement with Zarruq. In the balance of love and knowledge, Ibn ᶜAjība feels that love must always precede knowledge. Judging a saint's actions by the criteria of rational investigation and juridical norms, he contends, will always be misleading. Rather, love must shake the very facade of reason upon its foundation in the ego before true understanding can dawn. Further, one can only experience real love for God and for the Prophet through unconditional love for one's saintly guide.

In this way, he dismisses Zarruq's deep skepticism and inverts his judgment, for Zarruq had insisted that knowledge always takes precedence over love and that love is conditional upon knowledge. One cannot love God without obeying God's commands, and obeying is conditioned by knowledge of those commands. The same is true for love of the Prophet: true love of the Prophet is one's dedication to knowing about his character and actions and teaching this knowledge to others to uphold juridical norms. Reason, he taught, was an instrument to sharpen in order to keep love intense, focused within the narrow bounds of sincerity.

Ibn ᶜAjība could not rely on rational argumentation to dismiss the rationality of Zarruq. Instead, he appealed to a visionary encounter. He reported that he once met Zarruq in a dream, a dream as vivid and clear to him as if he had been awake. In the dream, their argument became heated. "I said to him, 'You have surely been harsh against those who hold allegiance to the saints [in your accounting for who] is a real and true disciple.' Zarruq countered, 'So what did I say?' I answered him, 'You said this and you said that,' recounting for him what critiques he had launched against them in his harshest moments. Zarruq replied, 'That is what stands in relation to the legal method of Imām Mālik.' Then I charged, 'The real Sufi does not follow the legal method of Imām Mālik or any other legal method. Rather the real Sufi grasps the *sharīᶜa* from its root source, and searches for reality in its deepest mines!' Then Zarruq admitted, 'As for whoever has reached this state or has been the companion of one who has reached this state, I have nothing to say to him.' So I retorted, 'By God, I have reached this state and I have been the companion of others who have reached this state!' Upon my saying this, the vision of Zarruq disappeared and he left me alone."[54] This dream vision expresses Ibn ᶜAjība's final assessment of Zarruq and his critical project most succinctly. Zarruq, as a jurist who is attentive to Sufi practices, can pronounce judgment only on actions that are within his jurisdiction. If the Sufi primarily follows Imām Mālik, then the limits of Mālik's legal method apply to him. However, if the Sufi primarily follows the Prophet in a way that is deeper than routine allegiance to Imām Mālik's exposition of the law, then the jurist in Zarruq has no jurisdiction over him.

In Ibn ᶜAjība's conception, the Muslim saint manifests the character, virtue, and light of the Prophet Muhammad. One who follows a saint, and strives to imbibe his presence and imitate his conduct, has a connection to the Prophet that is deeper and truer than adherence to any juridical method. Although a saint will not contravene the structure of legal rules and limitations, he should not rely upon them alone. Contravening them would be a disservice to ordinary believers, who rely on law to guide them. However, saints and their followers tap into a deeper current of Prophetic guidance. This current is suprarational, based on love and on seeing oneself in another, unbounded by egoistic restraints. Juridical norms have only a limited place, he feels, in this dimension, for they are distracting. If following juridical guidelines is like breathing air, he contends, the saint and his disciples must put them behind them if they are to dive below the surface of routine, ego-centered life. If pearl divers think obsessively about breathing air, how will they ever reach the oyster bed at the bottom of the sea?

Outside of dreamtime, however, Zarruq was not so easy to dismiss. He had addressed all of Ibn ᶜAjība's contentions in his theoretical writings in great detail. In his *Principles of Being a Sufi*, Zarruq had argued that being a Sufi does not exempt anyone from the jurisdiction of a discrete and specific legal method. Sufi devotion and legal judgment are two distinct dimensions of action, not two distinct jurisdictions or two separate areas of social life. Against the writings of Zarruq, Ibn ᶜAjība bolsters his argument by quoting the saints in his lineage, like Shaykh al-Darqāwī and Sīdī ᶜAlī al-ᶜImrānī. He demonstrates that he is speaking not as an individual or as a rival author, but as the representative of a robust spiritual community. In his explicitly written counter-critique, he is solidifying a long tradition of oral teachings that dismiss or minimize the impact of Zarruq's incisive critiques of the institution of sainthood as it developed in Morocco. Such dismissals must have been common, even in Zarruq's own lifetime. Certainly, Zarruq's experience in Fes shows that he did not find a sympathetic audience, let alone gain supporters.

Miracles at Law's Horizon

Zarruq's hostile reception in Morocco was a direct and personal challenge to his authority. He also received an indirect challenge (but a more lasting one) through the stories that were told about him. Each reinforced the other, and they resulted in a social boycott against Zarruq for the four years that he stayed in Fes. He found no powerful patrons in Fes who could mediate for him, very few friends, and no ready audience for his reformist ideas.

The extent of his isolation is revealed by the story of one of his miracles, as told by Aḥmad ibn Ghāzī (one of the few Sufis, scholars, or jurists who would meet with Zarruq). Such miracle stories display how Zarruq asserted authority, as a juridical saint, at the very horizon of legal jurisdiction. Such miracle stories hark back to Zarruq's youthful journey in exile from Fes to Tilimsān; when the clearly demarked borders of his identity as a juridical student broke down, miraculous occurrences flowed into the breach. Though he was now a mature man, an authoritative jurist with prestigious training from the Islamic heartland, Zarruq was again under intense pressure under a social boycott in Fes. When his reformist arguments, based on fusing Sufi training with legal rectitude, fell on deaf ears and his authority seemed to break down, miracles again flowed in to reinforce his authority. Once Zarruq petitioned Ibn Ghāzī to receive him and his many companions in Ibn Ghāzī's home, so he prepared a large quantity of food for the feast. "When the appointed time arrived, Ibn Ghāzī stood at the door of his home, waiting to greet the crowd of visitors. However, Zarruq arrived at his door alone. Ibn Ghāzī asked him, 'Sir, where are all your companions who were supposed to come? I have such a vast quantity of food prepared, and I fear it will all go to waste!' Zarruq answered him, 'Everything will be taken care of, if God wills, and nothing will go to waste.' Then he ordered Ibn Ghāzī to set out the food, and coming close to him said, 'Send away your servants so that only you and I are present.' The servants left the banquet hall. Then Zarruq rolled up his sleeves, picked up the food, each platter with a piece of meat and a handful [of couscous] and began to pass them behind him. Ibn Ghāzī heard a loud clamor coming from behind Zarruq; when he looked he saw a huge crowd of people, old and young, men and women. They were all extending their hands, asking 'My Lord, please give me some.' They occupied a vast expanse behind Zarruq, who gave each a meal. Then he turned to Ibn Ghāzī and asked, 'Is there anything left of the food you prepared?' He answered, 'No Sir, not a morsel.' Then Zarruq washed his hands and gave thanks to God."[55] When Ibn Ghāzī mustered up the courage to ask Zarruq who these crowds were who miraculously appeared at his feast, Zarruq replied, "These are the poor people of Tunis, who were in urgent need of a meal—the vast expanse where they were crowded is the courtyard of the congregational mosque of al-Zaytūna." Al-Zaytūna is the main mosque and madrasa of Tunis and all of the central Maghrib.

This miracle story reveals the depth of the boycott against Zarruq, overlaid with the ways Zarruq sought to establish his legitimacy in the face of it. Though he had few followers or friends in Fes, he claimed a devoted following in eastern towns like Bijāya, Tarābulus, and Tūnis. He claimed Moroccan saints were corrupt, but he counteracted this corruption with his lineage from eastern saints, bolstered by his scholarly training in Cairo's prestigious academies. The moral of this miracle is that Fes may be proud of al-Qarawiyyīn, but even more authentic is Qayrawān to the east; Moroccans may blame him for having betrayed al-Zaytūnī, but the people of al-Zaytūna considered Zarruq a real saint.

This miracle story also reveals how the polemical dispute between Zarruq and his contemporaries over the authority of sainthood involved the core virtue of "generosity." Ibn Ghāzī's story portrays Zarruq in one of the classic poses of a saint: the provider of sustenance to the needy. Although he refused to display such provision in public (in actual acts of feeding, providing rain, or protecting the poor) he could reveal his virtue of generosity in secret. He asserted that its secret nature safeguarded its sincerity against egoistic display and power-hungry hypocrisy.

Such an argument was clearly problematic from the point of view of contemporary Sufis in Fes and the general public that expected saints to be generous with demonstrative miracles. Zarruq failed to defuse the counter-critique imposed upon him by other saints and jurists in Fes. The depth of his isolation comes across in one of his compositions, a commentary on a poem by al-Shushtarī, the very commentary which ibn ᶜAjība later contested and dismissed. Al-Shushtarī was a Sufi poet of the highest caliber, specializing in metaphors of love and intoxication, like the more famous Ibn al-Fāriḍ.[56] At first glance, Zarruq's treatment of al-Shushtarī is rather strange, for he is highly critical of other poets who hold passionate desire and inebriating love to be the ultimate terms of God's relationship to humanity.[57] Yet Zarruq provides a detailed biography of al-Shushtarī, commends his learning and piety, and attempts to explain away or excuse the passionate metaphors of al-Shushtarī's most controversial poem. The poem's subject is "the goals of the Sufi path for those who strive to know God intimately." It details the ultimate goals and the means by which to reach the goals, and it mentions the role of saints who lead one to the goals through the means. "I intend to write about this poem that rhymes with the letter *nūn* by al-Shushtarī, in a condensed way in order to point out all the symbolic meanings contained in it, in overt and hidden forms. First, it seemed right to me to present an introduction to the readers, to familiarize them with this master and all the satisfying things that he has written. The author is named ᶜAlī ibn ᶜAbdullah al-Numayrī, known as 'al-Shushtarī.' He was a saintly guide and spiritual master, a jurist and scholar of the Prophet's sayings, a Sufi and a sage, a practitioner of complete discipline and was actualized in every nuance of spirituality."[58]

According to Zarruq's biography, the Sufi poet lived in Andalusia, in the town of Shushtar near the city of Lūsa (Sp. Llosa). He hailed from an aristocratic ruling family, but by natural disposition inclined to humility and the company of the spiritually impoverished of the Sufi community.[59] In his youth, he studied the Qur'ān and scriptural disciplines, then mastered jurisprudence and legal principles. He may have worked as a merchant for some time, traveling widely and engaging in theological debates. Then he worked as a scholar: "with his firm determination and lofty aspiration, he took part in many diverse scholarly disciplines." Then he took initiation from a saintly guide and devoted himself to purifying his heart. Zarruq downplayed the fact that he was a follower of the controversial philosophical Sufi Ibn Sabᶜīn, claiming that this is a "contention." Al-Shushtarī, he affirms, is free of blame from the charges that besmirched Ibn Sabᶜīn, and he denies that al-Shushtarī never engaged in that teacher's path of "divine incarnation and human union with God (*hulūl wa ittiḥād*), tending toward heresy and denying the true nature of God (*zaygh wa ilḥād*)." In contrast, Zarruq affirms that al-Shushtarī was a scholar and jurist as well as a Sufi, in his own image.[60]

It is surprising that Zarruq would expend such effort to acquit al-Shushtarī of the accusations against him. He was accused of believing in the presence of God in the existence of every thing. As a poet, he spread such ideas through his lyrics (which were often set to music and sung in devotional settings as well as in more popular venues). This anomalous treatment of the poet comes about because Zarruq saw in al-Shushtarī a reflection of his own suffering and alienation from the population where he lived.

Al-Shushtarī settled in the city of Tarābulus (Tripoli in Libya). The people of the city learned many scholarly disciplines from him and took him as a great teacher. Then they offered him the position of judge in their city, but he refused to accept the position. The people swarmed around him, urging him to take it up and even trying to coerce him, until they drove him crazy. They drove him to write these lines:

The one accused of following his own whims is satisfied in his distress
Leave him alone to waste his life practicing his arts.
Don't heap blame upon him, for your blaming him benefits you nothing
It's not of his religion to turn aside from whims and desires.
I swear to the one who mentions a ruby for his sake
The lover has already sworn to his beloved and by his right hand.
You are all so dear to me, but I have repented
from hypocritical judgments and their cosmetic beautification.
What is wrong with me, if when the dove calls from his thicket
[My wings] are forever clipped by [the voice of] his woes and his burdens.
Since you see my ardent weeping without tears
Know that the one crazed with love cries through his art not his eyes.

Al-Shushtarī makes a clever play on words involving the root *fa-ta-ya*. From this root comes giving legal decisions (*fatwa*) and also beautiful youthfulness (*fatiya*). He abjures from giving legal decisions because he is already in love with a beautiful beloved (God, the Prophet, or the principle of beauty they share); at the same time he counters that making juridical decisions is nothing but hypocrisy, presenting one's character as beautiful on the surface while never addressing the real quality of the heart within. Zarruq comments: "What I understand him to be expressing is his apology for opposing popular opinion and refusing to take up the position of judge. As if he were saying 'I haven't left it to show off my ascetic renunciation, nor because I desire anything other than the *sharīʿa*, but rather because it would by necessity dissipate [my sincerity] and invite hypocrisy." In Zarruq's portrayal, the people's praise of al-Shushtarī turned quickly to blame when he refused to acquiesce to their social expectations and demands. The people of Tripoli offered him social standing and wealth (as in the mention of a ruby ring), and he asked only to be left alone to teach, meditate, and sing poetry. From praising his knowledge, they turned to blaming him for following his own "caprice and selfish desires." If Sufi scruples led him to turn down the offer of being their judge, they quickly began to blame him for being a "heretical" Sufi.

From their initial welcome to their city, they ended up driving al-Shushtarī away. It is the fickleness of public opinion and the danger of succumbing to it that fed Zarruq's sympathy toward al-Shushtarī. In Fes, Zarruq was also harried by others whose accusations drove him into isolation. They praised his knowledge and learning but ostracized him for not giving them what they wanted, the juridical sanction for their practices of sainthood. Zarruq's discussion of al-Shushtarī provides a lens through which to see his response to the social boycott he faced in opposing the Sufis and scholars of Fes. If he were a Sufi, they expected him to join their saints; and if he were a jurist, they expected him to engage in worldly affairs without critiquing their saints. In either case, they denied him the dual role that he imagined for himself, to quest after sincerity in himself and insist on sincerity in others.

Even though he made a few allies in certain notable scholars (like Ibn Ghāzī, who spread this story about Zarruq's banquet), Zarruq appears to have convinced very few people in Fes of his saintly status. He certainly did not recruit any followers from the jurists of Fes, who, according to his reform program, would be the logical place for him to turn for students and disciples.[61]

God's Fools beyond the Law

Beyond this very limited following, Zarruq attracted the admiration of only a few unlikely followers from the "mad holy people" of Fes. The first of these is Ibrāhīm al-Afhām al-Zarhūnī. Very little is known of this man, from whom the pull of divine love had dragged his powers of reason (*majdhūb*). He was also known by the label *malāmatī*, meaning one who pays no attention to praise or blame in the eyes others. These two terms were often coupled in the same figure, to denote someone who acted "insane" by trespassing all bounds of conventional morality, either deliberately to hide their state of sanctity or unknowingly since their powers of discretion had been eclipsed. The hagiographic sources generously label this behavior "their personal absence from the world and absorption in divine unity" (*al-ghayba fi*ʾ*l al-tawḥīd*).[62]

Zarruq himself had written on this strange figure of the *majdhūb*. He displayed a marked ambivalence toward such people. He included them in his critique of Sufis, since they obviously stepped beyond the bounds of legal rectitude and owed nothing to scholarly achievement. He certainly did not see them as "real" saints to whom one could take initiation, no matter how authentic their divine madness might be in their internal state. However, they hovered on the outer horizon of applicability of his critique. They slipped beyond the jurisdiction of legal reasoning, since they had lost grasp of reason itself. "There is a community of Sufis who have appeared with divine distraction (*jadhb*) and behave like the insane. They cultivate such qualities until such distraction and irrational action becomes their habitual, natural character and they are unable to return to steadfast and regulated behavior. It becomes a burden for them to return to routine daily life. They are called to such a life by the apparently spiritual states that they see in other such irrational people and how society responds to them with wonder and acceptance. Common people, especially ignorant people who pursue worldly goals, are very fond of these folk who appear crazed. Such people are greatly affected by these displays of 'holy madness' and love those who display it. They protect these people and usually avoid acquiring religious knowledge and honoring the scholars; rather they tend to oppose the pious worshippers and the obligations they take upon themselves. Instead, they claim that these holy madmen are the true men of God who have left this world, and nobody else has a share in holiness. There is another group who do not respect the *majdhūb* at all and do not believe they are sincerely connected to God. It is safer for them to believe this, since this belief adheres to the outer form of the law and custom. The safest path is to reserve judgment entirely, neither following them nor denouncing them."[63]

Just as they were not worth being followed as saintly guides, they were not worth denouncing either, since they had no control over their actions. There is even something powerfully moving in seeing a person impassioned beyond self-control. In a state of possession or madness, one can "point to" religious truths, and this is what differentiates a *majdhūb* from a person who is simply insane. As the *majdhūb* becomes emptied of the habitual characteristics that make a social human being, he or she becomes a "receptacle for a meaning which is noble," though that nobility does not inhere in the *majdhūb*'s personality or person. Since reason is a tool necessary to understand scripture and legal obligations, one without reason is prevented from being a saint. One should admire them from a distance, and not take them as a guide or object of veneration.[64] However, "people naturally love children and fools; they seek the company and intercession of ascetics and recluses [who act like children in being helpless in the world], in preference to scholars and true Sufis, even though the latter are preferable if one has a true outlook."[65]

With such a perspective, one wonders why Ahmad Zarruq would accept someone like Ibrāhīm al-Afhām as a disciple. Perhaps it was simply his desperation, for very few with rationality intact were even talking with Zarruq, let alone looking to him as their guide. On the other hand, it is possible that Ibrāhīm al-Afhām claimed Zarruq as his guide without Zarruq's full assent. Taking into account his policy of "neither supporting or condemning" people like the *majdhūb*, he might not have rejected Ibrāhīm's request for an initiation. Hagiographic sources maintain that Ibrāhīm al-Afhām "was Zarruq's companion, and declared allegiance to his lineage with the goal of spiritual training and the cultivation of virtue (*tarbiya wa tahdhīb*)." However, Zarruq himself never mentions al-Afhām as his disciple. In view of al-Afhām's display of a model of "irrational" holiness beyond Zarruq's more constrained boundaries of authentic sainthood, it is hard to imagine him absorbing much of Zarruq's principles fused with juridical training.

Zarruq acknowledged the "low level" of these followers in Fes in the letters he sent to his followers back in the west after having left Fes for the final time. "Practice *dhikr*, even if only saying *praise be to God*. Recite the Qur'ān, even if only one verse. Fast, even for only a single day of Ramadan. Pray, even if just one prostration in the dead of the night. Give to the needy, even if just one morsel of food to a hungry dog—as long as you do it solely for the sake of God."[66] His advice is heartfelt, but shows none of the high and idealistic standards he had set for training disciples in his more formal writings.

Zarruq's ambivalence toward the *majdhūb* is equaled by Ibrāhīm al-Afhām's ambivalence toward Zarruq. He claimed Zarruq as a saintly guide, but in a conditional way. He had a previous initiation, in a visionary experience of the Prophet

Muhammad himself. The hagiographic record of his life explains: "He first of all saw the Prophet Muhammad in a vision while he was sleeping, and took initiation directly from his noble hand. The Prophet himself opened his spirit. Then he compounded this with a second initiation from Shaykh Zarruq."[67] In these reports, it becomes clear that Ibrāhīm al-Afhām had already laid claim to sainthood through an "*uwaysī*" visionary connection to the Prophet. He did not need or want Zarruq's reformist method of spiritual training, though he may have admired Zarruq, especially in his individual stand against the religious notables of the whole city. In his social isolation, Zarruq may have appeared a bit like a reclusive madman himself in the eyes of other *majdhūbs*.

It is doubtful that anyone would have recorded the name of Ibrāhīm al-Afhām if it were not for his one and only "disciple," another *majdhūb* named ᶜAlī al-Ṣanhājī. This holy madman achieved great fame in Fes, and his popularity preserved the memory of his "master," al-Afhām. ᶜAlī al-Ṣanhājī never met Zarruq, who must have left Fes before ᶜAlī al-Ṣanhājī encountered Ibrāhīm al-Afhām and, through his spiritual spark, left his reason behind. Through these *majdhūbs*, there occurred a strange "return of the repressed." These *majdhūb* followers perpetuated in Fes in Zarruq's name what he took such pains to critique and excise from Sufi practice.

The stories of ᶜAlī al-Ṣanhājī's many wild exploits give us a fuller picture of what kind of behavior constituted a *majdhūb* during Zarruq's time in Fes. "He acted like a fool and a buffoon, as if a mad love for the divine had dragged his reason out of him. He acted in *malāmatī* fashion. States of possession seized him at all times. He had no family and no fixed home. He would give reports on unseen matters and tell those who met him about their secret affairs. He paid no attention to either praise or blame from others."[68] His image is of a man both wonderful and dangerous. He had none of the social markers by which people in Fes knew each other, negotiated their relationship, and judged proper deference.

His name reveals that he was from a Ṣanhāja Berber background, which implies that he was not from Fes originally, but had come to the city from the countryside.[69] Immigrants to the city would be known either by their extended family, their neighborhood, or their occupation. ᶜAlī al-Ṣanhājī deliberately eschewed all these markers. People in Fes gave him the nickname "al-Duwwār," "the turner," since the most obvious characteristic was wandering in circles through the various quarters of the city, and nobody knew where he spent the night.[70]

His nickname "the turner" provides many other insights into his behavior. As a "raw human being" without social place, he constantly transgressed the boundaries of routine life and inverted the hierarchies that ordered civil life. As "the turner," he would circulate freely through people's homes, without any respect for social divisions, private property, or family propriety. Many stories are told of his walking into homes without knocking or asking permission, interrupting family life, and contravening the structure of gender norms in the household.[71] As a *majdhūb*, he claimed, his reason was alienated from him, and the routine norms of the law were lifted from his behavior. To a woman who denounced him for entering her home while she was not properly clothed, he retorted that he was like a child who knew nothing of her adult notions of propriety, desire, or shame.

ᶜAlī al-Ṣanhājī would deliberately transgress norms of purity and gendered behavior in ways similar to the role of the Qalandars in South Asian Muslim societies (who claim a status similar to the *majdhūb*), as documented by Katherine Ewing.[72] ᶜAlī al-Ṣanhājī would demand olive oil or lard from the vendors in the marketplace and smear it over himself in a deliberate soiling of his clothes and person.[73] With this practice, he would provoke not just disgust of the bourgeois respectable classes, but also their fear. He was known as "the turner" at another level, for he turned out people's secret deeds through his spiritual insight and set them circulating in public to shame the perpetrator. Sometimes he would do this without provocation and sometimes he would do it as retribution for someone's stinginess at his demands (namely for oil and lard).

This was but the beginning of ᶜAlī al-Ṣanhājī's campaign. Just as he destroyed privacy he also contravened private property. Often he would threaten to expose a person's dirty secrets unless they gave him money, which he would immediately redistribute to the needy. This type of charity by coercion has a long tradition behind it in Moroccan Sufi practice, and it was not a tactic exclusive to the *majdhūb*. The urban and scholarly figure of Abū al-ᶜAbbās al-Sabtī of Marrakesh had elevated this saintly critique of private wealth to an art form.[74] However, ᶜAlī al-Ṣanhājī practiced this technique with a particularly vivid inversion of norms. The man who was dirty and polluted could demand money by means of his inner purity, whereas the merchants and respectable people in clean clothes and ritual punctiliousness had to give up money to keep their inner dirt hidden away.

Death has obliterated all who came before
  and death is wiping out now all who remain
Death brings to the ground all of those
  who are saved with the damned without disdain
Oh you who have sinned in the past
  for what little time remains to good attain![75]

He would recite this little poem as a warning to the people and urge them to part with their money. He had no need to talk about obligatory alms or the juridical limits of ownership (*zakāt*).

By contravening the boundaries of wealth and status, ᶜAlī al-Ṣanhājī was a "populist." His person, emptied of reason and self-direction, became a vehicle for emptying the rich of wealth and redistributing it. He was particularly famous for walking into the palaces of the ruling aristocratic families as if they were back alleys. "ᶜAlī al-Ṣanhājī would walk straight into the homes of the ruling family of the Banū Marīn [and the Banū Waṭṭās]. As the women and children would rush to kiss his hands and feet, he would walk on without paying the least attention to anyone. They would urge him to accept fine objects and costly treasures as gifts, and the sultan himself would dress him in the finest clothes. When he would leave their homes, he would give everything away as charity."[76] Thus far, this narrative describes his social power and his control over others' wealth. But ironically, this control depends on his demonstrated lack of self-control. "Then he would circle among the stores of the olive oil sellers and plunge the sleeves of his old robe into the vats of oil and cover himself with grease. In this state, he would roam through certain quarters, screaming the name of Allah 'Ya Jalīl [O mighty One]!' Nobody knew where he spent the night, but the people of Fes held him in highest esteem, for they witnessed many of his miraculous actions that are innumerable." His reputation for being a saint depended on his miracles, and even more deeply on his trespassing routine social norms. It obviously did not depend on his holding a position of social respectability as a jurist or scholar or upon an authentic lineage of initiation leading to a respected saint. In this way, he was classified as "one of the *Abdāl*," that is one of the saints who "appear from nowhere" without social stability and known lineage.

This places ᶜAlī al-Ṣanhājī in the same class of "free radical" saints as al-Zaytūnī and his follower, al-Amīn al-ᶜAttār, who were also known as "one of the *Abdāl*" (although they professed allegiance to ᶜAbd al-Qādir al-Jīlānī). Their presence provoked the same social response of fear and wonder, the expectation of miracle, and the fear of vindictive reprisal. This social response to his awesome presence was dramatic. "When he died, multitudes descended upon his funeral procession and divided among themselves pieces of the poles of his funeral bier, his clothes and his prayer rug. The sultan, jurists and many others notables were present for his funeral."[77]

Despite this independent justification for his sainthood, ᶜAlī al-Ṣanhājī did have an "initiation" from Ibrāhīm al-Afhām, linking him back to Zarruq. If Ibrāhīm al-Afhām was a quiet, gentle *majdhūb* who could have conceivably sat in the company of Zarruq "for spiritual training," it is hard to imagine ᶜAlī al-Ṣanhājī sitting in his company or sensing any need for spiritual training based on juridical norms. In the only extant example of his writing, ᶜAlī al-Ṣanhājī claims that he wishes to "clarify points of contention in the way of the Lordly *Abdāl*," including himself in that category of saints.[78] In his words, these are people who are above disputing and arguing through the rational methods of jurisprudence and scriptural tradition. He saw himself as beyond the boundaries of Zarruq's type of discipleship, in which any claim to sainthood depended on legal rectitude and scholarly training. ᶜAlī al-Ṣanhājī's deliberately aberrant behavior, especially in matters of "sexual decency," provoked certain jurists to take action against him. He shocked people by falling into trance states in which his clothing fell off him and revealed his naked body. He even had female devotees who would follow him, giving greater publicity to his non-normative behavior and perhaps even staying with him against the wishes of husbands or male relatives.[79]

Majdhūb characters like ᶜAlī al-Ṣanhājī appeared on the Moroccan political stage at a crucial moment in the sixteenth century C.E.. Morocco teetered between two forces. The first was the weakening Waṭṭāsid empire that had found a tense coexistence with the Portuguese who controlled the coast, and the second was the ascendant Saᶜdian empire pushing up from the south. The Saᶜdian commanders' rhetoric of *jihād,* once taken over from the Jazūlīyya Sufi movement, threatened the Waṭṭāsid empire, the Portuguese, and anyone who supported the status quo. This made the situation very delicate for Zarruq's followers who lived within Morocco under Saᶜdian domination. They adapted to the Jazūlīyya paradigm in the positive sense of adopting practices and strategies that seemed to work in the new environment. They also adapted in the negative, defensive sense. The dominance of the Jazūlīyya community and the political agenda of the Saᶜdian rulers forced them to minimize their explicit allegiance to Zarruq so as not to be seen as traitors in the political tensions of northern Morocco.

The careers of Zarruq's followers in Morocco illustrate both the positive and the negative senses of adaptation. They had to adapt to local conditions of Sufi communities that cohered through their intense involvement in building local political dynasties and cultural hegemonies. Very soon after Zarruq's death, his followers in Morocco began to seek connections with the ascendant Jazūlīyya movement. These connections included political alliances and actual initiations with Jazūlīyya spiritual leaders. Within a few generations, the network of initiations that tied the two groups together became very dense, and it became difficult to distinguish Zarruq's followers from those who traced their allegiance to al-Jazūlī. It was mainly Zarruq's followers who sought out initiations with powerful Jazūlīyya saints, like al-Ghazwānī and al-Habṭī, and their circle of disciples.

Reflecting this political practice, the story arose that Zarruq himself had sought out initiation from al-Jazūlī. This story is found in the earliest hagiographic sources, but it is of doubtful historicity. It is always reported in the passive voice, revealing that it grew as a public perception rather than as a verifiable event. This is understandable considering that Shaykh al-Jazūlī had a disciple with a name very similar to Zarruq: Aḥmad al-Burnūsi, who is buried in the Sūs.[80] It would have been easy to conflate the two persons named "Aḥmad al-Burnūsī" and invent a fictitious initiation of Zarruq from al-Jazūlī.[81] By taking advantage of this conflation, the Moroccan followers of Zarruq argued that their own lineage was complementary to the Jazūlīyya lineage, in contradiction to the position of Zarruq's followers beyond the Saᶜdian border. These political and theoretical adjustments of Zarruq's early followers make up a complex phenomenon that will be illustrated through the story of ᶜAlī al-Ṣanhājī

ᶜAlī al-Ṣanhājī as a *majdhūb*, a holy madman, was an unlikely candidate for perpetuating Zarruq's reformist program in Fes. Nevertheless, it is through him that a community in Fes grew which looked to Zarruq as its founder. This is a supreme irony, for according to Zarruq's critical framework, ᶜAlī al-Ṣanhājī was not just an unlikely "saint" but was unfit for sainthood. However, through him grew one of the strongest Sufi communities in Fes, al-Zāwiya al-Fāsīyya. This was one of the only communities to institutionalize Zarruq's legacy, though in a partial form. Even as they portrayed Zarruq as the primary link in their initiatic chain, their own conception of sainthood and its manifestation in political and social activities had more in common with the Jazūlīyya community than with Zarruq's stringent reformist program.

To understand this seeming contradiction, we have to place ᶜAlī al-Ṣanhājī in the wider context of a social movement that appeared in northern Morocco. A *majdhūb* coalition formed during the years of unrest in which the Waṭṭāsid-Marinid dynasty struggled to hold on to power in Fes. Their *majdhūb* character far outweighed any formal initiations they might have to a Sufi lineage or any affiliation they might have with a saint. The coalition had a common social practice and a common display of sainthood, and they eventually settled on a common political agenda to get rid of the Waṭṭāsid-Marinid rulers. They decided to "withdraw spiritual support" from the Waṭṭāsid rulers and throw their weight behind the *jihād* movement. In this way, they followed the more dramatic example of al-Ghazwānī, marking the beginning of their alliance with the Jazūlīyya community.

The political activities of the *majdhūb* coalition must be understood within a world historical framework, for they withdrew spiritual support from the Waṭṭāsid rulers at a crucial moment in the configuration of power in the Mediterranean. The same concatenation of forces that limited Zarruq's teachings and lineage also affected the Portuguese sea-borne empire. The Saᶜdian *jihād* won popular support by attacking those ports held by the Portuguese. While they did not completely eject them from Moroccan territory, the Saᶜdian *jihād* did raise the Portuguese costs of defending their network of economic penetration into the interior of North and West Africa, and it toppled many local Moroccan strongmen who had acted as allies to the Portuguese.[82] In addition, rising Ottoman naval power in the Mediterranean made the Portuguese hold on the coasts more tenuous.

As a result, the Portuguese pushed farther south along the African coast in search of military strongholds and economic ports. As the Ottoman control of the Mediterranean denied them direct access to Asian products and markets, the Portuguese ventured around the South African cape and into the Indian Ocean. Soon, they applied their system of naval warfare and mercantile piracy (that they had developed against Moroccan coastal towns) to both sides of the Indian Ocean trade routes, on the coast of western India, and at the mouths of the Persian Gulf and Red Sea. In 1472 C.E., the King Alfonso of Portugal annexed Tangier and Asila, proclaiming himself king of Portugal and the two Algarves, one on this side and on the other side of the sea in Africa: the two "wests" (Algarve, Ar. al-Gharb) were Portugal and the kingdom of Fes.[83] Less than thirty years later, Vasco de Gama landed on the Malabar coast of southwest India (near Kozhikode, also known as Calicut). Having still failed to control Morocco, King Manuel I of Portugal declared all trade in the Indian Ocean basin to be a royal monopoly of the Portuguese crown, inaugurating a system of state-sponsored piracy against any ship that had not paid protection money at a Portuguese port-fortress.

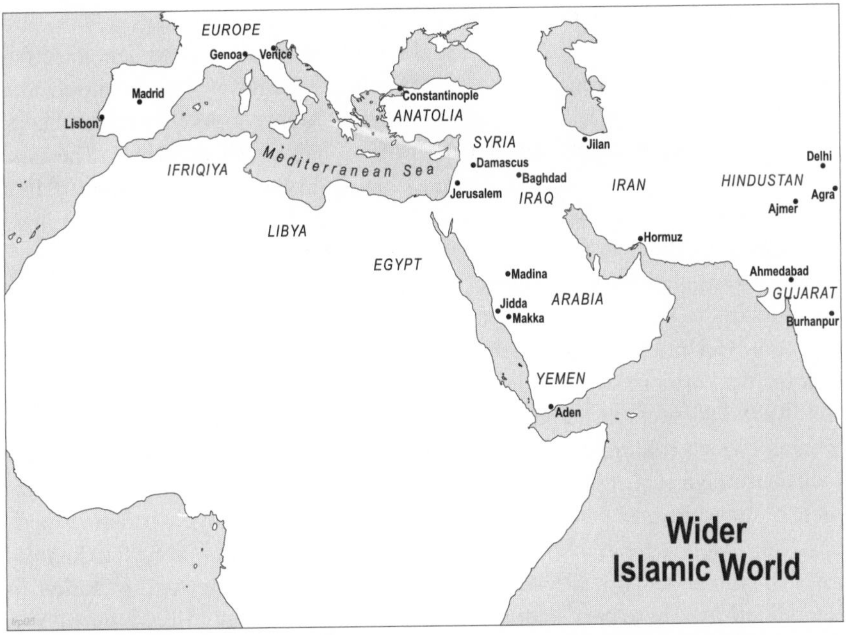

Map E

This opened up new possibilities for a sea-based crusade, as an extension of the Iberian *reconquista*. King Manuel I conceived of a renewed crusade to dislodge Muslims from the ports of western India. The Portuguese acted upon this plan during their initial foray into the Indian Ocean.[84] In 1517 C.E., they attacked the ports of Kamran and Zayla in the Red Sea, but were unable to invade Makka because the port of Jidda was too heavily fortified. They repeated a Red Sea incursion just three years later. Their goal had been to kidnap the body of the Prophet Muhammad, which they imagined to lie in state inside the Ka^cba (as Catholics embalmed saints for display in churches). In 1543 C.E. the Portuguese naval forces conducted raids in the Red Sea and threatened Jidda once again.[85]

Reports of such assaults near the holy cities reached Fes and incited riots against the last vestiges of the Waṭṭāsid rulers, who had affirmed a peace treaty with the Portuguese only five years before in a desperate bid to retain power.[86] As a result of this popular outcry, the Waṭṭāsids rejected the treaty and warfare erupted again between them and the Portuguese in northern Morocco. As the Waṭṭāsids taxed the people of Fes more heavily to support these military ventures, and as the tax base in the countryside shrank, popular support turned against them. This was the environment that pushed Zarruq's *majdhūb* followers in Fes to help lift saintly protection from the tottering Waṭṭāsid regime.

In earlier times, ᶜAlī al-Ṣanhājī used to walk into the homes of the ruling Waṭṭāsid aristocracy and redistribute their wealth to the poor and needy. This tacitly acknowledged their right to rule, even as he criticized their appropriation of the city's wealth through taxes and levies. However, as circumstances at home and in the wider world changed, ᶜAlī al-Ṣanhājī changed his policy to denounce the Waṭṭāsid elite. He once again acted as "the turner" in a novel way. He mounted a central point in the traffic arteries of Fes, a bridge which spans the river and connects the two halves of the city (at the dyers' market, al-Ṣabbāghīn). There he began to turn in a circle, as if invoking the entire city that spun around him. In a state of possession, he began to shout, "Get out, you children of the Marinids (Banū Marīn)! By God, we will not let you remain in our land!"[87]

ᶜAlī al-Ṣanhājī attracted several female followers. The most famous of them, Sayyida Amīna, began to take on social signs of sanctity, and she joined the *majdhūb* coalition. Her miracles graphically displayed her allegiance to those who were fighting the Portuguese. She would wake up in bed covered with bleeding wounds, "as if she had been participating in the *jihād*."[88] In her case, the bleeding of a woman (which routinely marks menstruating women off as dangerous and impure) became a sublime miraculous wound that distinguished her as an embodiment of the Moroccan people as a whole, injured in fights with the invading Iberians. This displays the remarkable ability of these *majdhūbs* to invert the dichotomies of routine ritual, especially in making outward impurity into a marker of internal purity. These persistent miracles aligned Amīna and ᶜAlī al-Ṣanhājī with the Saᶜdians and their supporters in the Jazūlīyya community, who built their reputation for leadership around *jihād*.

The *majdhūb*'s body is no longer the locus of a rational person bound by law, responsibility, and social custom. It becomes "empty" of these social meanings and can stand as a symbol of something greater, either the social whole or the workings of divine destiny. The miracles of ᶜAlī al-Ṣanhājī and Amīna illustrate this logic of the sacred, which allowed the *majdhūb*'s personality to take on political meaning in the shift of dynastic power. Their colleague, Abū Rawāyin from Miknās (Meknes), was known not just for being possessed by divine forces (*jadhb*) but also for a more crafty power to control the forces of destiny (*taṣrīf*).[89] He would practice spiritual extortion against the rich or against rulers by saying, "Quickly, buy from me your fortune and you won't come to ruin!" If they paid, he would say, "You are safe." But if they refused, he would pronounce, "You are cut off" or "You are killed," and shortly that would happen.[90]

In times of political uncertainty and upheaval, such threats from a holy madman gained extra potency. Abū Rawāyin was a colleague of ᶜAlī al-Ṣanhājī, though they did not share a formal allegiance in the same community. Abū Rawāyin had experienced his "spiritual opening" at the hands of a Jazūlīyya saint, Muḥammad ibn ᶜĪsā al-Fahdī.[91] The experience of repentance at the hands of this saintly guide (repentance ignited by his penchant for adulterous affairs with women) served to "free me from my confinement" and may have sparked his experiences of possession that left his reason behind. As a *majdhūb*, his emptied personality became a veritable barometer for political and military changes. He was a known proponent of *jihād* against the Iberians, but he would confound those who observed him by shouting out one day "I favor the Portuguese!" and the next day shouting "I favor the Muslims!" Soon it became apparent that "his favor" reflected who was winning in the wars at that particular time; it did not reflect his rational choice of whom to favor, but reflected instead divine destiny that granted either victory or defeat to the Muslims day by day.[92]

The shadowy figure of Abū Rawāyin lurked behind the scenes of many episodes as power tilted from the Waṭṭāsids to the Saᶜdians in northern Morocco. His seemingly irrational behavior was instrumental in prying loose support for the Marinid-Waṭṭāsid regime. In Fes, he convinced al-Miṣbāḥī, a saint who was a staunch loyalist, to "lift his spiritual protection from over the Marinid and Waṭṭāsid elite."[93] Hagiographic literature credits Abū Rawāyin with opening the way for the Saᶜdian conquest of Fes in 956 Hijri (1549 C.E.), and he was intimately involved in negotiating with the Saᶜdian forces.

This alliance between ᶜAlī al-Ṣanhājī and Abū Rawāyin signaled the beginning of more intimate connections between the followers of al-Jazūlī and Zarruq in Morocco. Upon ᶜAlī al-Ṣanhājī's death, Amīna and her "spiritual brother," ᶜAbd al-Raḥmān, "inherited" his spiritual state. ᶜAbd al-Raḥmān, known as "al-Majdhūb," institutionalized a Sufi community during the Saᶜdian era. He built a Sufi lineage around these *majdhūb* figures, and their initiation with Zarruq gave it legitimacy. As he built this lineage as a social institution, he built it around patterns set by the Jazūlīyya community rather than around Zarruq's reformist principles.

From the many disciples of ᶜAbd al-Raḥmān al-Majdhūb, one family was highly successful in building an institutional Sufi lineage, Abū al-Maḥāsin ibn Yūsuf al-Fāsī. He took his initiation with ᶜAbd al-Raḥmān al-Majdhūb and founded the Sufi community called "Ṭarīqa Zarruqīyya Majdhūbīyya."[94] He built this Sufi community upon the prosperity of his trading activities. In the preceding generations, Zarruq's immediate followers in Morocco had discontinued his critical project. Now, in the form of an institution, Abū al-Maḥāsin reclaimed Zarruq's scholarly and juridical prestige while disassociating himself from Zarruq's critique of sainthood and social movements. He also disassociated from the *majdhūb* character of his predecessors, even while enshrining that name in his institution. The hagiographic account of his life left by his son, entitled *Mirʾāt al-Maḥāsin*, purposefully minimized ᶜAlī al-Ṣanhājī's exploits. In this version of events, ᶜAlī al-Ṣanhājī simply passes on the blessing of Zarruq's lineage with a minimum of adventure. As it became a bourgeois institution, the "Ṭarīqa Zarruqīyya Majdhūbīyya" gradually lost both Zarruq's name and its *majdhūb* title and became known by the more neutral name "al-Zāwiya al-Fāsīyya." It grew into a Sufi community for the genteel and prosperous classes of Fes.

PART V. LEGACY

> Preservation of order is obligatory, and guarding carefully over the rights of common people is necessary.... For this reason, jurists have concurred that one must follow the leader (*imām*).... In the same way, they view *jihād* against Muslim rulers: one cannot disobey him even if he is a sinful person.[1]

ZARRUQ'S LEGACY IS a complex one. His immediate followers who advocated his reform movement encountered resistance at many levels in the emerging political and religious consensus of early modern Islamic polities. Despite this, Zarruq's texts continued to circulate and his figure loomed large in the hagiographic literature of North Africa. As we have seen, Ibn ᶜAjība in the eighteenth century was still confronting Zarruq's figure in his dreams and sparring with his critical ideas as if Zarruq were still alive and vocal. In the early twenty-first century, the figure of Zarruq continues to challenge and inspire Muslims in new ways. In our time, Zarruq still functions as a powerful symbol, something from a distant time or place that can nonetheless shape the current situation—"the legacy of the past when it fastens to the future," in the words of a contemporary Moroccan Qur'anic scholar and interpreter of dreams.[2]

How did Zarruq's ideals and writings survive, and how are contemporary conditions giving them a new context in which to flourish? This concluding chapter will venture some answers. After assessing how his reformist movement spread geographically beyond its initial crucible of North Africa, we will explore how his ideas persist chronologically into the present. His legacy may be more important than ever in the contemporary environment of reckless *jihād*. He argued that Muslims were legally bound to accept their political leader (*imām*) even if he was sinful. In contrast, they were not bound to follow a saint or heroic adventurer, for "the acknowledged leaders of Sufi communities have pronounced that the axial saint is known to exist but cannot be specified exactly in one appointed person."[3] This conclusion will address several points at which the evidence of Zarruq's life and writings impacts discussion of authority in the field of Islamic Studies and the broader field of Religious Studies.

9 Conclusion

With no fertile ground in Morocco, Zarruq's followers found positions in the madrasas of Laqqāna (in the Nile delta), at al-Azhar (in Cairo), and in Makka to perpetuate the form of juridical Sufi training that Zarruq had advocated. After 1535 C.E., these regions fell under Ottoman rule. In Cairo and the Ḥijāz, Zarruq's followers kept his intellectual spark and legal training alive, but they were gradually absorbed into scholarly families who won routine prestige under Ottoman patronage. From there, the Red Sea opened into the Indian Ocean basin, and Zarruq's personality was carried as far as South Asia. The far Maghrib that marks the confluence of the Mediterranean and the Atlantic is a long way from the Indian Ocean basin, and it is seldom that people imagine the two areas to be connected. These connections were very vivid and opened new opportunities for reformist juridical Sufis from South Asia.[1]

The most interesting mutation of Zarruq's legacy was in the Sufi community of ᶜAlī Muttaqī that thrived in the port cities that anchored the sea lanes between Makka, Yemen, and Gujarat (on the western coast of India). This community kept Zarruq's ideas alive in spiritual training and applied his ideas practically as critics of Sufis and their saints in South Asia who entered into political activities to support the early Mughal dynasty. Zarruq's legacy is evident in the illustrious career of ᶜAbd al-Ḥaqq Muḥaddith Dihlawī, who criticized not only the Mughal courtiers Abū al-Faḍl and Fayḍī (Pr. Abūl Fazl and Faizī) but also the ambitious Naqshbandī Sufi reformer Shaykh Aḥmad Sirhindī. This South Asian manifestation of Zarruq's teachings is a complex phenomenon full of its own fascinating narratives and demands a full book-length study to do it justice. However, Zarruq's legacy faded into the background in South Asia as the Mughal dynasty became fully established under the mature emperor Akbar, just as it had in Morocco as the Saᶜdian empire grew in strength. The rulers of these early modern empires were able to tap the cultural logic of sainthood in ways that supported their own innovative political designs. The concept of an absolute axial saint who channeled the flow of sacred power from God into the human community mirrored and supported the political rule of an absolute emperor who embodied justice and light and whose rule was above confirmation by mere jurists. Such a symbiosis between saintly authority and political power left little room for Zarruq's reformist ideals to fuse juridical and saintly authority.

Zarruq's legacy has mutated and been muted under the pressures of history. In Morocco, the initial furor over his critique of the Jazūlīyya movement and their helping to establish the Sa^{c}dian dynasty died down. His unlikely *majdhūb* followers settled down into the Zāwiya Fāsīyya, and its members became prolific historians, chroniclers, and hagiographers who built the literary archive of urban life in early modern Fes. Zarruq's program of reform failed to grow into a religious movement of any lasting force. Political events in North Africa foreclosed the possibilities of the reform movement he advocated, centered on the personality of the jurist saint in a highly rarified balance of Islamic legal training and Sufi discipleship.

However, Zarruq's legacy was not extinguished by the rise of early modern empires, European colonialism, and imposed modernity in the Islamic world. Rather, the figure of Zarruq continues to inspire contemporary Sufi leaders as they question the religious authority of modern reform movements and their politically extremist militant fringes. His ideas continue to hold sway over contemporary Muslims with a new relevance in the present that they may have lacked in the past. But we can only appreciate this modern application of his ideas after we assess what has been lost of the Islamic past.

Revival and Reform

In late fifteenth-century Morocco, Zarruq felt that his world was being fractured by political and cultural revolutions. In retrospect, these were only the first tremors of further revolutionary upheavals, centered in Europe but swiftly impacting the African and Asian regions where Muslims predominated. These revolutions have only accelerated through the nineteenth-century project of European colonial occupation, twentieth-century independence of nation-states, and the twenty-first-century domination by the global economy. Gone are the basic institutions that had framed Zarruq's life and work. Gone is the presumption that Muslims can form their own independent polities based on indigenous notions of political authority. Gone is the rule of Islamic law in nation-states ruled by Muslims. Gone is the system of madrasa education that cultivated the study of scripture, logic, law, and spiritual virtues side by side. Sufi communities remain, but they have been forcefully marginalized by European colonial regimes, post-colonial states that rule Muslim-majority nations, and Islamic revivalists like the Wahhabi movement. The *sharī^{c}a* still remains, though in an attenuated form that is more often reduced to a rhetorical flourish by preachers or an ideological rallying cry by political activists rather than as a shared reality of common values.

Although the basic institutions that shaped Zarruq's life are gone, his ideas and ideals remain. In fact, they take on a salience in the contemporary environment that they did not have before. Clifford Geertz, the American anthropologist and theorist of religion, is well-known for his writing about Muslim saints in Morocco. His approach employs saints as ciphers for religion as cultural system in premodern times; as modernization marginalizes saints in Islamic societies, Geertz observes that the gaps in authority are filled in by ideology and its appropriation of religious symbols to elicit mass support for radically new political regimes. Geertz, writing in the 1960s, assumed that ideology would lead to increasing "secularization" of Islamic societies, asking, "How do men of religious sensibility react when the machinery of faith begins to wear out?"[2] This prejudgment of the fact must now be thoroughly questioned as ideologies take on a more religious rhetoric with increasing popular disappointment in the promises of post-colonial secular nation-states in the Islamic world (and beyond). The rise of "fundamentalism" rather than inevitable secularization seems to be the dominant social force shaping Islamic societies today. These broad historical forces, channeled by more recent international political events since the first Gulf War in 1991, have given rise to *al-Qāʾida* and the attacks of September 11, 2001.

All these revolutionary changes stem from the technical, economic, and military dominance of Euro-American modernity and the subsequent Muslim loss of cultural pre-eminence. As scholars try to understand the ideological reaction to this dominance, the themes of reform and revival have shaped the literature on Muslims in the writing of Western observers as well as many Muslims. Scholars in Islamic studies have yet to reach a consensus on the terms "revival" and "reform." The terms cover a bewildering array of movements and attitudes and are rarely defined or critically discussed. However, certain dominant patterns emerge, patterns that the evidence of this study questions.

In an assertion with far-reaching consequences, many scholars locate the origin of Islamic reform in the Wahhabi movement in Arabia of the eighteenth century C.E.[3] Wahhabi ideals spread beyond Arabia in allied movements, known collectively as Salafi movements.[4] In this framework, reform becomes not only "scripturalist" in orientation, but corresponds to the political decay of Muslim states and appears to be a reaction to the advent of European colonialism.[5] With the Wahhabi movement as a defining origin, reform among Muslims becomes thoroughly anti-Sufi and diametrically opposed to the social, political, and doctrinal role of saints. Such reform seeks to "purge" Islam of foreign accretions and takes as its primary target "saint-worship" and the practice of Sufi communities as "saint cults," while rejecting even Islamic law (as it developed in the medieval period) as stagnant.

Unquestionably, Wahhabi and Salafi reform movements have gained real political and epistemological power in the modern world, especially after the establishment of an oil economy in the Arabian Gulf states. Yet scholars should not limit the category of "reform" to this type of movement. In contrast, the reform movement in this study had a very different philosophical orientation, ideological structure, and imaginative vocabulary. For Ahmad Zarruq and his followers, reform meant fusing fields of religious devotion and institutions of specialized knowledge that had become fragmented. They advocated a forceful fusion of saintly aspiration, juridical authority, and scholarly acumen. Such a fusion would limit or curtail certain practices as a natural consequence; the metaphor was not purging, but rather pruning. The primary agent of this reformist fusion was the saint who was also a jurist.

Some scholars have come to question the single "origin" of Islamic reform movements in the Wahhabi phenomenon. Yet many persist in seeing reform as a pre-eminently eighteenth-century C.E. phenomenon and position it as a reaction to modernism (in the form of European colonial domination or Muslim adoption of European technologies, organizations, and ideas to forestall colonial domination). This study questions such a framework, for the juridical saints articulated a paradigm of sainthood as the basis of a reform movement during a period prior to colonization (when even the commercial aspect of European domination was not yet fully established). The stimulus for this reform movement was not colonialism or even sharper competition with the rising technical prowess of European polities, but rather the rise of new centralizing political dynasties within Islamic societies.

With reform defined by the Wahhabi movement and contra-defined against European colonial imposition of modernism, it is no surprise that few scholars have looked for reform movements before the eighteenth century C.E.[6] Few have asked how reform movements operate from within Sufi communities, with saints as the primary agents of reform, for it seems absurd to scholars to ask whether saints and reformers have always been incommensurate and opposed, as this study has set out to ask. This intellectual myopia is reflected in the debate in Islamic studies over the status of saints and Sufi communities in the nineteenth century C.E. that did advocate reform. Some scholars have suggested a neologism, "Neo-Sufi," to suture over the assumed contradiction in these terms, reformer and saint.[7] Such a term suggests that a Sufi community suffused with reformist orientation is no longer "truly Sufi."

This study challenges the assertion that the origin for reform is the Wahhabi movement and the political condition of decline in the eighteenth century C.E.. Ahmad Zarruq and his followers initiated a movement of reform two centuries earlier. Some scholars have explored the more remote past of Muslims to locate reform movements, yet they most often posit their findings as examples of "fundamentalism," as did Geertz. This term, like "reform" itself, is often cited and seldom refined with analytic rigor. The penchant of scholars to include premodern reform movements, like the one documented in this study, under the rubric of "fundamentalism" forces us to examine how reform, fundamentalism, and religion overlap in modern scholarship.[8]

In the light of Zarruq's life story and discourse, this study suggests that the terms "reform" and "revival" should not be reduced to contemporary perceptions of "fundamentalism." The discipline of Islamic studies must be more attentive to variations in reform movements, variations over time periods, between regions, and among different communities. This study suggests that the Wahhabi movement did not uniquely set the standard for Islamic reform movements. Rather, it substantially modified the terms, techniques, and community base for reform movements, for prior reform movements were solidly centered in Sufi communities and rhetorically centered on the figure of saints. From this vantage point, after surveying the evidence of the career of Zarruq and his attention to the authority of the juridical saint, one might venture a hypothesis. The failure of Zarruq's type of "reform within Sufi communities" set the conditions for reform movements to flourish in the modern period that were "external to Sufi communities" and explicitly denounced saints. Marshall Hodgson validates this hypothesis (without venturing to prove it), when he noted that reform movements flourished in the form of Sufi communities in the era of "gunpowder empires," only to be overshadowed by the militant Wahhabi reform in a later period.[9]

Sufism as Part of an Integral Islam

Wahhabi and Salafi movements reduce Islam as a religion to a one-dimensional ideology. Many contemporary scholars, non-Muslim as well as Muslim, accept their ideologically charged assertions as the authoritative description of Islam. However, as this study has documented, Ahmad Zarruq saw the religion of Muslims in a more complex and multidimensional way. He offered a "thick description" (to use a useful phrase from Geertz) of the religion of Muslims, as a balance between *islām*, *īmān,* and *iḥsān*. Scholars in the field of Islamic Studies can learn from such a description that prevents "religion" from being reduced to a one-dimensional ideology.

This study has highlighted how Ahmad Zarruq did not privilege the term *islām* over other terms of religious meaning, like *īmān* and *iḥsān*. In his view, none of these domains excludes the others, but rather each depends on the others. Juridical Sufis, and Ahmad Zarruq in particular, explicitly described "religion" through these interrelated terms.

> The authority of an object depends upon its root principle and its foundation upon this principle according to evidence specific to it that guarantees its authenticity. This authority deflects anyone's repudiation of the essential reality of the object in question. The root principle of being a Sufi (*taṣawwuf*) is the dimension of virtue (*maqām al-iḥsān*). This is what the Prophet of Allah explicated with his words "to worship Allah as if you were seeing Allah, for if you cannot see Allah then surely Allah is seeing you." This is because all the meanings of sincerity of turning toward Allah return to this root principle and depend upon it. Around this principle they turn in all their variety, since its wording indicates the necessity of contemplation and worshipful observance (*murāqaba*). Likewise legal rulings (*fiqh*) centers on the dimension of submission (*maqām al-islām*) while jurisprudence (*uṣūl*) centers on the dimensions of faith (*maqām al-īmān*). Therefore, the discipline of being a Sufi is one of the integral parts of Muslim moral obligation (*dīn*) that Gabriel taught

to the Prophet Muhammad (upon him be blessings and peace) so that he could, in turn, teach his companions and followers (may Allah be pleased with them).[10]

Zarruq elaborated on these three terms, pushing their contextual meaning beyond theology into descriptions of human nature and the social structure of religious specialists. The three terms describe different levels of a person's being; they also describe different kinds of religious actions that address those levels of being.[11] The dimension of *islām* corresponds to outward actions and rituals located in the body or limbs. The dimension of *īmān* corresponds to beliefs and oral attestations located in the mind or tongue. Finally, the dimension of *iḥsān* corresponds to inward experience and intention located in the soul or heart. This multivalent description of "religion" ramifies into three areas to which different classes of religious specialists devote their attention (with their own disciplines of knowledge and their own authorities of power). Jurists are concerned with outward actions; they speak mainly about aspects of *islām*. Theologians, philosophers, and experts in jurisprudence theory (*uṣūlīyyūn*) are concerned with the objects of faith, belief, and dogma; they speak mainly about aspects of *īmān*. Sufis and saints are concerned with intent, sincerity, and its expression as virtue; they speak mainly about *iḥsān*.

In seeing his own "religion" in a network of interrelated terms, Ahmad Zarruq was typical of premodern Muslims thinkers in general. Yet he was also clearer and more persistent than others in articulating these three terms, contrasting them, and defining their mutual interrelation. This is because he interrogated the consensus about saints in his time. As a dissident to that consensus, he analyzed "religion" more thoroughly than most of his contemporaries, arguing that Sufi practices and sainthood (the outcome of attention to *iḥsān*) are integral to their religion, but must be limited and conditioned by legal norms and religious custom. In this argument, he analyzed the key terms of "religion" and demonstrated that *islām* is not the exclusive, all-encompassing term for their self-understanding. This is a crucial distinction between early modern reform movements within Sufi communities and modern reform movements that attacked Sufi communities.

Reformist Sufis and Fundamentalist Movements

This is a crucial distinction to bear in mind, especially because in other ways there are apparent continuities and similarities between Sufism and fundamentalist movements. The story of Ahmad Zarruq provides us with a lens through which to assess and evaluate these similarities. We have already seen how some later Sufis rejected Ahmad Zarruq and his ideals, claiming that he was nothing but a jurist who could speak only to concerns of outer behavior in ritual, social interaction, and political debate. We may recall that one Moroccan Sufi master, Shaykh al-Darqāwī, diminished Zarruq's ideals even though he held an initiation in the lineage of Zarruq; he said, "Shaykh Zarruq is a big deal among the literal-minded scholars and jurists, but to those who pay attention to interior spiritual realities he is insignificant."[12]

Shaykh al-Darqāwī dismissed him not only because Zarruq sharply criticized the way many Sufis organized their communities around saints, but also because Zarruq encouraged a self-conscious minimalism in the outer ritual practice of Sufi devotional exercises, as documented in chapter 6.

Zarruq desired to push Sufi communities to embrace only the "lowest-common-denominator" of Islamic devotion, in a way that challenged other Sufi communities. Zarruq reveals this in letters he sent to his followers back in Morocco, in which he wrote: "Practice meditation (*dhikr*), even if only saying *praise be to God.* Recite the Qur᾽an, even if only one verse. Fast, even for only a single day of Ramadan. Pray, even if just one prostration in the dead of the night. Give to the needy, even if just one morsel of food to a hungry dog as long as you do it solely for the sake of God."[13] This advice recommends "lowest-common-denominator" devotion (as it is called by one of my teachers in a term both observant and pejorative) that would not clash in any way with jurists' more external understanding of the demands of Islamic loyalty. In this sense, his advice affirms the words of his teacher, al-Ḥaḍramī, even it reveals none of the high and idealistic standards he had set out in his more formal writings for training disciples.

In this way, Zarruq's premodern movement shares a characteristic with other reform movements in the modern era that have forged Sufi rituals into lowest-common-denominator devotionalism among Muslims. If asceticism and supererogatory devotion are unhinged from discipleship to a saint or allegiance to a distinct devotional community, one gets lowest-common-denominator devotionalism. Zarruq's program of reform failed to grow into a religious movement of any lasting force, mainly because of the high idealistic standard he set. In the recent past, Islamic reform movements continued to impact Sufi communities in different ways that are far from the intricate balance Zarruq had imagined would fuse jurists and Sufis into one community.

Fundamentalist movements tend to grow out of the lowest-common-denominator devotional environment. Exemplary of this process is the *Tablīghī Jamā*ᶜ*at*, which is extraordinarily popular and powerful in the contemporary period.[14] The *Tablīghī Jamā*ᶜ*at* and other Salafi groups are the result of pressures to turn Sufi communities into mass movements of Islamic revival; these have been very important in the nineteenth century and have led the military defense of Islamic societies against European colonial incursions. Some scholars have advanced the label "Neo-Sufism" to describe such movements, though that label has dubious descriptive value. These mass movements attempted to overlay the *sharī*ᶜ*a* onto Sufi communities and suppress those elements of Sufi communities that were deemed to exceed the *sharī*ᶜ*a*. In this sense, they are on the surface similar to the reform of Sufi devotion advocated by Zarruq. Zarruq's formulation was more subtle if less forceful; he tried to infuse Sufi communities with the *sharī*ᶜ*a* while arguing that the *sharī*ᶜ*a* was only complete when integrated with Sufi spiritual and ethical cultivation.

We can conclude from the example of Zarruq that there are diverse paradigms of Islamic reform movements. Some preserve an integral role for Sufi practice and sainthood, while others might preclude both, even as they all exert pressure toward a lowest-common-denominator devotionalism. This conclusion parallels a major argument of this book, that Zarruq's life story reveals how various paradigms of sainthood in premodern Islamic societies were in competition, even as they shared common characteristics and drew on common sources.

In the contemporary context, lowest-common-denominator devotionalism seems to be the dominant interregional norm for Muslim communities. That it is simple and potentially uniform makes it a powerful symbol for Islamic unity in a time of political fragmentation. That it erases regional traditions and local particularities makes it fit the new globalization that is bringing different regions of the Muslim world into increasingly dense interaction. That it does not depend on traditional Islamic learning and scholastic complexities makes it possible to be transmitted through the Internet or democratic forms of rhetoric (like revivalist meetings, missionary speeches, or popular journals) where traditionally educated scholars are not found or are deemed too old-fashioned.

However, the fact that lowest-common-denominator devotionalism lacks the depth and subtlety of Islamic humanistic learning makes it an ideal vehicle to promote ideological, often fundamentalist, interpretations of Islam. Such interpretations of Islam are most forcefully promoted by Wahhabi and Salafi reform movements, which do not merely preclude Sufi practice and understanding but actively denounce them and often violently suppress them. And regardless of whether one supports or opposes Wahhabi and Salafi reform movements, one must admit that today they seem to dominate Muslim societies in a way never witnessed before.

This is why Zarruq's ideals have a new salience in the contemporary environment. His ideals of Islamic reform did not marginalize sainthood, but centered on it in the form of the juridical saint. However, its simplified exterior does make it a form of Sufism that is eminently compatible with today's climate of Salafi supremacy, in which more overt, robust, or ornate forms of Sufi devotion are increasingly attacked by Wahhabis and Salafis as "un-Islamic." For this reason, contemporary Sufi community leaders can make strategic use of Zarruq's legacy today in ways that his immediate followers could not.

Contemporary Sufi leaders, therefore, can advocate Islamic reform while challenging the dominance of the Wahhabi and Salafi forms of reform, or even their very authenticity. Contemporary Sufi leaders can outwardly conform to the simplified regime of reformist Islamic practice, while inwardly challenging the collapse of Islamic religiosity into a one-dimensional, ideological practice that can be easily manipulated by politically opportunistic extremist leaders. For this reason, some contemporary Sufi leaders are using Zarruq's ideas to reconstruct an integral Islam, in contexts outside the mass movements with no educational commitment like the *Tablīghī Jamāʿat*. Zarruq continues to be a pivotal figure in the public debate among Muslims about the authenticity of Sufism, the necessity of legal rectitude, and the danger of religious ideology. This debate has become even more heated in the contemporary political environment since the Iranian revolution, Afghan *Mujāhidīn* struggle, and the collapse of the Cold War international order.

In the Sunni Islamic world, there are a few institutions of traditional religious education that remain after colonial domination, like al-Azhar in Egypt and al-Qarawiyyīn in Morocco. In them, scholars still teach Zarruq's works in the context of juridical education. Jurists and muftis in these institutions have been vocal in denouncing the attacks of September 11, and in the decades leading up to those events they had disavowed the ideological interpretations of Islam that have been used to justify the attacks. In North America, we can find examples of how Zarruq's ideals are put into practice in a fuller expression. Here, the reformist pressure on Sufi ideals is tempered by access to education in "secular universities" that engender a respect for the general humanities that frame the teaching of traditional disciplines like Arabic language, literature, philosophy, and jurisprudence.

In this environment, Sufi leaders can engage in a reform project that is very similar to that imagined by Zarruq. Therefore, when we hear Sufi leaders like Hamza Yusuf take back the authority of being also Islamic jurists and communal leaders, we can hear deeper resonance with Zarruq's personality and teachings. Hamza Yusuf has said, "According to Islamic law, [Osama bin Laden] does not represent legitimate state authority. He has no authority to declare war on anybody …it is very dangerous for us to say that Osama bin Laden represents Muslim law because he does not. He does not have that authority. The only people who can declare *jihād* are legitimate rulers, and none of these groups has that legitimacy."[15]

The example of Hamza Yusuf is only one, if the most illuminating, example of how Zarruq's personality and ideals are crucial to this reformist project rooted in Sufi practice and traditionally moderate Islamic loyalty. Zarruq's legacy can deeply affect the way scholars analyze the present of Islam through the resources of its past. At stake is the very authority to decide what the practice of Islam will be in the future.

Appendix A

This list represents the lineage [*sanad*] of the initiatory handshake that spread in juridical Sufi community in Meknes and Fes by Muḥammad al-Ghasānī, one of the teachers of al-Qūrī and a colleague of ᶜAbdallah al-ᶜAbdūsī. Ibn Ghāzī received this initiatory handshake in Meknes, first from al-Ghasānī and a second time from al-ᶜAbdūsī.[1]

to Aḥmad ibn Ghāzī
from ᶜAbdullah al-ᶜAbdūsī
from Muḥammad ibn Muḥammad al-Ghasānī
from Muḥammad ibn Yaḥya (the father of al-Ghasānī)
from Muḥammad ibn ᶜAlī al-Marrākushī "ibn ᶜAliwat"
from Abū ᶜAbdallah al-Ṣadafī
from Abū al-ᶜAbbās ibn al-Banāᵓ
from Abū ᶜAbdallah al-Hazmīrī
from Khiḍr
from the Prophet Muḥammad.

Appendix B

This lineage represents the genealogy of the Qādirī *shurafā'* who settled in Fes. There are eight generations between those who left Iraq and those who arrived in Fes. Although the exact date of their settling in Fes is not clear, they were present by the late ninth century Hijri (late fifteenth century C.E.).[1]

ᶜAbd al-Qādir al-Jīlānī (died in the mid-sixth century Hijri/mid-twelfth century C.E.in Baghdad)
Ibrāhīm ibn ᶜAbd al-Qādir (died in 592 Hijri/1196 C.E. in al-Wāsiṭ, Iraq)
Muḥammad ibn Ibrāhīm (left Iraq when the Mongols conquered Baghdad in 656 Hijri/1258 C.E.)
Aḥmad ibn Muḥammad ibn Ibrāhīm (lived for some time in Madīna but faced resistance to his settlement in the Ḥijāz, returned to Baghdad and wrote a genealogical document in 671 Hijri/1272–73 C.E.)
Saᶜd (his place and date of death are unknown; he or his father had settled in Andalusia at Ḥiṣn al-Qāhira near Wādī Āsh [Sp. Guadix])
Muḥammad ibn Saᶜd (wrote a genealogical document certifying his family's descent in Wādī Āsh, then moved with his family to Granada)
Muḥammad Hafīd Saᶜd (known as "Grandson of Saᶜd" or Muḥammad ibn Muḥammad ibn Saᶜd; either he or his father moved the Qādirī family from Andalusia to Fes in the late ninth century Hijri/late fifteenth century C.E.)[2]
Muḥammad ibn Muḥammad al-Qādirī (wrote a genealogical document in Fes in 910 Hijri/1504 C.E.)[3]

Glossary of Names
(of Historical Personalities in This Study)

al-ᶜAbdūsī, ᶜAbdallah ibn Muḥammad ibn Mūsā ibn Muᶜṭī (d. around 859 Hijri/1455 C.E.). Jurist, Sufi, and preacher. Served as a head jurist of Fes and delivered sermons at the congregational mosque of al-Qarawiyyīn.

al-ᶜAbdūsī, Mūsā (d. 776 Hijri/1374–75 C.E.). A Sufi disciple of Ibn ᶜĀshir, along with Ibn ᶜAbbād. Mūsā al-ᶜAbdūsī died in Meknes and was the grandfather of ᶜAbdullah al-ᶜAbdūsī, Zarruq's grandmother's teacher.

Abū al-Faḍl and Fayḍī. Courtiers and literary authors. More commonly transliterated in Persian as Abūʾl Fazl and Faizī. Two brothers were important advisors to the Mughal Emperor Akbar (d. 1014 Hijri/1604 C.E.).

Abū Madyān, Shuᶜayb ibn al-Ḥusayn al-Anṣārī (d. 594 Hijri/1198 C.E. in Tilimsān). Sufi. Born near Sevilla, settled in Bijāya (Algeria).

Abū Rawāyin, Aḥmad (or Muḥammad) ibn Ḥussayn al-ᶜAbdī al-Sahlī (d. before 960 Hijri/1553 C.E.). Sufi and *Majdhūb*. Buried outside of Meknes.

Abū Yiᶜzza. Sufi. Known in Berber as Yallanūr, "Possessor of Light." The Sufi teacher of Abū Madyan and one of the major Sufi masters of Morocco before the organization of the Shādhilīyya community with its distinct branches.

al-Afhām, Ibrāhīm (d. first half of tenth century Hijri/early sixteenth century C.E.). Sufi and *majdhūb*. Buried at Jabal Zarhūn, north of Meknes.

Ajānā, al-Ḥasan (d. 939 Hijri/1532–33 C.E.). Sufi. A senior follower of al-Jazūlī.

al-Amīn, Muḥammad, known as "al-ᶜAṭṭār" (d. 863 Hijri/1459 C.E.). Qādirī Sufi. Lived in Fes and is buried at Jabal Zarhūn, near Meknes.

Amīna bint Aḥmad ibn al-Qāḍī (d.around 960 Hijri/1553 C.E.). Sufi and female *majdhūb*. She was a follower and inheritor of the spiritual power of ᶜAlī al-Ṣanhājī, along with her "spiritual brother," ᶜAbd al-Raḥmān al-Majdhūb. She is buried in Fes behind the tomb of ᶜAlī al-Ṣanhājī.

Anas ibn Mālik, Abū Hamza (d. around 91–93 Hijri/709–711 C.E.). Servant and companion to the Prophet Muḥammad. Source of many hadith reports about the Prophet's teachings and behavior.

al-Andalusī, ᶜAlī Ṣāliḥ. Sufi. Senior follower of al-Jazūlī. Administered the Jazūlīyya zawiya in Fes.

Banū Marīn. A tribal family of Berbers who moved into Morocco from Algeria and established the Marinid Dynasty that ruled from the mid-thirteenth century until 1465 C.E..

Banū Waṭṭās. A clan of the Marinid family, who served as ministers in the Marinid dynasty. Took over power upon the execution of the last Marinid sultan, ᶜAbd al-Ḥaqq II, during the sharifian revolution in Fes in 1465 C.E..

Dihlawī, ᶜAbd al-Ḥaqq (d. 1052 Hijri/1642 C.E.). Sufi and scholar. Known in India as "Muḥaddith Dihlawī," the hadith scholar of Delhi. His first Sufi initiations were Qādiri, but after studying hadith in Makka, he took initiation in Zarruq's community through ᶜAbd al-Wahhāb Muttaqī, the primary follower of ᶜAlī Muttaqī. Established an influential madrasa in Delhi.

al-Fāsī, Abū al-Maḥāsin ibn Yūsuf (d. 1013 Hijri/1604 C.E. in Fes). Sufi. Established the "Zāwiya Fāsīyya" based on the teachings of ᶜAbd al-Raḥmān al-Majdhūb, with Ahmad Zarruq as a major link in their chain of initiations.

al-Fihrī al-Sufyānī, Muḥammad ibn ᶜĪsā (d. around 930 Hijri/1523 C.E.). Sufi. A disciple of Abū al-ᶜAbbās al-Ḥārithī in the Jazūlīyya community.

al-Ghasānī, Muḥammad ibn Yaḥyā ibn Jabbār (d. 827 Hijri /1424 C.E. in Meknes). Sufi. See appendix A for his Sufi initiations that he spread through the juridical Sufi communities of Meknes and Fes.

al-Ghazwānī, ᶜAbdullah (d. 935 Hijri/1528–29 C.E.). Jazūlī Sufi. Principal follower and representative of al-Tabbāᶜ and powerful political leader during the Saᶜdian dynasty's rise to power.

al-Ghumārī, Ḥasan (d. 874 Hijri/1469–70 C.E. in Tilimsān). Sufi. Elder advisor to Zarruq in his youth.

al-Habṭī, ᶜAbdullah ibn Muḥammad al-Ṣanhājī al-Ṭanjī (d. 963 Hijri/1556 C.E.). Sufi. Disciple and representative of al-Ghazwānī. Known by his supporters as "the Religious Renewer [Mujaddid] of the Tenth Century."

al-Ḥaḍramī, Aḥmad ibn ᶜUqba, ibn ᶜAbd al-Qādir ibn Muḥammad ibn ᶜUmar ibn Aḥmad (d. between 889–895 Hijri/1494–1590 C.E. at Ṭabra in the Sahara). Sufi. Zarruq's spiritual master in Cairo.

Ibn ᶜAbbād al-Rundī, Muhammad ibn ᶜAbdullah ibn Ibrāhīm (d. 792 Hijri/1390 C.E. in Fes). Sufi, jurist, preacher. Also known by the tribal name al-Nafzī, and by the place name al-Fāsī.

Ibn ᶜAbd al-Raḥmān, Muḥammad. Sharīf, jurist, and tribal leader. From Tagmadert, he spearheaded the Saᶜdian dynastic military expansion in cooperation with the Jazūlīyya Sufi community.

Ibn Abī Ghālib, ᶜAlī (d. 801 Hijri/1398–99 C.E. in Fes). Surgeon and Sufi. Known popularly as "Bū Ghālib." His tomb in Fes is the location of the zawiya "Bū al-Quṭūṭ."

Ibn ᶜAjība, Aḥmad ibn al-Mahdī (d. 1124 Hijri/1809 C.E.). Sufi and scholar. Prolific author of the Darqawīyya Sufi community, a branch of the Shādhiliyya, whose chain of initiations includes Shaykh Zarruq.

Ibn al-ᶜArabī al-Ḥātimī, Muḥayy al-Dīn (d. 638 Hijri/1240 C.E. in Damascus). Sufi and philosopher. Born in Andalusia, traveled widely in North Africa.

Speculative thinker and theoretician of Sufi experience and saintly authority, Known as *al-Shaykh al-Akbar*, the "Greatest Master." In North Africa, known as "al-Ḥātimī" to differentiate him from the famous Mālikī jurist and Sufi, Abū Bakr ibn al-ᶜArabī.

Ibn ᶜĀshir, Aḥmad al-Anṣārī (d. 765 Hijri/1362 C.E. in Salé). Sufi and scholar.

Ibn ᶜAṭāʾillah, Tāj al-Dīn ibn ᶜAbd al-Karīm (d. 709/1309 C.E. in Cairo). Sufi and jurist. First author of texts in the Shādhilī Sufi community.

Ibn Ghāzī, Aḥmad. Sufi and jurist. Received an *ijāza* via Zarruq from teachers in Cairo and Arabia. Was one of Zarruq's few colleagues in Fes after his return from Cairo.

Ibn al-Futūḥ, Muḥammad ibn ᶜUmar (d. 818 Hijri/1415 C.E. in Meknes). Sufi and jurist. Born in Tilimsān, studied in Fes, then settled in Meknes. He is buried next to his companion, Ibn Ḥamd.

Ibn al-Ḥabbāk, Aḥmad (d. 938 Hijri/1531–32 C.E.). Jurist. Spokesperson for the jurists of Fes who confronted Zarruq upon his return from Cairo. Allied to the Jazūlīyya Sufi community and poisoned by order of Waṭṭāsid Sultan Aḥmad al-Waṭṭāsī.

Ibn Ḥamd, Abū Muḥammad ᶜAbdallah (d. 833 Hijri/1429–30 C.E. in Meknes). Sufi and jurist. His tomb in Meknes was famous as a pilgrimage point in the fifteenth century.

Ibn Khaldūn (d. 808 Hijri/1406 C.E. in Tunisia). Philosopher, courtier, and historian. Born in Andalusia, lived in North Africa. Wrote the definitive history of medieval Islamic polities, the *Muqaddima* and *Kitāb al-ᶜIbār* stressing how religious and political authority converge and diverge.

Ibn Wafāʾ, ᶜAlī (d. in Cairo). Sufi, jurist, and poet in the Shādhilī lineage of Ibn ᶜAṭāʾillah.

al-ᶜImrānī al-Jūṭī, Muḥammad al-Ḥafīd al-Idrīsī (d. around 871 Hijri/1466–67 C.E.). *Naqīb* or chief of the sharifian families in Fes during the late Marinid dynasty. Political leader of the sharifian revolution in Fes in 869 Hijri 1465 C.E..

al-Jīlānī, ᶜAbd al-Qādir (d. 563 Hijri/1166 C.E. in Baghdad). Sufi, *sharīf,* and scholar. The Qādirī Sufi community was established upon his reputation and by his descendants.

al-Jazūlī, Muḥammad ᶜAbd al-Raḥmān ibn Abī Bakr ibn Sulaymān (d. 869 Hijri/1465 C.E.). Sufi and leader. Founder of the Jazūlīyya Sufi community. Preached for *jihād* against Spanish and Portuguese invaders of Morocco and revolution against the Marinid dynasty. Buried first in Afūghāl and later in Marrakesh.

al-Karrāsī, Muḥammad (d. around 946 Hijri/1539–40 C.E.). Jurist and literary author. Born in Andalusia around 856 Hijri (1452 C.E.) and educated in Granada. Served as a jurist in Fes. Settled in Tetuan as the chief qāḍī.

al-Kharrūbī, Muḥammad ibn ᶜAlī al-Sfaqsī al-Jazāʾirī (d. 963 Hijri/1556 C.E.). Sufi and jurist. Principal successor and representative of Zarruq. Born in the Tunisian town of Sfax (south of Qayrawān), studied in Fes, settled in Tarābulus (Tripoli), and is buried outside Algiers.

al-Khaṣṣāṣī, Muḥammad. Sufi. Fellow disciple of al-Ḥaḍramī who traveled with Zarruq from Cairo to Fes.

al-Khaṭṭāb, ᶜUmar (d. around 943 Hijri/1536 C.E.). Jazūlī Sufi. Disciple of ᶜAbd al-ᶜAzīz al-Tabbāᶜ and master of ᶜAbd al-Raḥmān al-Majdhūb. Lived at Jabal Zarhūn, north of Meknes.

al-Laqānī, Muḥammad ibn al-Ḥasan ibn ᶜAlī ibn ᶜAbd al-Raḥmān (d. around 930 Hijri/1453–1529 C.E.). Jurist and Sufi. Known as "Shams al-Dīn." Born in Egypt in 857 Hijri and died in Laqqāna, in the Nile Delta region. Principal successor and representative of Zarruq. Brother of Nāṣir al-Dīn al-Laqqānī.

al-Laqānī, Nāṣir al-Dīn (d. mid-tenth-century Hijri/mid-sixteenth-century C.E.). Jurist and Sufi. Major successor and representative of Zarruq. Brother of Shams al-Dīn al-Laqqānī. Professor of Māliki jurisprudence at al-Azhar in Cairo.

"al-Majdhūb," ᶜAbd al-Raḥmān Abū Muḥammad ibn ᶜAyāḍ al-Ṣanhājī (d. 976 Hijri/1569 C.E. in Meknes). Sufi and *majdhūb*. Follower of ᶜAlī al-Ṣanhājī.

Mālik ibn Anas, Abū ᶜAbdullah (d. 179 Hijri/796 C.E. in Madīna). Jurist. Considered the "founder" [*imām*] of the Mālikī legal method, which came to dominate North Africa.

al-Marīnī, ᶜAbd al-Ḥaqq II (d. 869 Hijri/1465 C.E.). The last sultan of the Marinid dynasty in Fes. Executed during the sharifian revolution. Succeeded after a six-year revolutionary interval by the Banū Waṭṭās whose family had provided ministers under the Marinid dynasty.

al-Maṣmūdī, ᶜĪsā ibn ᶜAllāl ibn al-Qāḍī (d. 823 Hijri/1420 C.E. in Fes). Jurist and preacher. He studied under Ibn al-Futūḥ in Meknes.

al-Matīnsī (d. 875 Hijri/1470 C.E. in Cairo). Scholar.

al-Milyānī, Aḥmad ibn Yūsuf al-Rāshidī (d. 929 Hijri/1523 C.E.). Sufi. Disciple of Muḥammad al-Zaytūnī and Zarruq. Established a zawiya in Milyāna (in western Algeria).

al-Miṣbāḥī, Aḥmad al-Shāhid (d. around 956 Hijri/1549 C.E.). Sufi. Spiritual protector of Waṭṭāsid rule over Fes.

Muttaqī, ᶜAlī ibn Ḥusām al-Dīn al-Hindī (d. 975 Hijri/1567 C.E. in Makka). Sufi and scholar. Born in Burhānpūr south of Gujarat (the interior of the western coast of India). Renowned as a hadith scholar in South Asia. Spread the teachings of juridical Sufis in general and of Zarruq in particular to South Asia.

al-Qarmūnī, ᶜAbd al-Raḥmān (d. 864 Hijri/1459–60 C.E. in Fes). Qādirī Sufi. Descended from an Andalusian family from Carmona. Was a student and disciple of Ibn al-Futūḥ and Ibn Ḥamd in Meknes. Moved to Fes to study in the juridical Sufi circles of ^{c}Umar al-Ragrāgi and ^{c}Īsā al-Maṣmūdī.

al-Qūrī, ^{c}Abdallah ibn al-Qāsim (d. 872 Hijri/1467–68 C.E.). Jurist, preacher, and Sufi. Also know by the place names al-Lakhmī, al-Andalusī, al-Miknāsī. His family was from a town near Sevilla. Grew up in Meknes and moved to Fes. Served as chief mufti of Fes and preacher at al-Qarawiyyīn. Zarruq's first teacher and spiritual guide.

al-Ragrāgī, ^{c}Umar (d. 810 Hijri/1407–1408 C.E. in Fes). Jurist and preacher. Delivered the Friday sermons at the congregational mosque of al-Andalus in Fes. He was a teacher of ^{c}Īsā al-Maṣmūdī, who succeeded him at that position.

al-Sabtī, Abū al-^{c}Abbās (d. 601 Hijri/1204 C.E. in Marrakesh). Sufi. One of the patron saints of Marrakesh and moral exemplar for Moroccan Sufis.

Ṣahnūn, ^{c}Abd al-Salām ibn Sa^{c}īd, al-Tanūkhī al-Hamsi al-Qayrawānī (d. 230–31 Hijri/854 C.E.). Ṣahnūn was the *qāḍī* of al-Qayrawān (near Tunis) and wrote the legal text, *al-Mudāwwana*, which serves as the foundation of the Maliki juridical method in North Africa.

al-Ṣanhājī, ^{c}Alī ibn Aḥmad (d. around 947 Hijri/1540–41 C.E.). Sufi and *majdhūb*. Known as "al-Duwwār," "the turner." Buried outside Bāb Futūḥ in Fes.

al-Sanhūrī (d. 891 Hijri/1486 C.E. in Cairo). Scholar.

al-Shādhilī, ^{c}Alī Abū al-Ḥasan (d. 656 Hijri/1258 C.E. in Upper Egypt). Sufi. Founder of the Shādhilīyya Sufi community. Born in Morocco, established a community in Tunis, moved to Alexandria, and died in Upper Egypt while making the pilgrimage to Makka.

al-Shaykh al-Mahdī, Muḥammad (d. 964 Hijri/1557 C.E.). Sultan of Sa^{c}dian dynasty who unified northern and southern Morocco. Younger son of Ibn ^{c}Abd al-Raḥmān, Muḥammad al-Sharīf.

al-Shushtarī, ^{c}Alī ibn ^{c}Abdallah al-Numayrī. Sufi and poet. Follower of Ibn Sab^{c}īn and then Abū Madyan. Born in Andalusia, traveled widely in North Africa and died in Egypt.

al-Shuṭaybī, Muḥammad ibn ^{c}Ali ibn Aḥmad al-Andalusī al-Burjī (d. 963 Hijri/1555–56 C.E.). Sufi and scholar. Known as "al-Ḥajj al-Shuṭaybī." Took initiation from Zarruq and training from al-Milyānī. Established a zawiya at Tazaghdart (a village near the town of Ghafsay in the region of Tawanat), where he died.

Sirhindī, Aḥmad. (d. 1025 Hijri/1616 C.E.). Naqshbandī Sufi. Reformist Sufi who opposed "free-thinking" and Shi^{c}ī elements of the Mughal court under Akbar and his followers.

al-Ṣufyānī, Aḥmad al-Ḥārithī. A senior follower of al-Jazūlī.

al-Ṣughayyir al-Sahlī, Muḥammad al-^{c}Amrī (d. 918 Hijri/1512–13 C.E.). Sufi. Shaykh al-Jazūlī named him al-Ṣughayyir, "the little one." One of al-Jazūlī's earliest followers and primary representatives. Born in the Sūs.

Moved to the region outside of Fes, called Khandaq al-Zaytūn, along the banks of the river Wādī Laban, where he is buried.

al-Suhrawardī, ᶜUmar (d. 632 Hijri/1234 C.E. in Baghdad). Sufi. The saint who founded the Suhrawardīyya Sufi community.

al-Tabbāᶜ, ᶜAbd al-ᶜAzīz (d. 914 Hijri/1508–1509 C.E. in Marrakesh). Sufi. Principal follower and representative of Shaykh al-Jazūlī.

al-Tustarī, Sahl ibn ᶜAbdallah (d. 383 Hijri/993 C.E. in Iraq). An early influential Sufi.

ᶜUmar ibn al-Khaṭṭāb (d. 23 Hijri/644 C.E.). Second caliph and companion of the Prophet Muḥammad. In addition to his crucial historical importance in shaping the early Muslim community, he is the source of many hadith reports.

al-Wansharīsī, Aḥmad ibn Yaḥya (d. 914 Hijri/1508 C.E.) Jurist. Born in Tilimsān and died in Fes; he wrote the famous compilation of juridical decisions called *al-Miᶜyār al-Muᶜrib wa'l-Jāmiᶜ al-Mughrib.*

al-Waryāghalī, ᶜAbd al-ᶜAzīz (d. 880 Hijri/1475–76 C.E.). Preacher. Main preacher in the congregational mosque of Fes, al-Qarawiyyīn and inciter of the sharifian revolution in Fes.

al-Zarhūnī, Ibrāhīm al-Afhām. Sufi and *Majdhūb*. He claimed to have taken initiation from Zarruq in Fes, and most subsequent Sufis who claim Zarruq in their chains of initiation go through al-Zarhūnī.

al-Zawāwī, Aḥmad ibn al-Qāḍī (d. 920–30 Hijri/1514–24 C.E.). Sufi. Advocated *jihād* against the Iberians in Tunis and invited the Ottoman forces into the region to push out the Spanish.

al-Zawāwī, Majd al-Dīn Abū Muḥammad (d. 839 Hijri/1435–36 C.E. in Cairo). Sufi and jurist. Commonly known as al-Ṣāliḥ al-Maghribī [Righteous Man from the West]. Also know by his tribal affiliations, al-Ḥasanī al-Riyāḥī. Born in the central Maghrib in al-Madukāl, a town between Biskra and ᶜUmra, in 760 Hijri (1359 C.E.).

al-Zaytūnī, Muḥammad ibn ᶜAbdullah (d. between 910–20 Hijri/1504–1514 C.E.). Qādirī Sufi. Known as "The Blind Viper." Lived in Fes but traveled frequently east along caravan routes. Buried in al-Masīla in the area called al-Jarīd (now southern Tunisia).

Notes

Introduction

1. De Certeau, *The Mystic Fable* (1992), 154.

2. Integral Islam should not be confused with "Itegrism," the label applied to North African Islamic fundamentalist movements; see Burgat and Dowell, *The Islamic Movement in North Africa*, 8.

Part I. Sufism

1. Aḥmad Zarrūq, *Qawāᶜid al-Taṣawwuf* (1992), Principle 5.

2. Aḥmad ibn ᶜAjība, *Sharḥ ᶜalā Matn al-Ajrūmīyya li-ᶜAbdullah Muḥammad ibn Dāwūd al-Ṣanhājī* as reproduced in al-Ṭuᶜmī, *Ṭabaqāt al-Shādhīliyya al-Kubrā* (1996), 75–76. All translations from Arabic are by the author unless otherwise noted.

3. Ibn ᶜAjība, *Sharḥ ᶜalā Matn al-Ajrūmīyya* in al-Ṭuᶜmī, *Ṭabaqāt*, 74.

4. Ibn Khaldūn, *The Muqaddimah: an Introduction to History* (1967), 5.

1. Integral Islam

1. Ahmad Zarruq, *Kitāb Iᶜānat al-Mutawajjih al-Miskīn ilā Ṭarīq al-Fatḥ wa'l-Tamkīn* (1979). Hamza Yusuf has translated the text into English as "The Poor Man's Guide" and published it on CD and over the Internet.

2. Jack O'Sullivan, *The Guardian* (Monday, October 8, 2001). See also Carla Power, "The Muslim Moderator," *Newsweek* (Atlantic Edition), August 19, 2002: 57.

3. Murata and Chittick, *The Vision of Islam* (1994), xxvi.

4. In the past decade, some scholars in America like Carl Ernst, William Chittick, and Sachiko Murata have applied the intellectual method of "phenomenology of religion" to the religion of Muslims. They have found that "Islam" is not sufficient to describe the richness of the religion of Muslims. See Carl Ernst, *The Shambhala Guide to Sufism* (1997), xiv–xv, prefaces his discussion of "what is Sufism" with a discussion of how the term *islām* (in exclusion of *īmān* or *iḥsān*) came to apply to the religion of Muslims. Murata and Chittick, *The Vision of Islam*, xxv–xxxiv and 332–335, offer these terms from the textual source "the Hadith of Gabriel."

5. Ernst, *Sufism*, xiv–xv.

6. Murata and Chittick, *Vision*, 2–7, 37–42, and 267–276.

7. Aḥmad Zarrūq, *Qawāᶜid al-Taṣawwuf* (1992), Principle 5.

8. Zarruq, *Ḥikam Ibn ᶜAtaʾillah: sharḥ Aḥmad Zarrūq*, 8.

9. Hamza Yusuf, speech at Stanford University (May 4, 1997), sponsored by the Center for American Islamic Relations (CAIR), a continuation of the speech cited above. The Nizamiyya was the Sunni madrasa which the famous theologian and Sufi Imam Abū Ḥāmid al-Ghazālī administered and in which he taught, and it served as a model for the madrasa system of education throughout the premodern Islamic world.

10. Guennoun, *Dhikrayāt Mashāhir Rijāl*, 27.

11. Khaled Abou El Fadl, *And God Knows the Soldiers: The Authoritative and Authoritarian in Islamic Discourses* (2001), 154.

12. Abou El Fadl, *And God Knows the Soldiers,* 20.

13. Zarrūq, *Kitāb Iᶜānat* (1979). Hamza Yusuf calls this "The Book of Consolation," an alternate translation of the title.

14. The Shaykh's full name is Muhammad ibn Salek ibn Fahfu. His school has become a virtual village and permanent settlement, called Tuwamarat, near the city of Guerou. See the article written by Rami Nsour at http://www.zaytuna.org/specials/mauritantia.html.

15. See information contained on two websites: http://www.naqshbandi.org/about/biohmk.htm and http://www.sunnah.org/about/shaykh_muhammad_hisham_kabbani.htm. Hisham Kabbani is the North American delegated representative of Shaykh Nazim Adil al-Haqqani, a Cyprus-born Naqshbandi leader. David Damrel, "A Sufi Apocalypse" ISIM Newsletter [Institute for the Study of Islam in the Modern World at Leiden], (January 13, 2000) gives a brief history of the growth of this Naqshbandi community in North America.

16. See the interview in http://www.meforum.org/article/61, in reference to Hisham Kabbani's speech "Islamic Extremism: a Viable Threat to US National Security" in an open forum at the U.S. Department of State (January 7, 1999).

17. Muhammad Hisham Kabbani, *Encyclopedia of Islamic Doctrine* (1996), volume 1 "Beliefs" offers Kabbani's refutation of Salafī and Wahhabi ideology.

18. See the Internet URL: www.nfie.com/rafai.html.

19. *Quwwat Jadhb al-Taṣawwuf fi al-ᶜĀlam* (May 1997, Casablanca), a conference organized by the Butshīshīyya Sufi community, included a presentation on Aḥmad Zarrūq by a retired professor, Sīdī ᶜAzūzī, entitled "Zarrūq and Reform in the Shādhilīyya community," *al-Islāḥ ᶜind al-Ṭarīqa al-Shādhilīyya: al-Shaykh Zarrūq*.

20. Shaykh Fadhlalla Haeri, *The Elements of Sufism* (n.p.: Element Books, 1990), Chapter 11, "Sufism and Society." The text is available online at www.nuradeen.com/Reflections/ElementsOfSufism.htm. His name is sometimes transliterated as Fadhlalla and sometimes as Fadlalla.

21. O'Sullivan, *The Guardian* (Oct. 8, 2001).

22. Hamza Yusuf, "America's Tragedy: an Islamic Perspective" (Sept. 30, 2001, at Zaytuna Institute) republished at http://www.zaytuna.org/tragedy.html.

23. Yusuf, "America's Tragedy."

24. Zarrūq, *al-Naṣīḥa al-Kāfiya*, 144. See also Abou El Fadl, *Rebellion and Violence in Islamic Law*, 323, which discusses in detail the tension between obedience to unjust rulers and the preservation of social order in the interest of public safety.

25. Zarrūq, *Risālat al-Radd ᶜala Ahl al-Bidᶜa* (mss. Tunis: library 8631), folio 28.

26. Zarrūq, *Risālat al-Radd*, folio 30.

27. Mercedes Garcia-Arenal, "The Revolution in Fas in 869/1465 and the Death of Sultan ᶜAbd al-Haqq al-Marini." *Journal of the School of Oriental and African Studies* 61, 1 (1978), subjects this historical event to close scrutiny, looking especially at how firsthand accounts have been distorted in "versions of a traditional history composed over the years by agglomeration, repetition, and revision," which centered specifically around stereotypes of Jews in Fes.

2. Sainthood

1. William James, *The Varieties of Religious Experience* (1999), 293–294.

2. James, *Varieties*, 294.

3. Reginald Ray, *Buddhist Saints in India* (1994), 44–45. Ascetic practice disengages routine life in many dimensions, such as material consumption, economic production, social-familial obligation, or institutional-educational structures.

4. This assumes that saints-in-process mold themselves to hagiographic standards even during their lifetimes. However, hagiographic forces become even more important posthumously, as a saint's life is recorded and transmitted. Hagiographic forces can even "create" saints who did not live distinctive lives, or whose actual lives were unknown (or perhaps never existed as actual persons).

5. The use of "cultic" to describe these forces is Ray's, and it has long precedent in the sociology of sainthood. He desires to use it "in a restricted sense" that would not imply a dichotomy between popular religion and standard, elite religion. Due to the dangers of this dichotomy that habitually infects the term "cult," this study refers to "community" to describe this process by which followers relate to a saint through specific rituals or practices.

6. Victor Turner, *The Ritual Process* (1969). Ray does not list these three forces in this order; this study reorders them to highlight their compatibility with Turner's ideas and reveal their vector-like quality of motion and transformation. This emphasis on transformation as the key to "becoming a saint" also helps define how saintly authority may be different from other kinds of explicitly religious authority, like that of prophets, messengers, priests, healers, or scholars (who might all be rightly described as "holy persons" along with saints).

7. James, *Varieties*, 298.

8. Peter Brown, *The Cult of the Saints* (1981) set the standard for this project to take the Catholicism, projected retrospectively from a later era, out of these saints and out of the very concept of sainthood.

9. Richard King, *Orientalism and Religion* (1999), 8–34 and 96–97, has critiqued this modernist, Protestant construction of mysticism and its application to Asian (or non-Western) religions and documents how Protestant preconceptions were foundational in the post-Enlightenment construction of "the mystical." Ernst, *Sufism*, 4–8, notes that whether dismissed as psychotics or praised as those who actually recaptured the original experience of some primordial religion, Orientalist knowledge removed "saints as mystics" from the community of believers and the public life of Muslims. Saints or their Sufi followers who resisted this removal (by politically opposing colonial rule or modernization programs) were labeled as "fanatic."

10. Katherine Ewing, *Arguing Sainthood: Modernity, Psychoanalysis and Islam* (1997), 48–49, has critiqued the way Trimingham sets up true mysticism as private experience. Ernst, *Sufism*, 131–132, critiques his schema as stereotyped into a classical, medieval, and decaying early modern pattern. Cornell, *Realm of the Saint: Power and Authority in Moroccan Sufism* (1996), 249–250, makes a more specific critique of Trimingham's evolutionary schema, in that his terms "*tāʾifa* as opposed to *ṭarīqa*" do not apply directly to Moroccan evidence. Between these critiques, it may be time to put Trimingham to rest.

11. Clifford Geertz, *Islam Observed* (1968), 8–9, begins to outline such a theoretical position, in which the saint as a person is also concurrently the saint as a social role. However, he falls back on the bifurcation between individual mystic and political operator when he describes the Moroccan saint as a "marabout" who combines strongman politics with holy man piety. His general definition of "religion as a cultural system" is much more refined in tracing the interrelationship of person, ethos, and social structure within the dy-

namics of a religious belief system. See Geertz, "Religion as a Cultural System," in *The Interpretation of Culture* (1973).

12. Arthur Buehler, *Sufi Heirs of the Prophet* (1998), 13–14, uses "Friends of God" and "Protégés of God" as synonyms, to balance the dual dimensions of intimacy with God and empowerment from God.

13. John Stratton Hawley, *Saints and Virtues* (1987), xii–xxiv, offers "example, fellowship, and aid" as three broad characteristics that define the saintly person. He tries to posit sainthood as a category common to all religious traditions, yet falls back upon Vatican II documents to define these characteristics.

14. This study refrains from using "orders" for Sufi communities, or "monastery" or "fraternity" for a Sufi lodge and hospice, or "cult" for saints' followers and admirers, or "rosaries" and "frocks" to describe their apparel.

15. Ewing, *Arguing Sainthood,* presents an anthropological inquiry into Sufis in modern Pakistan that highlights the question of authority and power. Cornell, *Realm of the Saint,* documents the emergence of a paradigm of sainthood in Morocco (through various historical phases and through the agency of different communities) to its culmination in the politically powerful figures of the Jazūlīyya community.

16. Ernst, *Sufism*, 13–17.

17. The distinction is seen as selflessness or self-transcendence, opening the possibility that the person of the saint is a vehicle for divine presence in the routine world. Yet the distinction could come from many sources: ascetic practice, extraordinary knowledge, charity and social alleviation, even genealogy, can be the markers of this distinction.

18. Cornell, *Realm of the Saint,* 24, quotes Pierre Delooz to show that saints reside in "the social imaginary" through which they are recognized as saints who participate in patterns of social-religious meaning beyond their individuality. Whether all these people share some inner type of experience that can be called "mystical" (related to an expanded consciousness that breaks down the barriers of habitual, fragile, defensive ego) is a fascinating question. However, that experience cannot be used to define sainthood. James, *Varieties*, 453, offers a general but insightful summary of "mystical" experiences. "We pass into mystical states from out of ordinary consciousness as from a less into a more, as from a smallness into a vastness, and at the same time as from an unrest to a rest. We feel them as reconciling, unifying states. They appeal to the yes-function more than to the no-function in us. In them, the unlimited absorbs the limits and peacefully closes the account." Many people may have mystical experiences spontaneously or cultivate them through organized practices to more permanently change their consciousness, yet such people do not necessarily become saints; the category of saint cannot be reduced to "mystics" and their experiences.

19. Cornell, *Realm of the Saint,* 145–146 and 163.

20. The distinction between saint and Sufi is meant to be a functional definition to describe the situation pertaining to the medieval and early modern periods. This study does not address the origin of the terms or the multitude of "classical definitions" of the Sufi that highlight intuitive insight or illumination. Many other studies address those questions; Ernst, *Sufism,* 22–25, gives a concise overview of such classical definitions of "Sufi" as teaching tools rather than descriptive definitions, while pages 59 through 60 note how classical definitions often obscure the relationship between Sufi and saint.

21. In Islamic languages (as in the above definition) the person takes priority over an abstraction.

22. Sufis understand the Prophet to have received initiation and spiritual training from the angel Gabriel (Jibrīl) who acted as a mediator with and connector to divinity. Thus the lineage is the concrete form that defines and justifies the saint's position at the interface of divine and mundane (or sacred and profane) realms.

23. *Ṭarīqa* as a lineage is like a family genealogical tree that defines relationships in the present through shared ancestors in the past. Many respected scholars have translated *ṭarīqa* with the single term "order" to imply these three different nuances of meaning. However, this study avoids the term "Sufi order" since it retains the trappings of Catholic monastic orders and may cause conceptual blurring with many Western readers.

24. King, *Orientalism and Religion*, 18.

25. Many Western scholars saw Sufis and saints as expressions of "Islamic mysticism" seen through the lens of doctrine and intellectual systems, as in the scholarship of Julian Baldick, *Mystical Islam* (1989), Spencer Trimingham, *The Sufi Orders in Islam* (1971), and Annemarie Schimmel, *The Mystical Dimension of Islam* (1975).

26. Geertz, for instance, sees Muslims saints as abstract figures of Moroccan national culture even from a period before such a "nation" existed. Geertz, *Islam Observed*, 16–17, refers to Morocco and Indonesia in the premodern period by a confusing mixture of terms: as cultures, as regions, as societies, or as nations (all before a combination of European colonialism and nationalist protest created modern national boundaries and nation-states). In Morocco in particular, Geertz finds "scripturalism" to be contiguous with nationalism, while he projects fundamentalism into the remote past as essential to Moroccan spiritual culture.

27. Marshall G. S. Hodgson, *The Venture of Islam* (1958), 2:218 and 460–462; and Richard Eaton, *The Rise of Islam and the Bengal Frontier,* (1993), ch. 10, elaborates the metaphor of "rooting" with great insight.

28. The Hijri calendar is based on twelve lunar months to each year, beginning at the event of the Prophet Muḥammad's flight from Makka to Madīna (*hijra*) in the year 622 C.E..

29. The Mahdī, or divinely guided leader, is a figure projected to appear among the Muslims from the descendants of the Prophet Muḥammad to lead the community at the end of time (or during a crisis in time). This figure developed differently among the Shiᶜa than among the Sunnis, with some common elements. The figure of the Mahdi appears in this study especially in chapter 3.

30. Conversely, Mahdist movements were not unique to the tenth Islamic century and did not necessarily define themselves in relation to a specific year (or events presumed to occur around that year). However, there was an overlap of dynastic crises, increasing involvement of Sufi communities in political movements, and Mahdist rhetoric that suggests that the underlying calendar cycle had a role to play in the specific terrain of this period.

Part II. Rebel (introduction)

1. ᶜAbdallah al-Talīdī, *al-Muṭrib fi Mashāhir Awliyāᵓ al-Maghrib* (1987), 145.
2. Zarruq, *al-Kunnāsh fi ᶜIlm Āsh* (mss), 67.
3. Zarruq, *al-Kunnāsh*, 67.
4. al-Talīdī, *al-Muṭrib*, 145.

3. Promise

1. Zarruq's genealogy is unclear. He may have come from a lineage of Arabized Berbers from the region of Taza. His family *nisba* (tribal affiliation) was al-Burnūsī, perhaps referring to the Berber tribe of Barānis. His grandfather, at the latest, had settled in the Andalusian quarter of Fes, which absorbed most migrant families from surrounding countryside. He should not be confused with another saint named Aḥmad al-Zarrūq, whose tomb lies near the village of Tiliwān, outside of Fes.

2. Zarrūq, *al-Kunnāsh*, 57. She complained to Zarruq's father that he gave only one-third of his wealth for the upkeep of his son (his father's nickname, "al-Khaḍḍār," indicates that he was a greengrocer). He gave another third as charity to the muezzins of the Masjid al-Andalus, and the final third to his wife (which the grandmother perceived to be wasted upon the mother's extended family). Many thanks to Fredrick Colby for helping me acquire a copy of this manuscript and sharing his prior research on Zarruq.

3. Ostensibly, his grandmother had caught the wet nurse bragging to others that the young Zarruq was an orphaned descendant of the Prophet. The grandmother immediately took the child from her care and reared him herself. Lack of funds may also have been a consideration, beyond juridical rectitude.

4. Aḥmad al-Ṣumāᶜī, *Kitāb al-Muᶜzā fī Manāqib al-Shaykh Abī Yiᶜzzā* (1996), 282. The biography of al-ᶜAbdūsī will come in full later in this chapter. In the medieval and early modern periods, women from wealthy or urbane families often participated in religious studies and to a lesser extent rose to prominence in the social institution of sainthood. *Ṣāliḥa* (holy woman) is a broad term, encompassing those women given to juristic piety as well as those with other kinds of socially useful holiness. For women's participation in Sufi practices from the earliest period, see as-Sulamī, *Early Sufi Women: Dhikr an-Niswa al-Mutaᶜabbidat as-Sufiyyat*, trans. Rkia E. Cornell (1999).

5. Zarrūq, *al-Kunnāsh*, 60. Zarruq also studied with his grandmother's uncle, Aḥmad ibn Muḥammad al-Fishtālī, a jurist and saintly scholar.

6. As a major intellectual and saintly figure in Moroccan history, Zarruq is the subject of several biographies, none of which is comprehensive. The primary biography, ᶜAli Khushaim, *Zarruq the Sufi* (1976), which is also published in Arabic as *Aḥmad Zarrūq wa al-Zarrūqīyya,* contains a useful bibliography of Zarruq's writings, but the content is marred by factual and historical inaccuracies. ᶜAbdallah Guennoun, *Dhikrayāt Mashāhir Rijāl al-Maghrib: Aḥmad Zarrūq* (1954) is a monograph on Zarruq by the Moroccan literary historian, who does not attempt a comprehensive analysis of Zarruq's entire corpus or the historical context of his life.

7. This curriculum included texts on *uṣūlī* methodology, *uṣūlī* commentaries on books of Maliki legal decisions, and the study of hadith sources that the *uṣūlī* approach makes the mandatory foundation for any authentic legal decision.

8. Cornell, *Realm of the Saint*, 148 and 67–70 has coined the term "juridical Sufism" to cover a broad range of religious figures who are often labeled misleadingly as "orthodox" Sufis. Juridical Sufis are those who believe that juridical norms govern Sufi devotional practice and saintly behavior in society. In general, juridical Sufis admire Abū Hamid al-Ghazālī's text *Iḥyāᵓ ᶜUlūm al-Dīn* for having set these limits clearly while not compromising Sufi devotion. They also admire al-Muḥāsibī's scrupulous piety that fulfills the "rights of God" just as juridical rectitude fulfills the "rights of other people."

9. Ibn ᶜAṭāᵓillah lived in Alexandria and Cairo and was the key figure who firmly established the Shādhilī community in Egypt. From the perspective of the Egyptian com-

munity, he was the third "axial saint" in the lineage after al-Shādhilī and Abū al-ᶜAbbās al-Mursī. He was also the first Shādhilī master to compose literary works and act as an official jurist. He thus set the precedent for juridical Sufis who looked to him as an exemplar.

10. Scott Kugle (trans.), *The Book of Illumination: Shaykh Ibn ᶜAtā Aillah's Kitāb al-Tanwīr fi Isqāṭ al-Tadbīr* (Louisville, Ky.: Fons Vitae, 2005), 87. Ibn ᶜAṭāʾillah cites the Qurʾān, Surat al-Baqara, 2:189. "It is no good if you enter houses from around their backs, rather it is virtuous if you stay cautious and wary. Enter houses by their proper doors, and stay conscious of Allah that you might prosper."

11. Ibn ᶜAbbād al-Rundī, *Ghayth al-Mawāhib al-ᶜĀliya Sharḥ al-Ḥikam al- Aṭāʾiyya* (1970), 60–61.

12. Zarruq, *Ḥikam Ibn ᶜAṭāʾillah: sharḥ Aḥmad Zarrūq* (1969), 16. This is the seventeenth commentary of Zarruq on the Wisdom Sayings.

13. Zarruq, *Tuḥfat al-Murīd wa Rawḍat al-Farīd wa Fawāʾid li-Ahl al-Fahm al-Sadīd wa al-Naẓr al-Madīd* (mss.).

14. This study abbreviates this phrase (*taṣawwuf al-uṣūlīyyīn*) into the more compact "juridical Sufism."

15. Zarruq, *Ḥikam Ibn ᶜAtaʾillah: sharḥ Aḥmad Zarrūq*, 8.

16. Cornell, *Realm of the Saint,* 24 and 70–83.

17. Alfred Bel, *La Religion Musulmane en Berberie* (1983), 342, as quoted in Dale Eickelman, *Moroccan Islam* (1976), 25.

18. E. E. Evans-Pritchard, *Theories of Primitive Religion* (1965), 20, describes how "fetishism" originated with Portuguese colonization of West Africa, was elaborated by Compte's theory of social evolution, and persisted in French anthropology and psychology.

19. For example, see Ernest Gellner, *Saints of the Atlas* (1969). For critical perspectives on Western stereotypes, see Brian Turner, *Weber and Islam* (1974), 62, Cornell, *Realm of the Saint,* 19–25, and David Powers, *Law, Society and Culture in the Maghrib* (2002), 15–17.

20. Geertz, *Islam Observed,* 9, 20, 46, and 54.

21. Baldick, *Mystical Islam*, 34 and 66. Even as a religious studies scholar, Baldick does not respect any perceived "harmony" between jurists and Sufis. In his analytical framework, there was no tradition of juridical Sufis since "jurists" could not possibly be counted as "Sufis."

22. Hagiographic literature from this period does occasionally refer to a type of person called *Murābiṭ*, yet this term is used synonymously with *Mujāhid*, to describe someone living in a ribat or fortress, dedicated to warfare on the borders of Islamic territory, specifically in warfare against the invading Spanish and Portuguese. Neither Murabit nor Mujahid correspond to the Western anthropological construction of the marabout.

23. Sossie Andezian, interview with the author, at the Second International Conference on Middle Eastern and North African Popular Culture (Tunis, April 5, 2002); she is the author of *Experiences du divin dans a'Algerie contemporaine* (2001).

24. Geertz, *Islam Observed*, 35.

25. Cornell, *Realm of the Saint,* 444–446 outlined from earlier Moroccan history a type of saint called the "*qudwa*," which exhibits many of the same qualities as this ideal type of the "juridical saint." The juridical saint can be considered a refinement of the "*qudwa*" saintly type.

26. This is a particular expression of the *malāmatī* theme among Muslim saints who tried to hide their status as saints or take refuge from the popular expectation of sainthood through denial, obcurity, or even ill-repute. See Kenneth Honerkamp (trans.), *ᶜAbd al-Raḥmān al-Sulami's al-Risāla Malāmatīyya* (forthcoming).

27. Al-Qūrī's biography is found in Muḥammad al-Sharrāṭ, *al-Rawḍ al-ᶜAṭir al-Anfās* (1997), 333; Aḥmad Ibn al-Qāḍī, *Durrat al-Ḥijāl* (1971), 2:295; Aḥmad Ibn al-Qāḍī, *Jadhwat al-Iqtibās* (1973), 319; Muḥammad Makhlūf, *Shajarat al-Nūr al-Zakīya*, 1:261; and Muḥammad al-Hajwī, *al-Fikr al-Sāmi* (1995), 2:261.

28. Al-Ṣumāᶜī, *Kitāb al-Muᶜzā*, 282. This portrait is confirmed by another student of al-Qūrī's, Ibn Ghāzī in his *Fihris Ibn Ghāzī* (1984), 65.

29. Cornell, *Realm of the Saint,* 295–296 and 416, translates *Shaykh al-Jamāᶜa* as "paramount shaykh" to denote the axial saint who was the central authority of their community in both spiritual and political matters in the Jazūlīyya Sufi community (during the lifetime of al-Qūrī). The term was used in later generations to describe ᶜAbd al-ᶜAzīz al-Tabbāᶜ and ᶜAbdullah al-Ghazwānī in their roles of axial saint. The paramount leader of a Sufi community was normally considered "a saint" with the exception of two cases: if the leader was only a teacher (a transmitter of doctrine) or was a hereditary successor to the position (in a relationship known as *wirāthī* leadership). Leadership of the juridical saint in al-Qūrī's community was not hereditary, nor was it simply the leadership of a teacher (though the role of teacher was crucial to the public comportment of the juridical saint).

30. Al-Ṣumāᶜī, *Kitāb al-Muᶜzā*, 282.

31. Muḥammad al-Kattānī, *Salwat al-Anfās*, 2:116, cites *Fihris Ibn Ghāzī*. Al-Wansharīsī wrote the famous compilation of juridical decisions called *Al-Miᶜyār al-Muᶜrib wa'l-Jāmiᶜ al-Mughrib* (1983); see Powers, *Law, Society and Culture in the Maghrib*, 4–9.

32. Zarrūq, *al-Kunnāsh*, 65. His full name is Aḥmad ibn ᶜAlī ibn Ṣāliḥ "al-Fīlālī."

33. Zarrūq, *al-Kunnāsh,* 62.

34. In the Marinid period, access to education and judicial positions was often hereditary, so al-Qūrī could have been sure that any son would follow his footsteps and become a jurist.

35. His full name was Muhammad ibn Abdullah ibn Ibrāhīm ibn ᶜAbbād (but was also known by the tribal name al-Nafzī, and place names al-Rundī and al-Fāsī). His biography is found in Al-Sharrāṭ, *al-Al-Rawḍ al-ᶜAṭir al-Anfās*, 195–204, and Honerkamp, "Ibn Abbad: An exemplar of the Shadhili Path," in Eric Geoffroy (ed.), *La Voie Soufie des Shadhilis* (Paris: Maisonneuve & Larose, 2005).

36. Ibn ᶜAbbād, *Ghayth al-Mawāhib,* 41.

37. Cornell, *Realm of the Saint,* 258. Ibn ᶜAṭāʾillah was central to this circle of juridical Sufis, not only for his texts, which transmitted doctrine and methods of contemplation, but also as their prototype of a saint who was at the same time a jurist. During his lifetime, Ibn ᶜAṭāʾillah had come under some criticism for working as a state official in the capacity of judge while living a dual life as a saintly leader of the Egyptian Shādhilīyya community. See also Nancy Roberts (trans.), *The Subtle Blessings in the Saintly Lives of Abul-Abbas al-Mursi and His Master Abul-Hasan, the Founders of the Shadhili Order: Ibn ᶜAtaʾ Allah's Lata'if al-Minan* (Louisville, Ky.: Fons Vitae, 2005).

38. John Renard (trans.), *Ibn Abbad of Ronda: letters on the Sufi path* (1986), 49, and Cornell, *Realm of the Saint,* 246–248. For Ibn ᶜĀshir's personality, see al-Hafī, *Tuḥfat al-Zāʾir* (1988); for an English commentary on one of his works, see Aḥmad ᶜAlawī, *Knowledge of God* (1981).

39. Ibn ᶜAbbād's commentary on the *Ḥikam* was known as *Kitāb al-Tanbīh*, but has been published under the title *Sharḥ ᶜalā Matn al-Ḥikam* (1886) and most recently as *Ghayth al-Mawāhib al-ᶜĀliya* (1970).

40. Al-Sharrāṭ, *al-Rawḍ al-ᶜAṭir al-Anfās*, 196. Al-ᶜAbdūsī was a fellow disciple of Ibn ᶜĀshir. Ibn Qunfudh, *Uns al-Faqīr* (1965), 24, calls him "one of the oldest friends of

Ibn ᶜĀshir, and one of his best students." Mūsā al-ᶜAbdūsī was the grandfather of ᶜAbdullah al-ᶜAbdūsī, who was Zarruq's grandmother's teacher.

41. Ṣahnūn (ᶜAbd al-Salām ibn Saᶜīd al-Tanūkhī al-Hamsi al-Qayrawānī), *Sharḥ al-Mudāwwana al-Kubrā* (1999). *Al-Mudāwwana* was one of the most famous books of the Maliki juridical method.

42. Many thanks to Vincent Cornell for suggesting this metaphor of the icon, as well as encouragement and insight throughout the writing of this study.

43. Renard, *Letters*, 48.

44. These colleagues of Ibn ᶜAbbād include ᶜUmar al-Ragrāgī and al-Ḥasan Abarkan, both of whom were students of Mūsā al-ᶜAbdūsī. They traveled from Meknes for the *ḥājj* and ended up teaching in Tilimsān.

45. *Fihris Ibn Ghāzī*, 67.

46. *Fihris Ibn Ghāzī*, 77.

47. Ibn Futūḥ was instrumental in popularizing the teaching text in Maliki jurisprudence, *Mukhtaṣar Khalīl ibn Isḥāq*, which became a standard part of the teaching curriculum in succeeding generations.

48. *Fihris Ibn Ghāzī,* 75–77; and Ibn al-Qāḍī, *Jadhwat al-Iqtibas*, 317.

49. *Fihris Ibn Ghāzī,* 77. Al-Janātī learned the *Mudāwwana* from Mūsā al-ᶜAbdūsī and taught it to al-Qūrī.

50. *Fihris Ibn Ghāzī,* 71.

51. Ibn al-Qāḍī, *Jadhwat al-Iqtibas*, 502.

52. Al-Sharrāṭ, *al-Rawḍ al-ᶜAṭir al-Anfās,* 199.

53. ᶜAbdullah ibn Muḥammad ibn Mūsā ibn Muᶜṭī al-ᶜAbdūsī (the grandson of Mūsā al-ᶜAbdūsī who was discussed earlier) served as a leading jurist and delivered sermons at al-Qarawiyyīn and died around 859 Hijri (1455 C.E.) though Al-Ṣumāᶜī, *Kitāb al-Muᶜzā,* 278, claims he died one decade earlier according to a report of Zarruq.

54. Zarrūq, *al-Kunnāsh*, 61, is the source of above quotation as well.

55. Others in al-Qūrī's Sufi circle included his childhood friend and spiritual brother, Abū al-ᶜAbbās Aḥmad ibn Saᶜīd al-Ḥabbāk al-Miknāsī and his stepbrother, Muḥammad ibn Saᶜīd. Aḥmad took over as preacher at al-Qarawiyyīn after the death of ᶜAbdullah al-ᶜAbdūsī, while Muḥammad was a Sufi poet and jurist who had studied under a colleague of Ibn ᶜAbbād (named Muḥammad al-Milwānī). Ibn ᶜAbbād would praise this teacher, saying, "I don't know anyone in this age more knowledgeable than him about hearts." Al-Qūrī's circle included included Abū al-Qāsim al-Tazghirdī and Yūsuf al-Aghṣāwī.

56. *Fihris Ibn Ghāzī*, 68. Translations of all poetry from Arabic are by the author of this study unless otherwise noted.

57. *Fihris Ibn Ghāzī,* 71. Al-Qūrī's companion was named Aḥmad ibn ᶜUmar al-Mazgildī (who was a teacher at Madrasa Miṣbāḥiyya in Fes and was a disciple of al-Ragrāgī and al-Maṣmūdī, according to Ibn al-Qāḍī, *Jadhwat al-Iqtibas*, 127); the Arabic phrase for white magic is "*al-siḥr al-ḥalāl*." White magic, like alchemy, was a metaphor for the spiritual transformations that contact with a saint could spark.

58. Al-Ṣumāᶜī, *Kitāb al-Muᶜzā*, 282. For a discussion of the *Mudāwwana* as legal manual, see Powers *Law, Society and Culture in the Maghrib,* 11, and Mansour H. Mansour, *The Maliki School of Law* (1995).

59. Such students of scriptural disciplines composed the record of their teachers and texts in the genre of the *Fihris*, such as that of Ibn Ghāzī or Zarruq's *al-Kunnāsh* (which comprises a rough draft of his *fihris*). This genre stands in contrast to the works of Sufi disciples who would record their relation to past masters in genres of *Ṭabaqāt* (multigenerational biographies) or *Manāqib* (heroic spirituality of a single saintly figure).

60. Cornell, *Realm of the Saint,* 258. Ibn ᶜAbbād had "permission" to recite and transmit *The Litany of the Sea* (*Ḥizb al-Baḥr*) of Shaykh al-Shādhilī. An *ijāza* constituted "permission" to teach a text to others, traced back through generations of teachers to the author of a text itself. *Ijāza* documents (whether oral or written) were clearly different from a full Sufi initiation, traced back from disciple to master to an eponymous saint. Ibn ᶜAbbād may have had permission to teach the texts of al-Shādhilī and Ibn ᶜAṭāᵓillah, but those do not represent formal initiation into the Shādhilī lineage as would taking formal allegiance (*akhdh al-bayᶜa*) or wearing a cloak from a master's hand (*ilbās al-khirqa*). For the most recent research on Ibn ᶜAbbād's Sufi affiliations, see Kenneth Honerkamp's essay in Eric Geoffroy (ed.), *La Voie Soufie des Shadhilis* (Paris: Maisonneuve & Larose, 2005).

61. Al-Sharrāṭ, *al-Rawḍ al-ᶜAṭir al-Anfās*, 198. One of Ibn ᶜAbbād's followers, Abū Yaḥyā ibn al-Sakkāk, notes he was affiliated with the Shādhilī lineage "instinctively, spontaneously and approximately" in the same way that the philosopher Ibn Rushd was a Mālikī "not officially but rather instinctually."

62. This seems to have been the case with Ibn ᶜAbbād and with Zarruq as well. One of Zarruq's contemporaries, Muḥammad al-Zawāwī, saw the spirit of Ibn ᶜAṭāᵓillah in a vision, where the latter claimed al-Zawāwi as one of his disciples "because you love my speech in the *Ḥikam*." See Jonathan Katz, *Dreams, Sufism, and Sainthood* (1996), 158.

63. *Fihris Ibn Ghāzī*, 67. He was reportedly a student (and disciple) of ᶜAlī ibn Wafāᵓ, whose biography is found in al-Shaᶜrānī, *al-Ṭabaqāt al-Kubrā* (1988), 2:22–65, and through whose extended family this lineage grew in popularity in urban spaces of Egypt in the eighth and ninth centuries Hijri (fourteenth and fifteenth centuries C.E.).

64. Cornell, *Realm of the Saint,* 259, concluded that Zarruq was the first to bring to Morocco a clear affiliation with the Egyptian Shādhilī lineage through the figure of Ibn ᶜAṭāᵓillah, but it seems that this juridical Sufi community in Meknes was cultivating such a lineage one or two generations before Zarruq without publicly advertising their affiliations.

65. Cornell, *Realm of the Saint,* 251–257.

66. *Fihris ibn Ghāzī,* 87–88.

67. Ibn al-Qāḍī, *Jadhwat al-Iqtibas*, 317 and *Fihris Ibn Ghāzī*, 87–88.

68. The *khirqa*, or cloak, was the most distinctive piece of clothing that characterized Sufis, which was often invested from master to disciple. It was also seen as an investiture from the Prophet, who was known as "Master of the Dark Cloak" (*Sāḥib al-Burda*); with his cloak, Muhammad had sheltered his family and passed on his spiritual authority to his son-in-law, cousin, and closest follower ᶜAlī ibn Abī Ṭālib. One of the most popular Sufi devotional poems in North Aftica praises the Prophet Muhammad as "the Master of the Dark Cloak"; see Busiri, *Al-Burdah*, translated by Thoraya Mahdi Allam (1987).

69. Al-Sharrāṭ, *al-Rawḍ al-ᶜAṭir al-Anfās*, 195, cites Zarrūq, *Sharḥ al-Ḥikam al-ᶜAṭāᵓiyya* (from the fifteenth commentary).

4. Exile

1. *Zāwiya* literally means "a corner" or "a sheltered retreat." Zawiyas inside Fes were relatively rare, though present from the age of Abū Madyan onward. Those that dominate the urban topography today were not present then, or were only in their initial stages of growth. In the present, zawiya is often used as a synonym for *ribāṭ*. However, a ribat was a fortified settlement, often one founded by a Sufi master and community of disciples and admirers. A ribat was often a small town unto itself and was usually removed from large urban spaces. See Trimingham, *Sufi Orders*, 167–172.

2. Orientalist scholarship often asserted a strict dichotomy between scholar and Sufi, as in Gellner, *Saints of the Atlas*, 7–8. As historical evidence broke down this typology, it was replaced with the dichotomy between urban scholarly Sufi and rural charismatic Sufi. Both these dichotomies are misleading and depend on Orientalist presuppositions. The term "zawiya-based Sufi" is more useful: such a Sufi may be educated or not, scholarly in orientation or not, but most importantly he would rely on the institution of the zawiya.

3. Zarruq, *al-Kunnāsh*, 63–64.

4. Zarruq, *al-Kunnāsh*, 63. Muḥammad al-Amīn was known by his occupation, the pharmacist or spice merchant "al-ᶜAṭṭār," and also as the bleacher "al-Qaṣṣār." Al-Sakhāwī, *Dawᶜ al-Lamiᶜ*, 10:109, provides a short biography of him; some Moroccans who had taken allegiance to al-Amīn spoke to al-Sakhāwī of him in Cairo, but they did not specify that he was a Qādirī. One must be careful to distinguish him from another man of similar name who was a friend of Shaykh al-Jazūlī, called Abū ᶜAbdullah Muḥammad al-Qaṣṣār al-Qaysī. This distinction is specified in al-Fāsī, *Mumtiᶜ al-Asmāʾ* (1994), 55. Confusion between these two men has led many biographers to falsely assume that Aḥmad Zarruq frequented the circle of al-Jazūlī's followers, or took initiation from al-Jazūlī himself.

5. Zarruq, *al-Kunnāsh*, folios 63–65, provides this narration for the series of events that reveals al-Amīn's miraculous power, through the viewpoint of Zarruq's own family members. The narrative is repeated in al-Ṣumāᶜī, *Kitāb al-Muᶜzā,* 119–120.

6. Zarruq, *al-Kunnāsh*, 64.

7. al-Ṣumāᶜī, *Kitāb al-Muᶜzā,* 118.

8. al-Ṣumāᶜī, *Kitāb al-Muᶜzā,* 118.

9. al-Ṣumāᶜī, *Kitāb al-Muᶜzā,* 119.

10. al-Ṣumāᶜī, *Kitāb al-Muᶜzā,* 119.

11. Abū Yiᶜzza's correspondence with ᶜAbd al-Qādir is not limited to such visionary experiences; rather the story of their communications became a stock story of hagiography. Anonymous, *Rawḍ al-Nāẓir fi Manāqib ᶜAbd al-Qādir* (mss. Rabat: KhM 1224, part 2) reports that Abū Madyan met Khiḍr and through him accepted the mastership of ᶜAbd al-Qādir al-Jīlānī. The followers of Abu Madyan had long linked his saintly Berber master with the renowned but distant ᶜAbd al-Qādir, an Arab from Persian lands. Hagiographies picture Abū Yiᶜzza saying to a man who was getting ready to travel to Baghdad, "Be careful not to miss seeing a man in Baghdad who is from Persia but is descended from the Prophet's family, named ᶜAbd al-Qādir! Greet him with salams and pass on salams from me, and say to him don't forget Abū Yiᶜzza! By God, nobody has been born in Persia who can compare with him and his shadow cast from the east stretches all the way to the west!"

12. Al-Ṣumāᶜī, *Kitāb al-Muᶜzā,* 80. Zarruq called him "the leader of the seven *Abdāl*." See Ibn Maryam al-Tilimsānī, *al-Bustān* (1986), 50, and Ibn ᶜAskar, *Dawḥat al-Nāshir* (1976), 71.

13. Such an initiation "without mediation" (*bi-la wāsiṭa*) is given to a disciple by a spiritual master who is not physically present; the master may be long dead or far removed and meets the Sufi in a dream or vision. In the eastern Islamic world, such initiations are called *uwaysī* initiations, after Uways al-Qaranī, who is believed to have enjoyed a spiritual connection to the Prophet Muḥammad from a distance in Yemen, despite his never having met the Prophet in person. It is a characteristic of the Qādirīyya community to favor such "*uwaysi*" initiations. The eastern term "*uwaysi*" may have entered the Maghrib through the Qādirī community, for some Moroccan hagiographies use this term synonymously with the more typical Moroccan expression "without mediation"; see ᶜAbd al-Ḥafīẓ Ṭāhir al-Fāsī, *al-Tarjumān al-Mughrib ᶜan Ashhar Furūᶜ al-Shādhilīyya bi'l-Maghrib* (mss.), 41 mar-

ginal note. The tradition became ascribed to ʿAbd al-Qādir himself when he reportedly said it was not necessary to receive a *khirqa*, a cloak symbolizing initiation from a living master, in order to become his disciple; personal attachment to himself was perfectly sufficient. Such reports were transmitted in popular biographies of ʿAbd al-Qādir, like ʿAlī al-Shaṭṭanūfī, *Bahjat al-Asrār* (1991), and are quoted in *Encyclopedia of Islam*, new edition, s.v. "Kadiriyya."

14. Evidence from the Maghrib as well as from South Asia suggests this conclusion, but it is advanced here as a hypothesis. In South Asia, the Qādirī lineage grew around the person of Muḥammad Ghawth (who was known as ʿAbd al-Qādir the Second and claimed genealogical descent from Shaykh ʿAbd al-Qādir, but he is not to be confused with Muḥammad Ghawth Gwaliorī in the South Asian Shaṭṭārī Sufi community).

15. Muḥammad ibn al-Ṭayyib al-Qādirī, *Nashr al-Mathānī* (1977), 1:315. Parallel sources on the genealogy of Qādirīs in Fes confirm this report, such as Muḥammad ibn ʿAbdullah "al-Hawwāt" (al-ʿAlamī al-Ḥasanī), *Al-Sirr al-Ẓāhir* (n.d.).

16. This branch of the Qādirī family descended from ʿAbd al-Qādir's two sons, ʿAbd al-ʿAzīz and Ibrahīm, who died at the end of the sixth century Hijri (twelfth century C.E.). The descendants of ʿAbd al-Qādir al-Jīlānī moved from Baghdād due to the Mongol invasions of 1255 C.E. that killed many of the *shurafāʾ*. See appendix B.

17. Ibrāhīm Ḥarakat, *al-Siyāsa wa'l-Mujtamaʿa* (1987), 346.

18. al-Kattānī, *Salwat al-Anfās*, 1:143–144. Al-Kattānī also cites *Nashr al-Mathani* about the pillar at the mosque al-Qarawiyyīn that was associated with ʿAbd al-Qādir al-Jīlānī. It was removed from the mosque by the order of the Qāḍī Abū ʿAbdullah Ibn Aḥmad Bardala, due to some incident, on 20 Jumada al-Thani, 1104 Hijri (1693 C.E.).

19. Al-Kattānī, *Salwat al-Anfās*, 1:219. This is in the neighborhood of Zaqqāq al-Rumān inside the gate Bāb Guissa, just above the market of ʿAyn al-ʿAlūn.

20. Al-Kattānī, *Salwat al-Anfās*, 1:219. Idrīs ibn Muḥammad ibn Idrīs al-ʿImrānī is the author of these couplets.

21. His full name was Abū al-Ḥasan ʿAlī ibn Abī Ghālib, but he is known popularly as "Bū Ghālib." His biography is recorded in Al-Kattānī, *Salwat al-Anfās*, 2:17–24. The neighborhood was called al-Ṣirāwiyyīn; the area is now known as al-Qalīʿa and is located just inside Bāb Futūḥ.

22. From a locale known as Dār al-Gaytun, during the reign of sultan Abū al-Ḥasan or his son Abū ʿInān, in the late eighth century Hijri.

23. Al-Kattānī, *Salwat al-Anfās*, 2:20 cites ʿAbd al-Salām ibn al-Khayyāṭ al-Qādirī, *Manāqib ʿAbdullah al-Sharīf al-Wazānī*.

24. Al-Kattānī, *Salwat al-Anfās*, 2:22. The poet is Muḥammad ibn Idrīs al-ʿImrānī, apparently the father of the poet who adorned the wall of al-Khalwa al-Qādirīyya with his verses. See note 20 above.

25. Ibn al-Qāḍī, *Jadhwat al-Iqtibas*, 241. Thanks to Si Banānī, the bookseller at Sūq al-ʿAṭṭārīn, for informing the author about this proverb.

26. Al-Kattānī, *Salwat al-Anfās*, 2:19.

27. Ḥarakat, *al-Siyāsa wa'l-Mujtamaʿa,* 346.

28. This is the case in Fes and northern Morocco; other parts of the Islamic world witnessed an earlier formation of the Qādirī lineage as a Sufi *ṭarīqa* in different historical contingencies. These two Litanies of ʿAbd al-Qādir, along with many of his poems, have been collected in *al-Safīna al-Qādirīyya*.

29. Al-Zaytūnī and his followers may have learned of these Sufi practices from Qādirīs in Cairo, with whom they had contact via caravan travels. Despite their reputation

as institutional "free radicals," the Qādirīs were taking over a position that Rifāᶜī Sufis had been occupying in northern Morocco since the end of the sixth century Hijri (twelfth century C.E.); they seem to have acted as individual guides rather than representatives of an interregional Sufi lineage with any standardized practice; see Cornell, *Realm of the Saint,* 252–253. Still, they spread the fame Aḥmad al-Rifāᶜī, a powerful, foundational saint from Iraq who was also of sharifian descent. The Qādirīs juxtaposed the similar figure of their own eponymous saint and further spread the fame of Abd al-Qādir based on the previous work of the Rifāᶜīs. Al-Ṣumāᶜī, *Kitāb al-Muᶜzā*, 277, narrates a story that equates Aḥmad al-Rifāᶜī with ᶜAbd al-Qādir al-Jīlānī. Anonymous, *Rawḍ al-Nāẓir* (mss.) includes many of the descendants of Aḥmad al-Rifāᶜī among the early Qādirīs.

30. The Qādirīs did not create these stories, for they were in circulation among Abū Madyan's followers, perhaps as a way to explain their affiliation with a North African spiritual leader once they traveled to the east among people who had no Maghribi reference points. To portray Abū Madyan as a disciple of ᶜAbd al-Qādir was to give him a place in pan-Islamic spiritual cosmology, especially in Yemen, where Madyanīs interacted with Sufi communities with strong allegiance to ᶜAbd al-Qādir; see al-Ḥabshī, *Al-Ṣūfiya waᵓl-Fuqahāᵓ fi al-Yaman* (1976), 34–36. For an early Moroccan example of this equation, see al-Bādisī, *Manāqib al-Shaykh ᶜAbd al-Qādir al-Jīlānī wa Tabbāᶜihi* (mss.).

31. al-Kattānī, *Salwat al-Anfas*, 2:17.

32. Zarruq, *al-Kunnāsh*, 66. Zarruq implies that he had some role to play in this advocacy, since al-Zaytūnī "used to take me into confidence in his affairs." This would date the construction to the late 860s Hijri (1460s C.E.).

33. Sources do not specify al-Zaytūnī's place of birth, but it is doubtful that he was born in Fes. He is buried in al-Masīla in the area called al-Jarīd, possibly in the Tunisian oasis region of that name, through which caravan routes ran between Fes and Cairo. ᶜAbd al-Raḥmān al-Fāsī, *Ibtihāj al-Qulūb* (mss.) specifies that he died in 911 Hijri (1505–1506 C.E.), but there is doubt about the exact date. There is confusion in Fes about the burial of Abū ᶜAbdullah Muḥammad al-Zaytūnī. Many people, even scholars, conflate him with Abū ᶜAbdullah al-Makkī, who was also called "al-Zaytūnī" (and is buried in the neighborhood al-Ḥaffārīn in Fes). Zarruq's Shaykh al-Zaytūnī is mentioned in other sources: Muḥammad al-Mahdi al-Fāsī, *Mumtiᶜ al-Asmāᵓ*, 28; Ibn Zikrī, *Sharḥ al-Naṣīḥa al-Kāfiya* (mss.), introduction; and Muḥammad al-Mahdi al-Fāsī, *Tuḥfat Ahl al-Ṣidīqīyya* (mss.).

34. Ibn ᶜAskar, *Dawḥat al-Nāshir*, 71–72, mentions his travels several times on the caravan routes.

35. Cornell, *Realm of the Saint*, 243–245. Previously, followers of Abū Madyan in Morocco had built a Sufi lineage around the social institution of organizing the Hajj caravans. The operations of this "*ṭarīqa Māgirīyya*" seem to have been disrupted by the gradual encroachments of the Hilālī Arab tribes into the far Maghrib. The Qādirī saints were therefore reviving an institution in new political and religious circumstances. See al-Nāṣirī, *al-Istiṣqāᵓ* (1955), 4: 66 and 116, for the disruptions caused by the Shāwī Arabs in particular, and the Hilāī Arabs in general.

36. Ibn ᶜAskar, *Dawḥat al-Nāshir*, 72.

37. Ibn ᶜAskar, *Dawḥat al-Nāshir*, 71–72. This miracle aligns al-Zaytūnī with the heroic figure of ᶜAlī ibn Abī Ṭālib, the champion of the early Islamic community and the prototype for saintly virtue. ᶜAlī was reportedly helped in battle once by a swarm of bees. See Schimmel, *Deciphering the Signs of God* (1994), 195.

38. Al-Zaytūnī was in touch with contemporary Qādirīs in Tāza, Tilimsān, and Tarābulus. The Qādirīs had institutions in Cairo, including a large zawiya at the Qarāfa

cemetery with a congregational mosque named after ᶜAbd al-Qādir. Descendants of an Iraqi disciple of ᶜAbd al-Qādir built this mosque in the late thirteenth century C.E.. The site of al-Qarāfa cemetery contains the tomb of one of the sons of ᶜAbd al-Qādir al-Jīlānī, as reported by al-Ḥasanī, *al-Sirr al-Ẓāhir*, 61. See Cornell, *Realm of the Saint*, 297.

39. Al-Kattānī, *Salwat al-Anfās*, 1:191.

40. Al-Ṣumāᶜī, *Kitāb al-Muᶜzā,* 283, along with most other hagiographic sources, do not tell of al-Zaytūnī's miracles in detail precisely because they claim that "such miracles are too numerous to describe."

41. Cornell, *Realm of the Saint*, 19–24, thoroughly critiques the Western scholarly term "popular Sufism" and reveals its colonialist foundations.

42. On the surface, the Qādirī Sufis appear to conform to anthropologists' characterization of marabouts, with the moral severity, magical power, and aggressive piety that scholars like Geertz claim that marabouts exude; see *Islam Observed*, 43–55. However, close examination reveals that they do not conform to the stereotype of marabouts, under which Geertz lumps together "descendants of the Prophet, leaders of Sufi brotherhoods, or simply vivid individuals who had contrived to make something uncanny happen." Detailed examination of the Qādirī Sufi community reveals that these types of people (Sufi, sharif, saint, or rabble-rouser) are related in complex alliances, but are not reducible into one category.

43. Zarruq, *al-Kunnāsh*, 66. His full name was Muḥammad ibn Zimām al-Rakāᶜ. It is not clear if he was a teacher in a madrasa or solely Zawiya Bū'l-Quṭūṭ itself; see Muḥammad ibn al-Ṭayyib al-Qādirī, *al-Ṭurfa fi Ikhtisār al-Tuḥfa* (mss.), folios 101–110. Other literate participants in devotions at the *zāwiya* were ᶜAlī al-Kharrūbī and his son, Muḥammad, and Aḥmad al-Milyānī, who were major companions of Zarruq.

44. Zarruq included quotations from Ibn al-ᶜArabī (known in Morocco as al-Ḥātimī to differentiate him from the Maliki legal scholar Abū Bakr ibn al-ᶜArabī) in his early notebook, *Tuḥfat al-Murīd*.

45. Evidence from South Asian and Yemeni communities of Qādirīs suggests that members of this community actively discussed Ibn al-ᶜArabī's ideas and may have been crucial in promoting him as a saint, rather than as a philosopher.

46. Guennoun, *Dhikrayāt,* 41, cites Zarruq, *al-Kunnāsh*; see also Ibn al-Qāḍī, *Jadhwat al-Iqtibās*, 282.

47. The two most famous texts of Aḥmad ibn ᶜAlī al-Būnī are *Manba' Uṣūl al-Hikma* and *Shams al-Maᶜārif al-Kubrā*. His use of magical invocations on the names of Allah has been analyzed by two studies in German: Mohamed el-Gawhary, *Die Gottesnamen im magischen Gebrauch in den al-Buni zugeschriebenen Werken* (1968); and Dorothee Anna Maria Pielow, *Die Quellen der Weisheit: die arabische Magie im Spiegel des Usul al-Hikma* (1995).

48. Zarruq, *al-Kunnāsh*, 65. Abū Zakariyā Yaḥya was also known as "Ṣāḥib al-Ẓuhra" after a certain place where he lived or frequented.

49. On such magical prayer, see Scott Kugle, "Heaven's Witness: the uses and abuses of Muhammad Ghawth Gwaliori's ascension," *Journal of Islamic Studies* 14/1 (2003): 26–29.

50. The Marinid rulers did not see European merchants as a threat to their sovereignty. They relied on Genoese and Italian merchants as financiers and moneylenders even as the Portuguese were implementing their novel strategies of aggressive mercantilism.

51. Cornell, *Realm of the Saint*, 388, claims that the introduction to al-Tāzī's *Book of Jihād* shows an "unmistakable Jazulite influence," though he points out that al-Tāzī was

never a disciple of al-Jazūlī. This work was written after the fall of Asila to the Portuguese in 876 Hijri (1471–72 C.E.), which was almost a full decade after the events described here that led up to the sharifian revolution in Fes. After this revolution, open association between the Qādirīs of Fes and members of the Jazūlīyya community would have been possible; yet al-Jazūlī was not known to have had contact with the Qādirīs in Fes (though he might have associated with Qādirīs in Egypt).

52. Cornell, *Realm of the Saint*, 388; translation of this passage is by Vincent Cornell.

53. Cornell, *Realm of the Saint*, 390.

54. Zarruq, *al-Kunnāsh*, 65.

55. This particular Andalusian's claim to a sharifian genealogy also smacked of competition with the recent bid for social status by the Qādirī *shurafāʾ*, who looked to al-Amīn and al-Zaytūnī as their protecting saints.

56. This suggests that al-Amīn may have held controversial doctrinal views. His *uwaysī* initiations may have seemed suspect or may have suggested to skeptical outsiders that the Qādirīs cultivated direct visionary experience of the Prophet that possibly skirted the issue of the finality of the Prophet Muḥammad's revelation. Such claims to having direct visionary experience of the Prophet may also have helped spark Mahdist expectations.

57. Cornell, *Realm of the Saint*, chapter six, has thoroughly studied al-Jazūlī, filling out his biography and portraying him as the figure who set the paradigm for Moroccan sainthood in this early modern period.

58. Cornell, *Realm of the Saint*, 302, provides details of their regimen of renunciation, fasting, and initiation among al-Jazūlī's followers.

59. Cornell, *Realm of the Saint,* 290, discusses the ambiguities in al-Jazūli's "Tilimsānī" sharifian genealogy. This would make him very distant cousins to the Qādirī *shurafāʾ,* who shared with al-Jazūli the practice of cultivating a spiritual link directly with the person of the Prophet. Like leaders of the Jazūlīyya, the Qādirīs were often *shurafāʾ* or elevated the *shurafāʾ* to positions of authority, since their own center of devotion, ᶜAbd al-Qādir, was a sharīf. See Cornell, *Realm of the Saint,* 297, on the Qādirī uses of prayers of blessing upon the spirit of the Prophet.

60. Cornell, *Realm of the Saint,* 308. *ᶜIliyyin* is a Qurʾānic term that refers to the gardens of paradise.

61. Cornell, *Realm of the Saint,* 305. On development of an almost Shiᶜī paradigm of absolute spiritual authority in the later Jazūlīyya community led by al-Ghazwānī, see Cornell, *Realm of the Saint,* 361–368.

62. Cornell, *Realm of the Saint,* 307.

63. Garcia-Arenal, "The Revolution in Fas," 59. Garcia-Arenal made this claim after mistakenly conflating the identity of two different men with the same name. One was Abū ᶜAbdullah Muḥammad al-Amīn, a disciple of al-Jazūlī, who is distinct from Abū ᶜAbdullah al-Amīn al-ᶜAṭṭār, the Qādirī Sufi in Fes whom Zarruq befriended (see above note 4). Such a conflation allowed her to claim that the early Jazūlīyya community was active in Fes before the sharifian revolution. Further, she posits that al-Waryāghalī represented the Jazūlīyya community in Fes. However, there is no biographical data linking al-Waryāghalī to al-Jazūlī himself or to any of his followers. Her attempt to outline religio-political factions within Fes needs to be reconsidered, especially since the Qādirīs seem to be absent from her scenario.

64. Al-Kattānī, *Salwat al-Anfās*, 2:208 and al-Mahdi al-Fāsī, *Mumtiᶜ al-Asmāʾ,* 56, note 104. The links between the Qādirīyya community of al-Zaytūnī and the followers of al-

Jazūlī date to the period after the revolution in Fes. Al-Zaytūnī became a friend and ally of ʿAlī Ṣāliḥ al-Andalusī, a second-generation follower of al-Jazūlī, who founded the first zawiya of the Jazūlīyya community in Fes. The editor of *Mumtiʿ al-Asmāʾ* exaggerates this friendship to claim that al-Zaytūnī became "a disciple" of ʿAlī Ṣāliḥ; see al-Mahdī al-Fāsī, *Mumtiʿ al-Asmāʾ*, 78, note 152. Certainly, ʿAbd al-ʿAzīz al-Tabbāʿ strategically tried to incorporate the Qādirīs into the emerging Jazūlīyya movement, and this places ʿAlī Ṣāliḥ's friendship with al-Zaytūnī into the wider context of a political-devotional alliance. The zawiya administered by ʿAlī Ṣāliḥ al-Andalusī was near Madrasat al-Wād (so named since it was situated along the now extinct stream "Wadī al-Zaytūn" near the al-Andalus mosque).

65. Cornell, *Realm of the Saint,* 387, notes that certain phrases in al-Tāzī's propaganda poem seem to echo phrases in al-Jazūlī's own compositions. However, that document was written in 876 Hijri (1471–72 C.E.), after the sharifian uprising in Fes, and it reflects a situation in which the Qādirīs and the Jazūlīs could have come into close contact once Marinid control of Fes dissolved. Cornell's discussion of "Jazulite influence" on the Qādirī Sufis pertains to the post-revolution period. In fact, it was the revolution itself that set the two communities up as allies and partners.

66. Zarruq, *al-Kunnāsh*, 66–67. It would not be accurate to say, following Garcia-Arenal, that al-Jazūlī's followers helped to incite the revolution in Fes. The revolution in Fes started on 27 Ramadan 869 Hijri (May 23, 1465 C.E.) whereas al-Jazūlī died at least one and a half months later, in Dhū al-Qāʿida in 869 Hijri. The first mention of any of al-Jazūlī's followers coming to Fes was to announce his death after the revolution had already occurred.

67. Al-Nāṣirī, *al-Istiṣqāʾ,* 4:115.

68. Henry Munson, *Religion and Power in Morocco*, 19.

69. Aḥmad Bābā al-Timbūktī, *Nayl al-Ibtihāj fi Tatrīz al-Dibāj* (1899), 254. The position of *naqīb al-shurafāʾ* was also known by the Berber term *mizwār.*

70. Al-Nāṣirī, *al-Istiṣqāʾ,* 4:114. The ʿImrāni clan descended from Yaḥyā al-Jūṭī ibn Muḥammad ibn Yaḥyā al-ʿAddām ibn al-Qāsim ibn Idrīs ibn Idrīs (who was the first ruler of an Islamic polity in Morocco and a descendant of Ḥasan, the grandson of the Prophet). The story of how this ancestor resided in the city of al-Jūṭa, situated on the southern bank of the Sabu River outside the city of Fes, is found in Al-Sharrāt, *al-Rawḍ al-ʿAṭir al-Anfās,* 224, note 443. From him, all the branches of this family take their name, "al-Jūṭī." The branches include at least four major clans: at-Ṭālibī, al-Farjī, at-Ṭāhirī, and al-ʿImrānī; this last branch was the most dominant group in Fes during later Marinid times. Al-Qādirī, *Nashr al-Mathānī,* 2:341, provides a long discussion of the al-Jūṭī lineage. The leader of this clan at the time of the revolution was Muḥammad al-ʿImrānī al-Jūṭī.

71. Just as the Marinids introduced into Morocco the institution of the madrasa from Egypt and the eastern Islamic world, they also patronized the celebration of the birthday of the Prophet Muḥammad. Al-Nāṣirī, *al-Istiṣqāʾ,* 3:90 and 111, points out that the Marinid sultan Yūsuf ibn Yaʿqūb ibn ʿAbd al-Ḥaqq seems to have adopted the practice from the rulers of the city of Sebta (Sp. Ceuta). The practice had been spread from there to the Rīf in northern Morocco, and the Marinid sultan ordered the holiday celebrated in his realm during a campaign in the Rīf. The practice had begun in Egypt roughly a century earlier.

72. Al-Nāṣirī, *al-Istiṣqāʾ*, 4:84. About fifty years after the holiday became a regular celebration in Marinid lands, Ibn ʿAbbād ignored the celebrations. He chose to fast while others were celebrating the Prophet's birthday (contradicting the custom that fasting is not permissible on an "*ʿId*" holiday). His master, Ibn ʿAshir, found him fasting and refused to allow him to persist, but rather forced him to break his fast and celebrate the new holiday.

This incident occurred in the mid-700s in Salé, since Ibn ᶜĀshir died there in 765 Hijri. When Ibn ᶜAbbād subsequently moved to Fes, he had to sit with the Marinid sultan and his court (along with other religious notables, *shurafāʾ*, and Sufis) for the nighttime celebrations; he complied with these demands but reportedly resented them. Cornell, *Realm of the Saint,* 341–342, discusses the importance of this celebration to the paradigm of "sharifian Sufism" that depicts Muḥammad as the perfect, primordial human being and projects his descendants to be the rightful rulers of Islamic polities.

73. See Powers, *Law, Society and Culture*, 14, 170, and 202, who recognized the "seizure of power" by the Idrisid sharifian families of Fes as a pivotal moment in Moroccan history.

74. Anonymous, *Nubdha min Tārīkh al-Maghrib al-Aqsā* (mss.), 220. It is possible to surmise from references in the text that this history was written in 1058 Hijri (1648 C.E.) during the Saᶜdian era in Fes.

75. *Nubdha min Tārīkh*, 220. His father, Muḥammad ibn Muḥammad al-ᶜImrānī, had been the first assigned to that position as leader of the *shurafāʾ* by order of sultan Abū Sālim ibn Abī al-Ḥasan al-Marīnī.

76. *Nubdha min Tārīkh*, 220.

77. Al-Nāṣirī, *al-Istiṣqāʾ*, 4:98. Qāḍī al-Maṣmūdī was dismissed most likely due to his opposition to increasing taxation through illegal means. For his biography, see Ibn al-Qāḍī, *Durrat al-Ḥijāl,* 1:220.

78. In response to the public support in Fes for the members of the Waṭṭāsī family (and perhaps in fear of the public rallying around their cause), ᶜAbd al-Ḥaqq may have appointed a member of the Waṭṭāsī family as provisional and puppet wazir before appointing one from the Jewish community.

79. Al-Nāṣirī, *al-Istiṣqāʾ,* 4:98. Their names are recorded as Hārūn and Shāwil, but details of their biographies are obscure. "Appropriation of property" could refer to coercive collection of taxes or to the abolition of revenues that had formerly been ceded to the *shurafāʾ* and scholars as trusts (*ḥabs* or *waqf*).

80. Cornell, *Realm of the Saint,* 307–08 holds out the tantalizing possibility that al-Jazūlī's millenarian doctrines and elevation of the *shurafāʾ* to positions of spiritual potency may have inspired the *shurafāʾ* (and their Sufi supporters) in Fes to revolt against Marinid rule.

81. This narrative is based mainly on al-Nāṣirī, *al-Istiṣqāʾ*, 4:95–114, who himself synthesized information from many different sources. It also reflects the revisionist skepticism of Garcia-Arenal, "The Revolution in Fas," who subjects this historical event to close scrutiny, looking especially at how firsthand accounts have been distorted in "versions of a traditional history composed over the years by agglomeration, repetition, and revision" which centered specifically around stereotypes of Jews in Fes. See also Cornell, *Realm of the Saint,* 318.

82. There is disagreement over the full name of al-Waryāghalī; in some sources he appears as Abū ᶜAbdullah Muḥammad while in others he is cited as Abū Faris ᶜAbd al-ᶜAzīz ibn Mūsā. It is possible that he came from the Rīf region north of Fes, from the tribe of Banū Waryāghar. In Fes, he became a student of ᶜAbdullah al-ᶜAbdūsī, along with al-Qūrī. Garcia-Arenal tries to mark out political factions among the religious notables in Fes in this period, with al-ᶜAbdūsī supporting al-Waryāghalī's opposition to the Marinid dynasty. She does not notice, however, that the loyalist al-Qūrī was also a student and protégé of al-ᶜAbdūsī and was his immediate successor at al-Qarawiyyīn. Al-ᶜAbdūsī belonged to an older generation and cannot be claimed unambiguously by either faction.

83. Ibn ᶜAskar, *Dawḥat al-Nāshir*, 31. He is reported to have lived in Qaṣr Kutāma during the winter months, teaching at a madrasa, while in the summer months he traveled among the encampments in the northern region of al-Habṭ.

84. al-Timbūktī, *Nayl al-Ibtihāj*, 182, cites Zarruq, *al-Kunnāsh*.

85. Garcia-Arenal, "The Revolution in Fas," 45. The population of Jews had been increasing in Fes through immigration from Andalusia since 793 Hijri (1391 C.E.). There followed increasing economic and financial competition between the *shurafāʾ* and the Jews in the markets of Fes. Garcia-Arenal advances the argument that it was primarily economic reasons that motivated the *shurafāʾ* to first move the Jews out of the old city of Fes and then to attack their financial and administrative alliance with the Marinid regime during the revolution. She notes that conflict persisted between a community of "converted Jews" who became Muslim and thereby maintained their strength in the markets of Fes, even after other Jews were moved out in 641 Hijri (1243–44 C.E.); see *Dhikr Qiṣṣat al-Muhājirīn* (mss.). Many thanks to Fredrick Colby for providing a copy of this manuscript.

86. Garcia-Arenal, "The Revolution in Fas," 47, cites the *Riḥla* of ᶜAbd al-Bāsiṭ ibn Khalil, entitled *al-Rawḍ al-Bāsim fi Ḥawādith al-ᶜUmr waʾl-Tarājim*.

87. Sources differ as to the method and timing of the execution. Some say sultan ᶜAbd al-Ḥaqq was taken to a slaughterhouse and butchered like a sheep, others say that he was speared by his own army personnel, while others assert a more orderly procession to the public execution ground.

88. Garcia-Arenal, "The Revolution in Fas," 52, notes that the exaggeration of "a wholesale slaughter of Jews in Fes" seems to belong to the rhetoric which justified the revolution, the rhetoric of the righteous anger of the people of Fes, led by the sharifian nobles, against the Jews and their manipulation of the Marinid structures of rule. News of a general slaughter of Jews in such a cosmopolitan center such as Fes could not go unnoticed in Jewish chronicles, yet there is no corroborative evidence from contemporary Jewish accounts, and Garcia-Arenal notes that Jewish histories only slowly incorporated reports about "the Jewish wazir" and "the slaughter of the Jews" adopted from Muslim historical sources. She concludes that the *shurafāʾ* deployed the rhetorical trope of "the wickedness of the Jews" to justify the revolution and divert attention away from the question of whether uprising against the sultan was lawful or not.

89. Other sharifian republics also sprang up at this time. Shafshāwan in the north was founded by ᶜAlī ibn Rāshid (who died in 916–17 Hijri [1511 C.E.]) as a community ruled by a *sharīf* independent from the Marinid and Waṭṭāsid rulers with an open policy of *jihād* against the Iberians; see Cornell, *Realm of the Saint,* 395. The Saᶜdian movement to the south was also flourishing at this time under the leadership of Muḥammad ibn ᶜAbd al-Raḥmān of Tagmadert beginning in 914 Hijri (1509 C.E.). The movement won political successes and ultimately the governance of Marrākush (Pt. Marrakesh) through their *jihād* against the Portuguese in Agādīr, along the southern Moroccan coastline.

90. Zarruq, *al-Kunnāsh*, 67.

91. The manuscript text of Zarruq's autobiography housed in Rabat (in al-Khizāna al-ᶜAmma) is the unique copy extant in Morocco and is the one from which all researchers have worked (including Garcia-Arenal, Khushaim, Cornell, and myself). The Algerian copy of this text reproduces the Moroccan copy exactly: *Hadhā ma wujida min Kunnāsh al-Shaykh Zarrūq* (mss.) folios 65–95, as does the Tunisian copy (mss.) that has been recently published in Libya as Zarruq, *al-Kunnāsh: Ṣuwar min al-Dhikrayāt al-Ulā* (1980). It seems that the autobiography has been blurred for a long time, since the text, quoted in the six-

teenth-century hagiographic source Ibn ᶜAskar, *Dawḥat al-Nāshir,* is also printed in a garbled and incomprehensible way.

92. al-Ṣumāᶜī, *Kitāb al-Muᶜzā,* 132, quotes from another copy of *al-Kunnāsh* that is now apparently non-existent in manuscript form.

93. al-Ṣumāᶜī, *Kitāb al-Muᶜzā,* 132, and *al-Kunnāsh*, 67.

94. Garcia-Arenal, "The Revolution in Fas," 46, quotes the *Rihla* of ᶜAbd al-Bāsiṭ ibn Khalīl.

95. Garcia-Arenal notes that no evidence of any fatwa survives from any of the major players in this drama.

96. Zarruq, *al-Kunnāsh*, 62. His full name was Aḥmad ibn Saᶜīd al-Miknāsī.

97. Al-Qūrī died in 972 Hijri (1467–68 C.E.), three years after the revolution. However, no evidence exists to show that he ever re-entered public life in Fes.

98. al-Qādirī, *Nashr al-Mathānī,* 2:56, glosses the term *ghandūr* with the term *mulāᶜib*, meaning a hypocrite or one who pretends to play a role for which he is not really qualified.

99. Zarruq, *al-Kunnāsh*, 67.

Part III. Spirit (introduction)

1. Zarruq, *Qawāʾid al-Taṣawwuf,* Principle 25. The "giver of scripture" could refer to Muhammad the Prophet, or Gabriel the angel who gave him the scriptural message, or Allah who originated the message.

2. Zarruq, *Qawāʾid*, Principle 25.

3. Elizabeth Sirriyeh, *Sufis and Anti-Sufis* (1999), 11–12, and chapter 4.

5. Pilgrimage

1. Cornell, *Realm of the Saint,* 23–24; see also Turner, *Weber and Islam,* who offers an assessment of Weber's concepts but does not deal deeply with charisma.

2. Hamid Dabashi, *Authority in Islam* (1992), chapter 2.

3. Zarruq, *Risālat al-Radd ᶜala Ahl al-Bidᶜa* (mss. Tunis: 8631), folio 3.

4. Zarruq, *Risālat al-Radd*, folio 3, makes a subtle play on the Arabic root *ḥ-r m.* Those who do not respect the sanctity of spiritual masters (*ḥurma*) are forbidden access (*ḥurima*) to the ultimate goal.

5. Geertz, *Islam Observed*, 33 and 44.

6. Talal Asad, *Genealogies of Religion* 187, notes that Gellner, like Geertz, uses *baraka* as a cipher for the Christian notion of grace that was appropriated from the Greek term "charisma."

7. Geertz, *Islam Observed*, 45.

8. Geertz, *Islam Observed*, 52.

9. Islamic hagiographic literature makes a subtle distinction between sincerity and legitimacy. Authors record some saintly personalities who have sincerity without legitimacy, such as those whose reason is suspended in a holy madness (*majdhūb*) and those shadowy figures who have saintly character but no public recognition at all. These people have sincerity as saints, but have no legitimate way to pass their authority on to others after them.

10. Cornell, *Realm of the Saint,* 13–16. *Walāya* and *wilāya* are the "verbal nouns" related to *Walī* as a "personal noun." *Walī* denotes a person while *walāya* and *wilāya* de-

scribe the abstract qualities that characterize that person. Cornell translates *walāya* and *wilāya* (in their interrelatedness) as "Muslim sainthood." Ernst, *Sufism*, 59, also stresses the "relational meaning" of *walāya* and *wilāya* in defining an Islamic sainthood.

11. James, *Varieties*, 298.

12. Bruce Lawrence (trans.), *Nizam ad-Din Awliya* (1992), 95.

13. Stefania Pandolfo, *Impasse of the Angels: scenes from a Moroccan space of memory* (1997), 6.

14. Zarruq wrote his autobiography after 896 Hijri (1491 C.E.), in the last three years of his life. Clearly it is not a finished work, but rather a notebook of various ideas and problems that he could develop later into polished texts. There is doubt that Zarruq himself wrote the sections of this notebook that come after his autobiography, his *fihris*, and his discussion of initiation rituals. See the editorial discussion of Khushaim (ed.), *Al-Kunnash*, 7–8.

15. Zarruq, *al-Kunnāsh* (mss.), 67.

16. Zarruq, *al-Kunnāsh*, 67.

17. This is not evidence of maraboutic "hagiarchies," posited by Geertz, *Islam Observed*, 30–31 and 43–54. This role of saints as defenders of public order is not limited to saints in Morocco.

18. Victor Turner, *Dramas, Fields and Metaphors* (1974), 241, refines the basic ideas he laid out in *The Ritual Process* (1969).

19. Turner, *Dramas*, 196.

20. Zarruq, *al-Kunnāsh*, 67.

21. Zarruq, *al-Kunnāsh*, 67.

22. Zarruq, *al-Kunnāsh*, 68.

23. Zarruq, *al-Kunnāsh*, 68.

24. Zarruq, *al-Kunnāsh*, 68.

25. Zarruq, *al-Kunnāsh*, 68. Ibn Maryam, *al-Bustān*, 31–38 provides a biography of al-Ghumārī. He resided at night in the mosque of the *zāwiya* of Shaykh ᶜAlī al-Ḥalāwī. It was his habit to disappear during the day (sometimes to carry water for people in the market) and at night to reside in the mosque to recite the Qurʾān and move people to renunciation. He was once driven out of Tilimsān by opponents but was subsequently asked to return to his place.

26. Anonymous, *al-Taᶜrīf bi-Sīdī Aḥmad Zarruq* (mss.).

27. Zarruq, *al-Kunnāsh*, 68.

28. Zarruq, *al-Kunnāsh*, 69.

29. Zarruq, *al-Kunnāsh*, 69.

30. Lawrence (trans.), *Morals for the Heart*, 300.

31. Zarruq, *al-Kunnāsh*, 69–70.

32. Zarruq, *al-Kunnāsh*, 70.

33. Zarruq, *al-Kunnāsh*, 70.

34. Zarruq, *al-Kunnāsh*, 70.

35. Marvin Shaw, *The Paradox of Intention* (1988), offers a contemporary study of this inversion of practical logic in Buddhism, Christianity, and psychoanalysis, suggesting that the reversal of effort is a universal theme in spiritual development in all traditions.

36. Abdellah Hammoudi, *Master and Disciple* (1997), 89.

37. Zarruq, *al-Kunnāsh*, 71.

38. These tropes served to displace the reader's attention from the historical facts of the revolution in Fes, which are their direct antecedent. Zarruq himself seems to have "post-

dated" the events of his pilgrimage to the year 870 Hijri (1465–66 C.E.), in order to not correspond to the revolution, in order to erase its deep disruption of the life he had expected and taken for granted.

39. The passage of forty plays a consistently important role in the story of Islamic prophets: Noah endured forty days on the ark, Moses wandered in the desert for forty years, Jesus was tempted forty days in the wilderness, while Muhammad lived forty years before reaching a state of sincerity to receive revelation. Sufi communities adopted a passage of forty days for devotional retreats of social isolation and contemplation (*iᶜtikāf*).

40. Zarruq, *Sulūk al-Ṭarīq idha fuqida al-Rafīq*, (mss.).

41. Zarruq, *Sulūk al-Ṭarīq,* quoting a Prophetic hadith (*mūtū qabl an tamūtū*) and a *hadith qudsi* (*ḍiᶜ nafsaka wa taᶜālā*).

42. Zarruq, *Sulūk al-Ṭarīq.*

43. This hadith is quoted by Abu Ḥāmid al-Ghazāli in "The Beginning of Guidance" in Montgomery Watt (trans.), *The Faith and Practice of al-Ghazali*, 131.

44. Lawrence, *Morals for the Heart*, 137.

45. Zarruq, *al-Kunnāsh*, 72. According to Zarruq's account, al-Zaytūnī had questioned his character under the malicious effects of the jealousy of another disciple. In vindication, Zarruq notes sourly, the jealous disciple died within a year of his own return to Fes.

46. Khushaim, *Zarruq the Sufi,* 90, asserts that Zarruq composed his first commentary on the *Ḥikam* in 870 Hijri (1465–66 C.E.).

47. Anonymous, *al-Taᶜrīf bi-Sīdī Aḥmad Zarruq*, 279. Strangely, the author also mentions that Zarruq was accused (in the passive tense, without revealing his accusers) of the doctrine of Union with God (*ittiḥād*), which is the common accusation of jurists against Sufis.

48. Ibn ᶜAskar, *Dawḥat al-Nāshir*, 48–49, recorded the narrative that dominated Moroccan hagiography about Zarruq. Even those sources that present a positive picture of Zarruq (such as Aḥmad Bābā al-Timbūktī, and al-Ṣumāᶜī) do not cite Zarruq's own self-vindicating version of events, but simply elide his stormy relationship with al-Zaytūnī.

49. Zarruq reportedly wrote close to twenty commentaries on the *Wisdom Sayings* over the course of his life. Various versions were lost, stolen, or incinerated. Other versions he wrote for discrete communities of disciples in different urban centers across North Africa. Several manuscripts of various versions of his commentary have been preserved. Of these, the most popular are the fifteenth and the seventeenth commentaries, which have been published.

50. It is not clear when Zarruq left Fes for Cairo. His autobiographic narrative with firm dates in *al-Kunnāsh* ends at 870 Hijri (1465–66 C.E.), when he returned from Tilimsān, and does not provide a subsequent date for his departure to the east. Khushaim, *Zarruq the Sufi*, 17, asserts that he remained in Fes until 873 Hijri (1468–69 C.E.), but provides no textual or historical evidence for this claim. The fact that he took permission for his travel to the east from Ḥasan al-Ghumārī, his patron in Tilimsān, suggests that Zarruq left Fes at an earlier date, in 870 Hijri or shortly thereafter, and resided in Tilimsān until he could gather enough resources to continue east.

51. He gained the privilege of residing in the hostel for Moroccan students and professors called *Riwāq al-Sādāt al-Maghāriba*.

52. Al-Sakhāwī, *al-Ḍawʾ al-Lāmiᶜ*, 1:222. Zarruq studied the texts *Bulūgh al-Marām* and *Saḥīḥ al-Bukhāri* with al-Sakhāwī, and Arabic and juridisprudence with al-Jurjī, whom Zarruq recalls as "a jurist, an expert in legal philosophy, and a grammarian." He died in 896 Hijri (1490–91 C.E.). Al-Sakhāwī composed his huge biographical compendium, *al-Ḍawᶜ*

*al-Lāmi*ᶜ, to memorialize his own wide-ranging connections with other scholars, religious notables, and Sufis. This was a way of recording his own power as an authoritative teacher for posterity, by recording the greatness of others whom he met, who had studied under him, or who had come to pay him their respects. His compendium reads like Who's Who of religious authorities in the ninth Islamic century.

53. Zarruq, *Sharḥ Ṣaḥīḥ al-Bukhārī* (n.d.). His commentary tends toward a grammatical and literal reading of the hadith texts rather than providing a systematic "interpretation." He also wrote separate treatises on the study of hadith texts: *Juzʾ fi ᶜIlm al-Ḥadīth* (mss. location unknown) and *Risāla fi Taḥdīd Mustalāḥ al-Ḥadīth* (mss.).

54. Zarruq carefully preserved his *ijāza* documents that certified his knowledge of authoritative texts and gave him permission to transmit this knowledge to others. They are preserved in *al-Kunnāsh* along with a short summary of his autobiography in Zarruq, *Ijāzāt* (mss.) written in 877 Hijri (1472–73 C.E.). Khushaim erroneously claims that this is a copy of *al-Kunnāsh*.

55. al-Timbūktī, *Nayl al-Ibtihāj*, 70–74. It is not surprising that this author erases any mention of Zarruq's conflicts in Fes during the revolution and his break with al-Zaytūnī. Al-Timbūktī was a disciple in the lineage of Zarruq (two generations removed from Muḥammad al-Kharrūbī) and owed his scholarly reputation partly to the reputation of Zarruq in Morocco. For this reason, he tried to "purge" Zarruq's biography of any mention of political controversy and the subsequent legends that surrounded his expulsion from Fes. Ibn Maryam, *al-Bustān*, 99, followed this same strategy, for he was also a member of Zarruq's lineage as a disciple of Nāṣir al-Dīn al-Laqānī and tried to protect Zarruq's reputation as a juridical saint.

56. It is not clear that al-Sakhāwī engaged any disciples as a Sufi, either from among his students or from the population at large.

57. Zarruq, *Manāqib al-Ḥaḍramī* (mss. Rabat) folios 105–109. All quotations from this mss. copy in Rabat. Zarruq wrote this *Manāqib* as an appendix to his commentary on the *Ḥikam* that was completed in 889 Hijri (1484 C.E.) "in order to show that this era is not devoid of people who manifest blessings (*baraka*) in the world. Aḥmad ibn ᶜUqba [al-Ḥaḍramī] is the most prominent of them in his lofty station, the most advanced of them in his holy state, the chief of them in his pure virtues, and the greatest of them in his gifts of spiritual insight." Zarruq apparently wrote a longer version of this biographical account, preserved as *Manāqib al-Ḥaḍramī* (mss. Cairo)—many thanks to Prof. Denis Gril for alerting me to this text.

58. Although al-Ḥaḍramī was later known as a member of the Shādhilī community, his exact lineage remained ambiguous; the details of this ambiguity and its rhetorical importance will become clearer below.

59. Al-Sakhāwī, *al-Ḍaw*ᶜ *al-Lāmi*ᶜ, 2:5, reports that al-Ḥaḍramī stayed in Cairo for a time until he died in 895 Hijri (1590 C.E.) at a place called Ṭabra in the Sahara. However, Zarruq, writing of him in 889 Hijri (1494 C.E.), writes as if he were already dead.

60. Zarruq, *Manāqib al-Ḥaḍramī*, 104. In this commentary on al-Ḥaḍramī's proverb, Zarruq makes a clever play on words, exploiting the similarity between "snake" (*ḥayyatun*) and "while alive" (*ḥayyatan*).

61. Zarruq, *Manāqib al-Ḥaḍramī*, 104.

62. In this way al-Ḥaḍramī avoids the popular strategy of cultivating self-blame (*malāma*) which would play into this cultural logic of sanctity. By purposefully acting in ways that others may blame, the saint can avoid social status in a way that only increases one's perceived sanctity.

63. Zarruq, *Manāqib al-Ḥaḍramī*, 106.

64. Zarruq, *Manāqib al-Ḥaḍramī*, 106.

65. Zarruq, *Manāqib al-Ḥaḍramī*, 105. Al-Ḥaḍramī makes a clever word play between *wird* and *ḥadar*. *Wird* is a spring providing nourishment and shelter, but it is also the word for a Sufi's specific prayer (like "mantra" has become used in English). *Ḥadar* is a treacherous slope or steep incline, like the crests and troughs of rough waves, but it is also a term describing Qurʾānic recitation. This imagery of nature both nurturing and dangerous is also a play on religious rituals through which the Sufi can "leave worries and just plunge in."

66. Zarruq, *Manāqib al-Ḥaḍramī*, 105.

67. Zarruq, *Manāqib al-Ḥaḍramī*, 105.

68. Zarruq, *Sharḥ Asmāʾ Allah al-Ḥusnā* (mss), 249, paraphrases a teaching of Shaykh al-Shādhilī.

69. Literalists would surely denounce these texts and their authors, for they would see questions of how the cosmos was created and how human beings shared some continuity with the singular divine being as a threat to the ultimate authority of Islamic law.

70. The titles of four texts by al-Ḥaḍramī are preserved. *Ṣudūr al-Marātib wa Nayl al-Raghāʾib* [*The Emergence of Levels and the Fulfillment of Desires*] and *Bidāyat al-ᶜUqūl wa Nihāyat al-Nuqūl* [*The Beginning of Reason's Powers and the End of Tradition's Sources*] are cited in al-Ṣumāᶜī, *Kitāb al-Muᶜzā*, 283. Khushaim, *Zarruq the Sufi*, bibliography, notes the title *Kitāb al-Marāsid* [*The Book of Observatories*]. The title of an additional text, *Sāḥil al-Ishārāt* [*The Shore of Allusions*] is mentioned within the text of *Ṣudūr al-Marātib*. Zarruq wrote commentaries on *Ṣudūr al-Marātib* (cited below) and also *al-Marāsid* (no copy of the second commentary is known to exist). Zarruq also wrote a commentary on another work on existential realities by Muḥammad al-Tilimsānī al-Maqqarīʾ: Zarruq, *Sharḥ al-Haqāʾiq waʾl-Daqāʾiq* [*Commentary on the Book of Subtle Truths and Cosmic Realities*] (mss. location unknown).

71. Zarruq, *Sharḥ Ṣudūr al-Marātib*, 22, at the opening of chapter one. Many thanks to Muṣṭafā Nājī, a book lover in Rabat, for having provided me a photocopy of this rare manuscript from his private collection.

72. Zarruq, *Sharḥ Ṣudūr al-Marātib*, 20.

73. Zarruq, *Sharḥ Ṣudūr al-Marātib*, 2. Zarruq quotes this couplet from al-Maqarrīʾ (most likely from al-Maqarrīʾ's text *al-Ḥaqāʾiq waʾl-Daqāʾiq*).

74. Zarruq, *Sharḥ Ṣudūr al-Marātib*, 2

75. Guennoun, *Mashāhir Rijāl*, 41.

76. Zarruq, *Manāqib al-Ḥaḍramī*, 105, means that everything worthy of being taught as spiritual guidance was taught by the Prophet and is residual in the Prophet's legacy; nothing new is to be discovered, fashioned, or created by "skillful means."

77. Zarruq, *Qawāᶜid*, Principle 65. All citations from *Qawāᶜid al-Taṣawwuf* are by principle number rather than page number, to facilitate reference to the Arabic text, which has been reprinted so many times as to make page references misleading. Anas ibn Mālik was a servant to the Prophet Muḥammad as a young man and was the source of many hadith reports about the Prophet; he died around 91–93 Hijri (709–711 C.E.).

78. Zarruq, *Manāqib al-Ḥaḍramī*, 104.

79. Zarruq, *Qawāᶜid*, conclusion. This oral teaching of al-Ḥaḍramī was included by Zarruq as the seal of his text.

80. Zarruq, *Qawāᶜid*, conclusion.

81. Zarruq, *Qawāᶜid*, conclusion.

82. Zarruq, *Qawāᶜid*, conclusion.

83. Muḥammad al-ᶜArabī al-Qādirī, *al-Ṭurfa*. It is strange that al-Ḥaḍramī traces his spiritual method through his mother's inheritance but never reveals any further stories about her.

84. ᶜAbd al-Salām ibn al-Tayyib al-Qādirī, *al-Maqṣad al-Aḥmad* (n.d.), 302.

85. Zarruq, *Manāqib al-Ḥaḍramī*, 106.

86. Aḥmad al-Sharjī, *Ṭabaqāt al-Khawwāṣ* (1321 Hijri), 74–84, claims that most Sufi masters in Yemen trace their primary allegiance to ᶜAbd al-Qādir Jīlānī. The Qādirī lineage came to Yemen very early. In the lifetime of ᶜAbd al-Qādir, at least two Yemenis sought him out in Makka for training (though it is not clear if they saw him as a hadith teacher or a Sufi master, or both). These early Qādirīs are ᶜAlī ibn ᶜAbd al-Raḥmān al-Ḥaddād, who met ᶜAbd al-Qādir at the Kaᶜaba in 561 Hijri (1166 C.E.), and ᶜAbdullah al-Asadī.

87. Sufi communities spread in the Ḥaḍramawt region of Yemen in the seventh century Hijri, by the efforts of Shaykh Muḥammad ibn ᶜAlī "al-Faqīh al-Muqaddam," who died in 653 Hijri (1255 C.E.). He endeavored to spread Sufi training among the scholars of Ḥaḍramawt, who were previously renowned only for their abilities in law and prophetic traditions. See al-Ḥabshī, *Al-Ṣūfiya,* 23.

88. According to al-Qādirī, *al-Ṭurfa*, al-Ḥaḍramī had taken initiation from a master, ᶜAbd al-Kabīr al-Ḥaḍramī, who lived in Makka. Before coming to Egypt, he had also kept the company of at least three different shaykhs: Abū ᶜImrān Mūsā (who wrote a book called *al-Ḥalīf wa'l-Ḥalaf*), al-Sharīf Aḥmad al-Shāwī, and Abū Bakr al-Zalīᶜi (who wrote a book called *al-Khāl al-Muᶜajama).* However, none of their lineages are known. Al-Ḥaḍramī had possibly become a Shādhilī in Yemen, since that lineage had come to Yemen from Egypt earlier. However, all the Shādhilīs to whom al-Ḥaḍramī refers are Egyptian, so it is more likely that he acquired his allegiance once he left Yemen.

89. al-Qādirī, *al-Maqṣad al-Aḥmad,* 302, has subjected these lineages to historical and genealogical scrutiny and found them very weak. Al-Ḥaḍramī evidently conflated his master, Yaḥyā al-Qādirī, with a certain descendant of ᶜAbd al-Qādir, also named Yaḥya, but nicknamed "Sayf al-Dīn." However, this descendant of was five generations removed from ᶜAbd al-Qādir al-Jīlānī, leaving a large gap of time between the Yaḥya al-Qādirī whom al-Ḥaḍramī knew and Yaḥyā al-Qādirī the descendant of ᶜAbd al-Qādir. Later followers of Zarruq may have constructed this faulty lineage to substantiate al-Ḥaḍramī's simple claim to have been "a Qādirī."

90. Al-Ḥaḍramī claimed an additional Shādhilī lineage through ᶜAlī ibn Wafā', yet he never specified who were the necessary intermediaries between Ibn Wafā' and himself. Al-Qādirī, *al-Maqṣad al-Aḥmad*, 302, notes that ᶜAlī ibn Wafā' died seventeen years before al-Ḥaḍramī was born (so there must be at least one intermediary whom al-Ḥaḍramī neglected to specify).

91. Khushaim, *Zarruq the Sufi*, 102–103. Despite Khushaim, there is no way to affirm that this person named is the one al-Ḥaḍramī refers to as "my master" whom he met in Makka. The chart which Khushaim claims represents Zarruq's many Sufi lineages (in which Yaḥyā al-Qādirī plays a central role) pretends that his highly ambivalent situation is perfectly clear, and is therefore misleading. Zarruq's early followers were able to acknowledge his ambiguous relation to discrete Sufi lineages much more honestly than his later followers.

92. In *al-Kunnāsh*, he records that he took an *ijāza* from al-Sakhāwī in the treatise of al-Qushayrī, the books of al-Muḥāsibī, and *ᶜAwārif al-Maᶜārif* of al-Suhrawardī. In addition, al-Sakhāwī gave him an *ijāza* for the texts of Ibn ᶜAbī Jamra and the *Madkhal* of Ibn

al-Ḥājj. Zarruq took permission for the *Iḥyāʾ* of al-Ghazālī and *Qūt al-Qulūb* of al-Makkī from one of al-Sakhāwī's students, named Aḥmad ibn ᶜAbd al-Qādir al-Shāwī al-Ḥanafī (from the town of Shāwa that is situated between Cairo and Alexandria). Zarruq also took an *ijāza* in al-Bukhārī's hadith collection from this teacher who, like al-Sakhāwī himself, was initiated into the Qādirī lineage.

93. Zarruq, *al-Kunnāsh*, 73. Documentation of his *ijāza* in the texts of Ibn ᶜAṭāʾillah (including *al-Ḥikam, Kitāb al-Tanwīr, Tāj al-ᶜArūs, Miftāḥ al-Falāḥ* and others) does not explicitly name al-Sakhāwī. However, Zarruq follow the pattern set up by his earlier *ijāzas* and wrote the lineage out in condensed form, thereby implying that his *ijāza* for this set of Ibn ᶜAṭāʾillah's texts was from al-Sakhāwī.

94. Zarruq, *Qawāᶜid al-Taṣawwuf*, conclusion. On Ibn Abī Jamra, see Katz, *Dreams, Sufism, and Sainthood* (1996), 158–159.

95. Mohammed Benchekroun, *La Vie Intellectuelle Marocaine* (1974), 375, reports that more than six hundred students used to attend his lectures at al-Azhar. According to Guennoun, *Mashāhir Rijāl*, 21, Zarruq was named chief Mālikī jurist at al-Azhar and would teach from a raised chair as a symbol of his authority.

96. Zarruq, *Manāqib al-Ḥaḍramī*, 105.

97. Hagiographic sources differ widely in reporting Zarruq's lineage. Most judged him to be a Qādirī by initiation but at the same time assert that he was really a Shādhilī. Often they confuse his scholarly lineage as a pupil of al-Sakhāwī with a Sufi lineage in spiritual training. Al-Ṣumāᶜī, *Kitāb Al-Muᶜzā,* 280–281, cites his Sufi lineage as Shādhilī, running from al-Sakhāwī to Ibn ᶜAṭāʾillah (even though al-Sakhāwī was a Qādirī and he gave Zarruq a scholarly *ijāza* in Ibn ᶜAṭāʾillah's texts rather than an initiation, or *bayᶜa*, in ᶜAṭāʾillah's Shādhilī lineage). In the end, they all insist that Zarruq was "clearly a Shādhilī" without being able to document a stable chain of initiations.

98. Al-Ṣumāᶜī, *Kitāb al-Muᶜzā*, 350. Aḥmad al-Tadilī al-Ṣumāᶜī (or al-Ṣawmaᶜī according to the editor of *Kitāb al-Muᶜzā*) was concurrently a follower of al-Jazūlī. Still, he did not perpetuate the fallacy that Zarruq had been a disciple of al-Jazūlī, as did many later followers of Zarruq in Morocco (and as Khushaim repeats in *Zarruq the Sufi*).

99. Al-Ṣumāᶜī, *Kitāb al-Muᶜzā,* 350.

100. Al-Ṣumāᶜī, *Kitāb al-Muᶜzā,* 348–350, cites Ṭāhir ibn Zayyān ibn Qāʾid al-Zawāwī al-Maghribī, *al-Risāla al-Qaṣdiyya* (mss. location unknown). The term "triple *khirqa*" represents the ritual of initiation in the "triple lineage (*ṭarīqa*)." Wearing a cloak from the hand of a saintly guide was the outer sign of having undergone this ritual.

6. Sincerity

1. Zarruq, *Qawāᶜid al-Taṣawwuf,* Principle 26. The composition of that work will be detailed in the next section of this chapter.

2. Zarruq, *Qawāᶜid*, Principle 26.

3. Zarruq, *Risālat al-Radd* (mss.), folio 15.

4. Zarruq's legal commentaries include: *Sharḥ al-Muqaddima al-Qurṭubīyya* (mss.), *Sharḥ al-Risāla al-Qayrawānīyya* (mss.); *Sharḥ Mawāḍiᶜ min Mukhtaṣar Khalīl* (mss.).

5. Zarruq, *al-Naṣīḥa al-Kāfiya li-man khaṣṣahu Allah bi'l-ᶜĀfiya* (n.d.). Zarruq also composed a commentary on his own text, *Sharḥ al-Naṣīḥa* (mss.).

6. Zarruq, *al-Jāmiᶜ li-Jumal min al-Fawāʾid waʾl-Manāfiᶜ* (mss.). It is possible that Zarruq rewrote this text for disciples and companions at Tūnis or Bijāya, where he is known to have paused in his journey west in 878 Hijri (1473–74 C.E.).

7. The term *al-Jāmi*ᶜ comes up very early in Zarruq's experience, as recorded in his student notebook, *Tuḥfat al-Murīd*. From these early jottings, Zarruq developed this term through his many works. The highest aspiration of a saint is to become *al-Jāmi*ᶜ, the one who brings together law and sanctity. From this perspective, the goal of being a Sufi is not absolute self-transcendence, but rather self-effacement for the functional purpose of becoming the fulcrum between jurists and saints, between *iḥsān* and *islām*.

8. Zarruq, *Sharḥ al-Risāla al-Waghlīsīyya* (mss.). ᶜAbd al-Raḥmān ibn Aḥmad al-Waghlīsī was a Maliki jurist from Bijāya who died in 786 Hijri (1384–85 C.E.). His book is *al-Muqaddima al-Waghlīsīyya al-Jāmi*ᶜ*a fī al-Aḥkām al-Fiqhīyya* ᶜ*alā Madhhab al-Imām Mālik*.

9. Ibn al-Banāᵓ al-Sarqusṭī, *al-Mabāḥith al-Aṣliyya*, printed in the margins of Aḥmad ibn ᶜAjība, *Īqāẓ al-Himam fī Sharḥ al-Ḥikam* (n.d.). This poem was used for training disciples in the Jazūlīyya zawiya in Fes, see Ibn ᶜAskar, *Dawḥat al-Nāshir*, 98. Zarruq claimed that the author, Ibn al-Banāᵓ, was from an Andalusian family and lived and died in Fes sometime in the ninth century Hijri (fifteenth century C.E.). However, Zarruq had never read an historical or biographical account of the author himself.

10. Zarruq, *Sharḥ al-Mabāḥith al-Aṣliyya* (mss. Rabat), 135.

11. Ibn ᶜAjība, *Sharḥ al-Mabāḥith al-Aṣliyya*, 22.

12. Vincent Cornell, *The Way of Abū Madyan* (1996), offers a full English translation of the *qaṣīda in ra*ᵓ.

13. For examples of this genre, see Taqi al-Dīn Abū Bakr al-Ḥiṣnī, *Kitāb al-Qawā*ᶜ*id* (Riyadh: Maktabat al-Rushd, 1997), who died in 1426 C.E.. Two generations later, in Fes and Cairo respectively, see Aḥmad al-Wansharīsī, *Īḍāḥ al-Masālik ilā Qawā*ᶜ*id al-Imām Mālik* (Tripoli: Kulliyat al-Daᶜwa, 1991), and Jalāl al-Dīn al-Suyūṭī, *al-Ashbāh wa*ᵓ*l-Naẓā*ᶜ*ir fī Qawā*ᶜ*id wa*ᵓ*l-Furū*ᶜ *Fiqh al-Shāfi*ᶜ*ī* (Beirut: Dār al-Kutub al-ᶜIlmiyya, 1998).

14. Zarruq, *Sharḥ Qawā*ᶜ*id al-*ᶜ*Iyāḍ* "Commentary on the Juridical Principles of Qāḍī ᶜIyāḍ." The mss. no longer exists, but is mentioned in Zarruq, *Sharḥ al-Naṣīḥa al-Kāfiya* (mss.), 1.

15. The uniqueness of Zarruq's approach is clear when compared to how his elder contemporary, Muḥammad ibn Sulaymān al-Jazūlī, used the same terms in his ᶜ*Aqīda*, without importing the conceptual framework of juridical reasoning or the genre of juridical principles. ᶜ*Aqīdat al-Jazūlī* (mss.), folios 12–18.

16. Zarruq, ᶜ*Uddat al-Murīd al-Ṣādiq* (1996), 36–37, cites Ibrāhīm ibn Mūsā al-Shāṭibī, *al-I*ᶜ*tisām* (1997), 1:217.

17. This study will not attempt a detailed reading of all the textual tangents and ramifications, which are wide and deep and certainly deserve a fuller treatment. Istrabadi, *The Principles of Sufism*, introduces the text to an English reading audience, although *Qawā*ᶜ*id al-Taṣawwuf* demands a full study rather than a direct translation. Throughout this study, the English translation of *Qawā*ᶜ*id* is the author's own, and diverges from that of Istrabadi in many instances.

18. Zarruq, *Qawā*ᶜ*id*, Principle 3.

19. Zarruq, *Qawā*ᶜ*id*, Principle 4.

20. Zarruq, *Qawā*ᶜ*id*, Principle 5. See the conclusion of this study for a further discussion of this hadith.

21. Zarruq, *Qawā*ᶜ*id*, Principle 4.

22. Zarruq, *Qawā*ᶜ*id*, Principle 6.

23. Zarruq, *Qawā*ᶜ*id*, Principle 10.

24. Zarruq, *Qawāʿid*, Principle 11. However, it is not suitable for certain kinds of people, who will ruin themselves and other Sufis if they try to engage the discipline. According to Zarruq, the following kinds of people are not suitable: one prejudiced by reason of ignorance, one who pretends to be knowledgeable, one who speaks rashly in disputation, a stupid common man, a reluctant seeker of truth, or a person determined to imitate blindly the great man known in only a cursory way.

25. Zarruq, *Qawāʿid*, Principle 13.

26. Zarruq, *Qawāʿid*, Principle 15.

27. Zarruq, *Qawāʿid*, Principle 18. He echoes the *Ḥikam* of Ibn ʿAṭāʾillah: "Your being on the lookout for the vices hidden within you is better than your being on the lookout for the invisible realities veiled from you."

28. Zarruq, *Qawāʿid*, Principle 19.

29. Zarruq, *Qawāʿid*, Principle 20.

30. Zarruq, *Qawāʿid*, Principle 24.

31. Zarruq, *Qawāʿid*, Principle 36.

32. Zarruq, *Qawāʿid*, Principle 37.

33. Zarruq, *Qawāʿid*, Principle 73. He quotes Shaykh al-Shādhilī: "A spiritual master should provide you training through what gives you ease, not through what burdens you."

34. Zarruq, *Qawāʿid*, Principle 74. This single "root source" is most explicitly described in Ibn ʿAṭāʾillah, *Kitāb al-Tanwīr;* see Kugle (trans.), *The Book of Illumination*, 52–79.

35. Zarruq, *Qawāʿid*, Principle 58.

36. Zarruq, *Takallum fī al-Taṣawwuf al-Tisāʿī* (mss.). Although this manuscript text is not explicitly ascribed to Zarruq, it is copied amid a series of his other works. In addition, Zarruq is known to have written a short work on this subject that Khushaim cites by the alternate title, *al-Kalām ʿalā Anwāʿ Ahl al-Khuṣūṣiya*. Khushaim was unable to trace this work, which is evidently the same as the manuscript source cited here. In Principle 59, Zarruq divides Sufis into nine types without referring to this more Qurʾānic textual precedent.

37. Zarruq, *Qawāʿid*, Principle 11. Zarruq paid tribute to al-Ghazālī by writing a commentary on his statement of doctrinal belief; see Zarruq, *Sharḥ ʿAqīdat al-Ghazālī* (mss.).

38. Zarruq, *Qawāʿid*, Principle 66.

39. Zarruq, *Qawāʿid*, Principle 89.

40. Zarruq, *Qawāʿid*, Principle 93.

41. Zarruq, *Qawāʿid*, Principle 100.

42. Zarruq, *Qawāʿid*, Principles 126–143.

43. Zarruq, *Qawāʿid*, Principle 104.

44. Zarruq, *Uṣūl al-Ṭarīqa,* has been translated into English by Hamza Yusuf, *The Foundations of Our Path* (1987), and partially by Khushaim, *Zarruq the Sufi*, 128–130. It has inspired recent reformist writings in Arabic, such as ʿAbdullah Ḥassan Zarruq, *Manhajiya li-Dirāsat al-Taṣawwuf* (1993). The author is a contemporary professor of philosophy and Islamic thought in Sudan. His book has been sponsored by the Tijānī branch of the Qādirī lineage in Sudan. His academic training has been in Britain as well as Sudan, and he reinvents Zarruq's approach in an attempt to "restore the fundamentals" to Sufi practice, which he sees as the crucial element in revivifying Islamic civilization, especially in the midst of the resurgence of politicized Islam in Sudan as elsewhere.

45. Muḥammad al-Kharrūbī, *al-Durra al-Sharīfa fī Sharḥ al-Waẓīfa* (mss. Rabat KhA 2201), 33.

46. Ibn Maryam, *al-Bustān*, 47, cites a commentary that Zarruq wrote on his *Uṣūl al-Ṭarīqa* entitled *Mazīl al-Lams ᶜan Adāb Asrār al-Qawāᶜid al-Khams* [*Remover of Confusion from the Right Conduct regarding the Secrets of the Five Principles*], but the location of this mss. is unknown. Zarruq also wrote a letter, *Ikhtiṣār baᶜḍ Maktubāt al-Shaykh Zarrūq* (mss.), in which he restates the basic foundational sources of his spiritual way.

47. Zarruq, *al-Uṣūl waʾl-Fuṣūl al-Badīᶜa waʾl-Mabānī al-Rafīᶜa* (mss.). This manuscript collection contains the above-mentioned texts as well as the *Waṣiya* of al-Ḥaḍramī and the *Waṣiya* of Zarruq, which constitutes parting advice to disciples on how to act. See also the independent text of Zarruq, *Waṣiya fī Kayfiyat al-Sulūk waʾl-Akhdh ᶜan al-Ṣūfiya* (mss.).

48. Zarruq, *Kitāb Iᶜānat al-Mutawajjih al-Miskīn*, was completed in Bijāya in 883 Hijri (1478–89 C.E.).

49. Zarruq, *Taʾsīs al-Qawāᶜid waʾl-Uṣūl li-Taḥṣīl al-Fawāʾid li-dhū al-Wuṣūl,* the alternate title by which this text can be found in most manuscript copies.

50. Zarruq, *Kitāb Iᶜānat,* 36.

51. Zarruq, *Kitāb Iᶜānat*, 37.

52. Zarruq, *Kitāb Iᶜānat*, 37.

53. Zarruq, *Kitāb Iᶜānat*, 37.

54. Zarruq, *Kitāb Iᶜānat*, 96. The pithy rhyming aphorism that heads this quote is "*al-tawba miftāḥ, al-taqwā barāḥ, al-istiqāma iṣlāḥ*."

55. Zarruq, *Kitāb Iᶜānat*, 103–104.

56. Zarruq, *Kitāb Iᶜānat*, 104.

57. Abū Zayd al-ᶜAyāshī, *al-Anwār al-Sanīyya ᶜalā al-Waẓīfa al-Zarrūqīyya* (n.d.), 266–267. He cites this story from Yaḥyā ibn al-Bijāʾī's introduction to his commentary on the *Waẓīfa*, who had related the story from one of the most prominent followers of Zarruq, named ᶜAbdullah al-Ḥittāb. The *Waẓīfa* inspired many commentaries; Muḥammad al-Kharrūbī wrote one, as did his follower, Aḥmad al-Sāsī, *al-Ṭiryāq al-Fārūq li-Qirāʾ Waẓīfat al-Shaykh Zarrūq* (mss.).

58. Marginal note from the *Waẓīfa* bound with Zarruq, *Sharḥ Ṣudūr al-Marātib* (mss.). Muḥammad Al-Kharrūbī says it was in a dream vision, but ᶜAbdullah al-Ḥittāb says it was in a waking vision. Khushaim, *Zarruq the Sufi*, 133, claims that Zarruq's *waẓīfa* was written via "a direct dictation from the Prophet himself to Ahmad Zarruq." However, in Zarruq's vision, the Prophet gave him only the title once Zarruq had finished the composition himself.

59. Such prayers upon the Prophet proliferated among the Shādhilī community. Ibn Mashīsh and his disciple, Abū al-Ḥasan al-Shādhilī, were both of sharifian genealogy and initiated a tradition of Shādhilī invocations of blessings upon the Prophet that were more ornate and complex than the minimal customary blessing. For an English translation of the blessings on the Prophet by al-Shādhilī, see Elmer Douglas (trans.), *The Mystical Teachings of al-Shādhilī* (1993), 153–154. For an English translation of the invocation of blessing on the Prophet by Ibn Mashīsh, see Renard, *Letters*, 35–36. For an early commentary on the prayer by Ibn Mashīsh, see Muḥammad al-Kharrūbī, *Sharḥ Taṣliyat al-Quṭb Ibn Mashīsh* (mss.).

60. One of Zarruq's contemporaries in Fes, ᶜAli al-Ṣanhājī, claimed that the spirit of the Prophet Muḥammad gave him spiritual training directly without human intermediary, as

a result of his intense and constant offering of blessings and praise upon the Prophet. This is detailed in chapter 8.

61. Zarruq, *al-Uṣūl waʾl-Fuṣūl*, 456.

62. Douglas, *Mystical Teachings*, 75; In addition, pages 56–78 include English translations of al-Shādhilī's litanies (*aḥzāb*).

63. Zarruq, *Sharḥ al-Ḥizb al-Kabīr* (mss.); *Sharḥ Ḥizb al-Barr* (mss.); *Sharḥ Mughammadāt Ḥizbay al-Shādhilī* (mss.).

64. Khushaim claims that Zarruq wrote a commentary on al-Jazūlī's litany, *Dalāʾil al-Khayrāt*. However there is no manuscript evidence of its existence, he does not mention it in his own texts, nor do his immediate followers include it in his list of compositions. The only reference to such a commentary is in Ḥassan al-Kūhin, *Ṭabaqāt al-Shādhilīyya al-Kubrā* (1928), 123, which is a very late, uncritical, and unreliable source.

65. Zarruq, *al-Kunnāsh*, folios 74–75. Al-Ḥaḍramī did not provide Zarruq with the form of this ritual. He adopted this method of initiation from another spiritual guide, Muḥammad al-Farāwakhī al-Zawāwī, whom he had met in Makka and Madīna during his first pilgrimage in 874 Hijri (1470 C.E.). The chain of legitimacy for this initiation ritual traces back to the famous saint al-Suhrawardī.

66. Zarruq, *Qawāᶜid*, Principle 165.

67. Zarruq, *Sulūk al-Ṭarīq,* contains his strongest assertion of the possibility of spiritual training without a master, or even a companion.

68. Zarruq, *Qawāᶜid*, Principle 59.

69. Zarruq gives detailed descriptions of each kind of person and their interest in Sufi practice, with conditions they must keep. For the common person, Principle 60. For jurists, Principle 67. For hadith scholars, Principle 68 (note that Abū Bakr ibn al-ᶜArabī is the jurist and Sufi, not the philosopher and Sufi Ibn al-ᶜArabī al-Ḥātimī). For those engaged in devotional exercises, Principle 69. For ascetics, Principle 70. For philosophers, Principle 71. For scientists of nature, Principle 72. For Uṣūlīs, Principle 73 that has been quoted above.

70. Zarruq, *Qawāᶜid*, Principle 207. Along with the writings of Ibn ᶜArabī al-Ḥātimī, Zarruq warns against "the writings of Ibn Sabᶜīn, Ibn al-Fāriḍ, Ibn Ḥalā, Ibn Dūskīn, ᶜAfīf al-Dīn al-Tilimsānī, al-Aykī al-ᶜAjamī, al-Aswad al-Aqṭaᶜ, Abū Isḥāq al-Tujibī, and al-Shushtarī. Likewise, one must be cautious of reading certain portions of al-Ghazālī's *Iḥyāʾ* for "they can lead one into peril." One must avoid al-Ghazālī's texts *al-Nafkh* and *al-Taswiya* which "must be withheld from those who are not sufficiently equipped to understand them properly," and also his *Miᶜrāj al-Sālikīn* and *al-Munqidh min al-Ḍalāl*. Passages of *Qūt al-Qulūb* by Abū Ṭālib al-Makkī "have been criticized by scholars."

71. Zarruq, *al-Kunnāsh*, 76.

72. Ibn ᶜArabī al-Ḥātimī, *al-Bulgha fī al-Ḥikma* (1949), 4–5; and Aḥmad al-Rifāᶜī, *Hādhihi Ḥikam al-Rifāᶜī* (1883).

73. For translations of the *Ḥikam* into French and English, see Paul Nwyia, *Ibn ᶜAtaʾ Allah et la naissance de la confrérie Shadilite* (1990), and Victor Danner, *The Book of Wisdom: Ibn ᶜAtaʾillah* (1978), respectively.

74. This hyperbolic compliment among Arabic speakers invites a comparison with the *Mathnavī-yi Maᶜānavī* of Rūmī, whose poetic couplets and parables Persian speakers consider to be "the Qurʾān in Persian." Thanks to Dr. Aḥmad Qasṭaṣ of the Butshīshīyya Sufi community for this comparison.

75. Ibn Zaghdān (Abū al-Mawāhib Jamāl al-Dīn Muḥammad) wrote several books, including *Qawānīn Ḥikam al-Ishrāq ilā kull al-Ṣūfiya yujmiᶜu al-Afāq* (1999), which has

been translated in Edward Jabra Jurji, *Illumination in Islamic Mysticism* (1983); and *Faraḥ al-Asmāʾ bi-Rukhṣ al-Samāʿ* (1985), *Qānūn fī ʿUlūm al-Tāʾifa*, and his unfinished commentary on the *Ḥikam*. His use of the term *Qānūn* (rule or regulation) parallels Zarruq's use of juridical terms to elucidate spiritual illumination and the *Ḥikam*. Al-Shaʿrānī, *al-Ṭabaqāt al-Kubrā*, 2:67, records that Ibn Zaghdān held initiation into the Shādhilī lineage through ʿAlī ibn Wafāʾ.

76. Zarruq, *Sharḥ al-Ḥikam al-ʿAṭāʾīyya* (mss.).

77. The two brothers Shams al-Dīn al-Laqānī and Nāṣir al-Dīn al-Laqānī came to Misurata from Egypt, while Muḥammad al-Kharrūbī and ʿAbdullah al-Ḥittāb joined Zarruq from Tarābulus. The man who brought Zarruq to Misurata from Egypt and enabled him to settle there was a follower of his named Karīm al-Dīn al-Barmūnī, as recorded in al-Barmūnī, *Tanqīḥ Rawḍat al-Azhār*, 257–258.

78. His two youngest sons died at an early age, while the two eldest moved from Misurata after Zarruq's death to settle in Quṣantinīya (Constantine) in Algeria.

79. Khushaim, *Zarruq the Sufi*, 110. There is no evidence for Khushaim's claim that Zarruq intended to found a *zāwiya* or a separate lineage called "al-Ṭarīqa Zarrūqīyya."

80. Zarruq, *Risāla ilā Fuqarāʾ al-Muntasabīn liʾl-Ṭarīqa al-Zarrūqīyya* (mss.), 14–15.

Part IV. Law (introduction)

1. Zarruq, *ʿUddat al-Murīd*, 130.

7. Principles

1. Zarruq, *al-Kunnāsh*, 67.

2. Ibn Khaldūn blamed this rupture on the tribes of pastoral Arabs, known collectively as the Banū Hillāl, who settled in the far Maghrib and disrupted earlier economic and political relationships. He did not record the increasing domination of European powers over trade, which contributed to the disruptive potential of the Arab tribes, for it weakened the centralized states and gave pastoralists the ability to wrest the countryside and caravan routes from state control. The overt role of Portugal and Spain in the internal changes of Morocco became clearer in Zarruq's lifetime than it was in Ibn Khaldun's, roughly one century earlier.

3. Al-Nāṣirī, *al-Istiqsaʾ*, 4:85, citing the introduction (*al-Muqaddima*) to Ibn Khaldūn's universal history of civilization, written in 776–780 Hijri (1375–79 C.E.).

4. *Encyclopedia of Islam*, new edition, s.v. "Ibn Khaldun," by M. Talbi.

5. Ibn ʿAskar, *Dawḥat al-Nāshir*, 49–50.

6. Zarruq, *al-Naṣīḥa al-Kāfiya*, 143–149.

7. Zarruq, *Qawāʿid al-Taṣawwuf*, Principle 89.

8. Zarruq, *Qawāʿid*, Principle 89.

9. Zarruq, *Qawāʿid*, Principle 89.

10. Zarruq, *Qawāʿid*, Principle 104.

11. Zarruq, *Risāla ilā Fuqarāʾ al-Muntasibīn* (mss.), 14–15.

12. Zarruq, *ʿUddat al-Murīd*, 149.

13. Zarruq, *al-Jāmiʿ li-Jumal min al-Fawāʾid waʾl-Manāfiʿ* (mss. Rabat: KhA 2207d), 101.

14. Al-Timbuktī, *Nayl al-Ibtihāj*, 72, was the first to record that this title was applied to Zarruq. Guennoun, *Mashāhir Rijāl,* 13, claims that Zarruq is uniquely qualified for it.

15. Weston Cook, *The Hundred Years War for Morocco* (1994), 98.

16. Al-Nāṣirī, *al-Istiṣqā*ʾ, 4:117.

17. "Being at peace" (*salmā*) is a woman's name, but also refers to a state of resignation. Al-Ḥaḍramī plays on the conventions of love poetry, where the male lover must resign himself to the capricious demands of his desired woman. But the woman here is a spiritual state of peace, which demands ever-renewed resignation. Zarruq reports that he understood "being at peace" to mean the *sharīᶜa*, the outer structure of legal norms derived from what God gave in revelation.

18. Ibn Ghāzī, *Fihris,* 126–127, preserves the text of one such letter from 885 Hijri (1480–81 C.E.). Through the mediation of Zarruq, these certificates were granted to Aḥmad ibn Ghāzī, to his father (Mufti of Fes and preacher at Qarawiyyīn Mosque), to the famous jurist Aḥmad al-Wansharīsī, and to Muḥammad al-Maṣmūdī (the *Qāḍī al-Jamāᶜa* or chief judge of Fes).

19. Zarruq gave this work the full title *ᶜUddat al-Murīd al-Ṣādiq min Asbāb al-Maqt fi Bayān al-Ṭarīq wa Dhikr Ḥawādith al-Waqt* and completed its composition in Bijāya in 886 Hijri (1481–82 C.E.).

20. Zarruq, *Qawāᶜid*, Principle 128, had earlier ventured a similar definition of *bidᶜa* with a more condensed treatment of the subject.

21. Zarruq, *Risālat al-Radd* (mss.), folios 94–104. English translations of passages from this work are provided by Khushaim, *Zarruq the Sufi*, 191, and Cornell, *Realm of the Saint,* 335 and 381.

22. Two copies of this text exist in Tunis under slightly different titles. The first, *Bidᶜ al-Taṣṣawuf* (mss. Tunis: KhZ 19017), is a rougher draft, and the second, *Risāla Radd alā Ahl al-Bidᶜa* (mss. Tunis: KhZ 8631), is more polished.

23. Zarruq, *al-Nasḥ al-Anfaᶜ waʾl-Janna li-man iᶜtaṣama min al-Bidᶜ biʾl-Sunna* (mss.).

24. Ibn Khaldūn, *Shifāʾ al-Sāʾil wa Tahdhīb al-Masāʾil* (1996), offers an assessment of various opinions on Sufis from the perspective of critics affiliated with the scriptural and rational sciences.

25. Zarruq, *ᶜUddat al-Murīd*, 28.

26. This interpretation is in accord with the Khalīfa ᶜUmar al-Khattāb's statement about the *Tarāwih* prayers (which were not made mandatory by the Prophet): "What a good religious innovation (*bidᶜa*) this is!" He called these prayers "*bidᶜa*" even though they were established by the Prophet's example, because they were not made obligatory, and ᶜUmar meant to encourage them without claiming that they were an obligatory part of religion as practiced by the Prophet.

27. Kamalī, *Principles of Islamic Jurisprudence* (2000), provides full details of these five basic categories of juridical ruling that make up the *sharīᶜa.*

28. Other simpler examples of acts that are technically *bidᶜa* but are widely accepted by Muslims as positive religious acts include shaking hands after communal prayers, the celebration of the Prophet's birthday (*mawlid al-nabī*), and study of books of hadith reports.

29. Zarruq, *ᶜUddat al-Murīd*, 29.

30. Zarruq, *ᶜUddat al-Murīd*, 29.

31. Zarruq, *ᶜUddat al-Murīd*, 30–31.

32. Zarruq, *ᶜUddat al-Murīd*, 32.

33. Zarruq, *ᶜUddat al-Murīd*, 33.

34. Zarruq, *ᶜUddat al-Murīd*, 33.

35. Zarruq, *ᶜUddat al-Murīd*, 34, quotes the *Ḥikam* of Ibn ᶜAṭāʾillah: "You should not fear that the spiritual path will be ambiguous for you, you should only fear that your own dark desires will make it ambiguous for you."

36. Zarruq, *ᶜUddat al-Murīd*, 34–35.

37. Zarruq, *Qawāᶜid*, Principle 16.

38. Zarruq, *Qawāᶜid*, Principle 16. He quotes the early Sufi Sahl al-Tushtarī: "If after two hundred years, there is anybody left who believes in what we teach, let him hide it."

39. Zarruq, *ᶜUddat al-Murīd*, 58. He notes an oral teaching of al-Ḥaḍramī: "Since a sincere disciple is so hard to find between the furthest eastern lands and the furthest western lands, how can one expect to find a sincere saint?"

40. Zarruq, *ᶜUddat al-Murīd*, 41. Zarruq's reform project aimed to return to this earlier practice, as he advised that Sufi training must only consist of benefiting from the master's teaching and company which conferred his high-minded aspiration and spiritual state to others (*al-istifāda bi-himma wa ḥāl*).

41. Zarruq, *ᶜUddat al-Murīd*, 42.

42. Zarruq, *ᶜUddat al-Murīd*, 58.

43. This echoes the theory, stated most clearly in Schimmel, *Mystical Dimensions in Islam,* that the Sufi lineages took on institutional form and mass social function in response to the breakdown of the *khilāfat*, especially during the invasion of the Mongols and the sack of the Khalifal capital at Baghdad.

44. Zarruq, *Risālat al-Radd* (mss.), folio 1–2.

45. Zarruq, *ᶜUddat al-Murīd*, 34.

46. Zarruq, *ᶜUddat al-Murīd*, 54.

47. al-Ṣumāᶜī, *Kitāb al-Muᶜzā*, 273, confirms that this occurred in the year 870 Hijri (1465–66 C.E.) on the basis of Zarruq's account. However this event, like all the events Zarruq records in relation to the revolution in Fes, seems to have been postdated by one year. Al-Jazūlī died in 869 Hijri (1465 C.E.), a month after the revolution occurred in Fes.

48. Zarruq, *al-Kunnāsh*, 66, and reproduced in al-Mahdi al-Fāsī, *Mumtiᶜ al-Asmāʾ*, 28. The text of *al-Kunnāsh* actually reads "al-Ṣughayyir al-Ṣufyānī" which was another nickname of al-Sahlī. However, this person should not be confused with a later Jazūlī saint named al-Ṣufyānī, who was a follower of ᶜAbd al-ᶜAzīz al-Tabbāᶜ.

49. Zarruq, *Qawāᶜid*, Principle 52.

50. Zarruq, *Qawāᶜid*, Principle 52. To prove his point, al-Qūrī recited from the Qurʾān (al-Aḥzāb 33:30) warning the wives of the Prophet that the consequences of their misdeeds were of greater consequence than those of normal women. Further, he quoted a saying of the Prophet, when the latter admonished his uncle, saying "O ᶜAbbās, uncle of the Messenger of God, I shall be of no use to you when you stand before God—beg recompense from God for your soul!"

51. Zarruq, *Qawāᶜid*, Principle 53.

52. Zarruq, *Qawāᶜid*, Principle 53. To prove his point, Zarruq invokes the example of ᶜAbd al-Qādir al-Jīlānī who achieved sainthood by his piety and knowledge: his genealogical descent from the Prophet supported his acquisition of these virtues but was not the foundation or necessary condition for their acquisition. "ᶜAbd al-Qādir al-Jīlānī united in himself such loftiness of ancestry and nobleness of religious observance and knowledge as no one else in his time could do."

53. ᶜAbd al-Ḥafīẓ Ṭāhir al-Fāsī, *al-Tarjumān al-Mughrib*, 35.

54. Cornell, *Realm of the Saint*, 314–315, explains this misinterpretation through Jack Goody's research on the importance of semi-literate or formerly illiterate people in the transition from an "oral society" to a literate one.

55. Al-Nāṣirī, *al-Istiṣqāʾ*, 4:122–123.

56. Cornell, *Realm of the Saint*, 314–317.

57. al-Jazūlī, *Risāla ilā ᶜUlamāʾ al-Ẓāhir* (mss.).

58. Zarruq may have read this letter or al-Jazūlī's statement on doctrinal belief, *ᶜAqīdat al-Jazūlī* (mss.), but he never mentions any of al-Jazūlī's writings, in general or specific.

59. Zarruq, *ᶜUddat al-Murīd*, 116.

60. Zarruq, *al-Kunnāsh*, 66. In later chronicles, this conversation of Zarruq had been projected back in time and attributed to al-Jazūlī to acquit the saint of any pretensions of having been the Mahdi. Zarruq's argument with al-Ṣughayyir al-Sahlī is recast as a conversation between al-Jazūlī and al-Tabbāᶜ in order to read like this: On the night he was killed, some of his followers including al-Tabbāᶜ came to al-Jazūlī, asking him about he rumors that were being spread about his being the *Fāṭimī*. He replied, "They are only spreading rumors that will get them killed . . ." See Al-Nāṣirī, *al-Istiṣqāʾ*, 4:122–123.

61. "*Al-Fāṭimī*" refers to a person descended from Fāṭima Zahrā, the Prophet Muḥammad's daughter. Hadith reports contradict each other as to whether the Mahdi will be from the lineage of Ḥusayn or Ḥasan, the two sons of *Fāṭima*; so the term "*al-Fāṭimī*" is a compromise that avoids contentious arguments about the Mahdi's specific lineage. For a textual example of this equation of the *Fāṭimī* with the Mahdī, see Ibn Abī Maḥallī, *Mihrās Ruʾūs al-Jahla al-Mubtadiᶜa wa Madrās Nufūs al-Safla al-Munkhadiᶜa* (mss.), 1–11. For a general discussion of the traditions of the Mahdi's advent and a skeptical assessment of them, see Ibn Khaldūn, *The Muqaddima* (1967), 2:156–186.

62. Cornell, *Realm of the Saint,* 335, claims that Zarruq criticized al-Mughīṭī for creating this mass movement, rather than al-Jazūlī himself; however the sources of Zarruq portray him as equivocal on this issue.

63. Cornell, *Realm of the Saint,* 385. ᶜAbd al-ᶜAzīz al-Tabbāᶜ and other senior representatives of al-Jazūlī went into hiding at this time as well.

64. When this movement first took power, it was known as "the Sharifan Dynasty" (*dawlat al-shurafāʾ*). It became known popularly as "the Saᶜdian Dynasty" as it waned and was challenged by yet another sharifian family, the ᶜAlawī dynasty.

65. Al-Nāṣirī, *al-Istiṣqāʾ,* 4:122, uses the term *thawra* to mean "a political revolution." His usage is echoed by Cook, *Hundred Years War,* 112, in contrast to the more modest "uprising" of Cornell, *Realm of the Saint,* 314. The Arabic term is ambiguous and open to interpretation.

66. Cook, *Hundred Years War,* 110.

67. al-Ṣumāᶜī, *Kitāb al-Muᶜzā*, 273 cites Zarruq, *al-Kunnāsh*, 66. The verb *irtafaᶜa* (to be no longer valid) is crucial in this accusation, as it marks al-Mughīṭī's perception of a new spiritual dispensation in which the customs of Islam as articulated by jurists was no longer valid.

68. Zarruq, *al-Kunnāsh*, 87–88, and reproduced in Cornell, *Realm of the Saint,* 315.

69. al-Ṣumāᶜī, *Kitāb al-Muᶜzā*, 273 and Zarruq, *Risālat al-Radd* (mss.), folio 23.

70. Zarruq, *Risālat al-Radd*, folio 23.

71. al-Ṣumāᶜī, *Kitāb al-Muᶜzā*, 273.

72. This is true even though, as Cornell points out, these other followers were at loggerheads with al-Mughīṭī and had to stay undercover to avoid al-Mughīṭī's appropriation of al-Jazūlī's heritage (just as he appropriated al-Jazūlī's corpse).

73. al-Ṣumāᶜī, *Kitāb al-Muᶜzā*, 273.

8. Critique

1. He settled at a site called Khandaq al-Zaytūn in the region of Ahyayna.

2. Cornell, *Realm of the Saint,* 385. For their biographies, see al-Mahdī al-Fāsī, *Mumtiᶜ al-Asmāʾ*, 53–55.

3. Al-Mahdī al-Fāsī, *Mumtiᶜ al-Asmāʾ*, 72.

4. Cornell, *Realm of the Saint,* 392. Al-Ghazwānī's biography is also found in Ibn ᶜAskar, *Dawḥat al-Nāshir*, 96–99, and is treated in more detail in Vincent Cornell, "Mystical Doctrine and Political Action in Moroccan Sufism" (1992).

5. Cornell, *Realm of the Saint*, 394.

6. Zarruq, *ᶜUddat al-Murīd*, 63.

7. Zarruq, *ᶜUddat al-Murīd*, 63.

8. Zarruq, *ᶜUddat al-Murīd*, 63. Accusations of not following a discrete legal method (*madhhab*) is a cipher for following a Mahdī figure, who overshadows the jurists who had built legal methods and whose living guidance in effect eclipses the need for strictly following a legal method. On the followers of al-Tabbāᶜ not following a particular legal method, see Cornell, *Realm of the Saint*, 426. Similarly, the accusation of "being of the Shiᶜa" is a juridical interpretation of believing in a personified Mahdī. Accusations of the practice of various kinds of sorcery and divination were common at this time, as Ibn Khaldūn noted with dismay that the distinction "between sorcery and Sufism was blurring" in his era, as some Sufis developed a reputation for occult sciences and *sīmīyā* (theurgy of all kinds); see Katz, *Dreams, Sufism, and Sainthood*, 113.

9. These extreme jurists denounce without analyzing, opines Zarruq. They do not carefully sift out what is *bidᶜa* from what is authentic in Sufi practice, precisely because they have no experience in Sufi practice and no intimate knowledge of the tradition. Their denunciations are just as dangerous as the questionable practices of the socially activist Sufis they denounce.

10. Zarruq, *ᶜUddat al-Murīd*, 69.

11. The subtle difference was that the Shiᶜa projected that the Prophet's authority continued and extended through his bloodline. The Jazūlīyya held that the *shurafāʾ* at crucial points embodied this authority as axial saints (since al-Shādhilī was a descendant of the Prophet, as was al-Jazūlī) while its continuation was more predominantly spiritual, not genealogical.

12. Vincent Cornell, "Sovereignty of the Imāmate of the Jazuliyya-Ghazwniyya: a Sufi alternative to Sharifism?" *al-Qantara* 17 (1996), 440–441, quotes ᶜAlī Ṣāliḥ al-Andalusī's commentary on al-Jazūlī, *Sharḥ Rahbat al-Amān*.

13. Cornell, *Realm of the Saint*, 360–364.

14. Zarruq, *ᶜUddat al-Murīd*, 79, notes that this is the core of their "overweening partisanship" and lists ten scriptural and rational "facts" that disprove their claims to exclusive and absolute spiritual pre-eminence.

15. al-Ṣumāᶜī, *Kitāb al-Muᶜzā*, 219. This miraculous "learning" occurred at the tomb of Abū Yiᶜzza, who was also a saint famous for being an "illiterate" mountain Berber. Yet he

could distinguish Qur'ānic verses from other Arabic writing from the light that radiated from it in his perception.

16. Zarruq, *ᶜUddat al-Murīd*, 115. See Cornell, *Realm of the Saint,* 115–121, on the *ṭarīqa* built by the Maṣmūda Berbers. al-Mahdī al-Fāsī, *Mumtiᶜ al-Asmā'*, 31–36. provides a wide range of juridical opinions on the permissibility of shaving the head as a sign of repentance and initiation. Zarruq's disciple and successor, Muḥammad al-Kharrūbī, continued to critique the practice.

17. Zarruq, *ᶜUddat al-Murīd*, 100.

18. Zarruq, *ᶜUddat al-Murīd*, 97.

19. Cook, *Hundred Years War*, 169.

20. Zarruq, *ᶜUddat al-Murīd*, 101.

21. Zarruq, *ᶜUddat al-Murīd*, 101.

22. Zarruq, *ᶜUddat al-Murīd*, 103.

23. Zarruq, *ᶜUddat al-Murīd*, 78.

24. Zarruq, *ᶜUddat al-Murīd*, 78.

25. Zarruq, *ᶜUddat al-Murīd*, 76.

26. Zarruq, *ᶜUddat al-Murīd*, 78.

27. Zarruq, *ᶜUddat al-Murīd*, 119.

28. Zarruq, *ᶜUddat al-Murīd*, 124.

29. Ibn Tumart did not appeal to a new Prophet or new revelation. Rather in this movement, the figure of the Mahdī served to elevate the new ruler as a figure of radical justice, above the Maliki jurists, who were former claimants to religious legitimacy, and the al-Murābiṭ [Sp. Almoravid] dynasty that claimed suzerainty based on their support of the jurists.

30. Cornell, *Realm of the Saint*, 344–351.

31. Muḥammad Ḥajjī, *al-Ḥaraka al-Fikrīyya bi'l-Maghrib* (1976), 42–43. The key Jazūlīyya leaders in the Sūs were ᶜAbdullah ibn ᶜUmar al-Madaghrī and Barakat ibn Muḥammad al-Tidasī. These disciples of al-Jazūlī were already involved in organizing military resistance to the Portuguese economic and military penetration of the Sūs valley from their coastal forts around Agadir.

32. For instance, the first *khalīfa* of the Shiᶜī Fatimid dynasty took the title al-Mahdī, "The One Guided by God," while his son and successor took the rhyming title, "The One who Stands with the Command of God." These Ismaᶜīlī Shiᶜī rulers had intimate ties to the *shurafāᶜ* in northern Morocco and the southern oasis region of Tafilalt. Al-Mahdī had sought refuge in Sijilmasa before he set up his rule further east, and later from Egypt and the central Maghrib he tried to militarily incorporate Morocco into the Fatimid kingdom. The Saᶜdian movement repeated this pattern with slight variations.

33. Cook, *Hundred Years War,* 175–76, cites Muṣṭafā al-Jannābī, *al-Baḥr al-Zakhkhār wa'l-Aylām al-Tiyyār.*

34. Dahiru Yayha, *Morocco in the Sixteenth Century* (1981), 158–161.

35. His body had been buried there since 890 Hijri (1485 C.E.), when al-Mughīṭī died and his movement dissipated.

36. Zarruq, *Qawāᶜid al-Taṣawwuf*, Principle 145.

37. Zarruq, *ᶜUddat al-Murīd*, 165. Zarruq claims that Moroccans are like walnuts: hard on the outside but good on the inside. Still, he opines that most people in Morocco have "vicious manners and are stingy."

38. Ibn ᶜAskar, *Dawḥat al-Nāshir*, 49–50 and 21.

39. Zarruq, *ᶜUddat al-Murīd*, 187.

40. Qurᵓān, *Sūrat al-Ḥujarāt*, 49:12.

41. Zarruq, *Qawāᶜid,* Principle 104.

42. al-Kattānī, *Salwat al-Anfās*, 3:249 and Ibn al-Qāḍī, *Jadhwat al-Iqtibās*, 133. Aḥmad ibn al-Ḥabbāk came from the "Ibn al-Ḥabbāk" family of religious scholars of Fes.

43. His students included Riḍwān al-Januwī, ᶜAbd al-Wārith al-Yalsūtī (who were both disciples of al-Ghazwānī), and Abū al-Qāsim ibn Khajju (who was a friend of al-Habṭī). Once ᶜAlī Ṣāliḥ al-Andalusī had established a zawiya in Fes, young aspirants in the Jazūlīyya community established intimate ties to local scholars and jurists, who may have acted not just as their teachers and professors, but also as their protectors and patrons. In the case of Aḥmad ibn al-Ḥabbāk, these ties to the Jazūlīyya community eventually became so strong and overt that he attracted the suspicion of the Waṭṭāsid rulers: Sultan Aḥmad al-Waṭṭāsī ordered him to be poisoned in 938 Hijri (1531–32 C.E.), after the sultan returned from a campaign against the rising Saᶜdian movement.

44. Zarruq, *Qawāᶜid al-Taṣawwuf,* conclusion.

45. Aḥmad al-Ḥaḍramī, *Risāla ilā baᶜḍ Aṣḥābihi* (mss.).

46. Ibn ᶜAskar, *Dawḥat al-Nāshir*, 48–49.

47. Ibn ᶜAskar, *Dawḥat al-Nāshir*, 49.

48. Ibn ᶜAjība wrote commentaries on the *Ḥikam*, on *al-Mabāhith al-Aṣlīyya* (which have been published), and on al-Shushtarī's *al-Qaṣīda al-Nūnīyya*, all of which had been previously addressed by Zarruq's writings. In addition, he wrote a commentary directly on Zarruq's *al-Waẓīfa*.

49. Guennoun, *Mashāhir Rijāl*, 14–15.

50. Guennoun, *Mashāhir Rijāl,* 15.

51. Guennoun, *Mashāhir Rijāl,* 15.

52. Ibn ᶜAjība refers to al-Ḥaḍramī's works on existential philosophy, such as *Ṣudūr al-Marātib* (mss.). He does not acknowledge that Zarruq wrote commentaries on at least two of these texts; he may not have known of the existence of these commentaries.

53. Guennoun, *Mashāhir Rijāl,* 18, comments that if Ibn ᶜAjība had not concluded his assertions with "only God knows best" then his comments would have been a damning accusation against Ibn ᶜAjība himself in his dismissal of any meaningful role for the scholars and jurists.

54. Guennoun, *Mashāhir Rijāl,* 15.

55. Ibn ᶜAskar, *Dawḥat al-Nāshir*, 50–51.

56. Th. Emil Homerin, *From Arab Poet to Muslim Saint: Ibn Farid* (1994), introduction.

57. Zarruq, *Qawāᶜid*, Principle 134, mentions al-Shushtarī as a poet, while Principle 137 discusses the practice of writing lyric poetry as expressions of divine beauty. Zarruq repeatedly tries to excuse al-Shushtarī or minimize his poetic licenses, even in the stern presentation of his principles.

58. Zarruq, *Sharḥ al-Qaṣīda al-Nūnīyya liᵓl-Shushtarī* (mss.), folios 39–64.

59. Zarruq quotes Ibn Layūn's commentary on a text of al-Shushtarī, entitled *al-Ināla al-ᶜIlmīyya min al-Risāla al-ᶜAmalīyya fi Intiṣār liᵓl-Ṭāᵓifa al-Ṣūfīyya.* Ibn Layūn began this commentary with a biographical summary of al-Shushtarī's life. In addition to his poetry (in the form of *qaṣīda*, *zajal*, and *muqaṭṭaᶜāt*), al-Shushtarī wrote prose texts such as *al-Risāla al-ᶜAmalīyyah*, *al-ᶜUrwā al-Wuthqā*, and *al-Maqālīd al-Wujūdīyya*. Al-Shushtarī died in 668 Hijri (1269 C.E.) in the Egyptian town of al-Ṭīna, about eighteen miles from Dimyāt (Damietta), where he is buried.

60. Zarruq, *Sharḥ al-Qaṣīda al-Nūnīyya*, 41, cites al-Qūrī's teaching that "[t]o believe in someone is protection, but to critique someone is almost a crime. So if you know something to be right, follow it; if you do not know if something is right, then equivocate and let it be."

61. Zarruq attracted some of his former colleagues in the circle of al-Zaytūnī; some who had first taken initiation from al-Zaytūnī subsequently took a second initiation from Zarruq. This pattern suggests that al-Zaytūnī was no longer alive at the time, though it is unclear when he passed away. Ibn ᶜAskar, *Dawḥat al-Nāshir*, reports that al-Zaytūnī died in the 920s Hijri. However, he is inaccurate with death dates in general; he has a penchant for post-dating deaths to include famous persons in his chosen subject (saints of the "tenth century") even though they lived in the ninth century and died toward its end. There is no corroborative evidence to date al-Zaytūnī's death. Yet it is hard to imagine al-Zaytūnī's followers defecting to take a second initiation from Zarruq if the "Blind Viper" were still living. The two primary examples of this are Muḥammad al-Kharrūbī and Aḥmad al-Milyānī. Like most Moroccan Sufis who took allegiance to Zarruq, Aḥmad al-Milyānī valued him for the initiatory lineage he could provide. However, he shows no sign of having absorbed Zarruq's reformist teachings. Al-Kharrūbī was an exception to the general pattern.

62. al-Kattānī, *Salwat al-Anfās*, 2:221.

63. Zarruq, *ᶜUddat al-Murīd*, 48.

64. Zarruq, *ᶜUddat al-Murīd*, 132–133.

65. Zarruq, *Qawāᶜid*, Principle 158. Zarruq discusses the *majdhūb* and the *malāmatī* in Principles 157–161.

66. Zarruq, *Mimmā Kutiba bihi al-Shaykh Zarruq li-baᶜḍ Aṣḥābihi Naṣḥan* (mss.). This letter was written as "parting advice" to be spread among his companions and disciples in Morocco.

67. al-Fāsī, *Mirʾāt al-Maḥāsin*, 190–191.

68. Ibn ᶜAskar, *Dawḥat al-Nāshir*, 81, was the first source to record ᶜAlī al-Ṣanhājī's biography; it was subsequently expanded in al-Mahdī al-Fāsī, *Mumtiᶜ al-Asmāʾ*, 131–135, al-Sharrāṭ, *al-Rawḍ al-ᶜĀṭir al-Anfās*, 73–85, and al-Kattānī, *Salwat al-Anfās*, 2:219–221. His full name is ᶜAlī ibn Aḥmad al-Ṣanhājī, and he died at approximately 947 Hijri (1540–41 C.E.), and is buried outside Bāb Futūḥ in Fes.

69. Berbers (whether Maṣmūda or Ṣanhāja) had long since settled in Fes; however they would not be known by their tribal name if they were settled urbanites, as the example of Zarruq himself reveals. Al-Kattānī, *Salwat al-Anfās*, 2:220, claims that ᶜAlī al-Ṣanhājī was born in a place known as Ṣanhājat al-Ḥajar, left there when he was young, and after some years of wandering arrived at Fes.

70. He also was in the habit of revolving in a tight circle, in a sort of mad dance reminiscent of Jalāl al-Dīn Rūmī's whirling.

71. Al-Sharrāṭ, *al-Rawḍ al-ᶜĀṭir al-Anfās*, 76.

72. Ewing, *Arguing Sainthood*, 201–230, is especially attentive to how Qalandars, both men and women, assault conventional standards of gendered behavior which structure not just religiosity, but even normality.

73. He frequented the marketplace at ᶜAyn al-ᶜAlūn (near the Sharablīyyīn neighborhood of Fes), which is still a market for olive oil.

74. Cornell, *Realm of the Saint*, 80–92, and Ibn al-Zayyāt, *Kitāb al-Tashawwuf ilā Rijāl al-Taṣawwuf* (1984), 451–477.

75. Al-Sharrāṭ, *al-Rawḍ al-ᶜĀṭir al-Anfās*, 77.

76. Al-Mahdī al-Fāsī, *Mumtiᶜ al-Asmāʾ*, 133.

77. Al-Mahdī al-Fāsī, *Mumtiᶜ al-Asmāʾ*, 133.

78. Al-Sharrāṭ, *al-Rawḍ al-ᶜĀtir al-Anfās*, 77–79, notes that ᶜAlī al-Ṣanhājī wrote a text on the secret meaning of the letters of the alphabet, in which he provided a Sufi maxim describing the secret spiritual power of each letter. Along with his reputation for knowing the secrets of letters, he had a reputation for commanding "the beings of the unseen world" to do his bidding, in ways similar to al-Zaytūnī. In Zarruq's critique of occult practices, he notes that these two practices often went hand in hand.

79. Al-Sharrāṭ, *al-Rawḍ al-ᶜĀṭir al-Anfās*, 76. For an analysis of his relationship with one woman who became a *majdhūba* in her own right, see Kugle, *Sufis and Saints' Bodies: Mysticism, Corporeality and Sacred Power in Islam* (Chapel Hill: University of North Carolina Press, forthcoming 2007).

80. al-Qādirī, *al-Ṭurfa*, 101, reports that he is buried at a place called "Nararwalat" in the Sūs region of southern Morocco.

81. Al-Mahdī al-Fāsī, *Mumtiᶜ al-Asmāʾ*, 131. Other circumstantial evidence supported the proposition, for al-Zaytūnī became affiliated with the Jazūlīyya leader in Fes, ᶜAli Ṣāliḥ al-Andalusī. *Mumtiᶜ al-Asmāʾ*, 78, claims that al-Zaytūnī was a friend and companion of al-Ṣāliḥ al-Andalusī and that the two are buried together in the same graveyard. From this friendship, the author concludes that al-Andalusī was the spiritual master of al-Zaytūnī, implying that Zarruq was his disciple as well. This conclusion is not supported by any evidence; Zarruq had left Fes and the community of al-Zaytūnī before ᶜAlī Ṣāliḥ al-Andalusī ever set up a Jazūlīyya zawiya in Fes, for which see *Mumtiᶜ al-Asmāʾ*, 131.

82. Cook, *Hundred Years War,* 175. Saᶜdian economic policy focused on forcing local leaders and towns to offer them tribute through "charity and coercion" in order to siphon off tribute formerly collected by the Portuguese. They also strove to open the trans-Saharan trade routes into West Africa, to keep the circulation of gold in their control and away from Portuguese control along the coastlines.

83. Cook, *Hundred Years War,* 83. This was the same year Muḥammad al-Shaykh al-Waṭṭāsī took back Fes, crushing the Fesi revolution's early experiment with sharifian rule and provoking the Saᶜdian movement in the south.

84. Sanjay Subrahmanyam, *The Career and Legend of Vasco da Gama* (Delhi: Foundation Books, Cambridge University Press, 1997), 205–206. Vasco da Gama captured the Muslim vessel "the Miri" in 1502 C.E. that was returning to India from the *ḥajj*. He looted the vessel, massacred all the pilgrims including women and young people, and burned the ship; only seventeen children were spared. They were taken on the Portuguese vessels and forced to convert to Catholicism.

85. Salih Özbaran, *Ottoman Response to Portuguese Expansion* (1994), and Subrahmanyam, *Career and Legend*, 249 and 266.

86. In the battle of Bu ᶜAqba (also known as Wādī al-ᶜAbīd) in 1536 C.E. the Saᶜdians defeated the Waṭṭāsids and besieged Fes, driving the Waṭṭāsids into a formal treaty with the Portuguese in 1538 C.E..

87. Al-Mahdī al-Fāsī, *Mumtiᶜ al-Asmāʾ*, 130.

88. Al-Sharrāṭ, *al-Rawḍ al-ᶜĀṭir al-Anfās,* 87; see also Kugle, *Sufis and Saints' Bodies.*

89. Al-Mahdī al-Fāsī, *Mumtiᶜ al-Asmāʾ*, 129, claims that his full name was Aḥmad ibn Ḥussayn al-ᶜAbdī al-Sahlī, while Ibn ᶜAskar, *Dawḥat al-Nāshir,* 79–81 maintains that it was Muḥammad. He is buried outside of Meknes.

90. Cornell, *Realm of the Saint,* 173–176, has explained the logic behind this behavior that seems like gambling with destiny, in reference to famous Abū al-ᶜAbbās al-Sabtī, a patron saint of Marrakesh.

91. Ibn ᶜAskar, *Dawḥat al-Nāshir,* 76, and al-Mahdī al-Fāsī, *Mumtiᶜ al-Asmāʾ*, 80. Ibn ᶜIsa al-Fahdī was a disciple of Abū al-ᶜAbbās al-Ḥārithī in the Jazūlīyya community.

92. Al-Mahdī al-Fāsī, *Mumtiᶜ al-Asmāʾ*, 135.

93. Al-Mahdī al-Fāsī, *Mumtiᶜ al-Asmāʾ*, 130–133, and Ibn ᶜAskar, *Dawḥat al-Nāshir,* 80. He reportedly went to Qaṣr Kutāma, a city whose rulers, the Banū ᶜArūs, were from a sharifian family but were wavering between loyalty to the Waṭṭāsid regime and independence for themselves. Abū Rawāyin climbed the minaret of the central mosque and commanded the ruler of Qaṣr Kutāma to "buy your power from me or you'll be removed from your rule within a year," coercing them to break away from the Waṭṭāsid camp and leaving the tottering regime with one less ally just as Saᶜdian forces were pushing north to conquer Fes.

94. al-Fāsī, *Mirʾāt al-Maḥāsin,* 36. Abū al-Maḥāsin ibn Yūsuf al-Fāsī came from a successful merchant family from Fes that took the name al-Fāsī as they moved to Qaṣr Kabīr to pursue business interests; when he moved back to Fes his trading business thrived under the care of his extended family, and he founded a zawiya. *Mirʾāt al-Maḥāsin,* 190, provides a full discussion on the initiations and multiple lineages of ᶜAbd al-Raḥmān al-Majdhūb.

V. Legacy (introduction)

1. Zarruq, *Qawāᶜid*, Principle 89.

2. Pandolfo, *Impasse of the Angels*, 10, 183, and 196. She quotes Si Lḥassan, a Qurʾanic scholar, therapist, and dream interpreter from the southern Moroccan region of the Draᶜ River valley.

3. al-Qādirī, *al-Ṭurfa* (mss.), 101, marginal note.

9. Conclusion

1. Kugle, "Usuli Sufis: Ahmad Zarruq and his Followers in South Asia" in Eric Geoffroy, *La Voie Soufie des Shadhilis.* (Paris: Maissoneuve & Larose, 2005).

2. Geertz, *Islam Observed*, 3. Bruce Lawrence, *Defenders of God* (1989), argues cogently that religious ideology is the conceptual tool we need to understand "fundamentalist" movements, even though throughout the modernization of the eighteenth and nineteenth centuries in Europe and America, ideology was defined as the antithesis of religion.

3. The architect of this movement was the theologian Ibn ᶜAbd al-Wahhāb, and the movement was brought to power by his political ally, Ibn Saᶜūd, whose descendants continue to rule in Saᶜudi Arabia. See J. Zdanowski, "On Reconstructing the History of Wahhābī Arabia" (1995), and Michael Cook "On the Origins of Wahhābīsm" (1992), 191–202.

4. "Wahhābī" describes a distinct political movement driven by reformist theology that took power in Arabia, establishing the basis for the Saᶜudi state since the 1930s. "Salafī" describes a range of other movements outside of Arabia, the theology and ideology of which share many points in common with Wahhābīs. The late twentieth century has witnessed a convergence between the narrowly parochial Wahhābī movement and broadly international Salafī movements. This convergence is fueled by the oil wealth of Arabian Gulf states. Modern scholarship, beginning with British colonial historians, has often wrongly labeled international movements as "Wahhābī." Distinct movements in Bengal, northern India and Punjab, Indonesia, and West Africa have all been subsumed in scholarly treatment under the rubric of "Wahhābī" which are more accurately described as "Salafī."

5. John Voll and Nehemia Levtzion, *Eighteenth Century Renewal and Reform in Islam* (1987), 5–7. In this historiographic framework, the Wahhābī reform movement ushers in the modern period of Islamic history or even defines the modern period (since movements of revival and reform were more general than colonial encounters).

6. With the exception of those scholars who trace the pedigree of Wahhābī or "fundamentalist" movements to Ibn Taymiya. Such scholarship actually obscures the historical context and specificity of Wahhābī reform by projecting its "antecedents" into the late medieval period.

7. Fazlur Rahman, *Islam* (1979), 206. Rahman first coined the term "Neo-Sufism" in 1966 (based on observations by Hamilton Gibb about Aḥmad ibn Idrīss and the Idrīssīyya). In Rahman's formulation, Neo-Sufism described Sufi movements that abandoned the goal of ecstatic experience and "passing away" in favor of keeping elements of the social organization of Sufi communities but making them serve the ideals of "orthodox Islam." His rather offhand comment was adopted and elaborated by John Voll, *Islam: continuity and change in the modern world* (1982), 33, passim. The value of the term has been questioned by Rex O'Fahey and Berndt Radtke, "Neo-Sufism Reconsidered" (1993), 52–87, and also by Radtke, "Ijtihad and Neo-Sufism" (1994). For a general discussion of "Neo-Sufism," see Sirriyeh, *Sufis and Anti-Sufis*, 11.

8. Fazlur Rahman, *Revival and Reform in Islam* (2000), laid out a pedigree for "Islamic fundamentalism" that stretched back to Ibn Taymiyya, Abū Ḥāmid al-Ghazālī, and Aḥmad Sirhindī. Unfortunately, Fazlur Rahman passed away before he could write the final chapter of his study to specify the character of modern fundamentalism that justified including and engulfing these premodern figures. This study suggests that "fundamentalism" should be limited to religious ideologies of the twentieth century and disengaged from "reform," of which there are many premodern varieties.

9. Hodgson, *The Venture of Islam*, 3:159–161.

10. Zarruq, *Qawāᶜid al-Taṣawwuf*, Principle 5.

11. Murata and Chittick, *Vision of Islam*, 2–7, 37–42, and 267–276.

12. Guennoun, *Mashāhir Rijāl,* 15.

13. Zarrūq, *Mimmā Kutiba bihi al-Shaykh Zarrūq li-baᶜḍ Aṣḥābihi Naṣḥan* (mss.). His advice is heartfelt, but may not have been meant as the ultimate statement of his Sufi way. This letter was written as parting advice (*waṣiya*) to be spread among his followers in Morocco after he had left Fes for the final time. In Morocco, most of his disciples did not have access to education or juridical training that he required of full members of his reform movement, and this might account for the radical simplicity of his advice.

14. M. Khalid Masud (ed.), *Travelers in Faith: Studies of the Tablighi Jamaᶜat,* (2000), and Yoginder Sikand, *Origins and Development of the Tablighi-Jamaᶜat* (2002). *Tablighi Jamaᶜat* is currently the largest Islamic movement in the world in the scope of its membership and transnational activities. It advocates political revival without political parties, Islamic devotion without Sufi communities, and adherence to *sharᶜi* behaviors without Islamic jurisprudence. The *Tablighi Jamaᶜat* meshes with the new popularity given to other reformist Sufis, like Ibn Taymiyya and Ibn al-Jawzī, by twentieth-century Islamists who do not necessarily recognize these authorities of the past as "Sufis" despite their allegiance to the Qādirī Sufi community.

15. Hamza Yusuf, "America's Tragedy: An Islamic Perspective," (Sept. 30, 2001, at Zaytuna Institute) republished at http://www.zaytuna.org/tragedy.html.

Appendix A

1. He recorded the lineage of this initiatory handshake in Ibn Ghāzī, *Fihris Ibn Ghāzī,* 87–88, and is also mentioned in al-Ṣumāᶜī, *Kitāb al-Muᶜzā,* 358.

Appendix B

1. This lineage is recorded from al-Hawwāt, *al-Sirr al-Ẓāhir,* 71–79. On genealogical studies of the Qādirī shurafāᵓ in northern Morocco, see ᶜAbd al-Salām al-Qādirī, *al-ᶜUrf al-ᶜĀṭir fi Abnāᵓ al-Shaykh ᶜAbd al-Qādir,* and *al-Durr al-Sanī fi baᶜḍ man bi-Fās min al-nasab al-Ḥasanī* (Fes: Lithoprint, 1891); and Idrīss ibn Aḥmad al-ᶜAlawī, *Al-Durar al-Bāhiya wa'l-Jawāhir al-Nabawiyya fi'l-Furūᶜ al-Ḥasaniyya wa'l-Ḥusayniyya* (Fes: lithoprint, 1896); Muḥammad al-ᶜArabī ibn al-Ṭayyib al-Qādirī also wrote a treatise on the Qādirī genealogy, which may still be unpublished.

2. al-Hawwāt, *al-Sirr al-Ẓāhir*, 79, discusses the chronological ambiguity of when the Qādirīs actually settled in Fes. Later sources from the Qādirī shurafāᵓ spread the story that their ancestor "came when Granada fell" which was not until 897 Hijri. Other stories say that Abū ᶜAbdallah Muḥammad came to Fes to settle his people, then returned to Granada. So it must have been before Granada fell by some time. Memory of the events were condensed in later recollection to increase the drama of being driven out by the Spanish.

3. al-Hawwāt, *al-Sirr al-Ẓāhir*, 77. This genealogical document was witnessed and certified by certain Qāḍīs in Fes, as well as the head of the Ṭāhirī Jūṭī shurafāᵓ at that time, Abū Muḥammad ᶜAbd al-Wāḥid ibn Ṭāhir al-Ḥasanī, as well as the Naqīb al-Shurafāᵓ, Abū Muḥammad ᶜAbd al-Qādir ibn ᶜAbdallah al-Ḥasanī al-Jūṭī.

Bibliography

Manuscript Sources Written by Aḥmad Zarrūq (in Arabic).*

Arjūza fī Naẓm ᶜUyūb al-Nafs [A Verse Rendering of the text "Faults of the Self"]. Tunis: KhZ 17918, folios 34–45 and Tunis: KhZ 785, folios 167–185.

Baᶜḍ al-Qawāᶜid al-Fiqhīyya fī al-Muᶜāshara wa Ḥusn al-Sulūk [Some Juridical Principles for Civil Living and Cultivation of Good Values]. Tunis: KhZ 17918 folios 59–60.

Ḥizb al-ᶜAṣr [Litany of Afternoon Devotions]. Tunis: KhZ 16501, folios 143–145.

Ijāzāt [Credentials]. London: BL Add.9692.

Ikhtiṣār baᶜḍ Maktubāt al-Shaykh Zarrūq [Summary of a Letter of Shaykh Zarrūq]. Fes: KhQ 1371 part 6.

al-Jāmiᶜ li-Jumal min al-Fawāʾid waʾl-Manāfiᶜ [The Bringer-Together of Beneficial and Advantageous Pronouncements]. Rabat: KhA 2207 d, folios 85–101 and KhM 4661 part 1 and part 5; and Fes: KhQ 1364/4.

al-Kunnāsh fī ᶜIlm Āsh [Notebook on the Knowledge of Whatever]. Rabat: KhA 1385 k; and Tunis: KhZ 1911; and Algiers: al-Maktaba al-Waṭaniyya 363 part 10.

Mabādīʾ al-Ṭarīqa al-Ṣūfiyya [Foundations of the Sufi Way]. KhZ 17901 folios 87–88.

Manāqib al-Ḥaḍramī [The Saintly Virtues of al-Ḥaḍramī]. Rabat: KhA 1385 K folios 105–109; and Cairo, Dar al-Kutub.

Miftāḥ al-Sadād al-Fahmī Sharḥ Irshād Ibn ᶜAskar al-Baghdādī [The Master Key for Understanding in Commentary on "the Guidance" by Ibn ᶜAskar al-Baghdādī]. Tunis: KhZ 20054 and 19072 folios 17–21.

Mimmā Kutiba bihi al-Shaykh Zarrūq li-baᶜḍ Aṣḥābihi Naṣḥan [Exerpt of What Zarrūq Wrote to a Disciple]. Rabat: KhM 12241 part 6.

*This bibliography does not represent the complete oevre of Zarrūq. It documents only the manuscript copies of his texts consulted in this study. For a more complete bibliography of his writings, see Khushaim, *Zarruq the Sufi*. However, this bibliography does correct some errors in Khushaim's more comprehensive work. Those works of Zarrūq that have been published in Arabic are included below in the second section, while those published in English translation are included in the fifth section.

Muqtaṭafāt min Kalām al-Shaykh Zarrūq [Choice Selection of the Words of Zarrūq]. Rabat: KhM 7577 and 7210.

al-Nasḥ al-Anfaᶜ wa᾽l-Janna li-man iᶜtaṣama min al-Bidᶜa bi᾽l-Sunna [The Most Advantageous Advice and the Shield for those who seek shelter in the Prophet's Example from Inauthentic Practices]. Rabat: KhA 710 q part 4.

al-Naṣīḥa al-Kāfiya li-man khaṣṣahu Allah bi᾽l-ᶜĀfiya [Sufficient Advice for Those whom Allah has Selected for Wellbeing]. Rabat: KhA 182 d.

Naẓm Fuṣūl al-Sāmī [Versification of the Sublime Chapters]. Rabat: KhM 6647 b.

Risāla ilā Fuqarā᾽ al-Muntasabīn li᾽l-Ṭarīqa al-Zarrūqīyya [A Letter to those Renunciants Holding Allegiance to the Way of Zarrūq]. Rabat: KhM 12135 part 4.

Risāla ilā Ṣadīqayhi ᶜAbdallah al-Maghrāwī wa ᶜAbd al-Malik ibn Saᶜīd [Letter to His Two Trusted Friends al-Maghrawi and Ibn Said]. KhZ 2729 folios 95–98 and KhZ 19734 folios 2–13.

Risāla baᶜathahā min Miṣr ilā Ikhwānihi bi᾽l-Maghrib [A Letter that Zarrūq Sent from Egypt to his Fellows in Morocco]. Marakesh: Ibn Yūsuf 627 part 2.

Risāla fī Dhikr man ẓahara fī hādhihi al-Azmina bi-Ḥawādith lam tusmaᶜu min Qabl [A Treatise on Those who Appear in these Times Bringing Catastrophes Never Heard of Before]. Tunis: KhZ 17966 folios 57–60.

Risāla fī᾽l-Taṣawwuf [Treatise on Being a Sufi]. Rabat: KhM 10368.

Risāla fī Taḥdīd Muṣṭalaḥ al-Ḥadīth [A Treatise on the Definition of Terms in Hadith Studies]. Tunis: KhZ 7147 and 7052.

Risālat al-Radd ᶜalā Ahl al-Bidᶜa [Denunciation of those who Engage in Inauthentic Religious Practices] Tunis: KhZ 8631 folios 1–120 and KhZ 8178 folios 94–104. Same text unde the title *Bidᶜ al-Taṣawwuf* [Inauthentic Practices in Sufi Devotion] Tunis: KhZ 19017 folios 195–264.

Sharḥ ᶜAqīdat al-Ghazālī [Commentary on al-Ghazālī's Statement of Belief]. Rabat: KhM 4670 and Aḥmadabad: BJI 58 b. This work is also known by the alternative title *Ightinām al-Fawā᾽id fī al-Tanbīh ᶜalā Maᶜānī Qawāᶜid al-ᶜAqā᾽id li᾽l-Ghazālī.* Damascus: Maktaba Waṭanīyya 12192.

Sharḥ Asmā᾽ Allah al-Ḥusnā [Commentary on the Beautiful Names of God]. Rabat: KhA 1838 d.

Sharḥ al-Ḥikam al-ᶜAṭā᾽īyya [Commentary on the Wisdom Sayings of Ibn ᶜAṭā᾽illah]. Fes: KhQ 1336.

Sharḥ al-Ḥizb al-Kabīr [Commentary on the Great Litany of al-Shādhilī {known as The Litany of the Sea}]. Rabat: KhM 885 b.

Sharḥ Ḥizb al-Barr [Commentary on the Litany of the Land of al-Shādhilī]. Rabat: KhM 715 d; and Tunis: KhZ 3417.

Sharḥ al-Mabāḥith al-Aṣliyya fī al-Ṭarīqa al-Ṣūfiyya [Commentary on the Original Sources of the Sufi Way]. Rabat: KhA2284 d and KhM 7209 and 9332; and Fes: KhQ 1321/2; and Tunis: KhZ 9890; and Cairo: al-Azhar 23122; and Damascus: Maktaba Waṭanīyya 4015.

Sharḥ Mughammaḍāt Ḥizbay al-Shādhilī [Commentary on Obscure Expressions in two of al-Shādhilī's Litanies]. Rabat: KhA1383; and Cairo: al-Azhar 1032 al-Jawhari collection.

Sharḥ Mawāḍi^c min Mukhtaṣar Khalīl "Commentary on Some Passages of the Abridged Legal Treatise of Khalīl ibn Isḥāq]. Madrid: CDIX.2.

Sharḥ al-Muqaddima al-Qurṭubīyya [Commentary on the Introduction of al-Qurṭubī]. Fes: KhQ 1168; and Rabat: KhM 653, 6625, 883, and 9590; and Tunis: KhZ 9780 and 2390.

Sharḥ al-Naṣīḥa al-Kāfiya [Commentary on The Sufficient Advice]. Rabat: KhA 747 q.

Sharḥ Naẓm al-Dimyāṭī [Commentary on the Verses of al-Dimyāṭī]. Tunis: KhZ 507.

Sharḥ al-Qaṣīda al-Nūnīyya li'l-Shushtarī [Commentary on the Ode in Nūn by al-Shushtarī]. Rabat: KhM 10454 folios 39–64 and 5693 [this copy is badly damaged].

Sharḥ al-Risāla al-Qayrawānīyya [Commentary on the Juridical Treatise of al-Qayrawānī]. Rabat: KhM 3480; and Fes: KhQ 1168; and Tunis: KhZ 1845.

Sharḥ al-Risāla al-Waghlīsīyya [Commentary on the Legal Treatise by al-Waghlīsī]. Rabat: KhA 571 k and 1424 d; and Fes: KhQ 1364 part 5; and KhZ 1687 folios 1–62.

Sharḥ Ṣudūr al-Marātib [Commentary on The Levels of Emanation by al-Ḥaḍramī]. photocopy in private collection of the author, location of original is unknown.

Sulūk al-Ṭarīq idha fuqida al-Rafīq [Traveling the Path When You Have No Companion]. Cairo: al-Azhar. This text is also preserved in the commentary upon it: ^cAlī Muttaqī, *Hadha Hidāyat Rabbī ^cind Faqd al-Murrabī* [This is the Guidance of the Lord in the Absence of a Spiritual Guide]. Aḥmadabad: Pir Mohammadshah Dargah 70 dhayl; and Aligarh: Azad, Subhanullah Collection 297.7/51 farsi tasawwuf.

Ṭā'ifa min Kalām Shaykh Zarrūq [A Section of Zarrūq's Words]. Rabat: KhM 7571.

Tuḥfat al-Murīd wa Rawḍat al-Farīd wa Fawā'id li-Ahl al-Fahm al-Sadīd wa al-Naẓr al-Madīd [Gift of the Disciple and Garden of the Unique with Beneficial Points for the People of Acute Understanding and Extensive Reason]. Rabat: KhA 2587 d.

Takallum fī al-Taṣawwuf al-Tisāʿī [Discourse on Nine Levels of Being a Sufi] Rabat: KhM 7210 part 10. Khushaim cites this work by an alternate title, *al-Kalām ʿalā Anwāʿ Ahl al-Khuṣūṣiya.*

al-Uṣūl waʾl-Fuṣūl al-Badīʿa waʾl-Mabānī al-Rafīʿa [The Sources, their Excellent Ramifications and Lofty Foundations]. Rabat: KhA 3612 folios 424–438.

Waṣiya fī Kayfiyat al-Sulūk waʾl-Akhdh ʿan al-Ṣūfiya [Parting Advice on Traveling the Path and Taking Allegiance to the Sufis]. Rabat: KhA 3490 part 5; and Fes: KhQ 1371 part 3.

al-Waẓīfa [The Employment]. London: BL Add.7589 folios 117b–122a; and Marrakesh: Ibn Yūsuf 347; and Rabat: KhA 1060 d and KhM 3048, 7579 and 9480; and Cairo: al-Azhar 28939 al-Saqqa collection.

Published Works by Aḥmad Zarrūq

Ḥikam Ibn ʿAtaʾillah: sharḥ Aḥmad Zarrūq. ed. Maḥmūd, ʿAbd al-Ḥalīm and Maḥmūd Ibn al-Sharīf. Tripoli, Libya: Maktabat al-Najaḥ, 1969.

Ḥikam Ibn ʿAṭāʾillah: sharḥ Zarrūq. ed. Maḥmūd, ʿAbd al-Ḥalīm and Maḥmūd Ibn al-Sharīf. Cairo: [Dār] al-Shaʿb, 1969.

Kitāb Iʿānat al-Mutawajjih al-Miskīn ilā Ṭarīq al-Fatḥ waʾl-Tamkīn. ed. ʿAli Khusaim. Tunis and Libya: al-Dār al-ʿArabīyya liʾl-Kitāb, 1979.

al-Kunnāsh: Ṣuwar min al-Dhikrayāt al-Ulā. ed. ʿAli Khushaim. Tripoli, Libya: al-Munshaʾāt al-Shaʿbīyya, 1980.

al-Naṣīḥa al-Kāfiya li-man khaṣṣahu Allah biʾl-ʿĀfiya. ed. Muḥammad Āl Shaykh Mubārak. Riyadh: Maktabat al-Imām al-Shāfiʿī, n.d.

Qawāʿid al-Taṣawwuf. Beirut: Dār al-Jīl, 1992.

Sharḥ al-Ḥikam al-ʿAṭāʾīyya. ed. ʿAṭiya, Aḥmad Zakī. Benghazi: Kulliyat al-Ādab, 1971.

Sharḥ Ṣaḥīḥ al-Bukhārī. ed. ʿAṭiya,ʿIzzat ʿAlī and Mūsā Muḥammad ʿAlī. Cairo: Maṭbaʿat Ḥisān, n.d. Six volumes.

ʿUddat al-Murīd al-Ṣādiq min Asbāb al-Maqt fī Bayān al-Ṭarīq wa Dhikr Ḥawādith al-Waqt. Tripoli, Libya: Maktabat Tarābulus al-ʿIlmīyya al-ʿAmalīyya, 1996.

al-Waẓīfa al-Shādhilīyya al-Mashīshīyya. Alexandria: Maṭbaʿat Jurjī Gharzūzī, 1905.

Manuscript Sources by Other Authors (in Arabic or Persian)

Anonymous. *Dhikr Qiṣṣat al-Muhājirīn*. Rabat: KhA 270 k.

Anonymous. *Manāqib Aḥmad ibn Yūsuf al-Rāshidī al-Milyānī*. Rabat: KhA 1457 d folios 1–75.

Anonymous. *Munāqashāt al-Zarrūqī wa Ibn Abī Maḥallī wa'l-Sa'īd al-Jazā'irī*. Marrakesh: Khizāna Ibn Yūsuf 655.

Anonymous. *Rawḍ al-Nāẓir fī Manāqib 'Abd al-Qādir*. Rabat: KhM 12241 part 2.

Anonymous. *al-Ta'rīf bi-Nasab al-Shaykh Aḥmad al-Milyānī*. Rabat: KhA 1456 d.

Anonymous. *al-Ta'rīf bi-Sīdī Aḥmad Zarrūq*. Rabat: KhA 2100 d.

al-Andalusī, Aḥmad ibn Mūsā al-Murābī. *Tuḥfat al-Ikhwān wa Mawāhib al-Imtinān fī Manāqib Sīdī Riḍwān*. Rabat: KhA 114 k.

al-Andalusī, 'Alī Ṣāliḥ. *Miftāḥ al-Sa'āda li-Ahl al-Irāda*. Rabat: KhM 8967.

———. *Sharḥ Raḥbat al-Amān*. Rabat: KhM 5697.

al-Bādisī, Ḥassan ibn Abī al-Qāsim. *Manāqib al-Shaykh 'Abd al-Qādir al-Jīlānī wa Tabbā'ihi*. Rabat: KhM 12241 part 2.

Dihlawī, 'Abd al-Ḥaqq Muḥaddith. *Miftāḥ al-Futūḥ* [a Persian commentary on 'Abd al-Qādir al-Jīlānī, *Futūḥ al-Ghayb*]. Hyderabad, India: Oriental Manuscript Library and Research Institute 1771 farsi tasawwuf.

———. *Taḥṣīl al-Ta'arruf fī al-Fiqh wa'l-Taṣawwuf*. Rampur: RL 1347 arabic.

al-Fāsī, 'Abd al-Ḥafīẓ Ṭāhir. *al-Tarjumān al-Mughrib 'an Ashhar Furū' al-Shādhilīyya bi'l-Maghrib*. Rabat: KhA 4400 d.

al-Fāsī, 'Abd al-Raḥmān. *Ibtihāj al-Qulūb bi-Khabr al-Shaykh Abī al-Maḥāsin wa Shaykhihi al-Majdhūb*. Rabat: KhA 326 k.

al-Fāsī, Muḥammad al-Mahdi. *al-Jawāhir al-Ṣāfiyya fī Maḥāsin al-Yūsufīyya*. Rabat: KhA 1234 d.

———. *Tuḥfat Ahl al-Ṣaddīqīyya bi-Asānīd al-Ṭā'ifa al-Zarrūqīyya wa'l-Jazūlīyya*, also known as *Tufhah Ahl al-Taṣdīq*. Rabat: KhA 76 j and 2990 k.

———. *Rawḍat al-Maḥāsin al-Zāhiya bi-Ma'āthir al-Shaykh Abī al-Maḥāsin*. Rabat: KhA 976 j.

al-Fāsī al-Fihrī, Aḥmad ibn Abī al-Maḥāsin Yūsuf. *Risāla fī Jawāz al-Jahr bi'l-Dhikr* Fes: KhQ 1530 part 9.

———. *Risāla fī Mawḍū' Aqwāl al-Fuqahā' wa'l-Ṣūfiya fī'l-Samā' wa'l-Raqṣ*. Fes: KhQ 1530 part 10.

al-Ghazwānī, 'Abdallah ibn 'Ajala. *Jawāb Su'āl min Ṭarf al-Shaykh al-Habṭī*. Rabat: KhM 9467.

———. *Kitāb fī al-Taṣawwuf.* Rabat: KhM 732.

———. *Majmūᶜat Rasāʾil al-Ghazwānī.* Fes: KhQ 1504.

———. *al-Nuqta al-Azalīyya fī Sirr al-Dhāt al-Muḥammadīyya.* Rabat: KhM 324 and KhA 2617 k.

———. *Tahbīr al-Ajrās fī Sirr al-Anfās.* Marrakesh: Khizānat Ibn Yūsuf 342.

al-Habṭī, ᶜAbdallah. *Jawāb ᶜalā Masāʾil fīʾl-Taṣawwuf.* Rabat: KhM 5758.

———. *Jawāb Suʾāl awrada ᶜalayhi li-baᶜḍ Aṭbāᶜihi yuṭlabu fīhi al-Shuruḥ waʾl-Iḍāḥ Kalām Abī Ḥāmid al-Ghazālī fīʾl-Qalb wa Ḥaqīqatihi.* Fes: KhQ 1371 part 5.

al-Ḥaḍramī, Aḥmad ibn ᶜUqba. *Risāla ilā baᶜḍ Aṣḥābihi.* Rabat: KhM 12241 part 7.

Ibn ᶜAbbād, al-Rundī al-Fāsī. *Bughiyat al-Murīd min Ajlī ma quriba min Baᶜīd* [*al-Ḥikam* set to verse]. Rabat: KhM 11609 part 2.

Ibn Zaghdān, Abū al-Mawāhib Jamāl al-Dīn Muḥammad. *Qawānīn Ḥikam al-Ishrāq ilā kull al-Ṣūfiya yujmiᶜu al-Afāq.* Fes: KhQ 1030 part 2.

Ibn Zikrī, Muḥammad ibn ᶜAbd al-Raḥmān. *Sharḥ al-Naṣīḥa al-Kāfiya.* Rabat: KhA 807 d, and KhM 11555, 12362, 6771, 7335; and Fes: KhQ 1579.

al-Jazūlī, Muḥammad ibn Sulaymān. *ᶜAqīdat al-Walī al-Ṣāliḥ Sīdī al-Jazūlī.* Rabat: KhM 7245 folios 12–18.

———. *Risāla ilā ᶜUlamāʾ al-Ẓāhir.* Fes: KhQ 723.

———. *Mā Qāla al-Shaykh Muḥammad ibn Sulaymān al-Jazūlī.* Rabat: KhM 12241.

al-Kharrūbī, Muḥammad ibn ᶜAlī. *Ajūbat Asūlat Sīdī ᶜUmar.* Rabat: KhA 571 k. folios 31–62.

———. *al-Durra al-Sharīfa fī Sharḥ al-Waẓīfa.* Rabat: KhA 2201 part 3; and KhM 6646 part 8, 4506, 4670, 7506, 2829, 12217 part 7; and Fes: KhQ 1528 part 6.

———. *Kifāyat al-Murīd wa Hilyat al-ᶜAbīd.* Rabat: KhM 9901 part 1.

———. *Risāla ḥawl al-Fuqarāʾ.* Rabat: KhA 571 folios 31–62.

———. *Sharḥ al-Ḥikam.* Rabat: KhA 1796 d.

———. *Sharḥ Abyāt fī Taṣawwuf li-Ibn al-ᶜArabī al-Ḥātimī.* Rabat: KhM 6053.

———. *Sharḥ Taṣliyat al-Quṭb Ibn Mashīsh* (also known as *Sharḥ al-Ṣalāt al-Mashīshīyya.* Fes: KhQ 1425 part 3; and Hyderabad, India: Salar Jung Library add. 114.

al-Khayyāṭ, ᶜAbdallah. *Waṣiya.* Rabat: KhM 7410.

al-Lamṭī, Aḥmad ibn Mubārak. *al-Ibrīz fī Manāqib Sīdī ᶜAbd al-ᶜAzīz [al-Tabbāᶜ].* Fes: KhQ 1615.

al-Milyānī, Aḥmad ibn Yūsuf al-Rāshidī. *Ḥamla min Kalamihi fī al-Taṣawwuf.* Rabat: KhM 10764 part 1 folios 3–11.

Muttaqī, ᶜAlī. *Ḍābiṭa li-Uṣūl al-Ṭarīqa* [Fixing the Meaning of Zarrūq's Principles of the Path]. Rampur: RL, arabic 3083; and Aligarh: Azad, Subhanullah Collection 297.7/51 farsi tasawwuf.

———. *Dhikr al-Mawt li-tadarruk al-Fawt* [Reminders of Death for Gradually Passing Away]. Aligarh: Azad, Subhanullah Collection 297.7/51 farsi tasawwuf.

———. *Hidāyat Rabbī ᶜinda Faqd al-Murabbī* [My Lord's Guidance if One has no Master for Training]. Aḥmadabad, India: Pir Mohammadshah Dargah 70 dhayl; and Cairo: al-Azhar ᶜayn 5446 tasawwuf.

———. *Taᵓlīq ᶜalā Sharḥ al-Ḥikam al-Khāmis ᶜAshar* [A commentary on the fifteenth commentary of Aḥmad Zarrūq on the Wisdom Sayings]. Berlin: Deutsches Kulturbesitz 869. 6. We. 1757.2 folios 37a–50b.

al-Qādirī, Muḥammad al-ᶜArabi ibn al-Ṭayyib. *al-Ṭurfa fī Ikhtisār al-Tuḥfa.* Rabat: KhA 901 d folios 101–110.

al-Sāsī, Aḥmad ibn Qāsim. *al-Ṭiryāq al-Fārūq li-Qirāᵓ Waẓīfat al-Shaykh Zarrūq.* London: BL Add. 9484.

al-Shuṭaybī, al-Ḥajj Muḥammad ibn ᶜAli. *Miftāḥ al-Janna al-Mutawaffiq ᶜalā al-Kitāb waᵓl-Sunna.* Rabat: KhM 5908.

———. *Sharḥ Mabāḥith al-Aṣlīyya.* Rabat: KhM 4560.

al-Wazzānī, Mūsā ibn ᶜAlī. *Risāla Masᵓalat al-Quṭb.* Rabat: KhM 7585 folios 1–22.

Zakī, Muḥammad. *al-Mawārid al-Hāfīya fī Sharḥ al-Naṣīḥa al-Kāfīya.* Rabat: KhM 2191.

Published Sources (in Arabic)

Aḥmad, Muṣṭafā Abū Dayf. *Athār al-Qabāᵓil al-ᶜArabīyya fī al-Ḥayyāt al-Maghribīyya khilāl ᶜAṣray al-Muwāḥḥidīyyin wa Banī Marīn.* Casablanca: Dār al-Nashr al-Maghribīyya, 1982.

al-ᶜAlawī, Idrīs ibn Aḥmad. *al-Durar al-Bāhiya waᵓl-Jawāhir al-Nabawīyya fīᵓl-Furūᶜ al-Ḥasanīyya waᵓl-Ḥusaynīyya.* Lith. Fes: n.p., 1896.

al-ᶜAyāshī, Abū Zayd. *al-Anwār al-Sanīyya ᶜalā al-Waẓīfa al-Zarruqīyya*, published as an appendix of *Tanqīḥ Rawḍat al-Azhār.* Beirut: al-Maktaba al-Thiqāfiyya, n.d.

al-Barmūnī, Karīm al-Dīn. *Tanqīḥ Rawḍat al-Azhār wa Muniyat al-Sādāt al-Abrār fī Manāqib ᶜAbd al-Salām al-Asmar.* Beirut: al-Maktaba al-Thiqāfiyya, n.d.

Darnīqa, Muḥammad. *al-Shaykh ᶜAbd al-Qādir al-Jīlānī wa Aᶜlām al-Qādirīyya.* Tripoli, Lebanon: Dār al-Maᶜārif al-ᶜUmūmiyya, 1992.

al-Darqāwī, Mawlay al-ᶜArabī. *Hādhihi Rasāʾil Shaykh al-Darqāwi.* Casablanca: Dār al-Ṭibāᶜa al-Ḥadītha, 1970; reprinted from the original lith. from Fes.

Dihlawī, ᶜAbd al-Ḥaqq Muḥaddith. *Maraj al-Baḥrayn fī Jamᶜ bayn al-Ṭarīqayn.* Delhi: ᶜAbd al-Ḥaqq Muḥaddith Akademi, 1991; first published Karachi: Muḥammad Āᶜlā, 1968. In Persian.

al-Fāsī, ᶜAlī ibn Abī Zarᶜ. *Anīs al-Muṭrib bi-Rawḍat al-Qirtās.* Rabat: Dār al-Manṣūr, 1972.

al-Fāsī, Muḥammad al-ᶜArabī. *Mirʾāt al-Maḥāsin fī Akhbār Abī al-Maḥāsin.* Lith. Fes: n.d.

al-Fāsī, Muḥammad al-Mahdī. *Mumtiᶜ al-Asmāʾ fī Dhikr al-Jazūlī waʾl-Tabbāᶜ wa mā lahumā min al-Atbāᶜ.* Casablanca: Maṭbaᶜat Dār al-Najāḥ al-Jadīda, 1994.

Furāṭ, Aḥmad Ṣubḥī. "Al-Shaykh Aḥmad Zarrūq: ḥayātuhu wa athāruhu ᶜalā Ḍawʾ Kitāb al-Tadhkār li-Ibn Ghalbūn." *Majallat al-Buḥūth al-Tārīkhīyya* [Libya] 4, 1 (1982). 75–82.

Guennoun, ᶜAbdallah. *Dhikrayāt Mashāhir Rijāl al-Maghrib: Aḥmad Zarrūq, 23.* Tetuan: Maṭbaᶜa Krimadis, 1954.

al-Ḥabshī, ᶜAbdallah Muḥammad. *al-Ṣūfiya waʾl-Fuqahāʾ fīʾl-Yaman.* Sanᶜa: Maktabat al-Jīl al-Jadīd, 1976.

al-Hāfī, Aḥmad. *Tuḥfat al-Zāʾir bi-Manāqib al-Ḥājj Aḥmad ibn ᶜĀshir.* Salé: al-Khizāna al-ᶜIlmiyya al-Ṣabīḥīyya, 1988.

Ḥajjī, Muḥammad. *al-Ḥaraka al-Fikrīyya biʾl-Maghrib fī ᶜAhd al-Saᶜdīyyīn.* Rabat: Dār al-Maghrib, 1976.

al-Hajwī, Muḥammad. *al-Fikr al-Sāmī fī Tārīkh al-Fiqh al-Islāmī.* Beirut: Dār al-Kutub al-ᶜIlmīyya, 1995.

Ḥarakat, Ibrāhīm. *al-Siyāsa waʾl-Mujtamaᶜa fī al-ᶜAṣr al-Saᶜdī.* Casablanca: Dār al-Rushd al-Haditha, 1987.

al-Ḥasanī, ᶜAbd al-Ḥayy. *Nuzhat al-Khawāṭir wa Bahjat al-Masāmiᶜ wa al-Nawāẓir.* Hyderabad Dekkan: Dāʾirat al-Maᶜārif, 1988. Ten volumes.

al-Hawwāt, Muḥammad ibn ᶜAbdallah al-ᶜAlamī al-Ḥasanī. *Al-Sirr al-Ẓāhir fī-man abraza bi-Fās al-Sharf al-Bāhir min Aᶜqāb al-Shaykh ᶜAbd al-Qādir.* Lith. Fes: n.d.

Ibn ᶜAbbād, Muḥammad ibn Ibrāhīm al-Rundī. *Sharḥ ᶜalā Matn al-Ḥikam.* Cairo, al-Maṭbaᶜa al-Khayrīyya, 1886. Alternative title *Ghayth al-Mawāhib al-ᶜĀliya.* Cairo: Maṭbaᶜat al-Saᶜada, 1970.

Ibn ᶜAjība, Aḥmad ibn al-Mahdī. *Sayyidi al-ᶜĀrif Biʾllah Ibn ᶜAjība: al-Fihrasa.* Cairo: Dār al-Ghadd al-ᶜArabī, 1990.

———. *Sharḥ al-Mabāḥith al-Aṣlīyya.* Printed in the margins of Ibn ᶜAjība, Aḥmad. *Īqāẓ al-Himam fī Sharḥ al-Ḥikam.* Rabat: Dār al-Fikr, n.d.

Ibn al-ᶜArabī al-Ḥātimī. *al-Bulgha fī al-Ḥikma.* ed. Nihad Keklik. Istambul: n.p., 1949.

———. *Fuṣūṣ al-Ḥikam.* ed. ᶜAfifi. Cairo: Dār Iḥyāʾ al-Kutub al-ᶜArabiyya, 1946.

Ibn ᶜĀshir, Aḥmad. *al-Murshid al-Muᶜīn ᶜalā al-Ḍarūrī min ᶜUlūm al-Dīn.* Tunis: Maṭbaᶜat al-Manār, 1977.

Ibn ᶜAskar. *Dawḥat al-Nāshir li-Maḥāsin man kāna biʾl-Maghrib min Mashāʾikh al-Qarn al-ᶜĀshir.* Rabat: Dār al-Maghrib, 1976.

Ibn ᶜAṭāʾillah al-Iskandarī, Aḥmad ibn ᶜAbd al-Karīm. *Kitāb al-Tanwīr fī Isqāṭ al-Tadbīr.* Lith. Cairo: n.p., 1883.

Ibn ᶜAyāḍ, Aḥmad ibn Muḥammad. *al-Mafākhir al-ᶜAlīya fī al-Maʾāthir al-Shādhilīyya.* Cairo: al-Maṭbaᶜa al-ᶜAmir, 1315 Hijri.

Ibn Ghāzī, Aḥmad. *Fihris Ibn Ghāzī.* ed. Muḥammad al-Zāhī. Tunis: Dār Busdama, 1984.

Ibn Khaldūn. *Shifāʾ al-Sāʾil wa Tahdhīb al-Masāʾil.* Beirut: al-Dār al-Fikr al-Muᶜāṣir, 1996.

Ibn Maryam al-Tilimsānī, Muḥammad. *al-Bustān fī Dhikr al-Awliyāʾ waʾl-ᶜUlamāʾ bi-Tilimsān.* ed. Mohammed Ben Cheneb. Algiers: Diwān al-Maṭbuᶜāt al-Jāmiᶜīyya, 1986.

Ibn al-Qāḍī, Aḥmad al-Miknāsī. *Durrat al-Ḥijāl fī Asmāʾ al-Rijāl.* Alternate title *Dhayl Wafayāt al-Aᶜyān.* Cairo: Dār al-Turāth, 1971.

———. *Jadhwat al-Iqtibās fī dhikr man ḥalla min Aᶜlām Madīnat Fās.* Rabat: Dār al-Manṣūr, 1973.

Ibn Qunfudh, Aḥmad al-Qusamṭīnī. *Uns al-Faqīr wa ᶜIzz al-Ḥaqīr.* Rabat: al-Markaz al-Jāmiᶜī lil-Baḥth al-ᶜIlmī, 1965.

Ibn Zaghdān, Abū al-Mawāhib Jamāl al-Dīn Muḥammad. *Faraḥ al-Asmāʾ bi-Rukhṣ al-Samāᶜ.* Tunis: al-Dār al-ᶜArabīyya liʾl-Kitāb, 1985.

———. *Qawānīn Ḥikam al-Ishrāq ilā kull al-Ṣūfiya yujmiᶜu al-Afāq.* Cairo: al-Maktaba al-Azharīyya liʾl-Turāth, 1999.

al-Ifrānī, Muḥammad. *Nuzhat al-Hādī bi-Akhbār Mulūk al-Qarn al-Hādī.* Rabat: al-Maktab al-Ṭālib, n.d., second edition.

al-Jaznāʾī, ᶜAli. *Janā Zahrat al-Ās fī Bināʾ Madīnat Fās.* Rabat: al-Maṭbaᶜa al-Malakiyya, 1991.

al-Jīlānī, [c]Abd al-Qādir. *Al-Safīna al-Qādirīyya*. Tripoli, Libya: Maktabat al-Najāḥ, n.d..

al-Kattānī, Muḥammad ibn Ja[c]far. *Salwat al-Anfās wa Muḥādathat al-Akyās bi-man uqbira min al-[c]Ulamā[ɔ] wa[ɔ]l-Ṣulaḥā[ɔ] bi-Fās*. Lith.Fes: n.d. Three volumes.

Khushaim, [c]Alī Fahmī. *Aḥmad Zarrūq wa al-Zarrūqīyya: dirāsat hayyāt wa fikr wa madhhab wa ṭarīqa*. Tarabulus, Libya: al-Munsha[ɔ]āt al-Sha[c]bīyya, 1980.

al-Kūhin, Ḥassan. *Ṭabaqāt al-Shādhilīyya al-Kubrā*. Cairo: n.p., 1928.

Makhlūf, Muḥammad. *Shajarat al-Nūr al-Zakīya fī Ṭabaqāt al-Mālikīya al-Qāhira*. Cairo: al-Maṭba[c]a al-Salafiyya, n.d.

al-Makkī, Muḥammad Ibn al-Ḥusayn. *Ḥikam wa Akhlāq [c]Arabīyya*. Cairo: al-Dār al-Ḥusaynīyya lil-Kitāb, 1997.

al-Muḥāsibī, Ḥārith. *Kitāb al-Ri[c]āya fī Ḥuqūq Allah*. Gibb Memorial Series, New Series 15. London: Luzac, 1940.

al-Nāṣiri al-Slawī, Aḥmad ibn Khālid. *Kitāb al-Istiṣqā[ɔ] li-Akhbār Duwwal al-Maghrib al-Aqṣā*. Casablanca: Dār al-Kitāb, 1955. Six volumes.

al-Ni[c]amī, [c]Abdallah al-Amīn. "Zarrūq: al-Shaykh al-Murabbi." *Majalla al-Buḥūth al-Tārikhīyya* [Libya] 5, 2 (1983). 257–270.

al-Qādirī,[c]Abd al-Salām ibn al-Ṭayyib. *al-[c]Urf al-[c]Āṭir fī Abnā[ɔ] al-Shaykh [c]Abd al-Qādir*. Printed with *al-Durr al-Sanī fī ba[c]ḍ man bi-Fās min al-nasab al-Ḥasanī* and *al-Ishrāf [c]alā Nasab al-Aqṭāb al-Arba[c]a al-Ashrāf*. Lith. Fes: n.p., 1891.

al-Qādirī, Muḥammad ibn al-Ṭayyib. *Nashr al-Mathānī li-Ahl al-Qarn al-Ḥādī [c]Ashar wa[ɔ]l-Thānī*. Rabat: Dār al-Maghrib, 1977.

al-Qarāfī, Muḥammad. *Tawshīh al-Dibāj wa Hilyat al-Ibtihāj*. Beirut: Dār al-Gharb al-Islāmī, 1983.

al-Rifā[c]ī, Aḥmad ibn [c]Alī. *Hādhihi Ḥikam al-Rifā[c]ī*. Beirut: al-Maṭba[c]a al-Adabīyya, 1883.

Ṣādiq, Muḥammad Ḥajj. *Milyāna wa Walīyuha Sīdī Aḥmad ibn Yūsuf: dirāsa khāṣṣa bi-Madīna mutawassiṭa fī[ɔ]l-Jazā[ɔ]ir*. Bin [c]Aknūn, Algeria: Diwān al-Maṭbū[c]a al- Jāmi[c]īya, 1989.

al-Sakhāwī, Muḥammad ibn [c]Abd al-Raḥmān. *al-Ḍaw[c] al-Lāmi[c] li-Ahl al-Qarn at-Tāsi[c]*. Beirut: Dār Maktabāt al-Hayāt, 1966.

al-Sharjī, Aḥmad ibn Aḥmad. *Ṭabaqāt al-Khawāṣ Ahl al-Ṣidq wa[ɔ]l-Ikhlāṣ*. Cairo: n.p., 1321 Hijri.

al-Sharrāṭ, Muḥammad ibn [c]Īshūn. *al-Rawḍ al-[c]Aṭir al-Anfās bi-Akhbār al-Ṣulaḥā[ɔ] min Ahl Fās*. Casablanca: Maṭba[c]at al-Najāḥ al-Jadīda, 1997.

al-Shaṭṭanūfī, ᶜAlī ibn Yūsuf. *Bahjat al-Asrār wa-Maᶜdin al-Anwār*. Cairo: n.p., 1991.

al-Shaᶜrānī, ᶜAbd al-Wahhāb. *al-Ṭabaqāt al-Kubrā*. Beirut: Dār al-Jīl, 1988.

al-Sulamī, Abū ᶜAbd al-Raḥmān. *Kitāb Ṭabaqāt al-Ṣūfiya*. Leiden: E. J. Brill, 1960.

al-Ṣumāᶜī, Aḥmad. *Kitāb al-Muᶜzā fī Manāqib al-Shaykh Abī Yiᶜzzā*. ed. ᶜAlī al-Jāwī. Rabat: Maṭbaᶜat al-Maᶜārif al-Jadīda, 1996.

al-Sūsī, Muḥammad al-Mukhtār. *Kitāb min Afwaḥ al-Rijāl*. Tetuan: al-Maṭbaᶜa al-Mahdīyya, 1963.

al-Tādilī, Abū Yaᶜqūb Ibn Yaḥyā al-Zayyāt. *Kitāb al-Tashawwuf ilā Rijāl al-Taṣawwuf wa Akhbār Abī al-ᶜAbbās al-Sabtī*. ed. Aḥmad Toufiq. Rabat: Manshurāt Kulliyat al-Ādab, 1984.

al-Talīdī, ᶜAbdallah. *al-Muṭrib fī Mashāhir Awliyāᵓ al-Maghrib*. Tangier: Muᵓassasat al-Taghlīf liᵓl-Shamāl, 1987.

al-Timbūktī, Aḥmad Bābā. *Nayl al-Ibtihāj fī Taṭrīz al-Dibāj*. Fes: al-Maṭbaᶜa al-Jadīda, 1899.

al-Ṭuᶜmī, Muḥayy al-Dīn. *Ṭabaqāt al-Shāhilīyya al-Kubrā*. Beirut: Dār al-Jīl, 1996,

al-Wansharīsī, Aḥmad ibn Yaḥya. *al-Miᶜyār al-Muᶜrib waᵓl-Jāmiᶜ al-Mughrib ᶜan Fatāwī Ahl Ifrīqīya waᵓl-Andalus waᵓl-Maghrib*. Fes: Wizārat al-Awqāf, 1983.

Zarrūq, ᶜAbdullah Ḥasan. *Manhajiya li-Dirāsat al-Taṣawwuf: Uṣūl al-Taṣawwuf*. Omdurman, Sudan: Dār Jāmiᶜat Umm Durman al-Islāmīyya, 1993.

Published Sources (in English and European languages including translations from original texts)

Abou El Fadl, Khaled. *And God Knows the Soldiers: The Authoritative and Authoritarian in Islamic Discourses*. Lanham, Md.: University Press of America, 2001.

———. *Rebellion and Violence in Islamic Law*. Cambridge: Cambridge University Press, 2001.

Andezian Sossie. *Experiences du divin dans a'Algerie contemporaine: Adeptes des saint de la region de Tlemcen*. Paris: CNRS Editions, 2001.

Asad Talal. *Genealogies of Religion: Power in Christianity and Islam*. Baltimore: Johns Hopkins University Press, 1993.

Baldick, Julian. *Mystical Islam: An Introduction to Sufism*. London: I B Taurus, 1989.

Bel, Alfred. *La Religion Musulmane en Berberie*. Paris: Librairie Orientaliste Paul Geuthner, 1983.

Bell, Catherine. *Ritual Theory, Ritual Practice*. New York: Oxford University Press, 1994.

Benchekroun, Mohammed. *La Vie Intellectuelle Marocaine sous les Mérinides et les Wattasides*. Rabat: Imprim. Mohammed V, 1974.

Boxer, C. R. *The Portuguese Seaborne Empire, 1415–1825*. Manchester: Carcanet, 1991.

Brett, Michael. *Ibn Khaldun and the Medieval Maghrib*. Aldershot, England: Valorium, 1999.

Brown, Peter. *The Cult of the Saints: Its Rise and Function in Latin Christianity*. Chicago: University of Chicago Press, 1981.

———. *The Body and Society: Men, Women and Sexual Renunciation in Early Christianity*. New York: Columbia University Press, 1988.

Buehler, Arthur. *Sufi Heirs of the Prophet: The Indian Naqshbandiyya and the Rise of the Mediating Sufi Shaykh*. Columbia: University of South Carolina Press, 1998.

Bulliet, Richard. *Islam: A View from the Edge*. New York: Columbia University Press, 1994.

Burgat, François, and William Dowell. *The Islamic Movement in North Africa*. Austin: University of Texas Press, 1993.

Burke, Edmund, III. "Theorizing the Histories of Colonialism and Nationalism in the Arab Maghrib: Beyond Colonialism and Nationalism in North Africa." *Arab Studies Quarterly* 20, 2 (Spring 1998).

Burton, John. *An Introduction to the Hadith*. Edinburgh: Edinburgh University Press, 1994.

Chamberlain, Michael. *Knowledge and Social Practice in Medieval Damascus: 1190–1350*. Cambridge: Cambridge University Press, 1994.

Cigar, Norman, trans. *Muḥammad al-Qādirī's Nashr al Mathani: The Chronicles*. London: Oxford University Press, 1981.

Clancy-Smith, Julia. *Rebel and Saint*. Berkeley: University of California Press, 1994.

Cook, Michael. "On the Origins of Wahhābīsm," *Journal of the Royal Asiatic Society*, Series 3 2/2 (1992), 191–202.

Cook, Weston. *The Hundred Years War for Morocco: Gunpowder and the Military Revolution in the Early Modern Muslim World*. Boulder, Colo.: Westview Press, 1994.

Cornell, Vincent J. "The Logic of Analogy and the Role of the Sufi Shaykh in Post-Marinid Morocco." *International Journal of Middle East Studies* 15 (1983), 67–93.

———. "Understanding is the Mother of Ability: Responsibility and Action in the Doctrine of Ibn Tumart." *Studia Islamica* 66 (1988).

———. "Sovereignty of the Imamate of the Jazuliyya-Ghazwaniyya: A Sufi Alternative to Sharifism?" *al-Qantara* 17 (1996). 440–441.

———. *The Way of Abū Madyan: Doctrinal and Poetic Works of Abū Madyan Shu*ᶜ*ayb ibn al- Husayn al-Ansari*. Cambridge: Islamic Texts Society, 1996.

———. *The Realm of the Saint: Power and Authority in Moroccan Sufism*. Austin: University of Texas Press, 1996.

Dabashi, Hamid. *Authority in Islam: From the Rise of Muḥammad to the Establishment of the Umayyads*. New Brunswick, N.J: Transaction Publishers, 1992.

Danner, Victor. *The Book of Wisdom: Ibn* ᶜ*Ata*ᵓ*illah*. The Classics of Western Spirituality Series. New York: Paulist Press, 1978.

De Certeau, Michel. *The Mystic Fable: The Sixteenth and Seventeenth Centuries*. Translated by Michael B. Smith. Chicago: University of Chicago Press, 1992.

de Jong, Fred, and Berndt Radtke, eds. *Islamic Mysticism Contested: Thirteen Centuries of Debate and Conflict*. Islamic History and Civilization Series. Leiden: E J Brill, 1999.

Douglas, Elmer, trans. *The Mystical Teachings of al-Shādhilī: A Translation of Ibn al-Sabbagh's Durrat al-Asrār wa Tufḥat al-Abrār*. Albany: SUNY press, 1993.

Ernst, Carl W. *The Shambhala Guide to Sufism*. Boston: Shambala Publications, 1997.

Ewing, Katherine Pratt. *Arguing Sainthood: Modernity, Psychoanalysis and Islam*. Durham, N.C.: Duke University Press, 1997.

Evans-Pritchard, E. E. *Theories of Primitive Religion*. Oxford: Clarendon Press, 1965.

Garcia-Arenal, Mercedes. "The Revolution in Fas in 869/1465 and the Death of Sultan ᶜAbd al-Haqq al-Marini." *Journal of the School of Oriental and African Studies* 61, 1 (1978).

———. "Sainteté et pouvir dynastique au Maroc: le Résistance de Fes aux Saᶜdiens." *Annales ESC* 4 (July–August 1990).

———. "La conjonction du Sufisme at Sharifisme au Maroc: Le Mahdi comme sauveur." *Revue du Monde Muselman et de le Mediterreneé* 55–56 (1990).

———. "Pouvoir Sacré et Mahdisme: Aḥmad al-Mansur al-Dhahabi." *al-Qantara* 17, 2 (1996).

Geertz, Clifford. *Islam Observed: Religious Development in Morocco and Indonesia*. Chicago: University of Chicago Press, 1968.

———. *The Interpretation of Culture*. New York: Harper Collins, 1973.

Gellner, Ernest. *Saints of the Atlas*. Chicago: University of Chicago Press, 1969.

Geoffroy, Eric, ed. *La Voie Soufie des Shadhilis*. Paris: Maisonneuve & Larose, 2005.

Haeri, Fadhlalla. *The Elements of Sufism*. Dorset: Element Books, 1990.

Hammoudi, Abdellah. *Master and Disciple: The Cultural Foundations of Moroccan Authoritarianism*. Chicago: University of Chicago Press, 1997.

Hawley, John Stratton, ed. *Saints and Virtues*. Berkeley: University of California Press, 1987.

Hodgson, Marshall G. S. *The Venture of Islam: Conscience and History in a World Civilization*. Chicago: University of Chicago Press, 1958. Three volumes.

Honerkamp, Kenneth, trans. *ᶜAbd al-Raḥmān al-Sulami's al-Risāla Malāmatīyya* in *Three Early Sufi Texts*. Louisville, Ky.: Fons Vitae, 2004.

Hourani, Albert. "Islamic History, Middle Eastern History, Modern History." in Malcolm Kerr, ed. *Islamic Studies: A Tradition and Its Problems*. Malibu, Calif.: Udenda Publications, 1980.

Huff, Toby, and Wolfgang Schluchter, eds. *Max Weber and Islam*. New Brunswick, N.J.: Transaction Publishers, 1999.

Ibn Khaldūn. *The Muqaddima*. Translated by Franz Rosenthal. Princeton, N.J.: Princeton University Press, 1967.

Istrabadi, Zeinab. "*The Principles of Sufism*." Ph.D. thesis, Dept. of Near Eastern Lang. and Cultures, Indiana University, April 1988.

James, William. *The Varieties of Religious Experience: A Study in Human Nature*. New York: Modern Library, 1999.

Johansen, Julian. *Sufism and Islamic Reform in Egypt: The Battle for Islamic Tradition*. Oxford: Clarendon Press, 1996.

Jurji, Edward Jabra. *Illumination in Islamic Mysticism: A Translation, with an Introduction and Notes, of Qawānīn Ḥikam al-Ishrāq*. London: Oxford University Press, 1983.

Kabbani, Muhammad Hisham. *Encyclopedia of Islamic Doctrine*. Mountainview, Calif.: Al-Sunna Foundation of America, 1996.

Kamali, Mohammad Hashim. *Principles of Islamic Jurisprudence*. Cambridge: Islamic Texts, 2000.

Katz, Jonathan. *Dreams, Sufism, and Sainthood: The Visionary Career of Muḥammad al-Zawāwī*. Leiden: E J Brill, 1996.

Khushaim, Ali Fahmi. *Zarrūq the Sufi*. Tripoli, Libya: General Company for Publication, 1976.

King, Richard. *Orientalism and Religion: Post-colonial Theory, India and 'the Mystic East.'* London: Routledge, 1999.

Kugle, Scott. "Usuli Sufis: Ahmad Zarruq and His Followers in South Asia" in Eric Geoffroy (ed.), *La Voie Soufie des Shadhilis*. Paris: Maisonneuve & Larose, 2005.

———. *The Book of Illumination: An English Translation of Kitab al-Tanwir fī Isqat al-Tadbir by Shaykh Ibn ᶜAṭāʾillah al-Iskandari*. Louisville, Ky.: Fons Vitae, 2005.

———. *Sufis and Saints' Bodies: Mysticism, Corporeality, and Sacred Power in Islam*. Chapel Hill, N.C.: University of North Carolina Press, forthcoming, 2007.

Knysh, Alexander D. *Ibn ᶜArabi in the Later Islamic Tradition: The Making of a Polemical Image in Medieval Islam*. Albany: SUNY Press, 1999.

Lawrence, Bruce B. *Defenders of God: The Fundamentalist Revolt Against the Modern World*. San Francisco: Harper and Row, 1989.

———. *Shattering the Myth: Islam beyond Violence*. Princeton, N.J.: Princeton University Press, 1998.

le Tourneau, Roger. *Fez in the Age of the Marinides*. Norman: University of Oklahoma Press, 1961.

Mansour, Mansour H. *The Maliki School of Law: Its Spread and Domination in North and West Africa*. San Francisco: Austin and Winfield, 1995.

Masud, Muhammad Khalid, ed. *Travelers in Faith: Studies of the Tablighi Jamaᶜat as a Transnational Islamic Movement for Faith Renewal*. Leiden: E J Brill, 2000.

Mauss, Marcel. *Sociology and Psychology: Essays*. London: Routledge and Kegan Paul, 1979; first published in 1950.

al-Moudden, Abd er-Rahmane. "The Idea of the Caliphate between Moroccans and Ottomans." *Studia Islamica* 82, 2 (October 1995).

Munson, Henry, Jr. *Religion and Power in Morocco*. New Haven, Conn.: Yale University Press, 1993.

Murata, Sachiko, and William Chittick. *The Vision of Islam*. The Vision of Religions Series. New York: Paragon House, 1994

O'Fahey, Rex, and Berndt Radtke. "Neo-Sufism Reconsidered." *Der Islam* 70, 1 (1993), 52–87.

Powers, David S. *Law, Society and Culture in the Maghrib, 1300–1500.* Cambridge: Cambridge University Press, 2002.

Radtke, Berndt. "Ijtihad and Neo-Sufism." *Asiatische Studien* 18, 3 (1994), 909–921.

Rahman, Fazlur. *Islam.* Chicago: University of Chicago Press, 1979, second edition.

———. *Revival and Reform in Islam: A Study of Islamic Fundamentalism.* Ed. Ebrahim Moosa. Oxford: Oneworld, 2000.

Ray, Reginald. *Buddhist Saints in India: A Study in Buddhist Values and Orientations.* London: Oxford University Press, 1994.

Renard, John, trans. *Ibn Abbad of Ronda: Letters on the Sufi Path.* New York: Paulist Press, 1986.

Roberts, Nancy, trans. *The Subtle Blessings in the Saintly Lives of Abul-Abbas al-Mursi and His Master Abul-Hasan, the Founders of the Shadhili Order.* Louisville, Ky.: Fons Vitae Press, 2005.

Robertson, Elizabeth. "The Corporeality of Female Sanctity in The Life of Saint Margaret." in Renate Blumenfeld-Kosinski and Timea Szell, eds. *Images of Sainthood in Medieval Europe.* Ithaca, N.Y.: Cornell University Press, 1991.

Rodad, Ruth. *Women in Islamic Biographical Collections.* Boulder, Colo.: Lynne Rienner Publishers, 1994.

Roff, William. "Islamic Movements: One or Many?" in Willaim Roff, ed. *Islam and the Political Economy of Meaning.* London: Croom Helm, 1987.

Rogalski, J. "Ahmad Zarruq: Mystik und Rechtswissenschaft zwischen Maghrib und Mashriq im 15. Jahrhundert." *Wuquf* 1 (1986), 171–202.

Said, Edward. *Orientalism: Western Conceptions of the Orient.* New York: Vintage Books, 1978.

Sachedina, Abdulaziz. *Islamic Messianism: The Idea of Mahdi in Twelver Shi'ism.* Albany: SUNY Press, 1981.

Salvatore, Armando. *Islam and the Political Discourse of Modernity.* Berkshire: Ithaca Press, 1997.

Sayyid, Bobby S. *A Fundamental Fear: Eurocentrism and the Emergence of Islamism.* London: Zed, 1997.

Schimmel, Annemarie. *Deciphering the Signs of God: A Phenomenological Approach to Islam.* Albany: SUNY Press, 1994.

———. *Mystical Dimensions of Islam* Chapel Hill: University of North Carolina Press, 1975.

Shaw, Marvin. *The Paradox of Intention: Reaching the Goal by Giving up the Attempt to Reach It.* Atlanta: Scholars Press, 1988.

Siddiqi, Muḥammad. *Hadith Literature: Its Origins, Development, Special Features, and Criticism*. Calcutta: Calcutta University, 1961.

Sikand, Yoginder. *Origins and Development of the Tablighi-Jamaᶜat (1920–2000): A Cross-country Comparative Study*. Hyderabad, India: Orient Longman, 2002.

Sirriyeh, Elizabeth. *Sufis and Anti-Sufis: The Defence, Rethinking and Rejection of Sufism in the Modern World*. London: Curzon Press, 1999.

Streight, David, trans. *The Autobiography of the Moroccan Sufi: Ibn ᶜAjība*. Louisville, Ky.: Fons Vitae, 1999.

as-Sulami, Abū ᶜAbd ar-Raḥmān. *Early Sufi Women: Dhikr an-Niswa al-Mutaᶜabbidat as-Sufiyyat*. Edited and Translated by Rkia E. Cornell. Louisville, Ky.: Fons Vitae, 1999.

Tambiah, Stanley Jeyaraja. *The Buddhist Saints of the Forest and the Cult of Amulets: A Study in Charisma, Hagiography, Sectarianism, and Millennial Buddhism*. Cambridge: Cambridge University Press, 1984.

Trimingham, Spencer. *The Sufi Orders in Islam*. Oxford: Clarendon Press, 1971.

Turner, Brian S. *Weber and Islam: A Critical Study*. New York: Routledge, 1998; first published in 1974.

Turner, Victor. *Dramas, Fields and Metaphors: Symbolic Action in Human Society*. Ithaca, N.Y.: Cornell University Press, 1974.

———. *The Ritual Process: Structure and Anti-structure*. Chicago: Aldine, 1969.

Voll, John O. *Islam: Continuity and Change in the Modern World*. Boulder, Colo.: Westview Press, 1982.

Voll, John O., and Nehemia Levtzion, eds. *Eighteenth Century Renewal and Reform in Islam*. Syracuse, N.Y.: Syracuse University Press, 1987.

Weinstein, Donald and Rudolph Bell. *Saints and Society: The Two Worlds of Western Christendom, 1000–1700*. Chicago: University of Chicago Press, 1982.

Yusuf, Hamza. *The Foundations of Our Path*. Santa Barbara, Calif.: Zilzal Press, 1987.

Zdanowski, J. "On Reconstructing the History of Wahhābī Arabia," *Hemispheres* 10 (1995), 125–128.

el-Zein, Abdul Hamid. "Beyond Ideology and Theology: The Search for the Anthropology of Islam." *Annual Review of Anthropology* 6 (1977).

Index

The following terms are mentioned so often that they have not been documented page by page in the index: Fes, North Africa, and Zarruq. Terms in Arabic have not been given with diacritics in the index for the sake of simplicity.

SCOTT KUGLE is a scholar of Religious Studies and Islamic Culture. He received a Ph.D. in 2000 from Duke University for a comparative study of reform-oriented Sufis in North Africa and South Asia. He has taught courses at Swarthmore College on the Qur'an, ethics in Islamic law, and Sufism. He is currently a research fellow at the Institute for the Study of Islam in the Modern World in the Netherlands, focusing on issues of gender and sexuality in Muslim communities.